ETHNIC CONFLICTS AND THE NATION-STATE

The **United Nations Research Institute for Social Development (UNRISD)** is an autonomous agency that engages in multi-disciplinary research on the social dimensions of contemporary problems affecting development. Its work is guided by the conviction that, for effective development policies to be formulated, an understanding of the social and political context is crucial. The Institute attempts to provide governments, development agencies, grassroots organizations and scholars with a better understanding of how development policies and processes of economic, social and environmental change affect different social groups. Working through an extensive network of national research centres, UNRISD aims to promote original research and strengthen research capacity in developing countries.

Current research themes include Crisis, Adjustment and Social Change; Socio-Economic and Political Consequences of the International Trade in Illicit Drugs; Environment, Sustainable Development and Social Change; Integrating Gender into Development Policy; Participation and Changes in Property Relations in Communist and Post-Communist Societies; and Political Violence and Social Movements. UNRISD research projects focused on the 1995 World Summit for Social Development include Rethinking Social Development in the 1990s; Economic Restructuring and Social Policy; Ethnic Diversity and Public Policies; and The Challenge of Rebuilding War-Torn Societies.

Ethnic Conflicts and the Nation-State

Rodolfo Stavenhagen

 in association with

UNRISD

First published in Great Britain 1996 by
MACMILLAN PRESS LTD
Houndmills, Basingstoke, Hampshire RG21 6XS
and London
Companies and representatives
throughout the world

A catalogue record for this book is available
from the British Library.

ISBN 0–333–64801–3 hardcover
ISBN 0–333–64802–1 paperback

First published in the United States of America 1996 by
ST. MARTIN'S PRESS, INC.,
Scholarly and Reference Division,
175 Fifth Avenue,
New York, N.Y. 10010

ISBN 0–312–15971–4

Library of Congress Cataloging-in-Publication Data
Stavenhagen, Rodolfo.
Ethnic conflicts and the nation-state / Rodolfo Stavenhagen.
p. cm.
This book is one of the outcomes of the research project on ethnic
conflict and development undertaken by the United Nations Research
Institute on Social Development (UNRISD).
Includes bibliographical references and index.
ISBN 0–312–15971–4
1. Ethnic relations—Political aspects. 2. International
relations. 3. Culture conflict. 4. Conflict management. 5. World
politics—1985–1995. I. United Nations Research Institute for
Social Development. II. Title.
GN496.S7 1996
305.8—dc20   96–10553
                                                        CIP

10   9   8   7   6   5   4   3   2   1
05   04   03   02   01   00   99   98   97   96

Printed and bound in Great Britain by
Antony Rowe Ltd, Chippenham, Wiltshire

Contents

Introduction

This book is one of the outcomes of the research project on Ethnic Conflict and Development undertaken by the United Nations Research Institute on Social Development (UNRISD). The project began to take shape in 1990 with the purpose of studying the nature and characteristics of conflict between ethnic groups in the process of development. It was recognized that as a result of ethnic conflict, societies have had to face serious problems in their development process, sometimes even major setbacks. In some cases, violence has resulted and has become protracted or even endemic. Occasionally, ethnic violence has led to guerrilla warfare, terrorism and civil war. In the process, much needed resources have been syphoned off from development objectives, major social and demographic dislocations have taken place, national unity has been endangered, the legitimacy of governments and state structures has been questioned, human rights abuses have occurred and, in some cases, the involvement of outside actors has influenced national processes. To deal with such problems, countries have had to face the challenge of (sometimes major) institutional and, at times, constitutional changes. External interests, and what has sometimes been called the internationalization of such conflicts, have had an important impact on the course of events.

The team of scholars who met in Geneva in February 1990 to plan their work together had no inkling at that time how quickly the premisses of the research project would be borne out by the dramatic events that occurred shortly thereafter. Within a year the Soviet Union had collapsed and was replaced by the Commonwealth of Independent States. Ethnic and nationalist conflict became a major feature of post-Soviet space. Likewise, within a month of the research meeting held in Dubrovnik in 1991, the Federation of Yugoslavia disintegrated, being replaced by a number of independent countries and descending into the horrors of civil war and 'ethnic cleansing'.

While the study on Ethiopia was in progress, the revolutionary armies overthrew the central military regime, a new Ethiopian state was created, Eritrea became independent and other, unexpected ethnic conflicts arose, which made it necessary to revise the research project then in progress. Similarly, as our study on Lebanon was being carried out, the Taef Agreement in 1991 brought an end to the civil war in Lebanon.

The ethnic conflict in Burundi continued unabated during the research period, requiring an almost constant updating of data and an arbitrary cut-

off point. As research was being carried out on the conflict surrounding
the Babri mosque in Ayodhya, India, this monument was finally razed to
the ground by Hindu militants, which led to widespread rioting in different
parts of India – an outcome that UNRISD researchers had anticipated and
that they were able to observe during their study.

Equally dramatic were the events during the Gulf War of 1990–1, which
brought the plight of the Kurdish people in Iraq to world attention, a situation which had already been studied at the time for the UNRISD project.
In other areas covered by this project, important if perhaps less spectacular
changes were occurring even as the study was being carried out. These
various events testify to the importance of the research topic and the time-
liness of UNRISD's attention to these issues. At the same time, they
underline the difficulties involved in focusing ('getting a fix' as it were) on
a constantly moving object, a subject matter that changes while it is being
observed.

Given the various contexts of the study, as well as the heterogeneous
backgrounds of the researchers involved, it was neither possible nor desirable to impose a single methodological framework on all the case studies,
and it was felt that, as it turned out, a variety of approaches and complete
respect for the researchers' individuality would greatly enrich the
outcome, even while it reduced the possibility of more formal and quantitative comparisons between the case studies. While some case studies
involved several researchers, others were carried out by a single scholar,
who took sole responsibility for the work.

This book, though authored by the coordinator of UNRISD's research
project, is in the true sense of the term a collective endeavour. I wish to
make it quite clear that most of what is published in this volume is the
work of my fellow-researchers, without whose original contributions this
book would not have been possible. I am happy to acknowledge the participation in the project, as co-authors of this volume, of:

Gérard Chaliand, who wrote a book on the Kurdish problem,
Makhtar Diouf, who published a study on Senegal,
Jesús García Ruiz, who studied the situation in Guatemala,
Kamal Hamdan, who researched the conflict in Lebanon,
René Lemarchand, who wrote a volume on the conflict in Burundi,
John Markakis, who prepared a volume on the Horn of Africa,
Ashis Nandy, who studied the conflict in Ayodhya, India,
Okwudiba Nnoli, who analysed the situation in Nigeria,
Ralph Premdas, who prepared the monographs on Guyana and Fiji,
Mavis Putucheary, who presents a monograph on Malaysia,

Farida Shaheed and Abbas Rashid, who undertook the case study on Pakistan,

Valery Tishkov, who wrote about ethnic conflict in the former Soviet Union,

Danilo Türk, Silva Meznaric, Payan Akhavan and their colleagues who prepared reports and papers on Yugoslavia, and

Steve Levitsky, who did research on the ideology of racism in the United States.

The reader will appreciate that this is a collective effort. As a result of the preparation of a wealth of empirical and analytical material the coordinator's dilemma was not easy. One alternative would have been to prepare an edited volume, with monographic chapters by each of the authors, and an introductory essay by the editor. Many books on ethnicity and related problems are presented in this fashion. The other alternative, chosen in this case, was to bring the material together in a broader framework and present it in a topical, comparative manner. Only the reader will be able to judge whether this solution has been successful or not. Any shortcomings of this approach are entirely the coordinator's responsibility. The reader interested in a more exhaustive treatment of the various case studies is referred to the contributors' published volumes or unpublished reports on file at UNRISD (see the Appendix).

This book can be read horizontally or vertically, like a chart. The reader interested in a more comparative approach will follow the chapters sequentially. To obtain a fuller picture of the situation in any one country, he or she can also read the sections pertaining to each of the case studies in sequential order. Thus, a 'monographic' quality is preserved for the case studies, even though these are fragmented among the various chapters.

I have tried to prevent repetition, but at times this may have been necessary for greater clarity. The passages of this book which refer to specific case studies are taken to a great extent (except when indicated otherwise) from the reports prepared for UNRISD by the authors cited above. Whenever possible, the author's original text was respected and reproduced verbatim, rather than summarized or rewritten. However, in order to make it easier on the reader, I have avoided putting quotation marks round these passages. The original texts are deposited in the UNRISD archives. Some of the material, as mentioned before, has been published elsewhere. All other material used in this volume is acknowledged separately.

Chapter 1 is an overall introduction to the problematic of ethnic conflicts in the world today. Some of the theoretical and conceptual pitfalls concerning ethnicity are dealt with in Chapter 2. In Chapter 3 we look at the origin of ethnic conflicts in several of the cases covered by the UNRISD project, while Chapter 4 explores the crucial issue of how ethnic identities are structured and defined. The dynamics and evolution of conflicts in a number of cases is the subject matter of Chapter 5. In Chapter 6 we look at how ethnic conflicts affect some countries' economic development, as well as how unequal development in other cases can be a factor in these conflicts. Chapter 7 looks at how different kinds of policy pursued by governments deal with ethnic diversity within states, whereas Chapter 8 explores some of the international implications of ethnic conflicts. Chapter 9 considers the ideological underpinnings of racism and xenophobia, one of the lesser known ingredients of ethnic conflict in the industrialized West. A comparative look at how some of the ethnic conflicts studied in the project are being solved, and how some solutions have failed, is the topic of Chapter 10. Our final chapter summarizes the project's findings and ventures some conclusions.

Many people and institutions have contributed to this project. Besides the authors who wrote the various studies reported in this book, I am grateful to Dharam Ghai, director of UNRISD, whose vision and enthusiasm made this research possible, and whose support at all times was essential. El Colegio de Mexico, where I have been active for almost 30 years, provided the academic environment and support without which I would not have been able to pursue this project. I am also grateful to the Guggenheim Foundation and the Fulbright Fellowship Commission for providing grants that enabled me to spend the years 1990–3 at Stanford University as a visiting scholar, where much of the work that went into this book was carried out. To Stanford University in California, and particularly to Terry Karl, director of the Center for Latin American Studies, I owe a deep debt of gratitude for those very exciting and personally rewarding years in the little corner office at Bolivar House. A grant from the Jacob Blaustein Institute for Human Rights was crucial in supporting the research on the ideologies of racism and xenophobia, which is reported in Chapter 9. For their contribution to this research, I am also thankful to Steve Levitsky and John Bunzl. Last but not least, my thanks to Elia, Gabriel and Yara, for more than they can realize, to whom this book is dedicated.

1 The Ethnic Question in the World Crisis

The struggle of ethnic groups for recognition, equality or autonomy within the framework of an existing territorial state, or for independence from such a state, is not a recent phenomenon. Such endeavours, which are sometimes accompanied by violent conflict, have been inherent in the process of state-formation and nation-building which emerged in the Western world in the eighteenth and nineteenth centuries. While they were widespread in Europe during that time, they also occurred after the break-up of the Tsarist, Ottoman and Austro-Hungarian empires (and were, indeed, partly responsible for the disintegration of these empires) at the end of the First World War. Again, such struggles appeared in the aftermath of decolonization during the 1960s, within the successor states of the European empires in Africa and Asia. Once more, we are witnessing the re-emergence of ethnic conflicts as a result of the dissolution of the Soviet Union and the Yugoslav Federation in the early 1990s.

The counterpart of ethnic groups striving for recognition, equality or independence is the attempt by dominant elites to impose, preserve or extend their hegemony over other ethnies or over territory which they claim as their own. The ensuing confrontation between the in-group and the excluded, the majority and the minority, the dominant and the subordinate, between rival claimants to the power and resources of the state, has become one of the foremost contentious issues in political struggles and civil strife around the globe in contemporary times.

Public opinion is often severely shocked by the excessive violence that is frequently associated with such conflict, leading to massive loss of life, intolerable hardship for thousands if not millions of victims, massive violations of human rights and considerable material destruction. Many of the conflicts appear as confrontations between ethnic groups, and public opinion often refers to them as the expression of tribal hatreds or ancient enmities. But as we shall see, they are frequently, in fact, confrontations between politically mobilized ethnic groups and an existing state; it is only rarely that in such conflicts the state remains an innocent or neutral bystander.

There are currently several hundred ethnic conflicts of varying intensity on all continents, and international authorities, such as UN Secretary General Boutros Boutros-Ghali, have expressed their concern over their wider implications. From the perspective of the modern nation-state, the existence of ethnically distinct 'sub-national' groups, particularly when they are politically organized, always represents a potential threat, a destabilizing force. This is especially the case when power in the state rests principally with a dominant or majority ethnic group, or when the national society constitutes an ethnically stratified system. Indeed, it is the idea of the nation-state itself, a political concept which emerged in nineteenth-century Europe and which is still considered to be the main building block of the world system, that carries much of the responsibility for so many of the world's ethnic conflicts, past and present (and probably future ones as well). Whether this type of state was an historical necessity, the natural evolution of absolutist monarchies into modernity, or the peculiar creation of militant ethnic elites remains a matter of scholarly debate (Greenfeld, 1993). What resulted, however, is a world divided into a number of territorial-political units (called modern states) which have become the main actors in the international system. Yet within the borders of most of these states there exist numerous ethnic, national, racial, linguistic or cultural groups who either do not identify with the dominant model of the nation-state, or who are not accepted as full members of this state or the nation which it purports to be or represent, or who are actually excluded from it. In fact, the majority of independent states existing today are composed of more than one ethnic group, and this diversity poses challenges to governance and to the prevailing concept of the nation-state itself. One of the problems is that numerous states do not legally recognize the ethnic pluralism existing within their borders, and those that do are still struggling with ways to deal with diversity constructively (see Chapter 7). There is an inherent contradiction in the fact that the international system is made up on the one hand, of about 200 territorial states which have all the attributes of external and internal sovereignty, and on the other hand, of several thousand ethnic groups (the exact number is difficult if not impossible to determine and is a matter of debate), many of whom claim for themselves the characteristics of 'nationhood' and who either lack a state of their own or who do not feel represented by, or do not identify with, the state in which they live. For others, this situation does not appear to be an intractable problem and they may seek accommodation within the existing political framework.

Multi-ethnic states are more the rule than the exception, a reality that has multiple implications for democratic governance, as well as for international relations. Indeed, the problems derived from cultural and ethnic diversity within states has long ago ceased to be solely a domestic matter. Ever since the days of the League of Nations, the international community has been involved in the issues raised by the relations between ethnic groups and territorial states, especially with regard to the protection of the rights of minorities. As recently as 1992 the General Assembly of the United Nations adopted the Declaration on the Rights of Persons Belonging to National or Ethnic, Religious and Linguistic Minorities, thereby signalling the continued concern of the international community over the rights of culturally distinct peoples who live in independent states but who do not fully identify with the dominant cultural model of the nation-state. We shall see in later chapters that even in multi-ethnic states strong pressures exist to make the state conform to only one homogeneous nation, hence the traditional and powerful notion of the nation-state and its attendant political principle, nationalism.

Two rival conceptions of nationalism as the ideology of the modern nation-state have competed for historical legitimacy up to the present time. The first identifies the nation with all the people who form part legally of the territory of a sovereign state, regardless of their ethnic characteristics. Thus, all the permanent inhabitants of the United States are 'Americans' and they make up the American nation, just as all the citizens of the Swiss Confederation are Swiss, and all the diverse peoples of India are deemed to belong to the Indian nation. This may be labelled territorial or civic nationhood, and it is determined by the state itself through law and shared citizenship.

The other conception of the nation is based on ethnic criteria. Here the defining characteristics of membership are shared cultural attributes such as language or religion, as well as the idea of a common history rooted in the myth of common ancestry. According to this conception, membership in an ethnic nation is inherited, and though there may be some flexibility about how it is attributed or lost, it is cultural identity rather than formal citizenship that counts. As in civic nationhood, here too territory is a necessary referent; not so much as the space to which citizenship rights and legal systems apply, but rather as the historical homeland from which the ethnic nation emerges and to which it is forever tied. Ethnic nationalism strives to unify the ethnic homeland with the actual territorial unit over which a people ought to have a degree of control. Hence the idea of *Eretz Israel*, the concept of Greater Serbia, the struggle of indigenous peoples over their tribal territories or the mobilizing force of terms such as *Bumiputra* ('Sons of the soil') among the Malays.

Numerous ethnic conflicts express the underlying tensions between these two notions of the nation. We may cite, among others, the long struggle in Ethiopia which ended in the independence of Eritrea in 1993, the ongoing conflicts in Kashmir and Sri Lanka, the constitutional crisis in

Fiji, the war in former Yugoslavia, or the potential danger spots represented by the numerous Russian populations who now constitute national minorities in a number of former Soviet republics. Over time, however, these two seemingly contradictory and mutually exclusive conceptions of the nation may in fact converge. Numerous modern nations are in fact amalgamations of different constituent ethnic groups (such as the English), while states that were built on the avowed principle of territorial and civic – rather than ethnic – sovereignty have acquired in time a clear ethnic identity of their own (such as the French).

While it is true that there are many more ethnic groups, peoples or nations than constituted states, it is not as simple as it seems to identify and classify such groups. Scholars disagree on definitions, some governments may deny their existence altogether, whereas others impose strict legal criteria on ethnic groups and make them the object of specific policies. We discuss some of the pitfalls of ethnicity in the next chapter. At this point it should be noted that however defined, ethnic groups are historically given collectivities which have both objective and subjective characteristics, that is, their members acknowledge sharing common traits such as language, culture or religion, as well as a sense of belonging. Such groups exist over time, even as they emerge and may well change and disappear. Ethnic boundaries are socially constructed and may be more or less permeable. Again, individual membership in an ethnic group may be a matter of individual choice, or it may be strictly imposed and controlled by the group. Ethnic group identity is the result of internal factors (common lifestyles, shared beliefs), but also the outcome of the relations the group entertains with other distinct but similarly constituted groups and with the state in any given country.

Whether ethnic groups are called communities, nations, nationalities, peoples, minorities, tribes or ethnies is a matter of convention, yet it may have portentous legal and political significance. The republics of the former Soviet Union are made up of 'titular nationalities' and 'non-titular nationalities', who each have a different legal status which carries, among others, implications for economic privileges, educational facilities and social services. Membership in a 'tribe' in India or in Canada is established by law and carries legal implications. In Spain, the regional autonomy of Catalonia and the Basque country regulates the language of instruction in the schools as well as access to the civil service. In countries that recognize the existence of legal pluralism, members of different ethnic groups may be the subject of different, perhaps at times contradictory, legal structures. Indigenous 'communities' and their members are recognized and regulated in some Latin American constitutions. Some peoples are defined as minorities in some countries, and numerous minorities consider themselves as 'peoples', but current international law makes a clear distinction between 'minorities' and 'peoples', and categorically states that minorities do not have the same rights as peoples (see Chapter 8).

While small, geographically concentrated ethnic groups may be relatively homogeneous (such as an *adivasi* tribe in India or an indigenous community in the Amazon), other groups are dispersed and may number many millions (several minority nationalities in China, for example). A question that frequently arises is: who speaks for the group? This is no problem when an ethnic group has its own recognized political structure with legitimate authorities and decision-making processes. Very often traditional leaders enjoy widespread acceptance both within and outside the group, as for example among the Kurds and the religious communities in Lebanon. Elsewhere, ethnic leadership arises out of specific political struggles through modern mass movements or special interest organizations. Some of the ethnic nationalist leaders in Africa and other postcolonial states emerged during the years of anti-colonialist struggle. Not all members of an ethnic group may feel equally involved in a conflict that is defined and managed by an ethnic elite, particularly if the group is large, dispersed and internally differentiated. Thus, many Hutus in Burundi and Rwanda have thrown in their lot with the Tutsi leadership, and vice versa. Not all the Tamils in Sri Lanka approve of the objectives and tactics of the Liberation Tigers of Tamil Eelam (LTTE), just as not all Basques approve of Euzkadi ta Askatasuna (ETA) or all Ulster Catholics of the Irish Republican Army (IRA).

In this book we use the term ethnic group interchangeably with peoples, communities, nationalities and, at times, minorities. This is so basically to respect the terminology used by the authors of the UNRISD case studies themselves, but also because there is no overall consensus on the exact meaning of each concept. Whereas 'ethnic group' is legally and politically neutral, 'peoples' is widely used in legal and political literature, and carries particular implications in international law. The term 'minorities' also has specific meaning in international law, though it is used more widely because of its demographic connotations.

While some of the ethnic conflicts studied in this book are fairly recent, others have their roots in the complex historical evolution of the countries in which they occur, as we shall see in Chapter 3. Still, there is no disputing the fact that recent transformations in the world polity are partly accountable for the increased visibility of ethnically based conflicts. There are two principal world trends that have made a significant impact on these struggles and on the way they are perceived by outsiders.

One is the changing nature of the nation-state in a time of supra-national integration and the dwindling economic functions of central governments. It is no longer possible to speak about national economies in the way it was still fashionable to do so as recently as the post-Second World War period. The new global economy internationalizes productive processes, technology transfers, consumer behaviour, financial flows, banking activities, and so forth. International trade and currency exchange rates are increasingly regulated by regional and world-wide agreements (European Union, World Trade Organization). The imposition of the free market ideology leads everywhere to a drastic reduction of state intervention in the economy: governments divest themselves of costly, state-run enterprises, privatization is the order of the day, subsidies are cut or eliminated, and even basic investments in infrastructure are allocated in response to 'productivist' criteria rather than to collective development needs. In fact, the idea of development planning is no longer in vogue and long-term development strategies give way to short-term profit concerns. An example of this trend is the savage deforestation of the rainforests in the Amazon and Southeast Asia by international timber companies with devastating results for the environment and the survival of numerous indigenous and tribal peoples.

In these circumstances the state no longer controls the kinds of resources it can redistribute to ethnic and regional clienteles. Ethnic groups compete among themselves for these shrinking resources, as in the case of Nigeria, or they struggle for greater control over their own resources at the regional and local levels, as in the case of southern Sudan (see Chapter 6). When national resources are scarce, competition between ethnic groups may escalate, thus contributing to greater ethnic identity and awareness (for example, the struggle over preferential politics in the assignation of jobs in a number of post-colonial countries), or then again regionally specific ethnic groups may attempt to strike out on their own (for example, indigenous and tribal peoples negotiating development projects with international financing agencies directly, bypassing government bureaucracies).

On the other hand, competition and conflict over power at the political centre may not be as enticing to an embattled ethnic group when state resources are scant as when they are abundant. Moreover, when a major economic resource is to be found in an ethnic region, ethnic groups may find it in their interest to try to wrest control over these resources from the central state (as, for instance, the role of oil in the Kurdish rebellions in Iraq and in the Biafra war in Nigeria). Similarly, the separation of Slovenia from Yugoslavia was caused in part by Slovenia's perception that it was unfairly subsidizing the poorer parts of the federation. By reducing the scope of activity of the nation-state, the current tendency towards economic globalization provides opportunity and incentives for sub-national ethnic groups to become economic and political actors in their own right. Moreover, when the dominant elites in the political centre feel that they are subsidizing the periphery in an unequal relationship, it is the centre rather than the periphery which breaks away. After the independence of the Baltic countries, it was the Russian federation which first broke with the Soviet Union and not the peripheral republics that had been dominated by Russia. Economic dominance and political control by one ethnic group over another or others, do not always go hand in hand.

Just as the state-centred nation is no longer the principal locus of economic development, so also the mechanism of 'nation-building', long heralded as the main political process in the post-colonial world, has lost much of its appeal for numerous peoples who see themselves as excluded or marginalized from it, or worse, who see nation-building as a type of juggernaut under which their own cultures and identities will be quashed. To the extent that new territorial nation-states and the process generally described as modernization have been unable to provide for the identity needs of numerous distinct populations, ethnicity has again become a focal point of organization and mobilization for peoples and groups struggling for recognition, equality or basic human liberties (see Chapter 4).

Another tendency that has had an impact on the re-emergence of ethnic mobilization at the present time is the end of the cold war, and this has occurred at two distinct levels. On the one hand, a number of Third World conflicts were directly linked to US–Soviet world rivalry, and the participant ethnic groups were identified with the geopolitical interests of one or the other of the two Great Powers. This became especially clear in the protracted Ethiopian civil war, where the Soviets and the Americans supported first one and then the other of the ethno-political factions (see Chapter 9). Likewise, the legitimate grievances of the Miskito Indians were used by the US in its attempt to overthrow the Sandinista regime in Nicaragua during the 1980s. After the demise of the Soviet Union, ethnic conflicts in a number of countries were in fact shorn of their cold war baggage and became more 'ethnicized' as it were. Moreover, within the former Soviet Union ethnic conflicts have erupted which had either been suppressed earlier or had been non-existent during the communist period (see Chapter 5)

At another level, the end of the cold war helped produce what one might call a 'paradigm shift'. Sociological theorizing, under the influence of Marxism, had concentrated its attention on the analysis of social classes and their struggles, but had neglected the ethnic factor. This was particularly clear in studies on countries in the Third World. Marxist analysis steered away from the study of ethnicity and ethnic relations as these topics did not fit easily within the framework of historical materialism. Taking their cues from the theoretical literature of the period, the leaders of so many political organizations and movements in the Third World (many of them intellectuals by training and vocation) developed class-based ideologies of social and political dynamics in which ethnic references were carefully avoided, when not openly rejected as being contrary to the avowed purposes of furthering social revolution or obtaining national independence. This emphasis on class and related concepts (economic interest groups, elites, occupational categories) or on social and political institutions (the Army, the Church, the bureaucracy) actually prevented numerous scholars from effectively grasping the relevance and importance of ethnic identities and relating them meaningfully to social dynamics.

Theoretical approaches are also subject to changes in intellectual trends. For a number of years, the more orthodox approach to the study of socio-economic differences as expressed in the analysis of class has suffered declining fortunes, and perhaps as a consequence of postmodernist influences, more researchers have turned their attention to the sphere of culture and identity. Social realities are no longer considered to exist independently of their observers, to be described, analysed and interpreted in the light of competing theoretical frameworks, but rather they are now said to be invented, re-presented, constructed and deconstructed at every turn by ever-changing subjects.[1] In this context, a shift from class to ethnicity as the focus of attention by social scientists also signals the trend from a more positivist social science to a postmodernist approach. Thus, the re-emergence of ethnicity is both an observable social and political fact, as this book documents, as well as a social-scientific framework for the (attempted) understanding of continuing social processes.

As a result of the critique of the nation-state and the critique of class as sufficiently viable organizing principles, there has been a renewed interest in the resurgence of community, which is clearly addressed by the rediscovered importance of ethnicity-related issues. Local communities, often identified with a specific ethnicity, are frequently seen as the core of authentic, grassroots, unmediated democracy. There is, of course, a little romanticized utopia in this approach. Local communities, as anthropologists well know, are frequently quite hierarchical and undemocratic. Nevertheless, local communities may generate new or alternative approaches to development, and they often are able to mobilize resistance to invasive and destructive economic forces, as has been demonstrated, among others, by the tribal women involved in the Chipko movement for the protection of local forests in India.[2] Indeed, the struggle for the protection of the environment has become a major focal point of local-level activity by specific ethnic groups around the world, from indigenous peoples in the Americas to livestock herders in Africa to jungle and mountain tribes in Asia. Ecocide and ethnocide are two interlinked processes, and as a result, the struggle for the environment is a struggle for the survival of ethnic groups and their cultures as well. Local-level organization also emerges as a possibility for alternative development strategies in many parts of the world.

Ethnic and cultural diversity by itself does not necessarily lead to conflict between ethnic groups. This book focuses on conflict, but it does not argue that conflict is inherent in ethnic diversity, which it is not. To be sure, social conflict is inherent in human society, and under certain circumstances, as we shall see in later chapters, it takes the form of ethnic conflict. But this is not to say that in multi-ethnic states all social conflict necessarily takes on ethnic characteristics, nor that other forms of conflict disappear because of ethnic confrontations. However, as so many instances demonstrate, when ethnic conflicts become particularly acute, and especially when they turn violent, they easily displace and subsume other kinds of political and social, as well as economic, conflicts. A case in point was the protracted civil war in Lebanon, but there are many other examples, the most dramatic in the 1990s being the civil war in Bosnia-Herzegovina.

While ethnic conflicts usually pit a specific ethnic group against an ethnocratic state – that is, a nation-state controlled essentially by a majority or dominant ethnie, which is able to exercise cultural hegemony over the rest of the nation – there are cases of horizontal ethnic conflict between two or more groups, in which the political centre is not directly, or is only marginally, involved. The conflict between Mohajirs and Sindhs in Pakistan, which is described in Chapter 4, is at times of this sort. Similarly the various regional and local-level ethnic conflicts in Nigeria, outbursts of communal violence between Hindus and Muslims in India, or the long-standing tension between Indian-Guyanese and Afro-Guyanese in Guyana do not directly implicate the central state as one of the antagonists.

In general, there are different types of ethnic group and different kinds of ethnic conflict. In numerous cases, ethnic minorities who are marginalized or discriminated against may organize and mobilize in order to achieve full equality with the rest of the population. Such civic and political movements do not necessarily lead to conflict as described in the cases studied in this book, but they may evolve into conflict if the legitimate demands of the subordinate groups are not met. The most notorious instance of this kind of confrontation was the fight against apartheid in South Africa, which ended with the first democratic elections in that country in 1994. The struggles of the African-American people in the United States, or of the Roma (Gypsies) in numerous European countries, or the Burakumin in Japan, are of a similar nature. While the demands for non-discrimination and greater equality can be furthered peacefully in liberal democratic polities, they are frequently countered with repression and violence in authoritarian ones (for example, the plight of dissident religious groups in theocratic or totalitarian regimes). Sometimes, conflict and violence are generated by the dissemination of racist and xenophobic ideologies which target specific ethnic groups, as we shall see in Chapter 9.

A different kind of situation obtains when a subordinate ethnic minority demands recognition of its group rights by the state, which may involve specific legal status, cultural identity, territorial autonomy and other aspects related to the distinctiveness of an ethnic group within the wider polity. This has been the case of the Kurds in several western Asian countries, as we shall see in later chapters. It is also the case of the southern Sudanese population in their long-standing confrontation with the Arab Islamic north. Unmet demands for group rights may lead to attempts at political secession which, in turn, may evolve into full-fledged civil war, as occurred in Sri Lanka during the 1980s.

Indigenous and tribal peoples are usually considered to be a special case, whose situation may be similar to, but is not identical with, that of ethnic or national minorities. Basically, this is due to the historical process whereby indigenous and tribal peoples became the victims of conquest, colonization and settlement on their traditional homelands by ethnic outsiders who succeeded in establishing themselves as ruling classes or dominant elites in new states to which the former sovereign peoples then became subordinated. In some cases, as in Guatemala, the indigenous population is actually a demographic majority, and the denial of their group rights reminds one of the situation in apartheid South Africa. The refusal by the small dominant land-owning elites to recognize the democratic rights of the subordinate indigenous peoples led to a 30-year civil war, the end of which is not yet in sight (see Chapters 3 and 5). 'Low-intensity' ethnic conflict between indigenous peoples and the state occurs in many parts of the world, and given the extreme vulnerability of indigenous and tribal populations, it sometimes leads to genocide. Indigenous peoples also claim recognition of their cultural distinctiveness, their right to collective survival, and their sovereignty over their traditional territories and resources. The United Nations is currently drafting a Declaration on the Rights of Indigenous Peoples.

Other kinds of conflict occur between politicized ethnic groups that compete for state power or privileges, either within the framework of modern electoral politics or else by extra-legal means involving military coups, insurrections, genocide and revolutionary warfare. Numerous cases covered by the UNRISD project are of this type: the Indians and native Fijians in Fiji, the Malays and Chinese in Malaysia, the Hutu and Tutsi in Burundi, the Yoruba, Igbo and Hausa in Nigeria, the Africans and Indians in Guyana. None of the groups in these conflicts questions the legitimacy of the nation-state, nor do they apparently wish to secede from it at the present time.[3] They also recognize the need to accommodate at least some of the demands of their principal ethnic antagonists, with whom they usually maintain a functionally interlocking, even if conflictive, relationship.

A recent world-wide survey of 233 ethno-political conflicts classifies the antagonists involved in the following manner: 81 groups, labelled as *ethnonationalists*, pursue some type of separatist objective; 45 groups are described as *ethnoclasses*, generally of low status, who demand more equitable treatment; 83 *indigenous peoples* are concerned fundamentally about issues of group autonomy, whereas 49 *militant religious sects*, almost all of them Muslims, are involved in conflicts of various sorts; finally, 66 ethno-political groups are classified as *communal contenders*, either advantaged or disadvantaged, who seek power for themselves.[4]

If we understand why ethnic conflicts occur and how they evolve, which we attempt to do in the following chapters, then it should be easier to devise strategies and procedures whereby the negative effects of conflict, and particularly of ethnic violence, might be mitigated. It should also be possible to formulate policies that will deal constructively with ethnic diversity within a framework of democratic governance, justice and respect for human rights. We shall look at different kinds of ethnic policies adopted by the states studied in the UNRISD project, in Chapter 7. While ethnic conflicts – as distinct from violent confrontations, which are an extreme form of conflict – are not usually resolved once and for all (they have a strong tendency to rear their head anew at different times), it is possible to embark upon roads that can lead to conflict transformation and conflict management. In Chapter 10 we take a closer look at the way some of the conflicts studied in this book have been solved or are being managed.

Given the sometimes extreme, and unpredictable, violence of some ethnic conflicts, the international community has become increasingly concerned with the need for conflict prevention, or at least for the avoidance of warfare and violence, by attempting to channel potential and existing conflicts into peaceful and constructive avenues. As we shall have occasion to see in later chapters, ethnic conflicts do not emerge full-blown, but usually go through a period of incubation. This means that the potential for violence can be detected at an early stage, and if so, may be avoided. Among the characteristic signs of impending violence we might mention the increase in repressive measures by states against distinct ethnic minorities or against ethnic dissidents, the failure of democratic mechanisms for negotiation or power-sharing between ethnic political actors, the emergence of essentialist ethnic ideologies and tightly knit ethnic political 'vanguards', the rise in racist and xenophobic postures among the population, increasing economic and political disparities between ethnic groups, and legal arrangements designed to favour one ethnic group and exclude others.

Genocide and politicide become likely, according to some theorists, if (1) persisting cleavages exist among ethnic groups; (2) elites have a history of relying on repression to maintain power; (3) elites use their power to reward groups differentially for their loyalty; (4) the society has recently experienced a political upheaval, for example, a revolution or a defeat in war; and (5) exclusionary ideologies arise which define target groups as expendable.[5] These warning signals, if interpreted in time by perceptive agents both within and without a given country, might give rise to efforts at what is now being termed 'preventive diplomacy', in the hope of avoiding bloodbaths and forestalling violence. As we shall see later, numerous ethnic organizations formerly decried as outlaws, bandits or terrorists by governments and the groups in power, have later become legitimate interlocutors in the search for peaceful solutions, at times, however, only after violence has taken its brutal toll. The hope of 'preventive diplomats' is that the parties in conflict may be able to recognize in advance the high costs of violence and therefore opt for alternative solutions. Whether this is utopian thinking or *Realpolitik* can only be judged by the results of practical efforts in concrete situations.

In the aftermath of the global power confrontation between 'capitalism' and 'communism' as alternative world systems, some analysts imagine that humanity has reached a final stage of bliss with the triumph of Western-style liberal democracy, which is termed the 'end of history', while others augur an ominous new era of clashes between different civilizations.[6] The real world lies somewhere between these two extreme views. Even as the demise of communism has unlocked or actually engendered a number of acute ethnic conflicts in Eastern Europe, the Caucasus and Central Asia, the loosening of cold war ideological straitjackets has given greater salience to ethnic factors in many political conflicts in other parts of the world. Capitalist development continues to be unequal and polarized, both within countries as well as internationally, and the attendant social and economic differentiation frequently follows ethnic cleavages. These actually occur more frequently within civilizational spheres, rather than across civilizational boundaries. Ethnic nationalism reasserts itself around the globe, even as the modern concept of the nation-state is challenged by both economic globalization and an increasingly interdependent international system, as well as by local-level, regional and community-based identities. At the same time that universal human rights are becoming a truly global ideology, the collective rights of peoples, minorities and communities are asserted as a necessary ingredient for the recognition of the dignity and equality of human beings everywhere.

2 The Pitfalls of Ethnicity and Ethnic Conflict

Ethnic conflict appears to be a catch-all term, which covers a wide array of different kinds of social and political confrontations. In fact, it may not be appropriate to use the term 'ethnic conflict' in all situations currently so described. It is debatable whether the use of the word 'ethnic' actually aids the better understanding of the dynamics and underlying forces involved in conflictive situations or, on the contrary, whether the recourse to the presumed 'ethnic' identity of the groups and actors in such conflicts contributes more to a blurring of the basic issues. Such problems are often addressed in theoretical discussions, but they must also be dealt with in concrete situations and they have practical implications. Policy alternatives must consider whether ethnicity (that is, the nature and characteristics of ethnic groups and their members) is a factor when the management and possible solution of conflicts is dealt with. Politicians have to decide whether 'ethnic' criteria should be incorporated in electoral systems, power-sharing arrangements or the writing of constitutions and the adoption of legislations. The success of economic development strategies may depend on the way their hoped for results will benefit or harm different ethnic communities.

Even a cursory description of a conflictive situation in which different ethnic groups are implicated, however, entails the use of terms and concepts which do not always mean the same thing to everybody in all contexts. Thus, a first approach to the problem challenges us to address some of the pitfalls regarding the conceptual issues involved in the use of the terms 'ethnic conflict', 'ethnic group' or 'ethnicity'.

The specialized literature on this subject is vast. As in so many other areas of the social sciences, interested readers will soon appreciate that different theoretical approaches compete for their attention if not for their loyalty. Some of these may seem to be incompatible with each other and mutually exclusive. Others are soon revealed to be partial and incomplete on their own, but useful and sometimes penetrating when taken in conjunction with other complementary approaches.

Our starting point must be the observable fact that most of the world's countries are multi-ethnic, that is to say, that within the framework of existing state structures the population is divided into heterogeneous groups, which are distinguished according to certain ethnic attributes and may be referred to as *ethnies*. To the extent that the planet is divided into territorial units called states, there is no longer a single people anywhere who are not formally incorporated into a territory which some state claims as its own. It follows that when we speak about 'the ethnic question' we refer to the problematic of ethnic groups in relation to territorial states as these have developed historically.[1]

Ethnic groups are formed and acquire their identities (a process sometimes referred to in the literature as *ethnogenesis*) as the result of different historical processes. Thus, some ethnies have ancient origins and are able to trace their ancestry continuously from earlier times to the present. A number of Asian and European peoples and nations would fit this description. Other ethnic groups appear to have been constituted more recently and their formative process has perhaps not yet concluded, such as some peoples in the Americas and in Africa. Still others, who existed at one time, have disappeared from the face of the earth, either due to physical extinction or by way of sociocultural and political transformations which have contributed to their disappearance. We know of their existence through ancient documents, historical literature or orally transmitted myths and legends.

Some authors maintain that many modern nations have ancient ethnic origins.[2] Other scholars have shown how modern ethnies develop as a result of structural changes in their countries, particularly during the period of colonialism. Thus, for example, a number of African ethnies are the result of transformations which occurred during foreign domination and of specific policies carried out by colonial administrations. In India, historians have documented the attempt of the British Raj to recruit into service the so-called 'martial races', thus establishing conditions for distinctions and identities which in later years have led to tensions and conflicts. The widespread use of the 'tribal' category in India has also been attributed to British colonial policy. The Miskito Indians of Nicaragua, who entered into conflict with the Sandinista government for several years during the 1980s, do not appear to be of pre-Columbian origin as are other indigenous peoples of the Americas, but emerged during the process of socioeconomic formation of the Atlantic coast. Similarly, the *Metis*, a well-organized indigenous group in Canada, are the outcome of racial and cultural mixing during colonial times, as their name indicates. Palestinian national identity is the product of the twentieth century and is being reinforced constantly through the struggle of the Palestinians for self-determination.[3] Ethnogenesis and ethnic formation can thus be said to follow different paths under differing circumstances, as a result of internal and external factors within a complex web of interrelationships.

As a result of state formation in Europe from the sixteenth century onwards, some ethnies have become the dominant or majority people and have excluded others from participation in the state. These ethnies became nations and in some cases constituted nation-states. In fact, the territorial state often became the framework within which the nation arose. The European model of the nation-state structured the inter-ethnic relations between its constituent peoples. Later, this model of the state was transferred to the rest of the world, and it constitutes the institutional framework within which inter-ethnic relations are structured in contemporary times.

A number of countries which achieved independence in the process of decolonization during the nineteenth (Latin America) and twentieth (Africa and Asia) centuries consciously adopted the model of the nation-state to organize their political life. While in some cases it may be said that pre-existing nations were able to form their state and thus configure their national characteristics, in most contemporary countries the states were created first, and only then have the corresponding nations been formed out of the various ethnic groups which occupied their respective territories. Moreover, in some countries these nations were formed, or are still being formed, by immigrant populations. Thus, we may conclude that ethnies are transformed into nations when they manage to create state structures through varying historical dynamics, or else, when a constituted state structure becomes the framework which gives national form to one or various ethnies.

Nevertheless, there are ethnies in the world which for one reason or another (size, history, territory, collective consciousness, levels of organization) consider themselves and are considered by others as nations, even if they cannot boast a state of their own. These collectivities are often referred to as stateless nations or peoples. They may be part of a multinational state which recognizes them as nationalities and in which they may have a greater or lesser degree of autonomy; such was the case in the former Soviet Union and Yugoslavia. Frequently they may be considered as ethnic (or national) minorities without significant participation in state structures (the case of most tribal peoples, for example, or non-Islamic minorities in Islamic states). At times, an existing state will actually withhold recognition of such a group, or even deny its existence, when it feels threatened by the real or imagined demands that the minority may pose. This was the case of the Palestinians in Israel, and is that of the Kurds in Turkey. Some territorial minorities may be divided among various states. It is clear that often the nature and dynamics of the ethnic phenomenon is determined by state structures and policies, even among ethnies who do not achieve a territorial state of their own and who are therefore not generally referred to as 'nations'.

In order to place the ethnic question in an adequate analytical framework, it is necessary to attempt some clarity in the conceptual and terminological confusion which accompanies the concepts ethnie or ethnic group and similar, sometimes interchangeable terms such as people, nation, nationality, community and tribe. Neither the social sciences nor legal science nor popular usage have achieved a consensus regarding ethnic terminology. Furthermore, the terminology used by scholars frequently reflects regional or national intellectual traditions and dominant social and political ideologies. For example, colonial administrators discovered (some would say, created) 'tribes' in Africa and Asia, and this term is still being used widely in discussions about the ethnic question in these countries, even though many scholars (and not a few politicians) oppose its use on political and ideological grounds. Thus the use of the term 'tribe' reflects the nineteenth-century imperial idea that colonized peoples lacked governmental structures and adequate levels of civilization so that that their subjugation by the 'more advanced' states was perfectly justified within an evolutionary, Darwinian vision of history. It is still common to read references to 'tribal conflict' as something rather less rational and more unfathomable than the 'civilized' wars of modern nations. In anthropological usage, the term tribe originally refers to a people who possess a simple level of political organization; today it may refer also to an ethnically distinct segment of a wider structured polity, even in a modern urban environment. Thus, African cities are said to be populated by people of different tribal origins who sometimes organize themselves into tribal associations for economic and political activity.

In Eastern Europe political and intellectual debates centred for many decades on the terms 'nations', 'nationalities' and 'national minorities'. These concepts have their origin in the history of the Tsarist, Ottoman and Austro-Hungarian empires, and were developed as well as codified in legal documents and state policies during the communist period. Underlying the use of this terminology was a Marxist vision of stages of historical evolution in which fully-fledged 'nations' achieve formal statehood, whereas simple 'nationalities' (or worse, 'people without history' – the concept comes originally from Hegel) are destined to something less than statehood, if not to complete extinction. After the First World War, the Wilsonian principle of the self-determination of nations triggered a scramble for international recognition as nations by numerous minority and subordinate ethnic groups, a process which has not yet abated.

In contrast to the controversies in Central and Eastern Europe, the 'national question' was of relatively minor importance in Western Europe and North America, yet even here it has re-emerged in recent decades, sometimes violently. Great Britain, Spain, Belgium, Italy, Canada and other states have had their share of ethnic movements challenging the central nation-state. In the United Kingdom and the United States, 'race relations' is the term most frequently used to refer to the dynamics of relationships between different ethnic groups, basically between the White majority and the non-White minority or minorities. The widespread use of the concept 'race' in the Anglo-Saxon countries can be traced to the hegemonic ideology of White supremacy and racial stratification which developed in those countries in the nineteenth century, though it currently also involves the relations between natives or nationals and immigrants, principally from the Third World.

Ethnic terminology is different in Latin America, where indigenous communities (native American Indians) are thought to be at the lower end of a scale of socio-economic development within unitary nation-states. Although racial categories are sometimes employed, the concept of Indians or indigenous groups, as distinct from the 'national' populations, denotes basically a cultural and socio-economic category. It is held that in the process of 'development' and 'national integration' indigenous cultures will become assimilated or modernized and therefore will tend to disappear or melt into the national whole. The indigenous themselves prefer to be known as 'peoples' rather than 'populations', 'communities' or 'minorities', because as peoples they consider that they can claim for themselves certain rights according to international human rights principles. From this brief overview, we may conclude that ethnic terminology reflects not only a certain amount of conceptual confusion but also the various ideological frames of reference and the different theoretical approaches in which these terms are commonly used.

According to some scholars and, I might say, for the general public, the ethnic phenomenon is as old as humanity itself. From primordial times, the various nomadic or agriculturalist peoples around the world were said to be identified by name, language, customs, beliefs and territorial origins. And though many have disappeared or became transformed, others persisted over the centuries, identified as such from generation to generation. Ethnic identity or ethnicity, it is argued, expresses primordial, affective, deeply rooted sentiments of the human being. It is said that the identification of individuals with their group expresses some basic, innate human need, similar to that of life in the family.[4] In fact, a number of authors refer to ethnicity as a kind of kinship and to the ethnic group as an extended kin group. Kinship may be a real bond, based on blood ties, when descent from common ancestors can be traced. But usually it is fictitious, deriving more from shared beliefs about supposed common ancestry. Founding myths and stories are passed on from generation to generation and strengthen the bonds and identities of those who hold them dear. The important element, it is held, is that even if kinship is fictitious, the members of an ethnie assume it as if it were real.

This *primordialist* position is taken to extremes under the recent influence of sociobiology. Within the framework of this approach, some authors contend that ethnicity (the close ties that bind together the members of an ethnie) is based in genetics. That is, the persons who share a certain number of genes (it is not said how many nor which), will bond together and seek to reproduce their genes in the most efficient possible manner. This they achieve through the endogamy of the ethnic group, leading to a process of genetic selection which ensures greater opportunity for group survival.[5] If genetics accounts for ethnic identity and bonding, then it is easy to conclude that ethnic conflicts may be genetically determined. Such conflicts will then arise when an ethnically identified genetic population needs, in some mysterious manner, to ensure or expand its reproductive capability. This is mostly a *post-hoc* interpretation, for the ability of such a genetically-based model to predict specific conflicts is basically nil, unless we accept that the potential for conflict exists in any situation where two ethnically distinct populations interact.

Without going to the extent of accepting the existence of 'primordial sentiments' or genetic imperatives in order to account for the importance of the ethnic factor in the social life of human communities, it may be said simply that ethnic identities are a universal, recurrent phenomenon and constitute one of the basic forms of social integration. However, the *primordialist* approach cannot account for the dynamics of ethnogenesis (the formation of ethnies over time), nor does it tell us much about the internal and external structures of ethnic groups and identities. It will be necessary to look at some other theoretical approaches.

Beyond genetic imperatives and primal bonding instincts in humans, ethnic groups are sometimes defined by their persistence over time and their capacity for biological and cultural reproduction. Why and how do people bond in this fashion, not only at any one time with other members of the group but also, more importantly, with past and future generations?

One answer to this question is provided by the idea of *culture*. Ethnic identity and continuity are maintained as a result of the transmission within the group (through the processes of socialization, education, internalization of values) of the basic norms and customs which constitute the central core of the ethnic culture. In time, cultural patterns may vary, but this is usually a slow process and occurs over several generations. It does not alter the fact that the core culture is reproduced and transmitted from generation to generation through shared norms and values which are recognized as such. This, then, would explain the diversity and persistence of ethnies in time and space. It is through the mechanisms of cultural reproduction that the basic norms which structure the life of the group are defined. Each ethnic group so defined can be distinguished from others by its culture, or at least by certain cultural elements (more will be said about this below), whereas, on the inside, people 'belong' to a culture, are bounded by it and distinguish themselves from others who 'belong' to other cultures. Inherent in the notion of culture is the concept of ethnocentrism, the idea that those on the inside consider themselves to be better and superior to the outsiders. The 'we' and 'they' approach to inter-ethnic relations is fraught with potential conflict. If the outsider is seen as inherently dangerous, if the 'other' is rejected, feared, despised, excluded, demonized or dehumanized; or conversely, if the 'we' group is thought to be threatened, its survival endangered and its existence as a group undermined by the 'other', then conditions for conflict exist. Whether such conditions are sufficient for conflict to break out is another question. We are familiar with many societies in which such conditions exist but conflict does not break out. This is because in addition to conditioning elements, a number of other circumstantial factors must usually be present, the so-called triggering mechanisms of conflict emergence.

Anthropologists have learned that ethnic groups are not only defined by the content of their culture; indeed, some would argue that cultural content is actually irrelevant. What appears to be more significant is boundary-formation through social organization, that complex web of relationships whereby groups are formed, bounded and defined, and by means of which individuals become included or excluded. Ethnic group boundaries may be rigid and fixed, or else they may be permeable and flexible. In either case, the presence or absence of conflict is not easily deduced, for the presence of strong boundaries may either deter conflict or induce it, whereas weak boundaries may, under different circumstances, lead to similar contradictory results.

None the less, this *culturalist* or *normativist* approach raises many other questions. It may explain the persistence of the characteristic traits of an ethnie over time, but it neither explains their origin nor their variability nor the dynamics of ethnic change. Other theoretical approaches have attempted to answer these questions.

From another viewpoint, ethnies are groups placed in asymmetrical relationships to other groups within the framework of historically given social and economic formations. They occupy different niches in a wider social and economic system or different positions in a scale of wealth or power. According to this point of view, ethnic characteristics of social groups are the cultural response to the challenges raised by certain kinds of social and economic relations between different populations. This simply means that over time different peoples establish specific economic and social relations among each other within the framework of wider social and political spaces (market systems, territorial states, modes of production), and that the ensuing interaction generates particular cultural responses in every case, for example, nomadic herding peoples in symbiosis with sedentary agriculturalists, ethnically distinct traders in village or small town communities, European land-owners and native peasantries in a colonial setting, culturally specific occupational castes in ranked, hierarchical societies, etc.

This *structuralist* approach has been found useful in the study of interethnic relations in two distinct types of situations. In the first place, within the framework of colonialism, in which colonizers and colonized face each other as dominant and subordinate groups. The ethnic (cultural and biological) characteristics of the opposing groups become emblematic in the functioning and maintenance of the system of colonial exploitation and domination. Racism, other forms of discrimination and the cultural categorization of the population, contribute to perpetuate and accentuate ethnic differences that turn into markers of inequality and stratification. When such a situation prevails in the post-colonial period, it is sometimes referred to as *internal colonialism.*

Secondly, the structuralist approach helps us understand the dynamics of immigrant societies where ethnically distinct groups also become integrated differentially into new social and economic structures and are in turn categorized racially and culturally in answer to the needs of a segmented and fragmented labour market.[6] We have here a cultural division of labour, that is, the pattern whereby cultural differences between ethnic groups determine the nature of their members' insertion in the labour market (and therefore their access to resources and economic and social goods). But this differential insertion (which is the result of an historical process) in turn reinforces the cultural characteristics of the group. Gilroy, among others, has documented this process among Blacks in the United Kingdom.[7] This approach underlines the fact that ethnic identities as well as inter-ethnic relations depend to a great extent on the structural context in which they occur.

That the ethnic identities of groups may be the result of certain historically given economic and social structures is a persuasive argument in some contexts, but it does not explain the variability of the ethnic phenomenon, nor the currently crucial question of why ethnic conflicts arise when and how they do, why some groups assume their ethnicity more intensely than others, or why some ethnically based movements last longer and are more successful than others. Some scholars look for explanations to these questions not in social, economic and political structures, but in the motivations and behaviour of individuals. Group identities and behaviour can then be traced back to the preferences and rational choices of individuals rather than to the weight of custom, the norms and traditions of peoples or the imperatives of economic and political structures. *Rational choice theory*, derived from economics, states that individuals will act rationally to obtain their valued ends and maximize their benefits. If emphasizing their ethnicity will further these objectives, then rational individuals will be impelled to do so. This would explain why some individuals opt for ethnicity to achieve their individual ends, whereas others reject or ignore it.[8]

Ethnic groups are said to possess collective interests (the sum of the individual interests of their members), and they compete among themselves in a rational and calculated manner for these interests (resources, power, prestige, wealth, etc.). Consequently, ethnicity as a variable is the result of the rational interests of the members of the group; it is 'something' which can be taken or discarded by choice. The theories of rational choice as applied to inter-ethnic relations generally take ethnic differences between groups for granted, and use them as the starting point for their analysis, rather than as something to be explained.[9] Finally, a currently fashionable way in which students of ethnicity deal with some of the conceptual issues referred to is to deny any 'reality' to ethnic groups as such. What seems to be more important is the 'discourse' on ethnicity, that is, the way people invent or construct their ethnicity or that of others. This may be the result of political imperatives or ideological preferences, but once a 'discourse' or a 'narrative' is generated and becomes legitimized to some extent, it exerts considerable influence on the dynamics of ethnic relations and on human behaviour. For example, after having considered, for a long time, the nationalities in the Soviet Union as the historical result of a long process of ethnogenesis, Russian academics now prefer to see them as an intellectual construct, in which ethnic sentiment develops on the basis of historical differences in culture, as well as the myths, conceptions and doctrines that are formed in their context.[10]

The fashionable modernization theory in the social sciences predicts the progressive disappearance of ethnic and 'sub-national' identities and loyalties in the process of economic development and nation- and state-building. Accordingly, people will transfer their loyalties from the ethnic community to the wider society, to the nation, to economic and social class, to political parties. The emergence or persistence of ethnic conflicts may then be explained as an expression of incomplete or failed modernization. Some ethnic groups may feel threatened by modernization and will resist it, thus entering into conflict with the forces and groups that are promoting the modernization agenda. This is said to occur among so-called 'traditional' societies and cultures, whether tribal or indigenous. It is also true that efforts to constitute modern states have often been highly destructive of the nations and ethnies which were incorporated, often forcefully and against their will, into the process of political and economic development.[11] Under such circumstances, ethnic conflicts may express collective forms of resistance to the processes of assimilation, ethnocide and genocide.

More persuasive than the 'failed modernization' theory is the argument that the 'mass politics' associated with modernization generates ethnic mobilization and makes ethnic identities more relevant and potentially more useful in the competition and struggle over resources, wealth and power that are so characteristic of changing modern societies. Therefore, as societies change and modernize, ethnic identities may be strengthened and 'ethnopolitics' will become simply one more way of 'playing' politics.[12] Studies of the processes of migration and urbanization in various parts of the world have shown how urban immigrants tend to coalesce in ethnic neighbourhoods, to form and maintain ethnic institutions and to vote in ethnic patterns. Whereas at first glance this may seem to be a sort of traditional 'holding pattern' for ethnic groups in the face of insecurity and instability in the modern urban environment, a second look will show that this 'politicized ethnicity' actually emerges in the modernization process and is put to good use by 'ethnic brokers', who further their collective and individual interests. While modern 'ethnic ideologies' may be distinguished from the traditional cultural patterns of 'pre-modern' ethnic communities, they actually reinforce and build on each other. Modern ethnic ideologies are rooted in the traditional ethnic identities of the populations they relate to, and these in turn are often strengthened by the new meanings and symbols that the former provide.[13]

While so much ethnic conflict is confrontational and involves open inter-group hostility and animosity, frequently it takes the form of ethnic and racial competition for economic and political resources and collective goods (such as jobs, housing, education, budgetary allocations, land rights, etc.). In countries divided along ethnic and regional lines, a 'cultural division of labour' may occur, by which certain ethnies are traditionally identified with specific occupations to which they are attached for historical or geographical reasons. For example, in Guatemala the Maya Indians are mostly peasant workers on large estates managed by *Ladino* landowners. While an Indian may aspire to become a land-owner (of a small plot of individually held acreage), a *Ladino* (descendant of the European settlers) will never accept the status of rural labourer. In Burundi the Tutsi pastoralists and the Hutu farmers construct their respective identities in ethnic terms. Similarly, in Malaysia, the Chinese have been linked to 'modern' economic activities, whereas the native Malays were tied to traditional agriculture and have moved more recently into the civil service. Such a cultural division of labour does not necessarily lead to ethnic conflict if the economic activities of each group are kept separate or complement each other. It tends to lead to conflict, however, when the relationship between the ethnic groups is asymmetrical, when one of them holds political power while the other or others are excluded from it, or when the higher status group (for example, an ethnically distinct landowner) clearly exploits or oppresses an ethnic 'underclass' (for example, the Indian peasantry). Another source of conflict occurs when a distinct ethnic group moves into the economic preserve of the other and competes with it for the same 'collective goods'. In New York, for example, conflict has erupted on several occasions between African-Americans and Korean shopkeepers in traditionally Black neighbourhoods. Competition between Hispanics and Koreans also seems to have been a factor in the Los Angeles riots of 1992. When different ethnic groups occupy distinct 'economic niches', conflict tends to arise when 'niche overlap' occurs.

Another form of ethnic and racial competition is to be found in 'split labour markets', that is, where different racial or ethnic groups are paid different wages for the same work. Third World immigrants in the industrialized West tend to receive less pay than native Whites for the same activity. Of course, a similar kind of discrimination is exercised against women in most societies, regardless of whether they are ethnically or racially distinct from the higher-status group. The struggle for equality in the labour market may tend to drive wages down, as does labour competition in general, and will thus be resisted by the privileged ethnic group at the top. This kind of ethnic conflict is often found in relation to trade union activity. Again, when ethnic groups are seen to occupy specific 'economic niches', then a change in their status may lead to ethnic competition and conflict. The more asymmetrical the relationship between two economically differentiated ethnic groups, the higher will be the potential for ethnic conflict to arise. Also, the more two ethnically distinct economic niches overlap, the higher the potential for conflict to occur. The analysis of ethnic conflict within the framework of 'competition theory' has been shown to be a useful device for the understanding of such conflicts.[14]

In earlier times, it was generally considered that ethnic identity or ethnicity was something permanent, inherent, eternal, and that when given the chance, it would appear, or reappear, in political and social life. Later, ethnicity was to be subsumed under terms such as 'nation' and 'class' which were wider, more imposing identities. It was held that 'nation-building', a process widely hailed in the 1960s, would make sub-national identities, such as ethnic groups, disappear. Social groupings and their organizations based on class and occupation (industrial workers, middle sectors, business interests, peasants, intellectuals, etc.) were expected to become overriding and would relegate ethnicity to second place. This was considered to be not only inevitable in the process of 'modernization', but it was also held to be desirable. Ethnic attachments were somehow considered to be 'pre-modern', 'irrational' and a stumbling block in the process of development and nation-building.

However, as recent events show, under certain circumstances ethnicity and ethnic identities as mobilizing principles can make a comeback. Nationalism, it is said, 'rears its head', the 'spectre of tribalism' arises when something in the wider society breaks down. Nowadays, scholars tend to reject the idea that ethnicity is something 'there', permanent, which resurges naturally so to speak, when the ropes that hold it down are broken. A recent tendency in theoretical discussions underlines the fact that ethnicities are 'constructed', 'invented', 'imagined' under particular circumstances and for specific reasons and objectives.

1.   TYPES OF COLLECTIVE IDENTITY

When linked to an existing state or to recognized territorial boundaries, ethnic identities are often considered to be identical to 'national' identities. When such territorial identification is not directly relevant, then other criteria come to the fore. In his study for this project, Ralph Premdas shows how Guyana, for example, is split down the middle between Africans and Indians, each group identifying itself and the other by perceived *racial/biological* criteria. Tamils and Sinhalese in Sri Lanka are distinguished by *language* and *religion*. In Lebanon, *religion* is the major visible factor separating the actors in the protracted conflict which split that nation for so many years. However, as Kamal Hamdan reports, religion itself was not an issue in the civil violence, rather, it was economic and political power. Religion is also the distinguishing and dividing factor in the conflict in Northern Ireland, but the struggle is only partially about religion.[15] In one dramatic case of ethnic conflict, carefully studied by Ashis Nandy and his colleagues in India, the religious factor is indeed an issue in communal strife and violence (see Chapter 4).

Language is the visible factor in the political conflict between Flemish and Walloons in Belgium, whereas in Burundi, according to René Lemarchand, the complex and sometimes subtle distinction between Hutu and Tutsi seems to be more of a recent historical creation than linked to any observable objective criteria.

In some cases included in this study, ethnicities are an umbrella term for *regional interests*. John Markakis observes that in southern Sudan, for example, a number of distinct peoples who did not identify with each other in the past, are now joined as 'southern Sudanese' in their common struggle against northern dominance. Religion, language and territory do play their part here, but it is not yet possible to speak of a single southern Sudanese ethnic identity. Similarly, Markakis notes that in Ethiopia, regional interests were dominant in the recent civil war, and they subsumed a number of distinct ethnic identities; yet the conflict in both these countries has traditionally been framed in ethnic terms.

In Kashmir and the Punjab, as well as in north-eastern Sri Lanka, ethnic conflicts are regionally localized (though their consequences spill over into the country at large and even abroad), and controversy rages as to the political status of these regions (autonomous, independent, federated, etc.). Here the ethnic groups in conflict are clearly identified with their particular regions. The same holds for the conflict in Kurdistan, studied by Gérard Chaliand, or the war between Armenia and Azerbaijan in 1992–3 over the status of the region of Nagorno-Karabakh.

From the above discussion it becomes clear that the various criteria commonly employed to identify ethnic groups may be usefully classified into *objective* and *subjective* categories. By objective criteria we generally mean those attributes of a group that are independent of an individual's volition, that ascribe him to his group at birth or through the process of socialization. They serve to identify the group as such and to denote individual and collective membership in the group. Objective criteria are sometimes externally visible markers, such as racial characteristics, material culture or group activities. They are the specific attributes of an ethnic group independently of the individuals who partake of them. In contrast, subjective criteria refer to the psychological, affective, individual mental and emotional processes by which specific persons identify with a culture or an ethnic group, through which they assume a particular ethnic identity, and which guide their actions and behaviour as members of such groups.

The most commonly observed objective criteria, which are relevant in the various instances of ethnic conflicts referred to in this book, include the following:

1. *Language* is a powerful indicator of ethnic and national identity. National languages are deemed highly important by state-builders in the process of nation-building. When a dominant language (spoken by a dominant ethnic group) displaces other tongues, then the ethnic identity of the subordinate groups changes. Language policies are therefore important in processes of ethnic and cultural change. The struggle over language policies and language rights are often a major ingredient in ethnic conflicts. *Linguism*, as some authors have called it, was a crucial political issue for many years in India. Numerous linguistic minorities around the world are officially prohibited from using their language in public places, schools or in the communications media. Such is the case of the Kurds in Turkey. Consequently, language rights are often spoken of as a type of human rights and have become an issue in ethnic political mobilization around the world. Vernacular languages, when distinct from official or national languages, may be considered as a powerful integrating factor of ethnic identity and as potent markers of ethnic differences. It might be argued that the stronger the linguistic vitality of a people, the greater their political and social viability.[16]

2. *Religion* has historically been an important marker of the ethnic identity of a people. Whereas in contemporary Western societies religion is mainly a private matter, to be kept strictly separate from the public – mainly political – sphere (the separation of Church and state), in other societies religious practices are part and parcel of family and community life. Here religion conditions interpersonal behaviour, local and public institutions, legal process and the administration of justice, moral values and the norms of individual behaviour and customs. In urban industrialized society people interact independently of religion; their ethnic identities may not be related to religion at all, or only weakly. But in those societies in which religion intervenes in the various spheres of public life, it may become a hegemonic factor and thus determinant for ethnicity. The more all-inclusive a religion, the more it becomes an ethnic marker. The more the religious factor is interwoven with other elements of social life, the more important does religion become as a determining factor of ethnicity. Thus, for example, in Lebanon, being Christian or Muslim refers not only to a private expression of religious faith, but to community, and to collective behaviour and belonging. Similarly, the communal riots

which periodically shake the political foundations of modern India involve Muslims and Hindus not as individual believers, but rather as members of publicly distinct collectivities whose political histories are interwoven. Protestants and Catholics in Northern Ireland do not engage in conflict over their respective forms of worship, but over ideological differences associated with the distinct history of each religious group as a political and sociological community, and which can therefore be referred to as distinct ethnic groups, though many of the other visible attributes of ethnicity are absent.

3. *Territory* is the basis of the economic and political structures which are the fundamental units in the life of ethnies and nations. The territorial state is considered to be the determining element of the existence of a nation in modern times. Peoples who consider themselves to be nations aspire to have their own territorial state (Kurds, Palestinians, Tamils of Sri Lanka, Québecois, Basques, etc.). But even when no such state exists, identification with some territory considered as one's own becomes essential to justify ethnic identity and continuity. The Tamils fight for their homeland in Tamil Eelam, and claim original occupation of north-eastern Sri Lanka for 2000 years; indigenous movements from Australia to the Amazon defend their ancestral homelands; in Malaysia the *Bumiputra* ('Sons of the soil') defend traditional territorial privileges against the Chinese population; as do the native Fijians against Indian Fijians. Chicanos in the United States identify with 'Aztlán' (the mythical homeland of the Aztecs). In 1992, the Greek government launched a worldwide campaign against the international recognition of newly independent Macedonia, arguing that the name of this republic referred in fact to an ancient Greek territory ('Northern Greece', the birthplace of Alexander the Great). Nagorno-Karabakh is claimed by Armenia, and fought over by Azerbaijan.

The majority of the thousands of ethnic groups in the world are identified with some territory which is not only their vital environment, but also their real or mythical land of origin, sometimes imbued with sacred meaning. Serbia denies rights to the ethnic Albanians in Kosovo, because of the historically important (for Serbian identity) battle of Kosovo in the fourteenth century. Ethnies possessing a territorial base usually have more legitimate reasons to claim and conserve their identity than those who do not. Non-territorial ethnic groups, such as the Gypsies (Roma or Sinti), have a more difficult time in establishing their ethnic identity and obtaining international recognition. Some authors speak here of a 'primary identity', in contrast to the 'secondary identity' of peoples who do not have a territorial referent. Thus, in the United States, a distinction is generally made between 'territorial minorities' such as the Native Americans, Hawaiians and Mexican-Americans in the south-west, and the immigrant minorities of later generations, including involuntary immigrants (slaves from Africa). As world migration flows have increased considerably in recent decades, a new concept of 'diaspora communities' has been coined, which refers to emigrant groups that conserve certain links with their home country even while they establish a niche in the host country (Indians in Africa, Chinese in Southeast Asia, Turks in Germany, etc.). Generally, we may conclude that the stronger the territorial link, the stronger the ethnic identity of a group.

4. *Social organization* is the technical social science term which refers to the complex web of institutions and social relations that provide consistency to an ethnic group over and beyond the personal identity of its individual members. To the extent that the latter participate in the social organization of their ethnie, their dependency vis-à-vis the group and its collective values increases. Social organization establishes the boundaries of a group, it is the framework within which 'we' and 'they', 'insiders' and 'outsiders', are distinguished. Some scholars consider the (social) boundaries or limits of the group as a fundamental element in the definition of ethnicity.[17]

Social organization as a concept implies multiple levels and instances, so it may be present in greater or lesser intensity, and therefore its importance as a marker of ethnic identity may vary. In some situations, ethnic groups have numerous and complex interrelated and interwoven institutions and social relationships; that is to say, they are linked through 'multiplex' relations. But other ethnies have weaker institutions, and relationships between their members affect only a small part of an individual's lifelong social relations. A good part of these take place with members of other ethnic groups within the framework of political, social and economic institutions which are not necessarily identified with the ethnic group as such, or which are openly inter-ethnic. Obviously, if an ethnie is concentrated territorially, its social organization will probably be more viable than if the group lives interspersed with other groups within a wider space or territory.

Social organization as an ethnic group's attribute may be considered as a variable which makes the group more or less viable and therefore conditions its possibility for survival over time. The more structured the level of social organization, the stronger the ethnic identity of the group, and therefore the more likely its continuity.

5. *Culture*, in the widest sense of the term, constitutes a complex of distinctive elements of any ethnie. If we leave aside the factors mentioned

before (language, religion and social organization), which many scholars include in their concept of culture, then what remains relates mainly to (1) material aspects of culture, that is, cultural artefacts, and (2) value systems, symbols and meanings, norms, mores and customs, which are shared by the members of an ethnie and which distinguish the 'insiders' from the 'outsiders'. The social sciences (except anthropology) used to attribute minor importance to cultural phenomena, considering them to be of secondary significance, of being determined by other factors rather than being determining by themselves. In other words, cultural phenomena were deemed to be a 'dependent variable'. Thus, the cultural pluralism of many countries was not considered to be particularly significant, at least in relation to social institutions and the general processes of change (including economic and political development).

Currently, the pendulum has swung in the opposite direction. In the various poststructuralist approaches, culture has become the determining factor, and so-called structural phenomena are denied importance, when they are not actually argued out of existence. In other words, inasmuch as 'social structures' are but the result of some scholar's or theoretician's intellectual imagination, they are no more than artificial constructions rather than reflections of a non-existent reality. Within this perspective, culture means voluntarism and subjectivity. In the so-called postmodern condition, culture, particularly at the level of meanings, becomes an explanatory factor by itself. Thus, in reference to the ethnic question, it is sometimes held that the 'ethnic discourse' of social scientists, politicians, bureaucrats or ideologues actually 'creates' ethnies out of nowhere and imbues them with artificial life. A widely held opinion is that if only people did not talk so much about it, ethnicity would go away.

In relation to the problem of the criteria for the definition of ethnic groups, culture as a system of values and meanings is of paramount importance, but it cannot be decoupled from underlying structural phenomena. Culture defines the way of life which distinguishes one ethnic group from another. It is not possible to identify an ethnic group without its own culture. To the extent that culture is a dynamic factor subject to transformation due to a number of possible causes, cultural changes also condition the identity and viability of ethnic groups. Consequently, it may be argued that ethnies are cultural groups based on social structures (institutions and social relations). Culture and social structure (organization) are interrelated in a complex web of reciprocal relations and influences.

6. *Race* is sometimes considered as a category essentially different from ethnicity, because it refers to the inherited biological characteristics of individuals. This distinction is not adopted in this work, and here the

concept of 'race' as generally used in the literature will be subsumed under that of ethnie for the following reasons. First, from the point of view of human biology, there are no races, only populations that share a smaller or larger number of genetic characteristics. Slicing up the peoples of the world into any number of population segments or 'races' on the basis of a small number of genetically transmitted features is a purely arbitrary procedure which has no scientific value whatsoever. In the social sciences, as well as in everyday language, 'race' refers actually to the social and cultural construction of apparent biological differences.[18] 'Race' only exists to the extent that biological differences have meaning in terms of the cultural values and the social behaviour of people in any given society. Different racial groups are defined as such, and treated accordingly, in terms of socially constructed criteria. What makes 'race' a particularly significant marker of ethnic identity is that it commonly refers not only to the biological attributes of individuals (skin colour, facial features, body build, etc.), but also to the supposed social, cultural and psychological qualities that are associated with them. Therefore, when two interacting populations are distinguished by their 'racial' characteristics, these should be considered as attributes of ethnic differentiation, because they are culturally constructed. To be sure, not all ethnic differences are racial differences, but ethnic distinctions tend to be stronger and longer lasting to the extent that they include racial criteria.

In some cases, a single one of the foregoing elements may be sufficient to identify an ethnie, but usually a number of them come together and they reinforce each other. What is important is that the considered element(s) have meaning for the members of the group and be recognized by the rest of society or by other groups as determinant in the identification of the ethnie. Thus, for example, in the Sri Lankan conflict the Tamils are distinguished from the Sinhala by their language, religion, historical origin and according to some observers, also by their physical appearance. The Basques not only have their own language and are concentrated in a special region with its own historical traditions, but they also claim 'racial' similarities between their members, which supposedly distinguish them from other peoples in the Iberian peninsula.

The key idea of the preceding paragraph is that the 'objective' elements or attributes which have been mentioned must bear some 'meaning' for the group as well, and be recognized as such by others. This means that the objective characteristics (language, religion, race, etc.) are not simply attributes, the presence or absence of which can be attested, but they also turn out to be crucial in guiding and ordering the collective behaviour of those who share these attributes, both among themselves as well as with strangers. That is why the subjective factors of ethnic identity must also be considered as being fundamental for the existence and the definition of an ethnie.

As mentioned before, subjective factors, as distinct from objective attributes, have to do with cognition, affect, choice and will. They are thus essentially elements that pertain to the individual, although by being widely shared they may often be referred to as 'collective consciousness'. An individual's awareness of her ethnic identity is, of course, shaped by the shared identities of the group to which she belongs. An individual's choice to structure her identity in a different manner is at any rate a process which occurs after childhood, that is, after the collective identity has been imprinted upon the emerging rational human being. Thus the subjective elements in ethnic identity are always the result of the interplay between the individual's evolution and the group into which she is born or into which she is nurtured as a child. While there are marginal cases of new collective identities being created by charismatic religious or political figures, usually ethnic identities cannot be fashioned or invented out of whole cloth.

The crucial idea underlying the subjective factors of ethnicity is that of *identity*, a concept which comes to the social sciences from psychology and psychoanalysis. It refers basically to the fact that individual human beings need to identify with others in the process of socialization, that is, as social beings (non-social human beings do not exist, except as the proverbial 'wild men' or 'wolf-children' of literature). This will be discussed in Chapter 4.

3 How Conflict Came About

Public opinion may react with shock and surprise when the news media bring accounts of sudden confrontations between ethnic groups somewhere in the world. But ethnic conflicts do not arise spontaneously, and usually when they erupt in violence or have reached a level of intensity which draws the attention of the mass media, a period of preparation and incubation has passed. How do such conflicts arise? What are the factors which lead to these confrontations? Could they have been avoided? What interests do they address? And more to the point, who are the agents or actors in the conflict? And what are the social forces driving it?

When searching for the sources of contemporary ethnic conflicts it becomes clear that in many cases the roots of the confrontation can be found in the way a modern state, when originally established, related to the different ethnic groups within its borders, through constitutional arrangements, electoral systems, legislation or simply political culture and practice. Most post-colonial states adopted, at least formally, some kind of republican democracy in its parliamentary or presidential variety. How questions pertaining to the ethnic heterogeneity of the population were dealt with by successive governments (including colonial as well as sovereign administrations) has turned out to be directly relevant to the emergence or non-emergence of ethnic conflicts in later years. Most existing states are multi-ethnic or multinational. Ethnic diversity does not in itself signal the inevitability of conflict. It is only when ethnic diversity is politically mobilized to serve specific interests related to governance that the potential for conflict between ethnic groups becomes realized. A brief look at how conflicts arose in some cases will help us appreciate the factors involved in the emergence of ethnic conflicts around the world.

1. KURDISTAN

Perhaps the longest and oldest conflict included in the UNRISD project is the struggle of the Kurdish people for self-determination, or for at least a measure of liberty, equality and autonomy in the different states in which they live. This struggle has been studied by Gérard Chaliand, and his report was published in 1992.[1]

The Kurds have traditionally occupied a large mountainous area which covers parts of Turkey, Iran and Iraq, and a small fraction of Syria. While

they have never had an independent state of their own, the Kurds maintain a strong ethnic identity which distinguishes them from the surrounding Turks, Persians and Arabs. Nowadays the Kurdish population is
estimated at between 20 and 25 million, of whom 12 million live in
Turkey, 4 million in Iraq, 7 million in Iran and fewer than 1 million in
Syria.[2] Most of the Kurds are Sunni Muslims, but while they share their
religious identity with the other peoples of the region, the Kurdish language in its various dialects is quite distinct from the region's other major
languages (Turkish, Farsi, Arabic). The Kurds were incorporated into the
Ottoman empire in the sixteenth century, and because of their strategic
position along the Persian border, as well as their rugged mountain
terrain, they were able to maintain a certain degree of local autonomy
within the empire. When the Ottomans attempted to tighten their control
during the nineteenth century, they were met by a series of generally
unsuccessful Kurdish revolts. The first Kurdish nationalist stirrings
occurred at the turn of the century. After the First World War, when new
states were created from the ruins of the defeated empires, some Kurdish
leaders and intellectuals hoped for the establishment of an independent
Kurdish state. However, their aspirations were frustrated by the play of
the great powers and the opposition of Turkey and Iran. This may be considered the beginning of the 'Kurdish problem' in contemporary times.
By the Ottoman Peace Treaty of Sèvres (1920), the Kurds were granted
local autonomy and actually promised the possibility of independence at
a later stage. However, Kemalist Turkey steadfastly opposed these and
other provisions of the Sèvres treaty. Consequently, the Treaty of
Lausanne (1923) included Articles on the rights of minorities in Turkey
but did not mention the Kurds at all. The subsequent national boundaries
resulted in Greater Kurdistan being divided among five states – Iran, Iraq,
Syria, Turkey and the Soviet Union. Since that time, the Kurds have been
involved intermittently in political and sometimes military struggle for
their independent statehood or for local autonomy. The nature of the
conflict has varied from country to country and is related to the different
policies that each of these states has adopted regarding its Kurdish minority. Such policies have ranged from brutal repression, to forced assimilation, to political accommodation and, at least formally, in some instances,
local autonomy. The strategies and tactics of the various Kurdish organizations reflect these different policies, and so far this has prevented the
emergence of a unified Kurdish movement. Given the strategic geopolitical importance of Kurdistan in western Asia (particularly its oil fields), it
is not surprising that ever since the 1920s the Great Powers (Great
Britain, United States, France and the Soviet Union) have been deeply

involved in the Kurdish question. The conflict reached dramatic heights during the Gulf War (1990–1), when over two million Kurdish refugees from Iraq required international assistance and protection from the United Nations.

The Kurds are the fourth most numerous people in the Middle East, and certainly its largest ethnic minority. They also constitute one of the world's most numerous nations to have been denied an independent state. The contemporary origins of the Kurdish conflict can be traced to this denial of the principle of the right of peoples to self-determination. Some of the elements which were mentioned in Chapter 2 as conforming criteria of ethnic identity are certainly at the root of this conflict in Kurdistan: territory, language, culture and social organization all play their part in the identification of the Kurdish people, and they have become issues around which the conflict between the Kurds and the several states in which they live revolves. Moreover, the Kurds have a strong, historically rooted 'objective' identity, which is supported 'subjectively' through the process of political mobilization and the dynamics of the struggle in which they are engaged. In later chapters, we shall return to some of these issues in greater detail.

2. LEBANON

Also in the Middle East, the brutal civil war which raged in Lebanon from 1975 until the signing of the peace accord in 1991 had its roots in the long and complex dynamics of nation-building before and after the fall of the Ottoman empire. As Kamal Hamdan shows in his case study, the public administration of the region of Mount Lebanon in Ottoman times established the Druze (Muslim) and Maronite (Christian) communities as effective vehicles for the structuring of authority. Later, during the French mandate, this practice was continued, and the religious communities were further strengthened by differential economic policies.

By the National Pact of 1943, the Sunni Muslim and Christian Maronite elites agreed to share power and establish the framework for a period of political stability. However, they distanced themselves increasingly from the masses of the population, to such an extent that the Pact has been seen as a mechanism used by the elites to dominate and divide the rest of the population. Since that time, political life in Lebanon has been structured around the two principal religious communities. Developments since the Second World War tended to favour the Maronite bourgeoisie in terms of economic growth, social benefits and the political resources at their disposal. While each of the religious communities was in turn subdivided into other groups, when social and political unrest arose as a result of unequal economic development, regional geopolitics and what Hamdan terms the crisis of the middle class, the lines of conflict coalesced around these two religious communities. What began as intra-elite conflicts became inter-ethnic conflict. As the struggle deepened, the various sub-groups reaffirmed their own identity and in turn became political actors. The inability of the political system to accommodate social change in the process of mobilization and modernization strengthened the ethnic-religious identities that came to dominate the conflict from the beginning of the civil war in the mid-1970s. Outside intervention (mainly by Israel, Syria and the Palestine Liberation Organization, PLO) strengthened and exacerbated the situation until the state as such practically ceased to function and the national social structure was hopelessly fragmented. After a number of failed attempts and a political stalemate, an agreement between the warring parties in early 1991, brokered by external powers, seems to have taken hold. For how long, is anybody's guess.

The Lebanese case demonstrates that communal or inter-ethnic conflict is closely related to a number of interacting factors:

1. Pre-existing and generally recognized ethnic distinctions (in this case, religious differences).
2. These distinctions and attendant social and economic inequalities are rooted in the history of the country during the Ottoman empire, and were strengthened, if not actually fostered, by the subsequent colonial power, France.
3. Communal elites based their authority and power on the maintenance and manipulation of these ethnic distinctions, which in turn were used in political negotiations.
4. The strategies of economic growth tended to benefit one of the communities (Maronite Christians) at the expense of the other (Muslims).
5. External, regional political interests (Syria, Palestinians, Israel) further deepened communal conflict and promoted violence.
6. The major institutions of government (Parliament, judiciary) as well as the civil society (trade unions, employers' associations) were unable to function and provide alternatives to the inter-communal strife.
7. The actors in the conflict define themselves and each other in religious terms, but the conflict and the violence are not over religious issues, they are over control of political power and economic resources.

3. HORN OF AFRICA

The most serious challenges faced by states in the Horn of Africa have been posed by movements whose constituency is regional rather than ethnic, according to John Markakis' report. The conflict in Eritrea began in the early 1960s, and continued with escalating intensity for nearly three decades. It was a major contributing factor in the demise of two Ethiopian regimes during that period; the imperial regime which collapsed in 1974, and its military successor overthrown in 1991. The fall of the latter brought the conflict to a halt, with the Eritrean liberation movement in control of the region and assured of independence, its cherished goal. The conflict in southern Sudan is just as old, although it was interrupted by a decade of peace during the 1970s. It also has been a major destabilizing factor in the tortuous political history of Sudan, and the principal reason for repeated interventions by the military in the affairs of the Sudanese state. The conflict in that region shows no promise of ending soon, particularly since the avowed goal of the dissident movement is not to secede, but to reform the post-colonial state.

Neither region has a deeply rooted historical identity which can explain the rise of a militant political movement identified with it. Both are recent and typically haphazard creations of European colonialism, neither having had prior existence as an entity of any sort. Eritrea was put together by Italian colonialism; it comprised low- and highlands, and included pastoralists and peasants, Muslims and Christians, within its borders. Southern Sudan is a vast area inhabited by a variety of ethnic groups, which were first brought under one rule by British colonialism, which also attached their region administratively to northern Sudan. Neither region is ethnically or culturally homogeneous.

(a) Eritrea

As elsewhere in Africa, colonial rule in Eritrea and southern Sudan promoted a degree of regional integration through the establishment of institutions and processes that linked together the various districts and ethnic groups within each region, and provided them with a common interest in the existence of these very same institutions and processes. This trend was far more advanced in Eritrea than in southern Sudan. Initially, Italian colonialism nourished grand illusions of turning Eritrea into an African Eldorado, where peasants from the impoverished Italian south could be transplanted. Italy invested heavily in infrastructural development, providing Eritrea with an excellent road network, a railway system and a port at

Asab. In the 1930s, when Eritrea served as a base for the invasion of Ethiopia, the colony experienced phenomenal economic and urban growth, and many thousands of Eritreans served in the colonial army. The occupation of Ethiopia (1936–41) provided a further boost, which was maintained during the first half of the British military administration period (1941–52) while the Second World War lasted.

Eritrea is inhabited by a mix of ethnic groups, nine of which are officially recognized by the nationalist movement itself. One of the largest is of Abyssinian ancestry and represents the northernmost extension of the Tigrai branch, kin to the people who live in Tigrai province of Ethiopia, from whom they were separated when the colonial border was drawn. Christian and Tigrai-speaking, these highlanders till the land in a region plagued by soil erosion, drought and locust. The flanks of the Eritrean plateau and the surrounding lowlands are inhabited by several groups of pastoralists, all of them Muslim.

The ports and the lowlands have been under Muslim control ever since the rising tide of Islam flooded the region more than a millennium ago, surrounding and isolating Abyssinian Christianity in its mountainous stronghold. Throughout this period, the Eritrean highlands were the embattled northern frontier of Christian Abyssinia, ruled by local vassals of the Abyssinian crown, but seldom under its direct or effective control. Perennial conflict in this region found its ideological expression in religion, and has soured relations between followers of these two faiths to this day.

By 1945, Eritrea was already urbanized and counted thousands of industrial workers. It also had a large merchant class which had developed on the transit trade with Ethiopia and, to a lesser extent, Sudan. Generally speaking, in the early postwar period, Eritrea had reached a higher level of development than Ethiopia.

At the twilight of the colonial era, the future of the region became a matter for bargaining among third parties. Ethiopia made a determined bid for Eritrea and cultivated support among the people there and the Great Powers. Italy wanted to return to its former colony as the Trustee of the United Nations, Britain contemplated partitioning Eritrea in order to annex its western part to Sudan. The United States was concerned with the future of Eritrea, because it was in the process of acquiring a military base in Asmara, the country's capital, devoted to electronic intelligence, and was inclined to favour Ethiopia, whose government was anxious to become a US client. Hoping for a communist electoral victory in Italy, the Soviet Union initially supported the Italian bid, but when that hope was dashed in the 1948 elections, it supported Eritrean independence.

In the late 1940s, the people of Eritrea themselves divided on this issue, according to where each community perceived its interests lay. Understandably, the Muslims who made up half of the estimated one million population were, on the whole, loath to have any connection with Ethiopia, a country ruled by the traditional enemy, Abyssinia. There, their co-religionists were second-class citizens without access to the state and, in the traditional Abyssinian provinces, to land. The expressed preference of Eritrean Muslims was for independence, after a period of tutelage under the United Nations. However, the Muslim ranks were not solid. Certain pastoralist tribes, which lost traditional privileges with the emancipation of their serfs in the 1940s, supported Ethiopia in the hope that the imperial regime would restore serfdom.

Understandably also, Christians generally favoured a link with Ethiopia, whose cause was enthusiastically promoted by the Christian clergy in Eritrea. The clergy was mobilized by the ecclesiastical hierarchy, which was hoping the imperial regime would restore land and privileges the Church had lost during the Italian occupation. Christian enthusiasm was moderated by the fact that they belong to the Tigrai, the minor branch of the Abyssinian family, which had little power and few privileges in the state ruled by the Amhara, the senior Abyssinian branch. Proof of this was the fact that the Tigrai language was suppressed in Ethiopia along with all other tongues in favour of Amharigna. A small but vocal minority of Christians joined the Muslims in demanding independence. The late 1940s was a period of intense political strife in Eritrea, interspersed with violence. While the opposed camps fought for control of the colonial state, their rivalry found ideological expression in religion.

As it became clear in retrospect, the Christian political leadership in Eritrea saw the Ethiopian connection as a guarantee of their own political predominance in Eritrea. The Unionists, as they were called, certainly did not bargain for Eritrea to become simply another Ethiopian province, ruled by relatives of Haile Selassie. In the event, however, this is what happened, and the result was massive alienation of the Christians, who rallied belatedly to the Eritrean nationalist movement and ensured its eventual success.

Before this occurred there was a ten-year interlude (1952–62), when Eritrea was linked to Ethiopia in a federal scheme devised and imposed by the United Nations. The scheme provided for genuine Eritrean self-government and a democratic political system, complete with political parties, elections, a free press and trade unions; all of which contrasted incongruously with the medieval imperial reign in Ethiopia. Muslims and Christians in Eritrea were guaranteed parity in public employment. The official languages were Arabic and Tigrai, and each community was allowed to decide the language of instruction in the local school system. The imperial regime saw the federal scheme as the first step towards annexation. In a relentless campaign that involved intrigue, extortion, bribery and naked force, it emasculated Eritrea's autonomy, demolished the democratic experiment, destroyed its own ally, the Unionist Party, and finally annexed Eritrea in 1962. The first resistance movement, the Eritrean Liberation Front, had been founded two years earlier.

After the annexation of Eritrea, the imperial regime outlawed Tigrai, the language of the Christian community, and imposed Amharigna. This was resented even by the most ardent Eritrean supporters of Ethiopia, and alienated *en masse* the Eritrean student population, who now had to master two foreign languages – English and Amharigna – in order to complete secondary education. The students were the first group from the Christian community to join the rebel movement. The use of Arabic in education was squeezed out gradually in Eritrea by the simple technique of not providing for the education of teachers in that language, despite the pleas of Muslims that it is essential for the practice of their religion.

The Eritrean national movement had a distinctly sectarian origin. Founded in 1960, the Eritrean Liberation Front (ELF) was an exclusively Muslim affair for several years. This is understandable, since it was the Eritrean Muslim community that suffered first and most by the loss of self-government and the region's incorporation into Ethiopia, where Muslims had no access to state power and their religion was ignored. While the organizers and leaders of the ELF were former politicians, merchants and young educated people, its guerrilla fighters initially came from the pastoralist tribes of western Eritrea. For several years, the movement restricted its activities to the predominantly Muslim lowlands of Eritrea. The ELF sought and found support among the Arab states of the region, especially Syria, Iraq and the oil-rich Gulf states. After the fall of the first military regime (1958–64) in Sudan, the Eritrean rebels enjoyed unrestricted access to Sudanese territory, where they established clinics and rest houses, repair workshops and offices, and used Port Sudan to bring in supplies.

It was not until the mid-1960s that Christians began to join the movement, and the ELF was able to expand onto the highlands. There was considerable rivalry among ethnic groups for control of the ELF, and when elections to leadership posts were held in the 1970s, they were regularly fought on an ethnic basis. The Christians initially came from two social groups: students and workers. The former were affected not only by the banning of their language and the heavy-handed rule of the Amhara officials who came to govern Eritrea, but also by the political radicalism that infected the student population of Ethiopia as a whole and turned it into the imperial regime's most implacable opponent.

The workers were permanently alienated from the Haile Selassie regime by the brutal repression of the nascent Eritrean trade union movement in the 1950s. The subsequent stagnation of the Eritrean economy also affected them adversely. Eritrea entered the federal phase with a depressed economy, lack of domestic capital and widespread unemployment. Although Asmara was the second largest zone of industrial concentration in Ethiopia, Eritrea was fast falling behind the central region of Ethiopia, where the bulk of capital investment was concentrated. The local economy was never able to absorb the labour supply available in an urban sector that was proportionately more than twice as large as Ethiopia's, and many thousands of Eritreans were compelled to migrate to Ethiopia, Sudan and the Arab Gulf states to find employment. There, they were gradually brought into the network of ELF cells organized in these areas.

(b) Sudan

The region below the 10th parallel north, known as southern Sudan, occupies about one-third of the Sudanese Nile basin. It is home to many ethnic groups, the majority of which are grouped together under the name Nilotics, from the river that dominates their existence. The Dinka, Nuer, Shilluk and Anuak are the largest groups, belonging to the same linguistic family and sharing basic cultural features. Pastoralism is the traditional Nilotic vocation, though some groups, like the Shilluk and Anuak, turned to cultivation some time in the past.

Neither pastoralism nor cultivation produces a surplus, and Nilotic material culture is primitive. Trade was not a part of the local economy, nor was there any sign of urbanization in this region before the colonial period. Nilotic society is segmented in typical pastoralist fashion, and their political organization reflected this segmentation. Far greater cohesion was exhibited by the Azande, the major non-Nilotic group inhabiting the southwestern rim of the Nile basin. An agricultural society, politically centralized under a monarch, the Azande had imposed their rule in what is now Equatoria province before the colonial intrusion.

There was hardly a sign of development in southern Sudan during the colonial period. Preoccupied with developing an agricultural export economy in northern Sudan, where cotton became king, the British were content for the main part to maintain peace and collect taxes in the South. The pastoralist economy of the Nilotes was left unchanged. The South remained outside the framework of the colonial economy, producing nothing new, exporting little more than it did during the pre-colonial period, but importing more, including food, to meet the requirements of the non-productive population that gathered around the colonial administrative centres. In contrast with the central riverine region in northern Sudan, where a buoyant economy based on the production of agricultural exports underpinned a burgeoning urban sector, southern Sudan remained primitive and impoverished. At independence, the per capita domestic product in the South was only half the average for the whole of Sudan. Urbanization received no boost in the South. In fact, it was positively discouraged for a time by a colonial officialdom worried about the effects of 'detribalization'. Juba, the region's principal town, had a population of 9000 in 1956.

Though formally part of what was officially called the Anglo-Egyptian Condominium in the Sudan, the South was administered separately and purposely insulated from the North. The main thrust of the so-called Southern Policy applied by the colonial regime until the Second World War was to exclude Arab and Islamic influence, ostensibly in order to protect the primitive Nilotes from exploitation and abuse by northerners. In the nineteenth century, the South had been the hunting ground for Arab and European slave raiders and ivory traders from the North, an experience that had left indelible memories in the South and confounds its relationship with the North to this day. The purpose behind the Southern Policy was to minimize northern Sudanese influence in the South, in order to keep all options open for the eventual disposition of that region. One option was its incorporation into Uganda.

Accordingly, the South was made a closed area where permission was required for outsiders to reside or travel, the military Equatoria Corps recruited only southerners, and even northern Sudanese traders were squeezed out and replaced by Greek and Syrian merchants. Education in southern Sudan was entrusted to missionary groups, which combined this with proselytization. As a result, the spread of Islam and the Arabic language was blocked. Christianity and English gained ground, but neither of these became dominant in a region where the bulk of the population, which numbered nearly three million in the 1940s, remained attached to traditional creeds and had no contact with the English language. Nevertheless, the incipient southern Sudanese intelligentsia, which first emerged at the close of the colonial period, acquired a vested interest in these alien cultural attributes, which became rivals of Islam and Arabic, the twin themes of northern Sudanese nationalism.

The fate of southern Sudan was decided without reference to the opinion of its people, who hardly had the chance to know what was being decided, let alone to influence the decision. Nationalism had an early start in northern Sudan, where the Arab intelligentsia was inspired by the flowering of Egyptian nationalism in the interwar period. By the end of the Second World War, the nationalist movement had spawned two sizeable political parties which were already competing to inherit power from the British. After the end of the Second World War, Britain abandoned its earlier policy, and southern Sudan was integrated administratively with the North, with a view to merging this region into a united, centrally governed Sudanese state.

Northern Sudanese nationalism had no echo in the South. Given the isolation and retarded state of education in that region, a native intelligentsia had yet to make an appearance at the close of the colonial period. The 1952 revolution in Egypt forced Britain to make precipitate concessions to northern Sudanese nationalist demands for independence. Within a year, agreement was reached for Sudan to attain independence in 1956. There was no southern Sudanese representation in the negotiations, since there was no political organization in the region at the time. Nevertheless, the handful of southerners who had benefited from missionary education and were employed in lowly positions in the regional administrative service, had shown concern over the imminent prospect of Arab domination. The initial demand that came from this group was for independence to be delayed, in order for the South to have time to catch up with the North in education and other areas of development.

Southern fears of Arab domination seemed to be confirmed by the results of the 'Sudanization' of the civil service in 1954, in which southerners qualified for only eight subordinate posts out of 800. Southerners denounced this as the 'Arabization' of the state service, and the newly formed Liberal Party in the South immediately issued a call for federation. This was to become the rallying cry of the South and has remained a fixed item on the political agenda of the South to this day. Sudanization also affected the soldiers of the Equatoria Corps, now renamed the Southern Command. A dozen southerners had been raised from the ranks to become second lieutenants in the closing days of the colonial period. They and other rankers fully expected to fill some of the posts vacated by the departing British officers, but were bitterly disappointed when northerners arrived to claim them all.

To southerners it seemed their country was passing from British to Arab rule with only token participation on their part. The prevailing atmosphere of suspicion and anxiety was exacerbated when northern troops arrived in Juba, giving rise to rumours that southern units were going to be disarmed. In August 1955, when a southern unit stationed at Torit was ordered to the

North to take part in the independence celebrations, its soldiers mutinied and their example was followed by other garrisons in the South. An assault on northern army officers and civil officials soon turned into a slaughter of northerners generally, and more than 300 people lost their lives. Many of the mutineers fled to the bush, where they later formed the core of the Anya-nya guerrilla movement, which came to prominence in the 1960s. The southern demand for federation was ignored by the northern nationalist leadership, and Sudan attained independence in 1956 as a unitary state.

4. FIJI

This small Pacific island republic made headlines in 1987, 17 years after gaining independence from Britain, when a military coup overthrew a democratically elected government in the name of native Fijian ethnic nationalism. As Ralph Premdas reports, Fiji was colonized in 1874 when Chief Cakobau ceded Fiji to Britain. The Deed of Cession bound Britain to protect the Fijians from European commercial interests and to preserve the Fijian way of life. To halt the steady decline of Fijian customs, the first British governor of Fiji initiated three policies which laid the cornerstone of communalism. First, all land which was not yet alienated to Europeans – nearly 90 per cent of the country – was to remain under Fijian ownership. This policy curtailed economic development of the islands because growth depended on the availability of Fijian land for commercial exploitation. Land, then, became an issue. The second policy was the importation of labour to substitute for Fijians. From 1879, when the labour indentureship was inaugurated, to 1916, when it was terminated, over 60,000 Indians were introduced into Fiji. The Indian population thereafter grew steadily so that by 1945 they outnumbered the Fijians. From the policy of labour immigration, then, a new community was grafted onto Fiji. The final policy was the establishment of a separate Native Fijian Administration through which the British governed the Fijians indirectly.

Until the military coup in 1987, the idea of parity between the Fijians and the Indians prevailed, however imperfectly. Not a written constitutional law, the idea of parity had been embedded in Fiji's multiracial politics by practice whereby sectoral pre-eminence is distributed as follows:

1. The Fijians controlled the government, in particular, the Prime Minister's Office. They also owned 83 per cent of all the land.

2. The Indians dominated the sugar industry and intermediate-sized business.
3. The Europeans owned the very large businesses, such as banks, hotels, factories, etc.

Struggle over political representation, land rights and civil service posts set the stage for ethnic conflicts. Frequently, this struggle assumed the form of a threat of ethnic domination. Fijians propounded a doctrine of *paramountcy* to assert and safeguard their interests; While Indians sought a system of equality under which they could outcompete Fijians for the values of the polity and economy. The struggle was often cast in zero-sum terms so that the ethnic strife that was triggered seemed intractable.

Fijian paramountcy evolved as a mystique of imagined claims. Paramountcy itself is not mentioned in the Deed of Cession. It was used first to protect Fijian land and customs from European claims. Then, in the twentieth century, with the arrival of the Indians, it was interpreted to embody a new inter-group political dimension with increasing alarm and stridency, as an anti-Indian counter-claim. It emerged as a reaction to the perceived threat of Indian domination of Fiji. It has since retained this particularistic ethnicized connotation.

The situation in Fiji mirrors other, similar cases in which two or more clearly distinguished ethnic groups first become differentially related to the colonial administration, and later compete or struggle for political control and economic benefits within the framework of the post-colonial state. This has occurred, among others, in Guyana and Malaysia.

5. GUYANA

Although geographically part of the South American land mass, multi-ethnic Guyana falls culturally within the Caribbean insular sphere marked by plantations, mono-crop economies, immigrant settlers and a colour-class system of stratification. The country is populated by six ethnic clusters: Africans, East Indians, Amerindians, Chinese, Portuguese and other Europeans. A significant 'mixed' category also exists, consisting of persons who have any combination of the major groups. Even though objectively there is a wide array of racial mixes, a person is soon stereotyped into one of the existing social categories to which both 'blood' and 'culture' are assigned a defining role. From this, a society of ethno-cultural compartments has emerged with various forms of inter-communal antagonisms of which the African–Indian dichotomy dominates all dimensions of daily life. Whereas the original Amerindians were exterminated by the early settlers and the survivors pushed into the inaccessible jungle interior where they currently constitute a small minority, the two principal populations brought in by the British colonial administration, the enslaved Africans and the Indian indentured servants, are now engaged in a protracted struggle over control of the economy and the state. Guyana has been a typical colonial, enclave economy.

The persistence of European economic and political power for over three centuries has left permanent marks on Guyanese social structure. A pervasive colour-class stratification has evolved and permeates every stratum of Guyanese society. Partly because the various kinds of skill were bound up in status situations, and partly on a racial basis, the colour-class continuum of differentiation established the basis for the allocation of jobs, offices and prestige. As late as the 1950s this stratification system remained virtually unaltered.

Africans were transported to Guyana to meet the heavy demands for labour created by the establishment of sugar plantations. African slaves were brought as chattels and allotted to the plantations along the 270-mile coast of Guyana. After the emancipation of slaves, Africans abandoned the plantations and tended to concentrate in urban settlements, where they increasingly provided the staff for government service. The British later brought in indentured servants from India, who in time became the backbone of Guyana's rural economy. The Indian peasantry residing in villages developed the colony's rice industry. This provided the main economic basis for their upward mobility and improved status.

The different ethnic groups set up various voluntary associations to cater to the social, cultural and religious needs of their communities. This uni-ethnic pattern in the composition of voluntary associations persists to the present, extending to practically all kinds of clubs and groupings. The large economic organizations such as trade unions also became predommantly uni-ethnic like the cultural and religious organizations. This fact in turn reinforced ethnic exclusivity and exacerbated sectional divisions and fears. As mass political parties emerged after the Second World War, especially after 1955 when distinct Indian and African mass parties were launched, the voluntary associations would support and develop interlocking relationships with their *de facto* ethnically-based parties. Consequently, race relations were intensified and the segregation in the polity deepened.

Thus a deeply divided society emerged. The foundations of inter-ethnic rivalry were forged on the anvil of the colonial policy of immigration and 'divide and rule'. There was no evidence of any sort of inherent antipathy among the imported immigrants. It was, however, the manner in which colonial society was organized, stratified and exploited that triggered and sustained inter-communal fears and rivalries. In an interdependent communal order, the political balance was held at the beginning of the twentieth century by a colonial government originating in conquest, maintained by coercion, and perpetuated by a colour-class stratified order. A policy of 'divide and rule' prevented inter-communal collaboration between the two largest ethnic sections from evolving. Representation in the colonial councils left most Guyanese disenfranchised. This background set the stage for the ethnic conflict to follow, particularly during the period leading up to political independence from Britain in the early 1960s, and its aftermath.

In the Guyanese conflict, Ralph Premdas draws a distinction between *the predisposing factors* and the *triggering-igniting factors*. Among the former he includes (1) cultural pluralism; (2) lack of co-operation and overarching values and institutions; and (3) internal communal beliefs of the separate sections. The factors that triggered ethnic conflict were clearly identifiable but occurred at different times during the evolution of the problem. These factors were: (1) colonial manipulation; (2) the introduction of mass democratic politics; (3) rivalry over resource allocation; and (4) imported political institutions adopted at independence.

6. MALAYSIA

Malaysia is often cited as an example of ethnic harmony and absence of conflict. However, as Mavis Puthucheary reports, beneath the thin veneer of ethnic harmony there are considerable ethnic tensions which erupt from time to time and which have to be carefully monitored in order to keep them within the confines of manageability by the government. These tensions have reinforced ethnic boundaries and aligned the many different groups and subgroups into three large ethnic identities, Malays, Chinese and Indians, blurring important differences among the people within each ethnic category. In more recent years the alignment has been more clearly drawn with the Malays and other *Bumiputras* ('Sons of the soil') on the one hand, and the Chinese and Indians (the immigrants) on the other.

Early contact between Malay rulers and immigrant Chinese traders have been described as friendly and harmonious. Far from being resented, early Chinese entrepreneurs were actively encouraged to settle in the country. But this changed under colonial rule, when the Chinese established direct relations with British capitalists, and the colonial government set up political and administrative structures that dealt directly with the Chinese community while continuing to retain the traditional structures for dealing with the Malays. Colonial policy differentiated between the two groups, and each community was allowed to live almost independently of each other with minimum contact. In order to offset the economic advantages of the Chinese, the Malays were given special privileges with regard to jobs in the public sector and scholarships to receive training in the special school set up to train Malays for the Malay Administrative Service.

The 1930s was a period of political mobilization of cultural identities under the pressure of competition for allocation of resources. Ethnic conflict began to be expressed through Malay identification with the territory comprising the Malay States as their homeland, in order to justify claims to privileges against the Chinese population. The return of the British after the Japanese occupation of Malaya during the Second World War, the birth of Malay nationalism and the emergence of different political groups strengthened the process of ethnic awareness and increased tensions between the groups. Malay consciousness took on the appearance of a 'siege group identity', a process initiated by an increased level of ethnic group awareness as a result of threats to its existing power or privileges. British colonial policy in turn recognized and institutionalized ethnicity in politics and reinforced the saliency of ethnicity as the basis for political mobilization, partly in order to forestall the so-called communist threat.

As a result, the juxtaposition of the ethnic groups into two opposing forces tended to result in ethnic confrontation instead of co-operation, forcing individuals to think in ethnic terms. In the years leading up to independence, and in the period thereafter, serious efforts were made by all the political actors to work towards a consensus, or at least a compromise, on the different issues dividing the ethnic communities: education, language, citizenship rights, political representation, preferential economic policies, etc. For a while, this consociational arrangement seemed to work.

In 1959, the new Federation of Malaysia incorporated additional states, which brought a new dimension into ethnic relations. The singling out of the Malays as a group for special privileges was now to be extended to include a whole new category of persons. These privileges contrasted sharply with the denial of ordinary citizenship rights to the other communities and was therefore resented. The realignment of the population into two broad groups, the *Bumiputras* on the one hand, and the non-*Bumiputras* on the other, not only sharpened differences between the two groups but also changed the balance of power between them.

Subsequently, these tensions would explode on different occasions as ethnic riots, even as the major parties continued to attempt to maintain an unstable power equilibrium in order to preserve the unity of the country.

How these efforts were carried out and with what degree of success will be dealt with in later chapters.

7. BURUNDI

Repeated ethnic massacres from the 1960s to the 1990s have dramatically shaken this small eastern African country. In contrast to some other African societies, in Burundi ethnic differentiation between the two major population groups, the Tutsi (a demographic minority) and the Hutu (the majority), is also a vertical status distinction, with the pastoralist Tutsi being the dominant group and the mainly agricultural Hutu the subordinate one. As René Lemarchand observes, because of its long pedigree as an archaic kingdom, Burundi's existence as a national entity precedes by centuries that of some European states. Though now a republic, for as far back as can be remembered the monarchy served as the prime focus of popular loyalties. Its legitimacy as an institution was never seriously questioned. And yet, Burundi proved more vulnerable than most to the searing trauma of ethnic strife.

Tutsi power centred on the monarchy (*Mwamiship*) in the post-independence period, and early political conflict arose between rival princely factions which, partly as a result of the Belgian colonial administration's manipulations, coalesced around the two major competing political parties, the *Parti Pour l'Union et le Progrès National* (Uprona) and the *Parti Democrate Chrétien* (PDC). In 1965, Hutu army officers, perceiving that they were being squeezed out of the political arena by the Tutsi monarchy, staged a military coup, which was quickly repressed. Subsequently, many Hutu were assassinated, and soon the army overthrew the monarchy and established a republic. Thereafter, Hutu–Tutsi hostility became more intense, particularly after the Hutu revolution in neighbouring Rwanda. Another attempted Hutu insurrection in 1972 led to genocidal repression, a scenario repeated once again in 1988, and on a lesser scale in 1991.

Lemarchand argues that Hutu and Tutsi ethnic identities became crystallized as a result of these traumatic events. He also shows how each group in turn constructs the origins and nature of the conflict differently, and how ethnic identities are mobilized by the competing ethnic elites. From a society characterized by complex socio-political hierarchies, Burundi has now become greatly simplified, consisting of separate and mutually antagonistic ethnic aggregates. In a time of crisis Hutu and Tutsi emerge as the only relevant defining characteristics of group identities, reducing all other social roles to phenomena of marginal social significance. A whole range of social identities – associated with clan and family ties, patron–client networks, princely affiliations and court connections – seems suddenly to recede from the social horizon, leaving only Hutu and Tutsi in sight. Collective identities thus tend to shift back and forth from one level to another, from clan and lineage affiliations to ethnic identities. There can be little question that ethnic self-awareness has now asserted itself as the central element in the social landscape.

Simply stated, the conflict in Burundi involves principally Hutu against Tutsi. Beyond this elementary truth there are violent disagreements among participants and observers alike about almost every other dimension of the conflict, including the nature of Hutu and Tutsi identities, the root cause of their antagonisms, the scale of the human losses suffered by each side and how best to achieve a measure of social harmony between them. Some indeed might even question the existence of a Hutu–Tutsi problem.

The origin of the Burundi conflict does not fit into any of the easy categories which apply to some other cases. The two opposing ethnies are neither 'natives' and 'immigrants' (as in Fiji and Malaysia), nor are they two immigrant groups brought in and set against each other to serve the interests of a colonial power (as happened in Guyana). Neither of the two groups desires a separate state, regional autonomy or claims self-determination, as do the Kurds. While the colonial administration did in fact favour one faction against the other, the origin of the ethnic conflict cannot be attributed merely to colonial manipulation. Neither can it be phrased simplistically in terms of a class struggle between the oppressed Hutu and the dominant Tutsi. Burundi seems rather to be a case in which electoral politics has been thrust upon a traditionally stratified society, thus channelling different group interests (including the army as a powerful actor) into the political arena. The struggle is not about land, language, religion or specific cultural identity: it is more about political power. We shall return to some of these issues in later chapters.

8. NIGERIA

This most populous African country has a long and tragic history of ethnic strife, which erupted in attempted secession and brutal civil conflict in the 1960s: the Biafra war. After the end of this confrontation, the territorial unity of the state having been preserved, succeeding governments, both civilian and military, attempted to prevent major ethnic confrontations from erupting anew and have continued efforts to build and maintain national unity. Okwudiba Nnoli analyses the various factors involved in the persistent conflicts between Nigerian ethnic groups and discusses the policies which have been pursued in trying to cope with the centrifugal forces in the society. He considers that the search for harmony in the relations among Nigerian ethnic groups has gone on for over five decades. It has spanned various regimes, from colonial through civilian to military administrations. And it has seen periods of economic depression and the oil boom. Yet the ethnic problem has persisted. It has defied various solutions designed to resolve it. Among them are the military suppression of an attempted secession; the transformation of the federal structure of governmental administration from two protectorates to three regions, four regions, 12 states, 19 states, 21 states and now 30 states; the use of ethno-regional quotas in recruitment into governmental positions, the distribution of public projects, admission into educational institutions, recruitment into the armed forces, the award of public contracts, the banning of ethnic group-wide self-help associations; the use of constitutional devices to discourage the emergence of ethnic political parties; the creation of national institutions such as the National Youth Corps and the Federal Government (Unity) Colleges that transcend ethnic interests; and the use of such consociational democratic devices as the grand coalition in governmental administration, the zoning of political posts and the rotation of political posts among leaders of ethnic groups.

The major ethnic groups in Nigeria, mainly concentrated in their home regions, are the Hausa in the North, the Yoruba in the West and the Igbo in the East. Traditionally, relations between these peoples were peaceful and friendly. However, from the 1950s, conflict first arose in relation to the kolanut trade, when some Yoruba entered the trade in competition with the Hausa. The result was the emergence of scores of closely-knit Hausa communities in some Yoruba areas, which enabled the Hausa to control the trade. Similarly, following the unsuccessful attempts by the Yoruba to displace the Hausa as cattle landlords and dealers, the latter appealed for support, not in the name of the profession, but as Hausa. Thenceforth, Hausa and Yoruba ethnic chauvinism confronted each other in the cattle market. While during the early period of colonialism interactions between members of diverse linguistic groups were so positive that intergroup marriage was fairly common, when migrants from other ethnic groups to a host community increased in number and socio-economic competition with the hosts became more prevalent, relations became strained. In reaction, both migrants and hosts organized themselves along communal lines in order to safeguard their interests in the struggle for scarce and unequally distributed resources.

Nnoli argues that the increasing competition between ethnic groups and the attendant increase in ethnic solidarity and identity occurred as a result of capitalist development under colonialism, particularly in the urban areas. He explains, for example, that the Igbo migrated mostly because of population density and impoverished land. On the other hand, the coastal peoples were the first to receive education, get jobs in the civil service and foreign firms, enter into petty trading and serve as interpreters for the Christian missionaries. In the North, the situation was more complex, due to the already established states: the Muslim emirates. Here the British favoured indirect colonial rule, and for religious reasons related to the security of their system of domination, the Hausa rulers discouraged the migration of their subjects. Much of the emir's authority came from his religious role in society. Exposure of his subjects to Christian influences of the colonial order might have weakened this authority.

Hence, concludes Nnoli, the Hausa have lagged behind their Igbo and Yoruba compatriots in the acquisition of colonial socio-economic fortunes, leading to uneven development of the ethnic groups, which has exacerbated ethnicity in the country. Lagos, the capital, is in Yorubaland, and it had a disproportionate share of colonial activities causing the Yoruba who migrated there from the hinterland to acquire an early start over the other ethnic groups in acquiring a socio-economic foothold in the colonial order. This imbalance later caused antipathies between the Yoruba and Igbo.

These socio-cultural differences among the Nigerian ethnic groups assumed a tremendous significance for the emergence and persistence of ethnicity, states Nnoli, only because the colonialists placed emphasis on differences rather than similarities in intergroup interaction. During the independence struggle, the nationalist leaders tried to overcome these differences. The emergent Nigerian petty bourgeoisie led this struggle. They were the most strategically placed to wage it because they were located at important nodes in the communications network of the colony, had acquired education and other relevant agitational skills in the colonial educational system, were versed in modern organizational skills, were role models for their less privileged compatriots, were articulate enough to mobilize the latter behind their programmes and, most importantly, had an objective interest in nationalist agitations.

In reaction to the nationalist opposition the colonial government dismissed the nationalist leaders as self-seeking agitators who represented nobody but themselves and a few people in the urban areas. The nationalist leaders saw this colonial posture as a challenge to spread their nationalist activities to the rural areas in order to mobilize the vast majority of the population behind their demands as a show of force against the colonialists and to present evidence of their widespread support throughout the country. This nationalist effort to mobilize the rural population had the greatest significance for the spread of ethnic consciousness and identity throughout the country. Thus, in their mobilizational activities on behalf of Nigerian nationalism the Nigerian politicians were compelled to use emotive ethnic appeals, emphasizing the concrete benefits to be derived by the specific ethnic group in the post-colonial period.

While the emerging petty bourgeoisie resented colonial restrictions and pushed for real Africanization, the northerners, argues Nnoli, were afraid of southern domination in a post-colonial Nigeria for which they were not yet ready. This chauvinistic appeal was very successful in mobilizing the vast majority of northerners from various ethnic groups behind a particular vision of post-colonial Nigeria. The North lacked a significant crop of nationalist-minded bourgeoisie. Operating under the system of indirect rule in which wealth carried prestige but not necessarily political power, members of these classes sought political influence through accommodation with the local aristocracy, not anti-colonial militancy.

Personal political rivalries became regional struggles. By 1953 the three major political parties in the country had become associated with the three major ethnic groups: Igbo, Yoruba and Hausa-Fulani, respectively. By the time of national independence in 1960, Nigerian politics had become synonymous with the inter-ethnic struggle for power. Political power was widely perceived as an important instrument in the struggle among ethnic groups for the division of the national wealth. At both the regional and national levels, politics was seen as the election of representatives into positions of power that would enable them to transfer regional or national resources to the ethnic homeland. Constituents judged politicians by how much of such wealth they were able to secure for the homeland. In this circumstance, the persistence and growth of ethnicity in Nigeria was inevitable.

9. GUATEMALA

The roots of the ethno-political conflict, which has torn asunder Guatemalan society for the last 30 years, can be found, as in so many other cases, in the early colonial structure of the country. The Spanish conquerors established in the early sixteenth century a system of exploitation of indigenous labour, similar to that of Mexico and Peru and elsewhere in the Americas, which, with some variations, lasted for 300 years. The

Maya Indian peasants were forced to pay tribute in cash and kind, provide free or minimally paid labour to the land-owners, the colonial administrators and the Catholic Church under varying arrangements, and cultivate the crops which were imposed on them by the economic interests of the colonial elite.

The class distinctions between the colonial masters and the colonized peasantry became ethnic and cultural distinctions as well, as Guatemalan society coalesced around two major social categories: the 'Indians' and 'non-Indians' or '*Ladinos*'. In fact, these are cultural constructs more than biological distinctions, whose economic and political importance became more significant in the post-colonial period. Indians continued mainly to be tied to small, subsistence peasant communities, whereas *Ladinos* (often the mixed descendants of Indians and Europeans) became land-owners, engaged in trades and crafts and became increasingly linked to the emerging urban economy. The nineteenth century witnessed an expansion of export crops (mainly coffee), which entailed the rearrangement of land tenure systems, the increasing incorporation of migrant Indian labour in the plantation economy and the emergence of a Guatemalan bourgeoisie linked in various ways to international capitalism. Internal contradictions within the small ruling class coalesced along a 'Conservative' and 'Liberal' divide, whose political struggles continued well into the twentieth century. The Liberals, as elsewhere, were deemed to be 'reformers', whose 'reforms theoretically favored Indians by granting them equality before the law and access to more land and opportunity. In practice, however, most Indians had neither the resources nor education to take advantage of the opportunity. Liberalism simply exposed them to greater exploitation.'[3] During much of the nineteenth century, however, Conservative governments rejected the egalitarian policies of the Liberals, and running directly contrary to general world trends, their policy of protecting and segregating the Indian communities offered an alternative mode of development which put greater emphasis on subsistence than exports, and on the stability of traditional community social organization. Consequently, the expanding capitalist agricultural economy, though in need of Indian labour, remained in the hands of the *Ladino* social segment, while the subsistence peasant economy (particularly in the western highlands of the country) was linked to the persistence of an Indian identity (which was, moreover, ever-changing and in no way identical to the pre-Hispanic Maya). During the latter part of the nineteenth century, the Liberals regained power and renewed their attack on traditional Indian lands and communities, though on a lesser scale than occurred in El Salvador and in Mexico at about the same time. Indians resisted and sometimes revolted, and when this happened, state repression was swift, violent and effective.[4]

By the 1940s these policies had contributed to increasing Indian reliance on wage-labour on coffee plantation fostered partly by their diminishing land base. *Ladinos*, though in the minority, controlled most of the land. Ethnic tension, caused partly by this land dispossession and heightened by government attempts to control village government, permeated all aspects of rural Guatemala. In 1944, a democratic revolution, led by urban intellectuals and middle-class elements, achieved the overthrow of the dictator, Ubico, who had ruled with an iron fist since 1930. The new democratic regime of successive presidents, Arevalo and Arbenz, attempted to introduce political and economic reforms and modernize the country. The vagrancy law of 1936 (whereby Indians who did not own agricultural land had been forced to work on coffee plantations) was abolished, and in 1952 the government introduced agrarian reform legislation. While modest in its objectives and scope, the land reform programme affected the interests of the propertied class, as it promised to take excess land from the large estates to give to the landless peasants. Militant and revolutionary peasant organizations emerged to claim their rights, many of them with highly visible Indian membership, and often linked to competing political parties. Agrarian unrest spread throughout the country, and much of the conflict was ethnic in nature. Significant sectors of Indian communities readily, even eagerly, sought affiliation with such national institutions as the Campesino League and revolutionary partics.[5]

More significantly, the agrarian reform law adversely affected the interests of the US-owned banana companies, the largest land-owners in the country. By 1953, the US government was actively defending US business interests and taking on the Guatemalan government. In classic cold war style, Guatemala was denounced internationally as 'communist', it became the object of intense political and economic pressures, and in 1954 the CIA organized an invasion of Guatemala by disaffected military officers, which succeeded in overthrowing the Arbenz government, thus ending a ten-year experiment in democratic politics and ushering in three decades of almost uninterrupted military rule.[6]

10.   THE FORMER SOVIET UNION

Current national and ethnic conflicts in the successor states of the Soviet Union are the direct outcome of the legacy of the Bolshevik period and before that, of the Tsarist empire.

One widely-held interpretation of the current ethnic unrest holds that the disintegration of the Soviet empire has enabled the 'national revival' of the peoples of the former USSR. This interpretation presupposes that the major reason behind the USSR's disintegration as a multi-ethnic state was the diminished status and discrimination of the non-Russian peoples, whose culture and identity were forcibly deformed to conform to the official concept of the 'merging of nations' and of constructing a single 'Soviet people'.

Valery Tishkov questions this interpretation and provides elements for a different analysis. The revolution of 1917 took place in a huge country (22.5 million km²), in which the 1897 population census had registered 146 different ethnic groups or nationalities. The multi-ethnic composition of this enormous state was the result of several centuries of territorial expansion in the form of military conquests, colonization and development of new lands, initiated by the Principality of Moscow and continued by the Russian centralized state. The main ethnic component at the political centre were the eastern Slavic tribes who gave rise in later years to the ethnic communities of Russians, Ukrainians and Belorussians. But from its earliest stages, Russia's population also included Finns, Balts, Turkic and other non-Slavic groups. After the sixteenth century, the ethnic mosaic became more complex with the annexation of the Volga region to Russia, the colonization of Siberia and the Caucasus and later the incorporation of Central Asia. The Russian monarchy practised a policy of social oppression and cultural assimilation in relation to the non-Slavic populations, the *inorodtsi*. Many autochthonous peoples lost their lands in favour of the state, the landlords and the monasteries, the latter being the main means of spreading Orthodoxy among the *inorodtsi*.

Unlike other European empires, the Russian colonial metropolitanate was not separated from the colonized periphery by other geographical areas (land or sea). Moreover, the ethnic periphery was extremely diverse, comprising small groups of gatherers and hunters in Siberia and the Far East, to the relatively well-developed dynastic or religious states of the Transcaucasus and Central Asia. Russia also applied so-called indirect rule in its relations with the subordinate peoples, who to a great extent possessed different degrees of autonomy and self-government. After centuries of inter-ethnic relations, local elites, political and religious leaders had become closely allied with the all-Russian ruling elite. By the end of the nineteenth century, however, nationalist movements had begun to emerge in Russia's periphery, just as they had in the Ottoman and Austro-Hungarian empires.

After the overthrow of the monarchy in February 1917, Finland and Poland achieved their political independence. During the early years of the Bolshevik regime, independence was proclaimed by the Ukraine, the Transcaucasian republics of Georgia, Armenia, Azerbaijan and Abhkazia, and the Baltic countries (Lithuania, Latvia and Estonia). Movements for autonomy also sprang up among the Tartars and Bashkirs of the Volga area. At first, the Bolsheviks supported these movements for national self-determination, viewing them as allies in their struggle against the absolutist monarchy and the conservative centralist opposition. Among the first decisions taken by the victorious Soviets after the November revolution was a Declaration proclaiming the equality and sovereignty of all the peoples of Russia, their right to self-determination including separation and the formation of independent states, and the free development of national minorities and ethnic groups inhabiting the territory of Russia.

This policy was greeted with enthusiasm by the nationalist activists of the country's periphery and provided the new regime with the support it needed from among the non-Russian populations. In order to consolidate their power during the civil war, the Bolsheviks, even while they adhered to proletarian internationalism, actually embraced the doctrine of ethnic nationalism, a doctrine which was particularly attractive to the different peoples of this vast multi-ethnic country. It rested on two postulates: first, the recognition that an ethnic group with a set of inalienable characteristics, including its own territory, commonality of economic ties, common language and distinct socio-psychological features constitutes a 'nation'; and second, that a nation has to develop its own state, within the territory of which the members of the constituent group are declared to be representatives of an 'indigenous nation'. The nationalists of various of the peripheral ethnic groups took up this doctrine with enthusiasm and turned it back upon the Bolsheviks in order to bolster their drive for political independence. Soon, however, the Red Army re-established Soviet power over almost all of the territory, with the exception of the Baltic states. After consolidating their power, the Bolsheviks eliminated the right to secede from their programme and labelled the supporters of separate statehood for non-Russian peoples as 'bourgeois nationalists', a label with distinct negative connotations. Instead, the Soviet regime decided that national self-determination applied only to the state as a whole, but its constituent federated units were to be based on the principle of 'national statehood'. Accordingly, Soviet citizens were classified by 'nationality', an ethnic identity which became legally established as the years went by, and which individuals had no right to change. The administrative territories of the Soviet Union were defined according to the ethnic national principle, a situation which generated numerous practical difficulties such as defining internal borders, establishing the 'titular' and 'non-titular' nationalities of these territories (republics, regions), and accommodating the shape and size of the new territorial units to the needs of economic development planning.

By 1922 most of the new ethno-national units had been created, though changes continued to be made for political reasons in subsequent years. As could have been expected, new claimants for national titularity arose within the various territories leading to an emerging hierarchy of ethno-national units. Larger groupings were labelled as 'nations' and had a right to their own republic, whereas smaller ones were considered mere 'nationalities' and were assigned lower forms of national-administrative status. The establishment of Soviet power in Central Asia and the North Caucasus was accompanied by severe repressive measures and caused mass migrations of populations to other parts of the country and abroad, creating the first of a series of ethnic diasporas. Before the outbreak of the Second World War, the USSR annexed the three independent Baltic states as well as the western parts of Ukraine and Belorus (Byelorussia). By the time of its demise, the USSR contained 128 officially recognized ethnic groups numbering from a few hundred to several million people, organized into 15 union republics, 20 autonomous republics and 18 smaller autonomous regional units (*oblasts* and *okrugs*).

From the beginning, but particularly during Stalin's ruthless regime, Soviet nationalities policy was contradictory; there was a huge gap between the professed ideals and their actual implementation. The national leaders from the periphery who asked for greater sovereignty and independence were accused of 'bourgeois nationalism' and were liquidated in successive purges. At the same time, however, the central government and the Communist Party promoted measures to enlarge the political representation of non-Russian nationalities, to provide education and training for workers, executives and the intelligentsia among the 'native nationalities' in the republics, to promote non-Russian national languages and cultures. All of this took place, however, under the strict control of the Communist Party.

On the other hand, the building of socialism implied a process of social homogenization among the different nationalities and the creation of a 'new Soviet man'. This contradiction between the support for national cultural expressions and the *korenization* (nativization) of the civil service and economic productive activities, on the one hand, and the 'rapprochement' between the different nationalities and their integration into a new 'socialist' mould (the various republics were all deemed to be socialist in content and national in form), on the other, became an unresolved problem which lasted until the fall of the Soviet Union.

For a number of ideological and political reasons, certain peoples of the Soviet Union were labelled in their entirety as 'bourgeois' and therefore considered to be enemies of Soviet power. Moscow dealt harshly with them: the Cossacks were repressed and deported shortly after the Bolshevik revolution. The politicide of the rural middle class known as Kulaks in the early 1920s has been widely documented; in the 1930s, the rural population of the prosperous Kuban region was deported. Later, during the period of forced collectivization, millions of people from many different ethnic groups were deported or killed. A form of 'ethnic cleansing' was imposed in some areas, through deportations and mass resettlements, a process which contributed to change the ethnic cartography of the USSR. Many different nationalities became victims of these policies, the so-called 'punished peoples': Koreans, Kurds, Turks, Balts, Ukrainians, Volga Germans (who were accused of being Nazi collaborators during the Second World War), various Caucasian peoples. Some sources estimate that around 3.5 million people were forcibly removed from their homelands between 1936 and 1956. The conditions of life of the 'special settlers' were particularly difficult, and during the Stalinist years these repressed peoples suffered from enormous physical and moral traumas. In the late 1950s, many of the earlier restrictions were lifted and some of the deported peoples were rehabilitated and allowed to return home. But not only were the rehabilitation measures limited in general, in some instances the local population actually turned hostile to the returnees. It was only in 1989 and 1991 that the Supreme Soviet of the USSR and of the Russian Federation adopted decrees on the rehabilitation of repressed peoples, measures which, according to Tishkov, created more problems than they resolved (see following chapters).

11. CONCLUSIONS

From these brief introductions to a number of case studies included in the UNRISD project, it seems that some preliminary patterns emerge. First, it is difficult if not impossible to set the actual beginning of an ethnic conflict at any specific date. It would be more appropriate to speak of a period of incubation, of shorter or longer duration according to the circumstances. Secondly, it is equally risky to speak of a single causal factor that ignites ethnic conflict in any particular situation. It would perhaps be more suitable to refer to predisposing factors, which of course will vary from case to case, and the triggering factors which actually start the conflict at any particular time.

In the cases referred to above, both predisposing and triggering factors can easily be identified (see Table 3.1). In most of these cases, the role of the colonial state in setting the stage for the ethnic conflicts to come should not be underestimated. In the two African countries, Burundi and

Table 3.1

	Predisposing Factors	Triggering Factors
1. Kurdistan	Distinct ethnicity	Denial of self-determination
2. Lebanon	Distinct and structured religious communities	Intra-elite rivalry turns into ethnic conflict
3. Horn of Africa	Hegemonic control of culturally distinct centre	Resistance and repression of regional autonomic movements
4. Fiji	Immigration of Indian labourers	Native Fijians hold on to political power
5. Guyana	Indian and African workers brought in by colonial power	Economic and political rivalry between these two groups
6. Malaysia	Native Malays and Chinese immigrants occupy distinct statuses	Both groups struggle over resources and policy after independence
7. Burundi	Hierarchical relations between minority dominant Tutsis and majority Hutus	Politicized ethnicity exasperates ethnic identities
8. Nigeria	Differential position of regional ethnic groups under colonialism	Regions become power bases for national struggle
9. Guatemala	Majority subordinate Indian population is victim of discrimination	Revolutionary war against military regime involves Indians
10. USSR	Contradictory Soviet nationalities policy	Break-up of the USSR

Nigeria, inter-ethnic relations were customary and usually free of conflict. As an independent kingdom before German colonization, Burundi had established a kind of feudal system. Both the agricultural Hutu and the pastoralist Tutsi provided support for the legitimacy of the monarchy, which served as a powerful unifying bond and a symbol of power. It was not until direct Belgium rule was imposed after the First World War that anti-colonial resistance and internal political struggle became increasingly identified with the two major ethnic groups. As the monarchy lost its legitimacy in later years, both Hutu and Tutsi politicians struggled for power over the central state. With the formal overthrow of the monarchy in 1966 and the proclamation of the First Republic, Tutsi political hegemony was established.

The situation was different in Nigeria, where in pre-colonial times relations between culturally distinct peoples were usually symbiotic and co-operative, particularly between migrants and host populations. Different kingdoms did, to be sure, wage war among themselves, but as Okwudiba Nnoli points out, it was only after colonization that the present ethnic groups first acquired a shared consciousness. While colonialism placed the diverse peoples under a single administration (with regional variations), giving rise to Nigeria as a territorial entity, the colonial economy expanded and considerably modified productive and commercial activities. Thus it was that new urban nodes were created, and it was here, in the towns, that new ethnic relations emerged. Nnoli argues that 'ethnicity' is linked to the development of urban centres, new economic activities and different migration patterns, which developed as a direct result of colonialism.

Colonial domination created somewhat different patterns in societies where foreign peoples were brought in, either as slaves or indentured servants or simply as plantation labour. As we have seen, there are certain similarities between Fiji and Guyana. In both countries the British developed a plantation economy to which labourers from India were brought during the nineteenth and twentieth centuries. But whereas in Fiji, the natives obtained from the colonial administration certain guarantees regarding what they now consider as their 'paramountcy', thus effectively barring the immigrant community from real participation in political affairs, in Guyana the original Amerindians were displaced and marginalized early on. The plantation economy was first based on slave labour, but after the slaves were emancipated, the African population moved into the cities, the professions and the civil service, whereas the later waves of Indian immigrants settled in the rural areas to become plantation labourers, rice farmers and traders. Here the colonial administration dealt with two immigrant populations (excluding the Europeans who occupied the upper levels of the social and economic structure until after independence), neither of which could lay claim to original occupation of the land. Therefore, the struggle which emerged in later years involved ethnic groups whose identities were not linked to early territorial claims (as in Fiji), to regional concentration (as in Nigeria) or to ancient historical myths (as in Burundi), but rather to more recent and more visible ethnic markers (race, religion, culture), directly related to political competition over the resources of the state.

Original occupancy rights did, however, play an important role in structuring the relations of the British with the Malay 'Sons of the soil' (Bumiputras) and the Chinese immigrant community in Malaysia. Whereas the Chinese were not brought in as labourers by the colonial administration, their evolving relations with the Malays took place within the framework of British colonial interests.

A different set of ingredients can be seen as responsible for the emergence of the conflict between the Kurdish people and the various states to which they are attached. Here the predisposing factor was not direct colonial subjugation, but rather the creation of artificially drawn borders between Iraq, Iran, Syria and Turkey by the victorious allies after the First World War – borders which legitimized these new states and denied the Kurds a state of their own.

In some of the cases under scrutiny here, the territorial element is of particular importance. Kurds, Fijians and Malays derive their ethnicity from territorial attachments; Yoruba, Igbo and Hausa identities in Nigeria have regional roots. We shall see in later chapters how the 'territorial imperative' also operates in a number of other conflicts.

In Guatemala, as elsewhere in Latin America where indigenous populations were conquered by the Europeans, the native Maya peoples were incorporated into a hierarchical system of power and economic exploitation during colonial times (three centuries). After political independence in the early nineteenth century, the ruling land-owning classes, identifying themselves with their European ancestors and considering themselves to embody the emerging Guatemalan nation, continued to exploit and oppress the Indian peasantry, and to exclude them from effective citizenship. The political struggle between conservative and democratic forces in the mid-twentieth century led to a 'thirty years war' between revolutionary organizations and the military, in which the Indian peoples became mainly the victims and more recently also the active participants.

The recent history of the former Soviet Union gives us a somewhat different picture from those of the other countries dealt with in this chapter.

From early Tsarist times, the expanding Muscovite state incorporated vast expanses of adjacent territories and numerous distinct peoples identified by their different cultural, linguistic or religious characteristics. The Soviet Union inherited this empire, and while the early Bolsheviks declared their support for the national aspirations of the oppressed peoples in the periphery, in fact Soviet nationalities policy imposed even stricter control over them by the political centre, at times resulting in genocidal deportations and repressions (particularly during the 1930s). On the other hand, social and economic policies over the years fostered the emergence of local ethnic and national elites, strictly tied to the ruling political apparatus, who took over local administrative and economic positions. No wonder that when such a federation based on the ethnic territorial principle with its hierarchy of ethnic nationalities and administrative units imploded in the early 1990s, the resulting power alternatives (in the absence of any other choices: the virtual absence of a political party structure, a weak and disorganized civil society) were based on the national and ethnic structures which had been the traditional relays of political and economic control during Soviet times.

Among the factors triggering the conflicts in the countries related in this chapter is the emergence of ethnicity as a politically mobilizing element. In modern states, political parties (together with trade unions, employers' organizations and other associations) are the building blocks for the articulation of specific group interests, or for the political expression of different economic and social philosophies. In principle, a party system can only operate within the framework of a legitimate state and according to a set of rules generally agreed upon by the participants. Political parties are most likely to flourish in democratic electoral processes, but they also function in different kinds of authoritarian regimes. When the major constituency of a political party is a specific ethnic population, then political competition can easily become ethnic confrontation.

Horowitz recognizes that 'the main element that ethnic conflict introduces into party politics is the ethnically based party. When ethnic loyalties are strong, parties tend to organize along ethnic lines.'[7] We shall have more to say about this in later chapters, but in the cases mentioned so far, ethnic party politics has invariably played a crucial role in structuring the conflicts.

Thus, in Guyana the PPP and the PNC are identified with Indians and Africans respectively; in Burundi the PDC and Uprona represented rival Tutsi factions, while the Hutu organized the Parti du Peuple (PP); in Malaysia, 41 Malay groups came together to form the United Malays National Organization (UMNO), whereas the Chinese coalesced around the Malayan Chinese Associations (MCA), and these two political organizations were crucial in the struggles and bargaining relating to ethnic accommodation during the period of the creation of the Federation of Malaya. The Fijian-dominated Alliance Party and the predominantly Indian National Federation Party, channelled politicized ethnicity in Fiji before and after independence. In Nigeria, the Yoruba formed their ethnic party, the Action Group (AG), soon followed by the Hausa-Fulani Northern Peoples Congress (NPC), which left the older National Council of Nigeria and the Cameroons (NCNC), founded earlier to further the nationalist struggle in the entire country, as a vehicle for the Igbo ethnic group in the Eastern region of Nigeria.

Under the circumstances imposed by colonial rule and the formation of independent states, was the emergence of ethnic conflict inevitable? In the cases mentioned, this would indeed seem to have been the case. There are, however, some important differences that must be taken into account. Of the countries reviewed above, Fiji and Burundi were viable political entities before becoming European colonies. After decolonization, the basis for state legitimacy had been entirely modified, in the case of Fiji due to the presence of a large non-Fijian, Indian population claiming political representation and power for itself. In the case of Burundi, because the traditional monarchy could not cope with the forces of 'modernization': the increasing role of the army and party competition in electoral politics. Still, in both countries ethnic conflict might have been avoided if the right political decisions had been made in time, that is, the recognition by the dominant group of the legitimate demands of the subordinate or excluded ethnic group, even if that had meant the restructuring of state power.

In contrast, traditional state power rested with the northern emirs in Nigeria and the rulers of the Malay states in pre-colonial times, but their territorial units were much smaller than, and did not coincide with, those of the post-colonial state. The new states included additional territory and populations, and consequently the nature of the polity changed. In both Nigeria and Malaysia the struggle over control of the political centre and its resources would pit different ethnic groups with distinct claims against each other. Here the challenge *of* 'nation-building' meant creating a larger, overarching identity which would encompass these heterogeneous competing groups. But the challenge *to* nation-building came, on the one hand, from competing ethnic-regional claims and, on the other, from the drive towards ethnic hegemony by one of the groups. The Biafra war in Nigeria and the difficulties in the birth of the Malaysian Federation (including the separation of Singapore) underlined the fragility in the creation of new states and the building of new nations. The present borders of both these states are an historical accident, for they could as easily have been shaped differently in the transition towards post-colonial sovereignty, in which case relations between existing ethnic groups would certainly not have been the same.

A slightly different situation prevails in Guyana, where neither a pre-colonial polity nor a powerful indigenous ethnic group can lay claim to national legitimacy. Both immigrant groups – Africans and Indians – have an equal interest in the maintenance of the Guyanese state, but rather than seeking accommodation they have struggled for hegemony. The drive for ethnic hegemony seems indeed to be characteristic of bipolar states, that is, where two major ethnic groups of relatively equal size compete with each other in the political arena.[8]

Finally, it is difficult to assess what legitimate interest the Kurdish people can have in the four alien states – Iran, Iraq, Syria and Turkey – into which they were incorporated as a disadvantaged minority, as a result of Great Power manipulations after the First World War. Conversely, as we shall see in later chapters, these states developed their own models of national integration, which have led to direct confrontation with the Kurds over several decades. As may be seen from the above discussion, predisposing or incubating factors of ethnic conflict show many facets: the size, distribution and origin of the various ethnic groups; the political and economic relations they entertain over time; the policies of the colonial state, the nature of the transition to independence; the structure of the post-colonial polity, etc.

The survey does not support the hypothesis, often encountered in current political analysis, of 'ancient tribal hatreds', long suppressed, breaking out under certain circumstances. While mutual dislike and distrust between different ethnic groups may be present, harmonious and friendly relations between them are as much the rule as the exception in historical perspective. It is only when an imperial administration or the post-colonial state is able to structure certain relationships between these groups or communities, that conditions are created which may lead to tensions, antagonism, competition and conflict among them. But for this to occur, a number of mediating or intervening factors must also be present. This is dealt with in the following chapters.

4 The Structuring of Identities

In the cases discussed in Chapter 3, the actors or adversaries are clearly identified by all parties according to one or several ethnic criteria. In some cases, these are objective attributes that pertain to all members of the group or that characterize the group as a whole: language, race, religion or territorial concentration. Such criteria, however, are never sufficient to account fully for the identification of the individuals and collectivities involved in ethnic conflict. It is only when subjective (that is, individually held) beliefs, feelings and motivations concerning the significance of the objective attributes are present that ethnicity becomes mobilized and feeds into collective action. Such beliefs, feelings and motivations may be diffuse, loosely held sentiments, or again they may become ingrained values, shared by the community and structured in the form of systematic propositions, that is, they may be thought of as 'ethnic ideologies'. Frequently, such ideologies are handed down from generation to generation, they thrive on myth and legend, they are sometimes codified in books and laws and party platforms ('charters'), and they provide guidance, justification and legitimacy for the group's avowed purposes in the struggle in which it finds itself engaged. In general, these subjective elements are referred to as the 'identity' factors in the conflict and the struggles as 'identity conflicts'.

But contrary to some widely held perceptions, the objective ethnic attributes and the collective identity of an ethnic group are not permanent and unchanging features. And when ethnic conflict occurs, the attributes and the identity do not always happen to be there, ready-made, to provide a frame of reference for collective action. Rather, it is in the unravelling of the conflict itself that many of the features associated with the ethnicity of a given group acquire their particular importance. That is to say, ethnic identities become activated in a certain manner through the dynamics of the conflict. In some instances, identities are in fact constructed socially in the process, and identity formation or identity construction becomes a part of the conflict itself.

These issues have become crucial to the conflictual dynamics in a number of cases covered in this project. In this chapter some of them will be explored in more detail.

1. KURDISTAN

The term *Kurdistan* refers to the regions in western Asia occupied principally by the Kurds. This area consists mainly of mountain ranges, where the population engages principally in raising livestock and agriculture. A formerly flourishing handicraft industry has declined considerably in recent years. Demographic and political pressures, as well as military activities in Kurdistan, have forced many people into the cities and abroad, and the Kurdish diaspora is today one of the largest in the Middle East. Gérard Chaliand considers that Kurdistan passed from a formerly traditional economy to an underdeveloped, dependent economy.

Most Kurds are Sunni Muslims, who distinguish themselves clearly from the Shi'ites and other Muslim sects. There are several minority sects among the Kurds as well, some of whom, such as the Yezidi, have suffered persecution at the hands of the majority Muslims, and many of them have had to emigrate to Western Europe and elsewhere. The religious factor plays an important social and political role among the Kurds. During Ottoman times, the religious leaders (known as *Mufti*) exerted local influence, but since the abolition of the Caliphate in 1924, their influence has declined. Authority was vested in the village-level *mullahs*, who are the keepers of the cultural traditions and were for a long time charged with educational responsibilities. Their power, in turn, declined when the central government established state schools and sent civil servants into the Kurdish villages, mostly in Turkey and Iraq. A number of Kurds are also members of various Sufi brotherhoods, whose *sheikhs* or chiefs have produced numerous important political figures. Religious leaders traditionally occupy positions of wealth and power in the local social and economic hierarchy, and their prestige and influence may be transmitted through family lines from generation to generation. Some of the leaders of the Kurdish resistance in contemporary times, such as Mustafa Barzani and Jalal Talabani, come from traditional religious families who have occupied positions of pre-eminence for generations. As the influence of the *sheikhs* also declined under the impact of the secular state, and many of them were forced into exile by the Turkish government, they joined the nationalist cause and are to be found among the members of the various democratic and nationalist Kurdish political parties. There is also a Kurdish Islamic fundamentalist movement, known in Turkey by the name of Nurculuk (Disciples of the Divine Light), which is violently anti-communist and anti-Western, and rejects other non-orthodox Muslim sects as well.

Traditionally, rural Kurdish society was segmented into local territorial tribes, which in turn were made up of clans and extended families. The tribe was the largest local unit, and the persistence of inter-tribal conflict and rivalries well into the twentieth century is one of the factors which, according to Chaliand, prevent the emergence of a unified Kurdish nationalist movement, the other factor being, of course, the fragmentation of Kurdistan in four different states.

Conflicts between tribes, sometimes over land and resources, tend to turn into long-standing feuds in which vengeance or vendettas take precedence over other forms of conflict resolution. National states have tried, with variable success, to break the system of tribal vendettas and impose the national legal framework for administration of justice in the Kurdish areas. The traditional tribal chiefs, the *aghas*, in order to further their fortunes or preserve their privileges, develop relations with local state authorities, who thus can intervene in the dynamics of tribal politics.

2. GUYANA

As Ralph Premdas notes, the logic of the communal society implanted in Guyana pointed to a future of inevitable sectional strife. Not only were many layers of fairly distinct communal divisions erected, but in the absence of equally strong rival overarching integrative institutions, the immigrant groups viewed each other from the perspective of their respective compartments with misinformed fear and much hostility. African–Indian rivalry for the few scarce values of the colonial order would feature as a fundamental source of inter-communal conflict from the outset of the creation of the multi-tiered communal society. It would be sustained by a deliberate policy of divide and rule, but would be mitigated by the urban–rural pattern of residence especially of Africans and Indians respectively. Institutionalized division and embedded conflict were the defining features of the system.

Prior to 1950, when the People's Progressive Party (PPP) was launched, certain voluntary associations such as the League of Coloured Peoples (LCP) constituted the only building blocks from which a wider political consciousness would·evolve to challenge the colonial system. Indians and Africans formed the most active voluntary organizations during the early twentieth century. These organizations purported to act on behalf of all the members of their respective communities as a means of putting pressure on the colonial decision-making bodies to grant them political and constitutional concessions. Almost invariably, however, they pursued the narrow interests of their middle-class supporters, but did so by invoking the collective interests of their communal sections.

During the long struggle for independence, attempts were made by both major ethnic communities to join efforts across the communal dividing line. Particularly during and after the Depression, multi-ethnic trade unions and later 'national' political parties sought common ground in building a new multi-ethnic polity. However, for a number of complex reasons, these efforts were not successful in the long run.

The moment of opportunity to build a new basis of inter-group relations and a new society was lost when the two sectional leaders parted company, formed their own party and pursued their own ambition for personal acclaim and power. A new type of party emerged, constructed on the discrete ethnic fragments into which the old unified party had broken. Mass politics invited rival mass organizations to capitalize on ethnic loyalties for votes.

Notwithstanding the appeals of the two ethnically-based parties for supporters in all classes and from all races, the reality was that each party attracted virtually only Indians or only Africans. Sectional identification with the two major parties became a fundamental fact of contemporary Guyanese politics. *Apanjaat*, the local colloquial term for 'vote for your own kind', was the dominant factor which governed the political choices of nearly all Guyanese. Everyone expected an Indian to support and vote for the People's Progressive Party and an African for the People's National Congress. To a substantial extent the uni-ethnic composition of group leadership and group participation was traceable to the sectoral divisions in the social system. To ensure that they could at all times command the allegiance of at least a major segment of the voting population, the parties deliberately (but unofficially) pursued a policy of fostering sectional party identification.

The organization of the population into a network of sectional groups and the consistent surreptitious propaganda peddled by group activists exposed Indians and Africans literally to a single set of political views and attitudes after 1955. The resultant hardening of communal attitudes exacerbated by the activists of the party groups frustrated the efforts of the PPP and PNC to induce members of the other side to join with their parties.

More particularly, in terms of the present study, the hypothesis is advanced that in a cleavage-ridden state such as Guyana political parties engaging in competitive elections tend to accentuate ethnic differences. In Guyana, the country's political parties do not operate in an integrated political system with a pluralistic social infrastructure, and do not possess a racially overlapping membership. Party competition evokes the most hostile inter-community sentiments during elections. Each succeeding election campaign raises the level of inter-group distrust and fear to a new highpoint until, after several elections, inter-community differences become so intolerable that continued mutual coexistence among the sub-groups in the society is all but impossible. The intensification of racial animosities was substantially traceable to political campaigns waged by the parties during election years.

To the role of party organization and election campaigns is added the part played by the uni-sectional voluntary associations. The relationship between the parties and the interest groups had structured the political differences between Indians and Africans, reinforcing bifurcation in the Guyanese polity. Almost inevitably, the formation of voluntary associations followed ethnic lines in Guyana. The two major ethnic groups, Indians and Africans, had become not only predominantly rural and urban dwellers respectively, but simultaneously had become identified with specific occupations, because the economic interests of Africans and Indians had been separated by the historical patterns pointed out earlier. Since voluntary organizations tend to form around clusters of similar interests, unavoidably the intermediate associations became uni-sectoral in composition. In practice, all the major intermediate organizations reflected the historical development of separate economic and cultural interests among Africans, Indians, Portuguese and Chinese.

Throughout the 1960s, particularly during the 1962 budget crisis and the bloody 1963 and 1964 labour disputes that intensified inter-communal conflict, the parties maintained very close relations with the major associations. By prescription and precedent, all the major voluntary organizations had solidified their close relationship with the PPP and PNC. These associations were perceived by the population as belonging either to the 'Blackman party' or the 'Coolieman party'.

The spiral of intensifying ethnic conflict was slowly but inexorably exacerbated by the way the political parties organized the lives of their constituents, the manner in which election campaigns were waged, and the method by which voluntary associations were enlisted in the struggle for communal ascendancy, and led almost inevitably to cataclysmic inter-ethnic confrontation and civil war. Between 1961 and 1965, the screws of communal conflict were slowly tightened so that few people could escape being a co-opted participant in a system of mutual communal hatred. Inter-ethnic relations, especially between Africans and Indians, were increasingly marked by covert contempt and deceptive distrust. The elements of an impending explosion were registered first in the fear of ethnic domination of Indians by Africans and of Africans by Indians. A new drama was unfolding in which the main motif was a struggle for ethnic ascendancy compounded by a politically instigated terror of internal communal colonization. While inter-ethnic interaction was still carried on in the familiar routine of daily life, the same persons in the privacy of their homes and communities enacted a script of racist and communal antipathy, drawing every day perilously close to open conflagration. In public, the political drums continued surreptitiously to beat on the theme of ethnic claims and exclusivity; in public interaction each side had contrived a set of secret intra-communal symbols, idioms and nuanced expressions silently to communicate group solidarity erected on an understanding of collective contempt for the other side. Dual roles and divided personalities dwelt simultaneously in an ethnically split society. Forced to live together by the designs of a colonial conqueror, the sectional elements possessed no experience for inter-communal accommodation. Introduced mass politics was betrayed by sectional leaders jockeying for power. One cleavage after another that separated the ethnic segments – race, traditional values, religion, residence and occupation – was reinforced by a mode of modern mass ethno-nationalist politics which drove the society to the brink of self-destruction.

Each communal section became a virtual military garrison suffusing all activities with social self-assertions built on the dehumanization of ethnic opponents. Persistent ethnic struggle sharpened the negative stereotypes which communal groups held of each other. Indian views of their African compatriots became overladen by collective hate. Africans as a whole were portrayed in terms that made them objects of selfishness and ruthlessness. Africans reciprocated, deeming Indians to be uncivilized and selfish also. The stereotypes extended to derogations that bordered on outright racism.

In time, one factor above all – the ethnic enemy – took the centre-stage in intense group assertion. It occupied the very centre of the soul with an obsessive preoccupation, assigning to it all manner of causes of every conceivable social problem. Apart from shaping attitudes of intense collective hatred, the basis of any future inter-communal coexistence was crippled. Watertight ethnic compartments were created into which all normal emotions were now to be expressed.

The Guyanese who had been submitted to the intensifying tensions of ethnic compartmentalization, concludes Ralph Premdas, became a twisted, paranoid people. A stressful environment had been created, which was unconducive to healthy human development. It was not marked by ordinary struggle, but by hatred, jealousy and a single-minded obsession with subjugating and destroying the ethnic enemy. The stereotypes each Guyanese carried embodied traits which dehumanized entire communities.

3. BURUNDI

The conflict between the dominant Tutsi minority and the Hutu majority has led several times over the last few decades to horrendous massacres of Hutu and to political struggle among rival Tutsi factions. Lemarchand shows how Hutu identity has become politicized, especially in response to the Tutsi's denial that such identity exists at all.

When Hutu elites insist on being recognized as a political majority they are usually branded as 'tribalists' by their Tutsi opponents; for many Hutu, however, the label is exclusively reserved for the Tutsi, because of their 'Hamitic' origins and unswerving commitment to the supremacy of their kin. Adding to the confusion, some Western observers conclude that both sides are victims of 'tribal' enmities.

In terms of their respective numbers, physical characteristics and occupational ties Hutu and Tutsi are as different from each other as any other group in the continent. In one form or another, it is the *leitmotif* that runs through many of the official pronouncements of Hutu intellectuals, for whom these differences are treated as self-evident. In the absence of reliable census figures observers rely on population estimates dating back to the 1930s: today 85 per cent of an estimated population of perhaps 6 million are said to consist of Hutu, 14 per cent of Tutsi and 1 per cent of Twa (Pygmies). But perhaps as many as 20 per cent of Burundi's population today consists of Tutsi.

For many Hutu, the logic of numbers offers a devastating commentary on the methods used by the Tutsi minority to reduce the majority of the population into bondage: only through deceit and ruse could the Tutsi assert their political hegemony on a vastly more numerous population. Only by taking into account the objective characteristics of their physical traits ('tall and thin') and occupational ties (pastoralists) can one comprehend the social dimension of Tutsi hegemony according to the Hutu. Physical characteristics, however, are notoriously unreliable to distinguish Hutu from Tutsi. Given the extraordinary amount of nonsense that has been written about the 'short and stocky Hutu' and the 'tall, lash-thin and graceful' Tutsi, the point deserves the strongest emphasis.

Precisely because physical appearance is not an infallible guide to identity, ethnicity offers social actors opportunities for manipulation. It is one thing to stress the fluctuating character of social identities, and quite another to argue, as some Tutsi do, that ethnic differences simply do not exist, except in the form of imported 'tribal ideologies'. Until recently, even when confronted with the most dramatic evidence of ethnic conflict, the existence of separate ethnic identities has been consistently swept under the rug by the Burundi authorities. The assumption, presumably, is that by eliminating all public references to ethnic identities, ethnic discrimination will no longer matter as a policy issue or a source of inter-group conflict. Proceeding from the axiom that ethnic labels and stereotypes belong to the dustbin of colonial historiography, the official view has been that ethnic references are, at best, a figment of the colonial imagination, and at worst part of a neo-imperialist plot aimed at pitting one group of citizens against another.

In the crucible of the Hutu–Tutsi conflict other ethnic categories have simply disappeared. The hardening of the Hutu–Tutsi dichotomy presumably rules out alternative forms of social identity. What has vanished from the scene is whole gamut of social and political roles that once gave meaning and cohesion to membership in a 'national' community.

Inequality has always been a pervasive aspect of Burundi society. And yet, strange as it may seem, a convincing argument can be made for the view that inequality among individuals was a major source of social cohesion. Protection of the poor and the weak by the rich and the powerful was part and parcel of the normative frame of client ties. Social inequalities tended to generate their own mechanisms of social cohesion. Today, however, inequality has taken on a radically different connotation, not only because it is seen as morally objectionable by the Hutu masses, but because it enters the cognitive map of social actors primarily through an ethnic lens. Social inequality is thus increasingly correlated to ethnic identity. This is an unprecedented phenomenon in the history of the country.

No attempt to demystify the Burundi situation can fail to appreciate the chasm that separates the reality of ethnic conflict from the manner in which it is perceived, explained and mythologized by the participants. Reduced to its essentials, the conflict about the Hutu–Tutsi conflict revolves around three basic disagreements – over the significance of ethnicity as a source of tension, the nature of cultural differentiation between Hutu and Tutsi, and the role of history in shaping ethnic antagonisms. Behind these disaccords lies a construction of social realities rooted in part in the logic of numbers. As members of a ruling minority Tutsi elements are generally unmoved by charges of ethnic domination, and equally prompt to dismiss Hutu demands for full political participation as an intolerable expression of 'tribalism'. Ethnic differences between Hutu and Tutsi are said to be either irrelevant or grossly exaggerated. For the Hutu majority, on the other hand, Tutsi rule can only mean minority rule, which *ipso facto* tends to discredit their claims to power. For most Hutu nothing short of majoritarian democracy will do; yet precisely because it conjures up threats of Hutu domination, made all the more ominous by their shared sense of past injustices unavenged, this is what most Tutsi wish to avoid at all cost. In these conditions, how to establish the constitutional foundations of peaceful coexistence between Hutu and Tutsi is bound to remain a profoundly contentious issue. Thus emerges a narrative strategy which is also a discourse in the service of ethnic interests. The ethnic discourse is expressed in a number of widely shared myths.

Myth No. 1: Ethnic conflict as a carry-over of historic antagonisms

As already noted, presumptions of deep-seated, historically rooted ethnic antagonisms are a key feature of the Hutu discourse on ethnicity. Here the Tutsi as a group emerge as the incarnation of profoundly maleficent influences, fundamentally alien to Hutu culture, and traceable to the invasion of Hamitic elements from the north. Present-day conflicts, we are told, are the carry-over into the post-independence period of historic antagonisms: some are rooted in the efforts of Tutsi to dominate Hutu, others in the combination of ruse and cruelty which figures so prominently in Tutsi patterns of behaviour. Given these irreducible incompatibilities, all attempts at compromise are doomed.

Nowhere is this belief more widespread than among those who suffered most from the abuses and cruelties of arbitrary power – the Hutu refugees now living in exile, some in refugee camps in neighbouring African states, others in Europe. Tutsi rule did more than change Hutu identity; it made their collective selves synonymous with serfdom. By investing the original social meaning of the term *Hutu* ('social son') with a strongly negative and indeed totally misleading connotation ('slave'), and then obliterating its ethnic dimension, Tutsi are globally identified as the Hamitic 'bad guys' who radically transformed the social landscape, converting 'Bantus' into 'Hutus', free men into slaves.

Myth No. 2: Ethnic conflict as the direct outcome of colonial rule

It is not only among Hutu that history is recast as myth. That the Hutu–Tutsi problem is entirely the creation of the colonial state, and bears no relationship whatsoever to the structure of pre-colonial society, is treated as a self-evident truth by a number of Tutsi intellectuals. The quickest route to social harmony, some would argue, is to jettison once and for all the stereotypes inherited from the colonial era and look back to the pre-colonial past as a source of inspiration for the future.

All of which presumably shows how far 'tribal ideology' has contributed to the spread of the 'ethnic virus', thereby threatening the Tutsi minority with the prospects of genocide. It is clearly the European colonizer who first introduced this vector of disunity. Indeed, if so much of the country's recent history is written in blood, this is because the script was largely the work of European civil servants and missionaries eager to play one group off against another.

Myth No. 3: The 1972 killings as a Tutsi plot

For many Hutu a diabolical Tutsi conspiracy lies behind the physical liquidation of hundreds of thousands of Hutu civilians in the spring and summer of 1972. As in the case of most conspiracy theories, the aim here is to reduce an inherently complex and tragic sequence of events to the logic of a master plot. At the heart of the conspiracy, we are told, lay one single, overriding objective: to kill enough Hutu to achieve ethnic parity in the countryside.

Pending a more detailed account of the 1972 killings, suffice it to note that the consensus of opinion among impartial observers is that there is no basis whatsoever for assuming that the carnage came about in response to a masterplan drawn up well ahead of time, or that ethnic parity was ever considered as the ultimate goal. If there is any evidence of plotting it must be found among those Hutu politicians and army men who unsuccessfully tried to overthrow the Micombero government in April 1972. The intent physically to annihilate all Hutu elites and potential elites, and the degree to which this macabre endeavour was put into effect, leave no doubt as to its genocidal character. It is one thing, however, to view the 1972 killings as a Tutsi response to the perceived threats posed to their security by the Hutu attacks, and quite another to describe such killings as the outcome of a long-standing, carefully calculated plot aimed at the surgical 'equalization' of Hutu and Tutsi.

In a sense, of course, these considerations are immaterial. The important fact to remember is that the conspiracy theory has entered the consciousness of a great many Hutu as irrefutable proof of their victimization, indeed their dehumanization at the hands of Tutsi conspirators. As such it has become part and parcel of the 'mythico-history' which to this day informs their perceptions of Tutsi behaviour and mentality.

Myth No. 4: Ethnic violence as the outcome of external subversion

The theme of an 'imperialist plot' looms large in the discourse of Tutsi intellectuals on the 1972 slaughter. It crops up time and again in official and semi-offical pronouncements and in accounts of the 1972 and 1988 killings: only through the incitements of Hutu extremists operating in neighbouring territories could ethnic violence be unleashed on such scale; furthermore, external complicities, we are told, are 'clearly evidenced' by the role played by Rwanda in harbouring such extremists, and by Belgium in providing them with assistance.

Although there is little question about the existence of an externally-based Hutu opposition, exactly what role, if any, such an opposition may have played in engineering the massacre of Tutsi civilians in 1972 and 1988 remains unclear. What is beyond dispute is that subversive manoeuvres from the outside would have been of little consequence if ethnic antagonisms had not already created a potentially explosive situation within the country.

Reduced to its bare essentials, ethnic polarization in Burundi is reducible to a self-fulfilling prophecy inspired by the Rwanda model. Despite the far greater complexity of its ethnic map, and the absence of a rigid Hutu–Tutsi cleavage of the kind that characterized Rwanda society, Burundi could not be but profoundly affected by the political message of the Hutu revolution in neighbouring Rwanda. While providing the nascent Hutu elites of Burundi with the 'model polity' that some tried to emulate, it also gave the incumbent Tutsi oligarchy ample grounds for their incipient fears of Hutu domination.

Ironically, it is among Tutsi intellectuals that ethnicity performs a vanishing act in the name of instrumental rationality. Only by denying their collective identity *qua* Tutsi can they legitimately claim that (a) there is no real discrimination between Hutu and Tutsi, (b) that the quest for a political majority, as distinct from an ethnic majority, is the key to a healthy democracy; (c) that the verdict of history is entirely consistent with their present-day contention of basic social harmony between Hutu and Tutsi, and (d) that Hutu claims to represent the majority of the population are but a thinly veiled manifestation of 'tribalism', the bane of the African continent. There are significant ideological side-benefits to be derived from this set of assumptions: the threat of 'tribalism', coupled with the nefarious role played by the Belgian colonizer and his neo-colonialist offspring in fanning the flames of ethnic hatreds, can be readily translated into a radical, anti-imperialist discourse in which tribalism and neo-imperialism are but two sides of the same coin. Doing away with ethnic identity is seen by the Tutsi as the most rational course to ensure the perpetuation of ethnic hegemony.

Burundi is typically a case in which the affirmation of ethnic identity by one of the groups in conflict and the denial of ethnicity by the group in power, become discursive elements of the conflict itself.

4. AYODHYA (INDIA)

The conflict over the Ramjanmabhumi Muslim mosque in the northern Indian town of Ayodhya has been studied continuously by Ashis Nandy and his colleagues since its beginning. Predictably, the outcome was catastrophic, leading to massive communal riots in various parts of the country which produced hundreds of victims and has profoundly affected the Indian political scene. The facts are simple enough: On 30 October 1990, a few thousand men, largely members or sympathizers of ultra-Hindu organizations close to the Bharatiya Janata Party (BJP), converged here in response to a call given by a militant section to liberate what was according to them, the 'real' and 'only' Ramjanmasthān or the site of Lord Ram's birth, allegedly desecrated in 1528. They were bent upon *Karseva*, the tearing down of the mosque, in the name of Hindutva, the expression of Hindu nationalism or political Hinduism. Three hundred people damaged the temple, and five were killed by police. Two days later, 19 people were killed. Participant *karsevaks* were mainly upper caste, lumpenproletariat youth from other parts of India. Police only stopped them half-heartedly. Local Hindus did not participate at the beginning, though later some were drawn into the activity; many only gave passive support to the *karsevaks*, providing them with food and shelter. The police acted with considerable restraint, and were accused by some observers as having been merely bystanders. Some 300 marchers were able to occupy the temple, before they were finally removed by the police (another three people having been killed).

Things apparently went back to normal. But the agitation began anew in early 1993, when Hindu militants returned to Ayodhya and this time succeeded in razing the temple to the ground. Consequently, violence between Hindus and Muslims broke out in Bombay and other Indian cities, in which several hundred people were killed and much property damage occurred.

According to Ashis Nandy, the Ramjanmabhumi conflict can be explained in terms of the evolution of Hindu nationalism in the twentieth century and is not unrelated to the rise in communal violence in other parts of the country. The Hindus and Muslims of India do not constitute distinct ethnic groups in the conventional sense. Nor do they constitute, despite differences in their socio-economic and educational profiles, distinct socio-economic formations, with common political interests. After all, Hindus in India are 650 million strong, and the Muslims are more than 110 million. Such large aggregates, in a society as diverse as India, cannot but have internal divisions that are in some cases less and in other cases more significant than religious divisions. Even religious divisions within the two aggregates often bear 'peculiar' relationships with divisions within the other community. Thus, the Pranami sect in Gujarat (the one in which Gandhi was born) is closer to Islam than it is to many other sects within Hinduism; likewise, most versions of Sindhi Hinduism look very Islamic to many south Indian Hindus and many Muslim communities in Rajasthan, Gujarat and Bengal look disturbingly Hindu to many Muslims in other parts of India.

Such variations mean that all attempts to mobilize Hindus and Muslims *as* Hindus and Muslims must concentrate on broad ideological issues and subjective configurations of grievances, memories and cultural differences, specially engineered for mobilizational purposes. The social sources and political motives behind the Ramjanmabhumi movement are directly linked to the structure of consciousness within which the propaganda unleashed by the movement made sense to its consumers. These consumers, in turn, were not distributed randomly over all social segments; they came with a particular social profile.

To understand these sources and motivations, we shall have to provide a quick sketch of the growth of the political culture of Hindu nationalism. This growth has been paralleled in crucial ways by similar movements within South Asian Islam, Sikhism and Buddhism. The emergence of Hinduism as the religion of the majority community among urban, modernizing India has had its mirror images in the emergence of Islam as the religion of a minority community with roughly similar ideological and programmatic content. Both in turn have striking similarities with the emergence of Buddhist Sinhala majoritarianism and Sikh minority consciousness roughly along the same lines.

Hindu nationalism does not have a long history in India. The idea of Hindus as a single political community that could be called a nation is relatively new. Its beginnings can be traced to the middle of nineteenth century when, in reaction to the onslaught of aggressive modernism of mainly the Utilitarians and the Social Darwinists, Christian evangelism and exposure to European ideologies of nationalism, there began to crystallize out a wide variety of 'Hindu' responses in the public sphere of India.

These responses gained strength because the modern and secular ideologies, that came into India primarily through colonialism, began to be backed, from about the 1830s, by the colonial state, now trying to establish a closer link between colonialism and modernism and using the latter as an endorsement of the Raj's civilizing mission. The resulting feelings of inferiority, insecurity about the future and moral disorientation provoked responses that were often a strange mix of the classical, the folk and the imported Western categories which had produced the cultural and psychological disruption in the first place.

This new Hinduism – the political ideology of which was later to be given the name Hindutva – had a number of important features. First, it defensively rejected or devalued the little cultures of India as so many indices of the country's backwardness. Instead, the new Hindus sought to chalk out a new pan-Indian religion called Hinduism which would be primarily classical, Brahminic, Vedantic and, therefore, not an embarrassment to the modern or semi-modern Indians in touch with the more 'civilized' parts of the world. It was this high culture, more acceptable to the modern or Westernized Indians and to post-Enlightenment Europe, which was sought to make the basis of the new Hindu nation. The nationhood was also projected into the past and the Hindu cultural uniqueness was reinterpreted as merely the marker of a modern national ideology.

The Orientalists and the religious reformers created the impression of there being a 'real' Hinduism which transcended the 'trivialities' of the local traditions; the modernists and the missionaries delegitimized Hinduism as a lived experience and left open, for the increasingly insecure Indian *literati*, the option of defending only philosophical Hinduism as the real Hinduism.

Second, the redefined version of Hinduism allowed those who saw the new religion more as an ideology than as a faith, to use Hinduism as an instrument of political mobilization *à la* a European-style national ideology. This part of the redefinition of Hinduism derived strength from the fact that Indian culture was primarily organized around religion and it seemed natural to some Indians, sold on the new myth of the nation-state, to use Hinduism as a national ideology rather than as a repertoire of cultural categories in politics. In fact, Hindu nationalism had to reject a cultural-moral definition of Hinduism, the political possibilities of which were to be developed later by Mahatma Gandhi and others. The two strands of consciousness were never to be reconciled, despite the efforts of a number of individuals and parties. Occasional paeans to Gandhi notwithstanding, Hindu nationalism has continued to see Gandhism as a mortal enemy. Gandhi's Hinduism is bound to look to Hindu nationalists as openly anti-statist, anti-Brahminic, disaggregating, emasculating and hostile to modern science.

Third, Hindutva sought to masculinize the self-definition of the Hindus and, thus, militarize the community. The more the sense of cultural and personal impotency produced by the colonial political economy, the more pronounced became the attempts to give public shape to these masculinity strivings, to militarize the seemingly unmilitarizable. To bring about this change, the Hindu nationalists systematically began to use the newly discovered discipline, history. They did so not with the Orwellian conviction that one who controlled the past controlled the future, but with the enthusiasm of one who had introjected the colonial estimate of Indians as ahistorical, effeminate and irrational. Defensive about the traditional Indian emphasis on myths as the principal means of constructing the past, they enthusiastically used the colonial histories of communities identified by the British as martial – for instance, the histories of the Rajputs and the Marathas – and turned these sectional histories into powerful nationalist interpretations of the past.

The emphasis now is on the new version of Hindus emerging in the metropolitan India, with one foot in Western education and values, the other in simplified versions of classical thought now available in commodifiable form in the urban centres of India. This simplified version is expected to be a substitute or compensation for the loss of access to traditional social relations and life-styles, both in the growing urban jungles of modern India and in the cultural melting pots of the First World.

No wonder that from the beginning, the ideologues of Hindutva found that a majority of their supporters came from urban India and especially from among the same modern Indians who were unable to break into the high-status, oligarchic club of the fully Westernized Indians. To start with, the ideologues of Hindutva were a small minority in the public sphere, though their presence in the culture of Indian politics was never insignificant. But with increasing reach of the modern institutions, their influence grew. The major breakthrough came when the colonial state began to falter due to the growing politicization of the Indian middle classes. The reason for this visibility is not difficult to guess. The 'syncretism' that had once been so conspicuous in the Indian political scene had begun to look to many politicized Indians, thanks to the humiliations being inflicted by the colonial regime, as too compromising and obsequious to the colonial establishment. That syncretism had even failed to produce an adequate critique of the modern West. This is the cultural baggage with which the Bharatiya Jan Sangh, the forerunner of the BJP, entered the electoral arena in independent India for the first time in 1952. Its electoral performance was never spectacular until 1977, but almost from its beginning, the party carved out a small, reliable and steady support base among the urban middle classes and among sections of the twice-born castes. The BJP had been working assiduously to expand its upper-caste support by utilizing the ideology of Hindu nationalism. Its targets were primarily the numerically strong and politically mobilized backward castes.

Basically, the Ramjanmabhumi movement represents the recognition by the BJP, and the larger Hindu nationalist formation of which it is a part, that their day has come. The movement *is* an attempt to make short-term political gains, but beneath it lies the awareness that the BJP and its allies are no longer as peripheral as they once were. They have now broken into the mainstream of Indian politics.

As a consequence, the political culture of India is no longer merely an area of contention between the modern and the traditional, with the state clearly on the side of the former. It has become an area of contention between the modern that rejects or bypasses traditions and the modern that employs traditions instrumentally. This has opened up political possibilities for Hindu nationalism that were not open when the traditional idiom of Indian politics was *the* major actor in the culture of Indian politics and when a sizeable section of Indians were not insecure about their Hinduism. As Ashis Nandy argues, Hindu nationalism has always been an illegitimate child of modern India, not of Hindu traditions. Such a nationalism is bound to feel more at home when the main struggle is between two forms of modernity and when the instrumental use of traditions – the use of religion as an ideology rather than as a faith – is not taboo for a majority of the political class.

5. GUATEMALA

As elsewhere in the Americas, the indigenous peoples of Guatemala trace their ancestry to the populations that inhabited this territory before the arrival of the Europeans in the sixteenth century. They are distinguished from the rest of the population by language, custom and social organization. Guatemala's Indians number around five million, over 60 per cent of the country's total population. Their numbers have increased dramatically, from fewer than 150,000 shortly after the Spanish conquest. This demographic expansion contradicts the widely held view that Indians are bound to disappear in the process of economic and social modernization.

Indigenous or Indian identity is opposed in general to the 'white' or '*mestizo*' (mixed) identity of the non-Indian component of the population (also known locally as *Ladinos*). But internally, the indigenous group is diversified and highly fragmented. There are 26 different indigenous linguistic groups in Guatemala, and while most of them belong to the Maya family, linguistic differences also imply cultural distinctions and different subjective identifications. In contrast to the *Ladinos*, a person may be seen as, or consider him/herself as, just an Indian, but at the same time he/she will be a Quiche, or a Cakchikel or a Mam. The picture is further complicated by the proliferation in recent years of religious sects and denominations (over 600 different religious groups have been identified), so that people also identify themselves and others in religious terms. Indeed, religious identities have become important socio-political markers and relate to the dynamics of ethnic conflict in the country.

After centuries of economic exploitation and ethnic oppression during which indigenous identity was perceived more as a stigma in the wider society (and as an instrument of passive resistance by the Indians themselves), indigenous identities have now become mobilized and evolved into what might be termed 'ethnic ideologies'. Indigenous intellectuals (students, professionals, pastors, priests, leaders) consciously assume the role of 'producers of ideology'. Indigenous ethnic identities are no longer seen merely as a transitory phenomenon in the wider process of 'nation-building', but rather as 'structural' elements in the necessary redefinition of what constitutes the Guatemalan nation.

The distinction between Indians and *Ladinos* is also a socio-economic one. Indians are principally poor peasants (though this has also been changing lately), while *Ladinos* are mainly urban dwellers engaged in non-agricultural pursuits. The main area of conflict is the land, which for the Indians is a necessary means of subsistence, and for the *Ladinos* a symbol of status, power and wealth. Land-ownership is unequally distributed: about 2 per cent of all landholders own 62 per cent of the arable land, while almost 90 per cent of all farm operators account for less than 20 per cent of the land. The struggle over land and resources, which means a struggle over power, is at the bottom of the violent civil war which has destroyed Guatemala as a viable society over the last 30 years.

The concept of Indian (obviously a misnomer) grew out of the colonial domination of Guatemala's peasant societies and reflects the way the colonial system dealt with its subordinate, exploited populations. In the nineteenth century, as in other Latin American countries, the newly independent *mestizo* intelligentsia set about creating a cultural model for the new Guatemalan nation which consciously excluded the Indians (who were, after all, the majority of the population). Guatemalan 'nationhood' was defined in terms of the self-identity of the dominant white oligarchy, the sole owners of the land, the wealth, the power and the cultural symbols of the nation, a situation which lasted until the mid-twentieth century.

By this time, modern anthropology took up again the notion of 'Indian' as a descriptive and analytical category. Within a 'culturalist' perspective which was fashionable around the middle of the century, Indian identity had some essential, eternal qualities – directly descended from pre-Hispanic times – which would only change under the impact of outside, modern urban influences. Social change was seen as a process of 'acculturation' from the Indian (or *folk*) to the modern. Indian peoples were seen mainly as passive recipients of external stimuli, incapable of making their own history. National integration in Guatemala meant the incorporation of the Indians into *Ladino* society.

A later approach reformulated Indian ethnic identity in terms of unequal class relationships within a regional system of economic exploitation. Indians were members of peasant communities, structurally related to non-Indians through a system of land tenure, labour relations, unequal economic exchanges and differential access to status and power. Indian identity was not considered as a holdover from pre-modern times, but rather as a function of the Indian peasants' insertion into the economic system, described at the time as a form of internal colonialism. A more recent narrative polarizes the Indian and *Ladino* opposition into a kind of civilizational clash in which the only true Guatemalan identity is carried by the subordinate Indians, as against the 'false' national identity of the *Ladinos*. This interpretation turns the earlier approaches on their head, and instead of contemplating the assimilation of Indians and 'national integration' as its objective (which was, and to a certain extent still is, the government's aim), it proposes as its goal 'Indian liberation'. This stand has been adopted lately by a number of indigenous intellectuals and organizations, who develop the analysis into a powerful strategic political argument.

The emergence of an Indian political identity in Guatemala results from a long and complicated process in which several elements played their role. Mention must be made first of the Catholic Church. Long allied with the colonial system and the local ruling groups, the Church had become the country's largest land-owner in the nineteenth century, when it lost its pre-eminence to the emerging liberal bourgeoisie. Forced to take a political backseat, the Church re-emerged in the 1950s, at the forefront of the struggle against 'communism'. Feeble attempts by a progressive government to implement land reform and social legislation favouring the Indian peasantry were cut short by a military coup in 1954, engineered by the United States and supported by the Church.

In order to re-establish its hegemony over the population, the Church used numerous foreign priests and missionaries, who spread out into the Indian rural areas to carry their message. But not being tied to the local power structures, as the dwindling supply of local priests were, these Catholic missionaries soon understood the social and economic realities of the country and many of them threw in their lot with the peasantry, helping organize farm-labour unions, credit societies, rural co-operatives and peasant associations. During the process, they stimulated an awakening of Indian ethnic consciousness. This was accelerated when a progressive current in Catholic thinking, the Theology of Liberation, achieved a certain presence in the rural Catholic networks, through the establishment of Christian Base Communities.

A second important element has been the rapid growth of Protestant evangelical missionary activity among numerous Indian communities. Small nuclei of Protestants had contested Catholic terrain ever since the nineteenth century. Their influence increased through the efforts of the Summer Institute of Linguistics, an American missionary organization, which for many years worked closely among a number of indigenous groups in Guatemala (as elsewhere in the region). In recent years, dozens of Protestant evangelical sects from the United States have made converts among Guatemala's Indians. Many of them are being financed by conservative economic groups in the United States, who see their role not only as struggling for souls, but mainly as fighting communism and the Marxist-inspired Theology of Liberation. The success of these numerous proselytizing sects among the Indian communities (as well as in the urban areas) is due to the severe social and cultural disorganization in many of the Indian communities as a result of 30 years of civil war and repressive government policies, as well as to the impact of modern mass media evangelical campaigns in which these religious groups excel. Religious conversion and growing religious fragmentation in once homogeneous communities contribute to the reshaping of traditional Indian identities at the local level.

The process of religious change has stimulated the emergence and growth of a new religious phenomenon: the appearance of a Maya Church, based on the recovery of ancient Maya religious practices, rituals and symbolic representations. Active in this new movement are mainly young, articulate representatives of Indian communities who may have been members of Catholic and or Protestant organizations, and who now challenge the 'right' of these traditional establishments to use Indian communities as recruiting grounds for their converts. They claim religious legitimacy for Maya beliefs and practices and attempt to achieve respectability by raising them to the level of a 'Church', in direct competition with Catholicism and Protestantism. While not yet widespread, this religious phenomenon is one more expression of a changing Indian ethnic identity in Guatemala.

After the overthrow of the democratic regime in 1954, small leftist revolutionary organizations attempted in vain to gain a political foothold over the next 30 years. It was only after suffering one defeat after another and severe repression at the hands of successive military dictatorships that they acknowledged the need for the support of the indigenous communities. Some of the revolutionary organizations began creating a rural indigenous base in the 1970s, where despite horrendous military repression (massacres, scorched earth counter-insurgency tactics, massive human rights violations, forced relocations of hundreds of thousands of people), they began to recognize the cultural and religious characteristics of the indigenous peasantry not as an obstacle, but rather as a resource for revolutionary mobilization. Participation in revolutionary movements by Indians *qua* Indians and not only as a 'dispossessed rural proletariat' also stimulated the emergence of a new Indian political identity.

A Guatemalan anthropologist and writer has documented this process. According to Arias, the traditional control of Indian communities was in the hands of a group of men known as *principales* (elders), who achieved their position by ascending through the ranks of the civil–religious hierarchy of their community and who often used their position to gain control of land or Indian labour. From their ranks came those known as *costumbristas*, the defenders of the 'customs', particularly the traditional Indian agricultural and religious rituals. As the agricultural land base in Indian communities decreased and as the externally driven commercial activity increased, Indians involved in the commercial sector began to consolidate their economic power by buying and selling outside of the markets controlled by the *principales* in their own communities. This allowed them to free themselves from the subjugation imposed by the latter through ceremonial services and religious rites, mechanisms that had impeded their accumulation of capital. They confronted the *costumbristas'* traditional beliefs. They found support in the Catholic organizations. The reduction in the political power of the *principales* was equivalent to redefining the community in relation to its own history. The *costumbristas* embodied the link to the ancestors and the ancestral link was what justified the right to land the community considered within its domain. But as the community's land base eroded and residents sought other ways of making a living, the world-view of the agricultural past ceased to provide an adequate ideological framework for defining community relations. The *costumbristas'* displacement in the mid-1960s implies the gradual displacement of agriculture as the indigenous populations' *modus vivendi*.

In the 1970s, Indian communities continued to search for new values to re-establish their commonality, their identity and their place in the new environment. They sought a substitute for the ancient sacred bonds, now eroded by the rapid changes their communities had experienced. From these roots a literacy campaign was born in 1972, which lasted a few years. Literacy programmes, inspired by the Brazilian educator Paulo Freire's methodology, became a means whereby the Indian peasants acquired a new awareness of their problems and began forging a new identity. A number of specifically Maya cultural associations were also organized in the early 1970s by Indian intellectuals, and a number of cultural congresses and seminars were held.

The economic crisis of the mid-1970s produced much hardship for many indigenous peasants and generated increasing internal socioeconomic differentiation within the Indian communities. An emerging Indian bourgeoisie allied itself with the country's conservative and extreme right-wing elements, and claimed for itself an Indian representation in the national political system (seats in congress, control of local government, demands for the establishment of an Indian political party). This was strongly contested by the *Ladino* power structure.

At the same time, poor Indians became more and more involved in social and economic struggles, which were more often than not violently repressed by the military governments (see Chapter 5). Social and political awareness increased after the devastating earthquake of 1976, which left thousands of victims and a million homeless people. Indians took part in demonstrations, protest marches, peasant and miners' strikes, as well as in the organization of the Committee for Peasant Unity (*Comité de Unidad Campesina*) in 1977, which was to play a decisive political role in subsequent years. By the mid-1970s many Indian communities were divided among three groups: the traditional *costumbristas*, the commercial sector (emerging bourgeoisie) and the radicalized peasants, who no longer recognized either of the two other groups as their natural leaders.

Ethnic identity had been transformed in the search for political force. Now, identity was a tangible, verbalized, phenomenon, around which the articulation of political practices was sought. But the symbolic practices, the worldview, and the unconscious codes had been discarded without the formation of new ones to substitute for them. Thus, in concrete practice, just as identity was being talked about more openly, it was experiencing its deepest crisis.[1]

By the late 1970s and early 1980s, even as the Indian bourgeoisie leaned more towards the traditional political party structure, the radicalized Indian *campesinos* leaned more towards revolutionary mass organizations and joined the revolutionary movement in increasing numbers.

6. THE FORMER SOVIET UNION

The Soviet regime spent much effort and considerable resources to achieve what was officially termed the 'complete solution of the nationality question'. Even while centralized control over the non-Russian nationalities was iron-clad, the development of education in the republics and among the small indigenous peoples was strongly encouraged (textbooks were developed for 57 ethnic groups), cultural activities were promoted and national cultural institutions were established and supported. As a result of the policy of 'nativization', the major Soviet nationalities had developed their own intelligentsia and managerial personnel as well as an influential party bureaucracy. From the 1960s onwards, the gap that existed in the social structure of the main ethnic groups was practically abolished as a result of quotas and preferences in the sphere of education and in the process of urbanization. In fact, educational standards and the proportion of persons with university diplomas and academic degrees grew more rapidly in the various non-Russian republics than the national average, which also meant a faster rate than the majority Russian population.

Over the last few decades, population growth among the non-Slavic peoples was also considerably higher than among the Russians, Ukrainians and Baltic nationalities. Moreover, beginning in the 1970s Russians emigrated increasingly from areas of Central Asia and the Transcaucasus, whereas their presence increased in the Baltic states, the Ukraine, Belorus and in Kazakhstan. Consequently, in the former areas the local 'titular nationalities' expected to obtain increasing control over the institutions of power and the distribution of resources, whereas in the latter areas, as a result of the changing demographic balance, the titulars feared losing control in their 'own' republics and becoming subject to an even greater degree of acculturation in favour of the Russian culture.

When the Gorbachev reforms weakened the power of the political centre and the dominant ideology itself was challenged by those who had wielded it for so long, the nationalities policy of the Soviet Union was undermined by the national elites who had become its main beneficiaries. Ethnicity as a basis of group solidarity and ethnic nationalism as a political doctrine effectively challenged Gorbachev's vision of a new multi-ethnic post-socialist Soviet Union. It was, according to Valery Tishkov, a kind of 'national answer' to the nationality question. Emblematic of the political changes of the times was the fact that at the 1989 session of the Congress of People's Deputies the president of the USSR, Mikhail Gorbachev, had to pledge allegiance not to the 'people' as he had insisted, but to the 'people*s* of the Soviet Union', as the Congress decided. That small 's' marked the profound historical change which was taking place in the country.

Gorbachev's policy of gradual political liberalization and administrative decentralization was challenged first by the Baltic republics, where nationalist movements openly advocated secession (arguing the illegality of their annexation by Stalin in 1940), soon followed by similar movements in Georgia, Azerbaijan, Ukraine and Moldova. While the conflicts between the centre and the periphery were mostly of a vertical and political nature, they were also accompanied by some sporadic displays of inter-communal violence and ethnic conflicts at the lower levels – mainly between non-Russian titular nationalities and local minorities in several republics (Meshketian Turks in Uzbekistan; Armenians in Azerbaijan; Gagauz, Ukrainians and Russians in Moldova; Uzbeks in Kirgizia). The leaders and activists of the deported peoples from Stalin's time (Crimean Tartars, Volga Germans and others), began formulating their programmes to restore or establish their own statehoods. Leaders of autonomous republics started movements to raise their status to the level of union republics in order to avoid their 'double' subordination to the all-Union centre and the republican centres.

The ethnic policy of the *perestroika* period failed, and Gorbachev's political enemies used it as their main argument to abolish the Soviet Union altogether. While this event can be considered as a great victory for the leaders of the principal non-Russian groups who were able to dismember the USSR peacefully, the irony of the situation is that the disintegration of the Soviet Union was actually initiated by the Russian Federation. By taking over all the principal functions of government and control over all resources held by the Soviet government, the Russian Congress of People's Deputies, led by Boris Yeltsin, declared its sovereignty in June, and then again in October 1990, depriving the central Soviet government of any real existence. The rest is history: Gorbachev's failed attempt to obtain consensus on a new 'Union Treaty' which would have preserved the Soviet Union, the attempted military coup in August 1991 and Yeltsin's counter-coup after which the USSR (and its president, Gorbachev) were effectively dismantled. Thus Russia, not the other republics, was the key actor in the demise of the USSR. But this process rested on the same ideological foundations of earlier Marxist-Leninist nationalities policy: the principle of national self-determination (by existing ethnic territories) up to and including secession.

Precisely because of the long-standing contradiction between the 'ethnic territorial' and the 'administrative territorial' principles, ethnic conflicts are not absent from the independent states which emerged after the disintegration of the Soviet Union, including within the Russian Federation (a major war erupted between Moscow and the break-away Chechen republic in December 1994). Why and how these conflicts develop is intimately related to the way ethnic and national identities have been constructed. We shall look at some of the cases studied by Valery Tishkov and his colleagues at the Institute of Anthropology of the Academy of Sciences in Moscow.

Central Asia

After acquiring their independence unexpectedly with little, if any preparation, the states of the Central Asian region (Kazakhstan, Uzbekistan, Kirgistan, Tajikistan and Turkmenistan) are now searching for new formulas and socio-political foundations of national development, and for their own niche in the new geopolitical space. Inasmuch as the disintegration of the USSR took place under the slogan of the doctrine of ethnic nationalism, it is only natural that the proclamation of so-called 'national states' within the borders of the former union republics should be made on behalf of the 'titular' ethno-nations: the Kazakhs, Uzbeks, Kirgiz, Turkmen and Tajiks. These groups are mainly socio-cultural structures of the Soviet period, who in the past 70 years have undergone an extremely intensive process of 'nation-building'. This process was attended by radical changes: economic modernization, promotion of universal education and the establishment of prestigious institutions of 'national statehood' based on a new powerful stratum, the administrative, creative and scientific-technical intelligentsia. It was precisely these 'successes' of Soviet nationalities policy, and not just the centralization of the Soviet regime and the ideological and cultural control of the Russian-speaking centre, that made possible the powerful thrust of the Central Asian periphery towards national self-determination. Yet it was also this process which generated a major problem which the new post-Soviet states have to tackle in developing their statehood, namely the status and fate of the non-titular nationalities, who constitute 30–50 per cent of the population in each of these new states. Most of them are Slavs, mainly Russians, and their new identities in the newly independent states is a major problem.

The Russians who emigrated into these areas during the Soviet period were at first mainly associated with industrial modernization and urban growth. Later they were joined by deported peasants from Russia and the Ukraine and by farmers under the virgin lands scheme in the 1950s. The rising proportion of Russians in the total population levelled off in the 1970s, partly because immigration slowed, and mainly because of higher birth rates among the local nationalities. Ethnic distinctions corresponded roughly with socio-economic and professional differences. Having occupied higher status and higher income jobs before the era of *perestroika*, in recent years the position of the Russians has deteriorated. They are now faced with the pressing problem of finding a new niche in the changing economic and socio-cultural situation. In Kirgistan, for example, Russians feel that in the process of privatization they have less of a chance to make good than the Kirgiz. Their professional opportunities are also limited to the extent that they are not fluent in the national language.

In the former USSR, Russians enjoyed for decades the comfortable status of a people dominating all the major socio-cultural areas. The Russian language and culture were reference components of all culture which was transmitted forcibly from the centre to the periphery via the education system, the mass media, party and government structures, and especially via the system of training managerial and intellectual elites, and military service. In these circumstances, Russians residing in the union republics had no compelling motivation to learn the languages of the titular nationalities and integrate into the non-Russian ethno-cultural environment. All levels of education were available in Russian, the media and cultural activities were predominantly Russian, and Russian was the language of office work and the social services. As a result, in Central Asia, Russians basically retained their cultural profile, even if about half of them were already second-generation immigrants.

Although there were intensive inter-ethnic contacts and a high level of linguistic russification in all former Soviet republics, in this region the Russians and the titular populations kept at a cultural distance from one another and were in effect isolated communities with their own social niches and circles of everyday contacts. Russians have preserved their traditional culture in everyday life, rites, behaviour, especially in rural areas. Most Russian folk traditions and rites are performed strictly within their own communities and their Muslim neighbours often do not even know of their existence. Nowadays, the Russians have an increasingly keen ethnic consciousness and are worried by the disregard of the state authorities for their national, cultural and religious requirements, and by the growing Islamicization and traditionalism in official circles. The vigorous manifestation of sovereignty in the realm of language, which has been a major instrument for the titular group to assert its dominant political and socio-cultural status, has proved to be an especially sensitive issue for the local Russians. In Uzbekistan and Kirgistan, the Russians are worried about new laws which establish Uzbek and Kirgiz respectively as the sole state language.

The deterioration of inter-ethnic relations in Central Asia in recent years has been mainly caused by the upsurge in ethnic nationalism among the representatives of the titular groups and by inter-clan and inter-regional disputes that climaxed in a series of ethnic conflicts and even, in the case of Tajikistan, in a devastating civil war. Ethnic minorities deported to the region in an earlier period (such as the Meskhetian Turks in Uzbekistan) and groups of the autochthonous population living outside their own native republics, were the main victims of this violence. While the violence was not generally targeted at Russians, one of the features of the present-day social climate is that the blame for past injustices and crimes committed by the centre is now projected on the Russians. Anti-Russian sentiment is often fanned by politicians and ethnic activists in order to rally and consolidate the 'indigenous nations', rent as they are by internal dissension.

At the same time, Russians who suffer the consequences of the current economic crisis which principally hits the urban population, feel that they are being 'ousted' from prestigious jobs and 'forced' out of the republics in which they live. The enactment of the laws on language and citizenship, the shrinking of opportunities for children to be educated in their mother tongue, anti-Russian nationalist rhetoric and the actions of local radicals and fundamentalists affecting the Russians' everyday affairs evoke a painful psychological reaction among the Russians.

The situation surrounding the Russian community in Central Asia is pregnant with conflict. While the Russians feel that they have always played a progressive role in the life of the peoples of Central Asia, the local population in general does not share this opinion. Their assessment of the role of the Russians is more negative.[2] Many Russians feel that their national pride is being affronted, and they feel defenceless about this. While the local Russians are not generally happy about the agreements which led to the break-up of the Soviet Union and the establishment of the Commonwealth of Independent States, they expect Russia to protect their interests in the political, legal and economic fields. The Russian leadership has expressed concern about the fate of the Russian population in the 'new abroad', and membership in the CIS may be seen as a kind of a guarantee for the Russian diaspora.

Tishkov concludes that the new socio-cultural and political status of the Russians in the former Central Asian republics has led a considerable number of them to adopt ethno-political positions that are significantly at variance with the stand taken by the leadership of the republics in which they live and by a large proportion of the titular nationalities. Judging by all the signs, the overwhelming majority of the Russians living in the newly emerged independent countries are unprepared and unwilling to accept the status of an ethnic minority. Well aware that the exodus of Russians would jeopardize their economic projects, the leaders of these countries have now taken a number of steps to assuage the fears of their Russian population, ensure their safety and raise obstacles in the path of Russian emigration. While in some countries Russians have formed their own national organizations or joined with local nationalities to organize democratic and civil associations, on the whole the political inertia of the Russians in Central Asia is largely a result of their despair regarding the prospects of their continued presence in the region. Emigration aspirations are preponderant most everywhere, and emigration has in fact increased in recent years.

7. CONCLUSIONS

What emerges from the analysis of identity formation in such disparate cases as Burundi, Guyana and India is the fact that modern politicized ethnic identities are forged on the anvil of the post-colonial state. Here we do not have the 'ancestral tribal enmities' that the mass media seem to discover periodically in the Third World, but rather the articulation of group objectives and strategies that will be played out on the political scene, within the framework of a modern party system and highly contested periodic elections. It would, however, be a mistake to reduce the politicization of ethnicity only to the instrumental ends of the 'ethnic entrepreneurs' or the party hacks who are able to mobilize their followers around 'ethnic' issues. As the authors of the three studies on Burundi, Guyana and India show with great clarity, the 'ethnic discourse' – whether it is the self-perception of the Hutu as a victimized indigenous people in Burundi, the mutual stereotypes of Africans and Indians in Guyana, or the search for a Hindu national identity in India – reflects a multi-layered problematic:

1. In more than one instance, it addresses the deep-seated affective, psychic identity needs of a population.

2. It emerges as a result of the breakdown of traditional society in which, for better or worse, different ethnic groups had an established and recognized position in a system of reciprocal and relatively stable relationships.

3. Furthermore, the ethnic discourse develops in support of (India), or in opposition to (Burundi), the nationalist ideology of the modern state, and therefore relates to the various differing and sometimes competing concepts of the 'nation'.

4. Ethnic identities in fact compete with 'national' identity for the people's loyalties and involvement.

In a different way, the emergence of a new Indian identity in Guatemala is also the result of colonial and post-colonial history. Long denied and suppressed, indigenous identities reappear as the result of the complex interplay of numerous factors: the exclusionary prevailing model of the nation-state in which Indians could not find their rightful place; the failure of democratic, 'class-based' organizations to take into account the cultural specificities of Indian peoples; the destruction and disorganization wrought by decades of violence and repression; the rivalry between different religious groups battling for the Indian 'soul'; the struggle for land, resources, justice and dignity at the local level, and the struggle for political representation at the national level. The changing ethnic identity of Indians in Guatemala, while based on objective attributes and subjective attitudes, is a new, modern political phenomenon related to the socio-economic transformations of the country in the international system.

The situation of the Russian population in the newly emerged sovereign states of Central Asia after the demise of the Soviet Union underlines the changing role of ethnic identities. Having been formerly associated with the dominant nationality, the Russians have now become a vulnerable socio-cultural minority in all these countries. Their position is somewhat analogous to that of the European expatriates in post-colonial Africa and Asia. While for the most part they remain culturally Russian, to the extent that taking a nationality is an individual choice, many of them, particularly those of mixed origin, have decided to declare themselves members of the titular nationality of the country of their citizenship. Tishkov sees that there are unquestionable advantages for Russians to move to the category of the titular non-Russian nationality (particularly within the Russian federation), and he predicts a decline in the percentage of the population declaring itself Russian.

As all the cases studied in this chapter show, the mere existence of shared attributes among the members of an identifiable ethnic group (language, religion, biological features, national origin, etc.) is apparently not enough to fire the common ethnic imagination at all times and under all circumstances, let alone trigger ethnic conflict and violence. But how and why does ethnic identity, as a subjectively perceived factor, become such a mobilizing force?

Any individual's identity is established at first in childhood through identification and differentiation with the mother, later with the kin group, and still further down the road with the wider community and its social institutions. Identification theory in psychology, explains how, through shared identification, individuals are linked and will act together to preserve, defend and enhance their common identity. Ethnic identity refers to an individual's consciousness of belonging to, and identification with, the group of which he or she becomes a part in the process of growing up, the internalization of values and symbols shared with other members of the group, and the common beliefs regarding the origins, descent, characteristics, specificity and destiny of the group. Ethnic identity may have a highly affective content, or it may be more 'intellectual' than emotional; it may at times be merely ritualistic. Ethnic identity may also compete with other identities, such as class or nation. It is essential in the construction of an individual's self-image, and it may be charged with positive or negative values. This will depend upon the position of the particular ethnic group within the wider society, and of the life experience of the individual. When an ethnic group has a history of persecution and discrimination, identities may become positively reinforcing ('Black is beautiful') or negatively stigmatizing (e.g. Jewish self-hatred).[3] Ethnic identity or consciousness may also be external, as when others are aware of the existence of an ethnic group even when it has not crystallized as such. For example, the assimilated Jews in Germany during the 1930s had relatively little consciousness of their Judaism and considered themselves as more German than anything else, until the racist policies of the Nazi regime made them highly 'visible'. In Japan, the Burakumin caste is almost indistinguishable from other Japanese, but the discrimination of which they have traditionally been the victims has strengthened among their members a group spirit and collective identity, thus producing a process of 'ethnicization'. Dark-skinned immigrants in the United States or the United Kingdom will immediately be categorized as 'Blacks', and even if they had no 'black' identity before, they will soon learn to assume it.

Identification theory posits that at an early age infants identify with their parents and then come to internalize certain values and attitudes derived from this process of identification. As the individual grows, there develops an image of the 'self' which (s)he shares with other individuals in the family, the locality, the community. In later years, adults will thus acquire a shared identity and require a secure sense of identity in order to navigate the social environment in which they find themselves. A secure identity will provide them with a sense of well-being, whereas a diffuse identity or a lack of a secure sense of identity, will lead to what is commonly termed an 'identity crisis', and sometimes to personality breakdown. Individuals, then, will tend to identify with general modes of behaviour and share values and attitudes with others, by which their individual sense of identity finds support and strength. Such general modes of behaviour and shared values refer to culture and ideology.

As Bloom notes, a threat to ideology or culture is a threat to identity, and equally, an enhancement of ideology or culture enhances identity. Inasmuch as most, if not all, identities are social, that is, shared with other individuals, group identifications become crucial in maintaining cohesive social systems, and this creates the potential for the group to act together to enhance and protect that shared identity. As individuals become socially and politically active, identifications transcend the immediate family or locality, and are made with more diffuse symbolic entities, such as the ethnic group, the religious community, the social class or the nation. To paraphrase Bloom, who specifically refers to 'National Identity': '[Ethnic] identity describes that condition in which a mass of people have made the same identification with [ethnic] symbols – have internalised the symbols of the [ethnic group] – so that they may act as one psychological group when there is a threat to, or the possibility of enhancement of, these symbols of [ethnic] identity.'[4] In a similar vein, Volkan suggests that children, who at about three years of age begin to develop a cohesive sense of self, use 'cultural amplifiers' (usually inanimate objects) to identify with or reject particular ethnic groups to which they either feel they belong or from which they distinguish themselves (for example, material symbols such as flags, ethnic costumes and foods, music, etc.). The sharing of ethnic traits coalesce in adolescence, when the adolescent's horizons expand beyond the family and neighbourhood. At this point, states Volkan, identifications have lasting effects on the adolescent's involvement with ethnicity and nationality.[5]

Identification theory may help us understand why Hutu and Tutsi in Burundi, Blacks and Indians in Guyana, Hindus and Muslims in India, behave the way they do in specific contexts. This last condition is important, because the group identifications referred to only occur within the same environmental circumstances. Bloom argues that only under such conditions will there be a tendency for a group of individuals to make the same identification, to internalize the same identity.[6] In other words, there is nothing in an ethnic identity as such which predisposes the ethnic group to conflict. Only under certain circumstances do ethnic identities become salient and mobilized, and very often they emerge in the course of the conflict itself.

5 The Dynamics of Conflict

It would be arbitrary to attempt to pinpoint any single event as the starting point of an ethnic conflict. As we have seen in previous chapters, conflicts may have a variety of underlying causes, conditioning factors and triggering events. It would be equally hazardous to predict the evolution of conflicts along any standard path. While ethnic confrontations may share some common features, each one is unique to the circumstances in which it occurs. The main difference between ethnic conflicts and other kinds of social struggle is their 'intractability', the fact that they appear to be almost impossible to solve. The conflicts studied in the UNRISD project are also characterized as being protracted; they persist over the years, intensify and wane, change over time, and sometimes peter out through the exhaustion of the antagonists, only to arise anew at a later date. A typical example of this process is the struggle of the Kurdish people. Exceptionally, such conflicts are solved through the political or military defeat of one of the parties and the victory of the other, or through negotiations. We shall have more to say about conflict resolution in later chapters.

1. KURDISTAN

The Kurds were mentioned as a distinct people by Greek writers of ancient times. They were conquered and converted to Islam by the Arabs. By the sixteenth century, most of the Kurdish areas had fallen under the domain of the Ottomans, while some remained subordinate to the Persians. Until the beginning of the nineteenth century, Kurdish emirates maintained a large degree of local autonomy within the empire. During the nineteenth century the Ottoman policy of attempting to strengthen a more centralized state led to a number of Kurdish revolts, which were all defeated in time. Even in that period, the imperial rivalries in the region between Russia and Britian influenced the outcome of these struggles, as British interests supported the Turkish empire against the emerging Kurdish nationalists. Several Kurdish uprisings against the Shah of Persia were equally unsuccessful.

Kurdish nationalism, as an intellectual political movement, emerged at the beginning of the twentieth century. Gérard Chaliand divides recent Kurdish history into four phases. During Phase 1 (1920–45), the Kurdish population was divided into four and even five nationalities and became the object of either stringent assimilationist or openly repressive policies by the major new states in western Asia: Turkey, Iran and Iraq. Large-scale Kurdish insurrections took place in Turkey in 1925, 1930 and again in 1936–8, which were brutally repressed. Thousands of Kurds were deported, and the existence of Kurds as such in Turkey was officially denied. They were referred to as 'Mountain Turks'. Some of the Kurdish areas remained off-limits to foreign visitors until 1965.

Kurdish revolts also occurred in Iraq between 1920 and 1931, as a result of the creation of the Iraqi state by Great Britain. A Kurdish religious leader, Sheikh Mahmud Berzendji, headed a nationalist movement and proclaimed himself the King of Kurdistan in 1922. His movement was not successful and failed to marshall the support of the international community. In Iran, a Kurdish tribal chief, Simko, opposed the government in Tehran as early as 1918, and attempted to gain the support of Turkey and Britain for his cause. He was defeated in battle in 1922, and murdered by goverment agents in 1930. Most of the revolts during this period were led by religious chiefs.

Phase 2 (1945–58) was marked by the establishment of the Kurdish republic of Mahabad in Iran (1946), to date the only instance of a fragile Kurdish independence. During the Second World War, northern Iran was jointly occupied by the Soviet Union and Great Britain. After the war, the USSR wished to extend its influence beyond its southern border, whereas Great Britain was committed to maintaining Iran's territorial integrity and its own political influence over the central government. During those years, the Kurdish Democratic Party of Iran (KDPI), a local nationalist group, succeeded in obtaining Soviet support for the creation of the Autonomous Kurdish Republic of Mahabad in January 1946. The experience was short-lived. As a result of international agreements, Soviet troops withdrew from Iran, and after the re-establishment of the central government's authority in Mahabad with help from Great Britain, the leaders of this short-lived republic were executed in 1947.

After this defeat, the KDPI reorganized as a left-wing party, and maintained links with Iran's Communist Party. As a result of the overthrow of the Mossadeq government in Iran by the CIA, the KDPI was weakened by government persecution and internal conflicts, but continued its struggle for regional Kurdish autonomy within a democratic Iran.

The overthrow of the Hashemite dynasty and the proclamation of the republic in Iraq in 1958 inaugurated Phase 3 (1958–75) in the history of the Kurdish question. For the first time, Iraq formally recognized the existence of two peoples in the nation: Arabs and Kurds. This recognition was on paper only however, and soon the Kurds in Iraq, under the leadership of Mustafa Barzani, began their struggle for regional autonomy, first with the support of the Soviet Union, later with that of the Americans.

The Baathist government in Baghdad, which seized power in a coup d'état in 1963, first engaged in massive military activities to defeat Barzani's rebellion, while at the same time it recognized the national rights of the Kurdish people and proceeded to decentralize its administration of Kurdish areas. Despite severe internal dissensions, the Kurdish forces (*Peshmergas*) successfully resisted the Iraqi army and obtained a ceasefire agreement in 1966. Between 1966 and 1969, Mustafa Barzani headed a Kurdish autonomous region in northern Iraq. Severe fighting erupted again in 1969, resulting in thousands of victims and refugees. A major Iraqi offensive in 1974–5 finally broke the back of the Kurdish resistance.

In Turkey during this period, despite the fact that the Kurds probably represent almost a quarter of the total population (estimates vary), the government continued its anti-Kurdish assimilationist policies, initiated by Kemal Atatürk in the 1920s. While Kurdish politicians did participate in national politics, though not *qua* Kurds, any attempt to develop a Kurdish identity was severely repressed, a policy which provoked different expressions of local Kurdish resistance. Numerous Kurdish politicians in national political parties were pushed aside, and even legally prosecuted, for supposed 'regional and separatist' activities. No wonder that the first organized nationalist Kurdish activities were channelled through small left-wing parties, which usually viewed Kurdish demands through the then fashionable Marxist dogma on the class struggle, the union of all labouring classes and the need for socialist revolution, in which the Kurdish question would be automatically resolved. The first openly Kurdish nationalist parties were founded during the 1970s, mostly as clandestine or semi-clandestine operations. Most of them had a pro-socialist ideology, but internal divisions led to the proliferation of splinter groups and weakened their overall effectiveness. The Kurdish Workers Party (PKK), which was to become the most important of these groups, grew out of student activity at the University of Ankara in 1974.

Phase 4 (1978–91) of the Kurdish resistance, according to Gérard Chaliand, began with the fall of the Shah of Iran in 1978 and the Iran/Iraq war (1980–8), during which each of the antagonists wanted to use the Kurds on the other side for its particular political purposes.

In Iraq, a rival organization to Barzani's Kurdish Democratic Party (KDP), the Patriotic Union of Kurdistan (PUK), was established in 1977 under the leadership of Jalal Talabani, one of Mustafa Barzani's fiercest rivals. The PUK was able to bring several other parties under its influence and waged a major struggle against the KDP in the late 1970s. In the early 1980s Talabani attempted unsuccessfully to negotiate an agreement with the Iraqi government, while receiving support from Iran.

As a result of the Iraqi army's brutal operations in Kurdistan (including the 5000 victims of a gas attack on the Kurdish town of Halabja in March 1988), the two major Kurdish parties and several smaller ones agreed to create the Kurdish Front of Iraq. The end of the war between Iran and Iraq freed the Iraqi army to launch a major offensive against the Kurds that same year. During this operation almost 500 Kurdish villages along the Turkish border were wiped out, 77 were attacked with chemical gases and over 100 000 refugees fled the area, joining the more than 300 000 Kurdish refugees from the Iraqi government's war on the Kurdish people.

Now, the Iraqi government embarked upon a particularly repressive phase of its policy towards the Kurds: the forced displacement of Kurdish populations and the massive destruction of Kurdish mountain villages (3500 according to Kurdish sources, cited by Chaliand), including the use of chemical gases which caused thousands of victims. The Kurdish drama in Iraq reached its crisis during the Gulf War (1990–1), when about two million Kurdish refugees required the protection of the United Nations. For the first time since 1920, the international community finally decided in 1991 to intervene on behalf of the Kurdish people, as the Security Council approved a call for humanitarian aid.

After the fall of the Shah, the Kurds in Iran had hoped for autonomous status for Kurdistan in Iran, but the Ayatollah Khomeini declared a *fatwa* against the 'atheistic people of Kurdistan' and sent his revolutionary guards to occupy the region and control all administrative positions in the area. The Iranian government also supported the local Kurdish land-owners against the peasants, who were mainly affiliated with the KDP of Iran.

During the 1980s the Kurdish Workers Party (PKK), aiming to achieve independence for Turkish Kurdistan, began to carry out guerrilla activities, which were violently repressed by the Turkish army. While the outlawed PKK engaged in a number of terrorist acts against so-called Kurdish collaborators and the civilian population, which led to internal divisions and conflict with other Kurdish parties and organizations, it later abandoned these tactics and was able to establish a solid popular basis of support in a number of urban areas. It also received aid from Kurdish organizations in Iraq, which provoked a number of Turkish attacks on Kurdish bases in that country, creating friction between the two states. Since 1983, this struggle has produced several thousand victims, and at the beginning of the 1990s it seemed that the armed conflict in Turkey would most probably escalate. International pressure finally led the Turkish government to recognize the identity of the Kurds in 1991, but this political decision has so far not mitigated the level and intensity of the conflict, according to Gérard Chaliand.

As these brief paragraphs show, the Kurdish question has had a complex history of struggle, alliances, betrayals, hopes and shattered expectations over the years. Seen in historical perspective, there is an overall unity to the Kurdish struggle, but in fact at any one time it consists of several parallel conflicts: among Kurdish parties and leaders both within countries and in different countries; between Kurdish and other organizations; between Kurdish parties and the various governments of the region; between these states over the Kurdish issue; and finally, between outside powers concerning their particular geopolitical and ideological interests in the case. Perhaps no other ethnic conflict in the world is as complex as the Kurdish drama, and few other people have suffered so much for so long as a result. As Gérard Chaliand concludes, 'among the numerous oppressed minorities, the Kurds have by far paid the heaviest price over the last sixty-five years'.

2. LEBANON

The brief civil war in Lebanon in 1958 was the first generalized confrontation between the different Lebanese factions since the communal violence of 1860. This was not only an internal crisis, as it reflected the general conflictive situation in the Middle East and the international rivalries associated with the cold war. For about six months, between May and October, a majority of Muslims and a minority of Christians fought the government of President Chamoun, a Maronite Christian, who had attempted to amend the constitution allowing him to remain in power after his legal mandate ended that year.

While this was not the only reason for the revolt, Chamoun's attempted power seizure exposed underlying tensions in Lebanese society. Ever since independence and the pact of 1943, the Maronite Christian elites had tried to impose their own concept of Lebanese nationalism on the rest of the country, whereas the Muslim elites had turned towards Pan-Arab nationalism.

The accumulated frustration, created by increased economic inequalities and the national identity problem, led to a mass movement, composed of a majority of Muslims, against Chamoun, who was supported by the West.

His successor, President Chehab, tried to mend fences with the Muslim community, but his policy of appeasement did not last long. The situation was further complicated by Egypt's military defeat by Israel in 1967. The situation was ripe for a political return of the traditional Maronite leadership, which succeeded in derailing all concrete proposals to reform the system. Consequently, both internal and external factors of destabilization combined to set the stage for the break-out of war in 1975.

A major fact in this drama was the increasing military presence of the Palestinian resistance in south Lebanon after 1967, and the subsequent arrival of various Palestinian resistance organizations after their liquidation by King Hussein in Jordan in 1970. The Palestinian presence contributed to a new fundamental political cleavage in the country, in addition to the other communal cleavages. Numerous battles between the Palestinians and the Lebanese army culminated in a major confrontation in May 1973, a general rehearsal for the civil war which erupted in 1975. The Palestinian presence also provoked increasing Israeli military involvement, particularly the bombing of villages in south Lebanon, where the victims also included Lebanese civilians. This military activity created a flow of refugees to the capital and the Palestinian refugee camps. The Muslim elites played the Palestinian card in internal politics, particularly after 1970, when President Frangieh tried to monopolize political power in benefit of his Maronite political clientele. This attempt further alienated the Muslim Sunni elites. The Palestinian presence challenged the national identity of the country, but squabbles over identity were only an epiphenomenon: the real struggle was over political power, in which the Maronite elites attempted to maintain their control of the system, whereas the Muslim elites hungered for greater participation in the exercise of power.

The crisis was further aggravated by the progressive deterioration of the social situation (inflation, labour unrest, declining standards of living), on which the political Left was able to build a large-scale popular mass movement which included members of the different religious communities. During the 1960s and 1970s, Beirut became a mosaic of religious and ethnic groups, each population concentrating in homogeneous neighbourhoods: Maronites, Greek Orthodox, Druzes, Sunnis, Shi'ites and Palestinians (some of whom lived in refugee camps), as well as Syrians, Armenians and Kurds.

As a result of the break-down of the institutions of the state and the social crisis, these groups acted as more or less self-contained communities, and became increasingly hostile towards each other. Political polarizations set the so-called Islamic Progressives against the Christian

Conservatives, the International Left against the Fascists, the 'real' Lebanese against the 'traitors and foreign agents'. Loyalties and definitions were in flux: soon the Christians saw themselves as resisting the Islamic Revolution inspired by Iran, and the Muslims saw themselves as defending Islamic and Arab identity against Israel, the West and their local Christian allies. How did these political-cultural oppositions turn into open warfare in the mid-1970s?

Kamal Hamdan identifies three phases in the escalating warfare. At first, the various groups and parties had their local neighbourhood militias for defensive purposes, engaging in occasional individual violence. Some of these militias had emerged in the 1950s, during an earlier civil conflict. Then there were the three larger 'territorial' militias, the Lebanese Forces, the Amal and the Progressive Party, each one attempting to secure and control a specific urban space identified with a particular community. The Palestinians had their own militia. Finally, there were the larger militias which struggled over the power of the state itself: the religious Islamic Hizbollah, and General Aoun's Christian national army. The distinction between these three types of militia were not always clear-cut.

Soon the capital, Beirut, was divided between the Muslim-controlled areas in the west and the Christian-dominated areas in the east. The militias, regardless of their particular ideologies, attempted above all to keep control of their respective community's territory. Grand political discourse aside, the power of the militias rested on their control of certain restricted neighbourhoods only, which were communally segregated from each other and remained the power-base for each community's dominant elites. In the end, the political violence expressed the social rivalries between communal groups. Between 1975 and 1990 more than 100 armed groups and sub-groups went active in Lebanon. They represented not only the large local actors, but also the small and medium-sized groups identified with neighbourhoods, regions or simply families. While only a small number of these militias became politically significant, by the time the war ended in 1990, about a dozen armed groups were still active. While only about 30 000 people are estimated to have been actively involved in the fighting at any one time, and around 100 000 altogether – that is, no more than 3 per cent of Lebanon's total population – many more were involved as sympathizers, family members and supporters of the various groups.

Just as the country fragmented into separate disputed and communally held territories, so each of these in turn became the scene of factional fighting. The civil population never had a chance, being herded by the militias into communally controlled spaces, or exposed to uncontrolled violence if they were caught on the wrong side of the demarcation line.

But these communal territories were never able to develop stable and functioning institutions, and suffered more from internal strife than from external aggression. A sort of self-apartheid and segregation kept the Muslims from the Christians, and then divided the Christians among themselves and the Muslims in turn. Self-imposed communal segregation did not create appropriate forms of stable institutional life and governance.

If political autonomy was not particularly successful, economic autarchy within the communal territories was even less possible to impose. The territorial militias were in fact actively engaged in trade and exchanges between territories, which was a source of revenue for them. Many individuals continued to cross between eastern and western Beirut for economic reasons, even if at considerable risk to themselves.

Towards the end of 1990, after 15 years of civil war, the country was divided into seven major communal territories:

1. Israel's self-declared security zone in southern Lebanon, controlled by a Christian army;
2. southern Lebanon north of the 'security zone', a collection of mainly Shi'ite Muslim villages, and a number of economically strategic points;
3. the region around the port of Sida, made up principally of Sunni Muslims and the 'Progressive Islamic' political coalition;
4. The Druze region strategically placed between southern Lebanon and the capital and on the east–west, north–south communications network; by far the best-run of the communitarian territories;
5. the southern rim of greater Beirut, first controlled by the Palestinians, later by Hizbollah, includes large masses of impoverished Shi'ites concentrated in shanty-towns. In the absence of effective national government, Hizbollah developed its own public services and institutions with aid from Iran;
6. the Christian enclave of eastern Beirut and its immediate area, includes the most prosperous part of Lebanon and covers about 20 per cent of the country's land mass, including about an equal share of the total population. This is the core of the Christian 'mini-state' which the Maronite leaders attempted to set up after they failed to control the central state. Despite its early unity, by 1988 this territory had split into two rival Christian factions.
7. The rest of the country, including West Beirut, which contains about 25–30 per cent of the country's Christians, was controlled by the Syrians, but several communal groups, both Muslim and Christian, also had their local strongholds here.

Whereas each community tried to consolidate its hold over the territory it controlled, they were relatively unsuccessful in setting up stable governing institutions, let alone economic organizations. While at the beginning of the war in the mid-1970s the principal cleavage was between Christians and Muslims, towards the end of the 1980s most of the confrontations took place among different power groups within these two communities. Thus, inter-communal conflict turned into intra-communal fighting. At the same time, a younger generation of militant leaders challenged the authority of the traditional community elders and extremist positions on all sides became common. The earlier division between ideologies of the 'Left' and the 'Right' were overtaken by more 'fundamentalist' positions on both sides. A subtle demographic shift in the composition of the militias also took place: a younger (mostly under 18 years of age), less well-educated group of recruits, many of them refugees from the 1982 Israeli invasion and the fighting in the east, displaced the early core of mainly urban middle-class, relatively well-educated, ideologically motivated militants. This contributed to making the violence more unpredictable and arbitrary.

The Lebanese national army was involved in these struggles from the start. First, each one of the major communal groups wanted to use the army for its own purposes, and ran into the resistance of the other group. Afterwards, the army itself split into different factions, associated with the various communal groups, and effectively ceased to be an instrument of national unity. Officers and enlisted men of Christian or Muslim persuasion deserted to join their respective militias, only to return when conditions changed.

Uncontrolled, arbitrary violence played a significant role in this war. Again, the nature of the violence changed over time. At the beginning, selective violence by each one of the major groups could be seen as an instrument of certain political objectives, as a dependent variable. In time, however, the violence became an 'independent' factor, following a logic of its own. The different militias engaged in brutal, destructive encounters, without any apparent political objective except to harass the rival group in its territory. In fact, they all knew that they could not win such a war, and they did in fact respect the various territorial boundaries, particularly in the Beirut metropolitan area. The escalation of violence followed a tit-for-tat pattern, in which each group saw in the immediate enemy a mirror image of itself. In these battles, the no-man's land of central Beirut (which was not clearly claimed or controlled by any of the factions) became the preferred target of the destructive violence of all the factions in the area, as if by destroying the unifying metropolitan centre each territorially bounded community could enhance its own image and local power.

3.   THE HORN OF AFRICA

(a)   Eritrea

We have already seen in Chapter 3 that the Eritrean Liberation Front (ELF) was founded in 1960 by Muslims who felt threatened by Ethiopia's annexation of their country. In later years, the growing influx of Christians, especially radicalized students, created intolerable strains within the ELF, whose conservative leadership was suspicious of Ethiopian infiltration and feared loss of control over the organization it had founded. The radicals forced a split in the nationalist movement, and created a second organization under their control, which eventually became known as the Eritrean People's Liberation Front (EPLF). The new organization forged an amalgam of socialism and nationalism as its ideology, proclaimed its mission to be a social as well as a national revolution, and its goal Eritrean independence. Independence was not a negotiable issue, and in order to put it beyond discussion, the EPLF defined Eritrea's position as colonial and claimed the right to self-determination exercised by all colonized people. Inevitably, the two movements clashed, and a civil war was fought between them during the early 1970s. They were still locked in internecine conflict when the imperial regime was overthrown in 1974.

The military faction that took power in Ethiopia was committed to the preservation, not only of the territorial integrity of the Ethiopian state, but of its highly centralized and authoritarian character as well. Consequently, no serious attempt was made to engage the Eritrean nationalists in negotiations. Instead, an all-out effort was made to subdue them by greater force. A savage battle fought inside Asmara at the end of 1974 produced horrors that turned the majority of Eritreans against Ethiopia. From now on, the nationalist tide mounted, and within two years the ELF and EPLF had seized control of the region, with the exception of its capital and the two ports on the Red Sea. But by 1978, the regime was able to recover most of Eritrea from the nationalists. The latter were forced to retreat to inaccessible regions, from where, however, they could not be dislodged despite determined Ethiopian efforts.

The destruction wrought in that region provided the nationalist movement with a steady stream of recruits, while weapons of increasing sophistication were routinely captured from the Ethiopian army. While repulsing the Ethiopian offensives, the rival Eritrean fronts fought their own internecine struggle. This ended in 1981, when the EPLF, by now far the stronger of the two, defeated and drove its rival out of Eritrea. After several years on the defensive, the EPLF was able to go on the offensive in the mid-1980s, against a regime that had failed to gain legitimacy in a country stunned by a second famine within a decade and threatened by economic paralysis. The regime was further distracted by the rebellion in Tigrai province, where it was losing control of the area and the land routes to Eritrea. After a series of stunning defeats in the late 1980s, the Ethiopian army once more was left besieged in Asmara and a couple of other towns, with the rest of Eritrea under the control of the EPLF.

The EPLF now concentrated on a diplomatic offensive abroad, designed to win support for its proposal to settle the issue by means of a referendum in which the people of Eritrea would exercise the right of self-determination and decide their future. After three decades of desperate struggle, the Eritrean cause began to receive grudging recognition. The final scene of the drama occurred in 1991, when the regime in Addis Ababa collapsed under the assault of the Tigrai rebels and their allies. The Ethiopian army in Eritrea disintegrated, and the EPLF assumed complete control.

Three decades of warfare had a devastating impact on the region, whose population was estimated at 2.6 million by the 1984 census, but is considered twice as large by the EPLF. A large part of this population was widely dispersed, and the local economy was shattered. One positive result, from the viewpoint of the nationalists, was the adherence of all sections of Eritrean society, regardless of ethnic, religious, linguistic and other differences, to the nationalist cause. A very strong consciousness of common identity and solidarity was forged in the struggle, so that now it became possible to speak of the emergence of genuine Eritrean nationalism.

(b) Sudan

In southern Sudan it was Christianity that came under attack. Missionary schools were taken over by the state in the first few years of independence, Friday replaced Sunday as the day of rest in 1960, missionary activities were restricted from 1961, and all foreign missionaries were expelled from southern Sudan in 1964. A plan for education adopted in 1961 was premissed on total Arabization. Northerners took over all school supervisory posts in the South, and later the region's secondary schools were removed to the North. Southerners in public service came under pressure to take Muslim names and to send their children to Quranic schools. These moves drove the budding southern Sudanese intelligentsia to embrace the Anyanya movement in the 1960s.

The resistance movement in southern Sudan made its appearance in 1963, following five years of military rule, a period during which normal political activities were outlawed, and the military regime proceeded with its policy of achieving 'national integration' by promoting Islam and Arabic and restricting Christian religious activity. The Sudanese military and security forces had a free hand in dealing with suspected opponents of this policy, and were ruthless in their treatment of the southern intelligentsia, particularly those who had been involved in political activity earlier. Educated southerners and political activists fled to Uganda and Zaire, where they established the political arm of the movement, the Sudan African National Union (SANU). Others went into the bush to form the guerrilla organization that became known as the Anya-nya.

The two wings of the southern movement were linked only tenuously. The political activists abroad were not involved in the creation of the Anya-nya, and had no influence in the guerrilla movement. They tried to solicit support abroad, particularly among Africans, portraying the conflict as racial and relying heavily on the theme of Arab oppression of black Africans. They succeeded in enlisting strong support among Christian missionary bodies and Church organizations in the West, which took up the southern cause and raised a chorus of protest internationally. However, the southern activists abroad gradually neutralized themselves through interminable squabbling and factionalism, in which tribalism played a conspicuous role.

For some years, the guerrilla force consisted of several poorly armed bands, formed along ethnic lines and operating in their home districts, with little communication or coordination between them, or a common leadership. Even so, they posed a challenge to the Sudanese army which moved *en masse* to the South, where it massed in small towns, venturing out on retaliatory expeditions that rarely engaged the rebels, but frequently brought destruction to communities suspected of harbouring them. The Anya-nya made considerable progress during the second half of the 1960s. The guerrilla bands were gradually integrated into a unified military structure, whose organizational format nevertheless was based on ethnicity. In contrast to the rebellion in Eritrea, the southern Sudanese movement was innocent of ideology. No great effort was made to conceptualize its goals in the ideological context of nationalism, and the closest southern propaganda came to abstraction was a feeble attempt to play on the theme of Arab victimization of Africans. The motto of a short-lived publication produced abroad was *Negritude and Progress*. The leadership of the guerrilla force did not formulate a specific programme, nor did it ever specify the goal for which it was fighting, other than to pledge to rid the South of

Arab domination. Many voices spoke for the South, including several factions of political activists organized in Sudan and abroad, and they were seldom in agreement.

The attitude of southerners towards the Sudanese state, as distinct from the Arab hegemony, remained quite ambivalent. At a conference held in Khartoum in 1965, various southern factions presented proposals ranging from independence to federation, and were easily outmanoeuvred by the northerners, who were unanimous in rejecting all such demands. The common denominator of southern political opinion, was self-government for their region, and this is what they settled for in 1972.

The offer of regional autonomy brought the conflict in southern Sudan to a negotiated end in 1972; the only instance of peaceful conflict resolution in the Horn, albeit a temporary one. It came at a time when Anya-nya military effectiveness was at its peak, and the state's presence in the South had eroded to the point where the insurgents were proceeding to fill the vacuum with an alternative administration. It was the realization that a military solution was not a realistic option, and awareness of the political danger a protracted, unwinnable struggle posed for his regime, that brought President Nimeiry to the negotiation table in Addis Ababa in 1972. On the other side, supporters of the rebels, including the religious bodies abroad and the regime in Addis Ababa, urged them to negotiate.

With the Addis Ababa Agreement the South did not win equal status with the North in a federal system, but attained a significant measure of self-government within a unitary state. The three southern provinces formed a region with its own legislature and executive authority to manage regional affairs. The language issue was resolved by making English the 'principal' language in the South, while Arabic remained the official language of the state. Freedom of religion, and regional control of education, offered assurances of protection against enforced Arabization.

The Agreement satisfied the outstanding demands of the social groups in the South that had led the movement. The autonomy of southern regional civil service guaranteed a monopoly of state posts to the southern intelligentsia, thus removing a major grievance. Additionally, they were guaranteed a share of civil posts in the central government. Most of the Anya-nya fighters were inducted into the Sudanese army in separate units stationed in the South, others joined the regional police and prison services, while their leaders became army officers, and the top commander of the Anya-nya became a general in the Sudanese army. Finally, a promise was given that development in the South would be promoted by a special development plan financed by the central government and foreign aid.

The Addis Ababa Agreement brought peace to southern Sudan for a decade. However, it brought no development. The Sudanese economy declined steadily under the Nimeiry regime, and the central government was unable to fulfil its financial obligations to the South. The Agreement allowed the state president considerable freedom to intervene in the affairs of the regional government, and Nimeiry intervened destructively in southern affairs. He imposed his own candidates for regional office, repeatedly dissolved the regional government, ordered changes in the boundaries of the southern provinces, and in 1984 divided the region itself into three separate units, in a blatant move to reduce southern solidarity and political power. In doing this, he exploited ethnic and provincial rivalries which had mounted steadily within the region during the 1970s. A major political cleavage emerged between the Dinka pastoralists, the largest ethnic group which accounts for roughly half the population of southern Sudan, and the sedentary groups of Equatoria province, who feared Dinka domination.

The second round of the civil war had started in 1983, when the Sudan Peoples Liberation Movement (SPLM) made its appearance. Its origins were not dissimilar to those of the Anya-nya. In fact, many of the actors were the same, since they came from the ranks of the Anya-nya fighters who had been integrated in the Sudanese army ten years earlier. The ranks of the guerrilla force were filled mainly from the Dinka ethnic group, and within a year of its founding the new movement was operating aggressively throughout the South.

The SPLM's growth was ensured by Nimeiry's next desperate move in search of political support. As his political fortunes declined, along with a downward slide of the economy, the dictator courted the support of the fundamentalist Muslim Brothers, the implacable opponents of southern autonomy. At their behest, he flirted with theocracy, initiated constitutional changes towards the imposition of an Islamic republic and imposed the strict Muslim shariah law on a bewildered population. Although it was not clear whether it applied in the South, the first victims of the draconian law were southerners living in the North. This signified the final abrogation of the Addis Ababa Agreement, and it cost Nimeiry the support of most southern Sudanese, as well as many secular-minded northerners. The SPLM now won broad support among southerners, and considerable sympathy in the North for carrying the fight against the increasingly oppressive regime in Khartoum.

The SPLM, whose leadership displayed a degree of political sophistication missing in the old Anya-nya, distanced itself from the latter's exclusive preoccupation with the South. It was no longer just a southern Sudanese movement, but a movement that represented all regions and peoples of Sudan, particularly the marginalized and underprivileged groups. For the SPLM, the enemy was the political system that had ruled Sudan since independence, and the political factions that had created and maintained it for their own benefit. The ousting of Nimeiry in 1985 through a popular uprising and the return to civilian rule did not change the situation. The war continued, and now the government began to arm certain ethnic groups to fight the SPLM. In an appalling return to the horrors of the nineteenth century, southern children were abducted and kept or sold as slaves.

By this time, the Sudanese economy was close to bankruptcy, basic services were faltering even in Khartoum, famine was threatening the entire country and was already taking a rising toll in the South. Having lost all hope of winning the war, the Sudanese army leadership itself demanded that the government bring the war to a negotiated end, and the government was forced to begin negotiating in earnest. In July 1989, just when negotiations with the SPLM seemed about to bear fruit, another military coup took place, led by middle ranking officers with strong Muslim fundamentalist connections. Its apparent goal was to abort the negotiations and to continue the effort to subdue the SPLM by force.

After some months of equivocation, the fundamentalist orientation of the new regime became obvious. The National Islamic Front (NIF) emerged as the dominant political force in Sudan. The shariah law was reimposed and Sudan was declared an Islamic republic. The war in the South continued. Supplying the towns became nearly impossible, and a huge civilian population that had sought refuge in them was starving. The population of the war-torn region was decimated by famine, disease and violence. Millions of southerners were forced to leave their homes. A large number took refuge in the North, where they live in appalling slums, while others crowded into refugees camps in Ethiopia.

(c) Comparison

The evolution of the conflict in Eritrea and southern Sudan followed the same escalating pattern. The regimes in Addis Ababa and Khartoum adopted policies aimed at wiping out all resistance and integrating the regions into a centralized, unitary state. Force was the main instrument used in the effort to subdue the rebels. Accordingly, the military and security apparatus in Ethiopia and Sudan expanded disproportionately in size, consuming a steadily increasing share of the budget, and gaining virtual autonomy from political control until, eventually, the state itself was brought under military rule. The escalating use of force had

ambivalent effects. On the one hand, it contained the challenge and preserved the state and the power monopoly of the ruling groups for a long
time. On the other, state violence fanned the flames of resistance and
expanded its scope by driving potential victims to join the ranks of the
rebels. Military operations laid waste whole districts, drove people off the
land, produced successive waves of refugees, disrupted the process of production and distribution of food, and caused massive starvation. Moreover,
years of uninterrupted warfare saddled the state with enormous foreign
debts and brought it to the verge of bankruptcy.

The resistance movements that emerged in Eritrea and southern Sudan
were truly regional in character. From the outset, their frame of reference
was the regional entity that had been carved out by colonialism, and all
groups living in it were perceived as having common interests threatened
by groups in control of the state. This perceived commonality was not
based on ethnic affinity, religious affiliation or linguistic unity, since the
population of both regions is quite diversified along these lines. Moreover,
ethnic and religious divisions were strongly manifested in the internal
political life of these movements, and at certain times greatly weakened
them. Nevertheless, such divisions were transcended in the effort to resist
the absorption and subordination of these regions in states controlled by
ethnic groups that regarded themselves as culturally superior, denied
others access to power and monopolized the material and social resources
controlled by the state. In the course of the long struggle, regional solidarity evolved into a consciousness of a common identity that can, at least in
the case of the Eritreans, be called national.

4. FIJI

More than once in recent years, collective racial violence has spilled
over into the public arena threatening to envelop the entire fragile
system in conflagration. In particular, 1968 is remembered in this regard;
electoral competition cultivated racial sentiments to unprecedented
heights, and the fear that one day all restraints would be removed in a
racial confrontation haunted political leaders. It finally happened in May
1987 when the Fiji military forces staged a coup d'état which removed
the elected government of Timoci Bavadra. The event that triggered the
military intervention was the removal from power via the electoral
process of Fijian High Chief Ratu Mara and his Alliance Party after a
decade and a half of uninterrupted rule. The military architect of the
coup cried 'Fiji for Fijians' in removing the first truly multi-ethnic

political party from power. The critical issue in the coup turned on inter-ethnic relations.

We have already mentioned the concept of Fijian paramountcy in Chapter 3. It is noteworthy in this regard that the paramountcy claims which became by Fijian convention linked to the Deed of Cession found their way by interpretation onto the preamble of the 1970 Fiji constitution. The preamble cited the Deed of Cession as conferring special position to the indigenous Fijians. It was inevitable that, at least to Fijians, this meant that the political paramountcy idea was recognized and accepted by the constitutional Founding Fathers.

In contrast, the Indian sector of the population demanded electoral equality, and its claim was couched in terms of the 'common' roll (one man, one vote) as distinct from the 'communal' roll (sectional representation). Because the Fijians were governed under a separate native administration, the Indian demand for a common roll challenged European control of the colonial council and was interpreted as an attempt to introduce Indian political domination of Fiji. When the Indian population first exceeded the Fijians in 1946 and became a clear majority in the entire population by 1966, the menace of Indian hegemony became as ominous as it was allegedly real. The growing Indian economic and educational ascendency compounded the problem and seemed to provide the foundations for effective takeover.

While constitutional agreements provided the broad structural bases for co-operation in Fiji, some other factor was necessary to link the leadership of the two major parties (one Indian, one Fijian) so that they could consult each other and collaborate informally in running the government. Ralph Premdas uses the term 'comity agreements' to refer to the varieties of informal devices by which communal leaders work out a *modus vivendi* to accommodate each section's interests. Without comity agreements a constitution could become a source of conflict and continued communal animosity.

The honeymoon that followed the making of the 1970 constitution and the elections in 1972 that confirmed the Alliance Party and Fijian political paramountcy did not last long. A comity agreement faces dual danger from 'outbidders' and criticisms alleging conspiracy between elites. In late 1975, the leaders of the two parties faced intense pressures from these two danger points. The leadership of the Alliance Party was challenged by criticisms that it presided over a government that was inimical to indigenous Fijian interests and promoted continued Indian economic progress in Fiji. Similarly, the leadership of the National Federation Party was challenged by an Indian 'outbidder'. Towards the end of 1975 and early 1976, it appeared that the criticisms by the Fijian and Indian outbidders had started to have their desired effects. A newly organized Fijian Nationalist Party took aim at all of the major concessions constitutionally given to the Indian section, even challenging the continued presence of Indians in Fiji. Equally significant, it would cause the Alliance's moderate multi-racial posture to change. In the remaining part of the decade the growth of new strains between the Alliance and Federation parties threw the entire set of understandings of the 1970 constitution in turmoil.

In the 1977 election, the Fijian Nationalist Party competed for the votes of Fijians, drawing substantial numbers away from the Alliance and reducing the percentage of its vote. The significance of these elections pointed to the possibility that Fijian parliamentary and political paramountcy could be undermined by the correct combination of electoral actors. The 1977 general elections signalled that Fijian political paramountcy was no longer acknowledged by Indians. A struggle for power was now on. Alliance acts of discrimination against Indians would increase.

In 1975, a Royal Commission was appointed to study the electoral system, and its report called for a modification of the current communal system of representation. The changes were more equitable towards Indian interests, but they were rejected outright by the ruling regime. The set of deals and compromises which the constitutional Fathers struck in 1970 had been eroded so thoroughly by the mid-1980s that only a bare constitutional skeleton devoid of its spirit continued to exist. Comity between the Fijian and Indian political elites had been destroyed. Balance in the distribution of power and privileges was superseded by a fierce zero-sum struggle for dominance of the state. The 1987 coup merely made formal a constitutional funeral that was long overdue. Both the Fijian and Indian party leaders acted in a way that contributed to the undermining of the constitutional balance that was formalized in 1970. Fijian leaders succumbed to 'outbidders', resorting to administrative practices that negated the Indians' equal access to state opportunities and resources. Access to land as perceived by the Indians was diminishing; the government returned Crown land to the Fijian domain instead of making it available to the land-hungry farmers. Indian access to scholarships and promotions was circumscribed, frustrating them and making them feel like second-class citizens. Budgetary allocations were tilted consistently in favour of projects benefiting Fijians. The latter, in turn, feared for their paramountcy privileges. Should Indians assume power, Fijians would also face the prospect of seeing their traditions eroded and chiefly system discarded. Fijians land and values were equally threatened. The loss of power could then have far-reaching repercussions for the survival of the Fijians as a people. To them, then, the paramountcy doctrine seemed to safeguard their future. Vital interests were at stake for both the Indian and Fijian community.

The primary triggering instigators of this process of erosion came from the 'outbidders' in both the Indian and Fijian section. To battle against the 'outbidder', moderate leaders were driven to co-opt the 'outbidder's' programme, thereby destroying their own moderation and becoming extremist. Old compromises and comity relationships were quickly eroded. The balance was overturned. Instability became endemic in the pluralistic society inviting military intervention.

The 1987 general elections were the fifth in Fiji's history since independence. Next to the two old-established parties, the Indian-based National Federation Party and the Fijian-based Alliance Party, there was one major addition among the party contestants, the Fiji Labour Party (FLP), born out of the confrontation between the government and the unions in 1985. The FLP was able to persuade an enfeebled Federation Party to join it in a coalition arrangement.

The victory of the Labour–Federation coalition was a signal event in Fiji. For the Alliance, its loss signalled a fundamental violation of its political eminence which it thought was 'embedded in the Deed of Cession' and premissed in the concept of balance. Almost as soon as Timoci Bavadra's new government was sworn in, a grumble commenced about alleged Indian dominance in the government. Bavadra himself was Fijian and he took the sensitive portfolios of Fijian and Home Affairs which covered institutions close to native Fijian interests. In a cabinet of 14 members, six went to Fijians, one to a General Elector, and seven to Indians.

It would take the deliberate and systematic instigation of latent Fijian fears by a small contingent of disaffected Alliance leaders to arouse Fijians to mass action. At meetings and demonstrations organized and led by the Alliance, Fijians were told that the Bavadra government was a front for Indian interests and that their immediate objective was to deprive Fijians of ownership and control of their land. Labelled the Taukei Movement, the meetings picked up momentum at first from small, half-hearted gatherings, then included road blocks, fire-bombings and outright racist appeals to Fijians. Soon the streets of Suva and Lautoka, Fiji's largest cities, were in control of the demonstrators. Less than three weeks after taking office, the Labour–Federation government was in dire straits, jolted and steadily destabilized to the point where the regime was paralysed.

Whatever were the motivations, inspirations and surreptitious manoeuvrings involved in the making of the coup, the fact remained that Bavadra and the Labour coalition were unceremoniously evicted from office just 33 days after peacefully assuming power. The coup leader,

Lt.-Col. Rabuka, echoed the fears and demands of the Taukei demonstrators. The military junta proclaimed that 'Fiji was for Fijians', and that in their own land, Fijians would not be dominated by an alien race. Only a Fijian-run government could protect Fijian interests. To this end, the military announced that the old constitution was abrogated and a new one would be prepared to guarantee Fijian political paramountcy in perpetuity. A new constitution was soon drafted to entrench Fijian paramountcy and institutionalize Indian, European and Chinese political inferiority.

The evidence clearly shows that at least four interests combined to instigate Fijian mass mobilization against the government:

1. a minority of frustrated Alliance dissidents who were ex-ministers of the outgoing government assumed the instigator leadership role;
2. the small number of Fijian chauvinists who generally tended to support the Fijian Nationalist Party and other Fijian extremist groups;
3. representatives of multinationals who feared nationalization; and
4. the US government, which was displeased with the potential loss of a reliable ally in the Pacific islands.

The military coup provided the occasion and opportunity for a full vetting of Fijian communal grievances. While Rabuka wielded *de facto* power following the coup, the Governor-General and the ousted Labour–Federation Party met between mid-May and mid-September 1987 to work out a compromise for a new political order, embodied in the Deuba Accord. Rabuka was unhappy with the inter-ethnic terms of the Deuba Accord, however, and felt impelled to stage a second coup in September 1987 to preserve the original extreme Fijian chauvinist expectations of the first coup.

From that moment on, Fiji was to be ruled by a military administration. Rabuka declared Fiji to be a republic, effectively severing its ties with the Commonwealth. However, given the difficulties of holding together the new governing group, Rabuka decided to lift military rule in December 1987, passing power over to the president. In all of this, it is clear that a *de facto* authoritarian state with a distinctive ethnic slant was grafted onto Fiji's erstwhile open society. Even while the civilian interim government used the rhetoric of constitutional review and the need to restore democracy, the Fiji military forces were busily engaged in establishing a pervasive repressive apparatus in Fiji. In 1990 a new constitution was promulgated, and with this single event Fiji is now the only state in the international community with a political system based on outright racism. The constitution was not based on majority rule; it was a document forged in the service of ethnic supremacy. The ramification of racism was manifested pervasively in the institutions that were established. In every area of political and economic life, the explicit priority assigned to Fijian interests above others was based on ascribed traditional and biological characteristics, much of this as fictive as they were self-serving. The claim to indigenous rights served to justify oppression and discrimination against other groups. It was not enough simply to assert equality, but by a crude calculus of power, it seemed necessary to devalue the dignity and rights of other communities. If all of this had achieved its purpose of protecting Fijians from domination in their own land, giving them as a whole access of equal economic opportunity and conferring equal political power among Fijians, it could, in part, be justified. However, the evidence suggested that the new dispensation dealt harm not only to non-Fijians, but also to most lower stratum Fijians. A definitive class and status dimension seemed to be built into the new constitutional order so that those lower income and lower status Fijians who had so enthusiastically supported the military intervention of Lt.-Col. Rabuka in the expectation of obtaining a just deal were about to be systematically excluded and frustrated. The justification for this ethnically separatist authoritarian order was the claim to paramount rights of Fijians as the indigenous peoples of Fiji.

The new constitution institutionalizes the political representational inferiority of non-Fijians who constitute a majority in the country's population. By decree, Fijians are now more than equal to non-Fijians.

5. BURUNDI

The struggle began before the independence of Burundi in 1961, in the rivalry between the two principal political parties, the *Parti de l'Union et du Progrès National* (Uprona) and the *Parti Democrate Chrétien* (PDC). Each of these parties was associated with a rival Tutsi faction, and the Belgian administration clearly favoured the PDC.

The leader of Uprona was Louis Rwagasore, who, as the king's eldest son, was in an ideal position to claim a share of the legitimacy surrounding the Crown; and he enjoyed the support of the Hutu masses. In the 1961 legislative elections, the Uprona candidates emerged victorious and Rwagasore was expected to become prime minister. However, shortly afterwards, Rwagasore was assassinated, the victim of a PDC plot. Perhaps no other event has weighed more heavily on the destiny of Burundi.

Rwagasore's death was the first in a series of crises leading inexorably to a sharp polarization of ethnic feelings. Until 1965 the *Mwami* (monarchy) remained the most important stabilizing element in the power equation. As the polarization of ethnic loyalties gathered momentum the growing concentration of power around the throne gave a measure of stability to the political system; by the same token, as the imperative of political centralization became increasingly difficult to resist, the legitimacy of the monarchy declined in proportion. By 1965 the monarchy was no longer seen as the solution; for a number of Hutu and Tutsi politicians it had become a major part of the problem. The youth wing of the Uprona Party, *Jeunesses Nationalistes Rwagasore* (JNR), whose Tutsi bias became increasingly apparent, eventually emerged as the spearhead of an incipient, urban-based movement towards Tutsi hegemony.

The Kamenge riots, in January 1962, provided the JNR with a unique opportunity to establish its credentials as a radical organization. The *Jeunesses* went on the rampage, many Hutu were killed and much property was destroyed. In time, party, parliament and civil service became major diffusion points for the spread of ethnic rivalries, thus expanding the scope of Hutu–Tutsi polarities far beyond the political arena. As ethnic rivalries intensified, attempts by incumbent Tutsi elites to eliminate their opponents by legal or extra-legal means led to a nightmarish sequence of plots and counterplots, accompanied by acts of terrorism and threats of assassination. The Hutu felt increasingly discriminated against and pushed aside from effective participation in the political system as a result of the concentration of power in Tutsi hands.

The explosion came in October 1965, when a group of Hutu army and gendarmerie officers staged an unsuccessful coup. The mutineers took a huge gamble and lost – but the losses went far beyond the extermination of the thousands of Hutu that followed in the wake of the aborted coup. What was lost was an opportunity for the Hutu leadership to share in the exercise of power. After the extensive purges of the army and gendarmerie, and the physical elimination of every Hutu leader of any standing, power became the exclusive monopoly of Tutsi elements. Groups of Tutsi soldiers and youth set about the grim task of restoring 'peace and order'. An estimated 5000 Hutu civilians lost their lives in the capital alone at the hands of local civilian defence groups organized under the supervision of the army and the governor. Besides bringing about the physical elimination of the entire first generation of Hutu leaders, one of the most significant consequences of the abortive coup was the near collapse of the government machinery built around the Court. Indeed, at the end of 1966, the military overthrew the monarchy, seized power and proclaimed the First Republic.

While the new government proclaimed 'Unity and Revolution' as its aim, what emerged instead was a very weakly structured governing apparatus largely dominated by Tutsi elements, with the extremists holding the key positions within and outside the army. In such circumstances state–society interactions took the predictable form of increasingly brutal encounters between a Tutsi-dominated army and the Hutu opposition. To bolster their own political fortunes, some Tutsi factions played on latent Tutsi fears of a Hutu rebellion and the restoration of the monarchy.

For some Hutu elites the writing on the wall was now unmistakably clear: armed rebellion was the only meaningful alternative to Tutsi hegemony. After another failed attempt at insurrection in 1969, which cost many lives, a major Hutu uprising took place in 1972. Within hours of its outbreak, a reign of terror was unleashed by Hutu upon the Tutsi, and then on an even more appalling scale by Tutsi upon Hutu. The killings went on unabated for several months. By then almost every educated Hutu element was either dead or in exile. Some conservative estimates put the total number of lives lost at 100 000, others at 200 000. Approximately 150 000 Hutu refugees fled to neighbouring territories.

For the next 15 years only Tutsi elements were qualified to gain access to power, influence and wealth. To an even greater extent than before, what was left of Hutu society was now systematically excluded from the army, the civil service and from higher education. Never before had the Hutu as a group been so thoroughly reduced to the status of an underclass.

In 1976, yet another coup brought a new military regime to power. This one proclaimed 'National Unity' as its immediate goal: the need to restore the secular cohesion of Burundi society. However, exhortations to national unity did little to alter the stranglehold of Tutsi elements on the apparatus of power. From 1976 to 1979 the country remained firmly under the control of a Supreme Military Council consisting of 30 officers, all of them Tutsi. The Uprona now became an all-embracing, strongly structured instrument of political mobilization, the major vehicle of Tutsi interests. To allay charges of ethnic discrimination in the recruitment of party cadres and civil servants, an imaginative solution was found in the official banishment of all references to ethnic identities, with the additional provision that all such public or private references could be grounds for charges of incitement to 'racial hatred'.

Concurrently, a new system of education was put into effect, based on the use of Kirundi, the traditional language of the Barundi people, as the sole medium of instruction in primary and secondary schools. Thus, access to the language of the elites – French – was *ipso facto* reduced to those 'privileged' families where parents already spoke French, in short to Tutsi families. 'Kirundization' thus tended to perpetuate a highly dichotomous pattern of socialization, which inevitably played into the hands of the Tutsi elites.

In 1987, yet another group of young military officers proceeded to seize power in a bloodless coup: the 1981 constitution was suspended, the National Assembly and Central Committee of the Uprona dissolved and the Third Republic proclaimed. For all the hopes raised by the advent of the Third Republic, little was done to adjust policies to expectations, which was nowhere more apparent than in the rising expectations of the Hutu masses and their bitter disappointment upon discovering that, in spite of official statements to the contrary, nothing would substantially alter the realities of Tutsi supremacy. In 1988, a local incident of Tutsi abuse triggered a burst of Hutu violence in a rural commune. Ethnic hatred suddenly turned into a blind fury directed at every Tutsi in sight. The restoring of 'peace and order' by the army proved even more horrendous. Assisted by helicopters and armoured vehicles, the military unleashed their retribution with appalling brutality.

The confrontation with the army took an enormous toll. Although the exact number of Hutu victims remains a matter of speculation, informed estimates suggest that 15 000 may not be too wide of the mark. It is a safe assumption that the total number of casualties would have been substantially higher without the massive exodus of tens of thousands of Hutu peasants to Rwanda. As a result of international pressures, a consultative commission, including an equal number of Hutu and Tutsi, was appointed by the government to investigate the circumstances of the massacre and make appropriate recommendations to promote 'national unity'. Shortly thereafter, the cabinet was reshuffled, with the number of Hutu ministers increasing from six to 12, and a Hutu becoming prime minister. In the wake of the massacre a number of liberal reforms were introduced, a Charter of National Unity was adopted which formally proclaimed the advent of a new era, dedicated to the construction of a society free of prejudice and discrimination; and a new constitution, overwhelmingly approved by way of referendum, now set specific limitations on the powers of the executive, stipulated the conditions of multi-party democracy and enshrined the sanctity of basic human rights. The Report of the National Commission for the Study of the Question of National Unity (1989) is an impressive joint Hutu–Tutsi effort to chart a new course towards unity. For the first time in the history of independent Burundi an official statement was issued which explicitly recognized the centrality of the Hutu–Tutsi problem.

The Hutu were divided as to what to do. The principal line of cleavage here was between those Hutu who, willingly or not, accepted the terms of the compromise outline in the Report of the Commission on National Unity, and those who rejected it out of hand as a thinly veiled attempt to perpetuate Tutsi hegemony. The former cast their lot with the official, ethnically-mixed, though Tutsi-dominated, Uprona, the latter with the all-Hutu Palipehutu party. A third group, identified with the Front des Democrates Barundi (Frodebu), sought to enlarge the scope of reforms and prepare the ground for a genuine multiparty democracy in which both Hutu and Tutsi would have a meaningful share of power.

Despite this promising beginning, however, not much changed at the local level. Renewed killings occurred in November 1991, with an estimated 3000 Hutu killed by government troops. Since then, the cycle of violence has continued. In the first free and widely monitored elections in decades, held in June 1993, Frodebu unseated the long-ruling Uprona government. Four months later, fearing the consolidation of what they perceived to be Hutu power, the Tutsi-dominated army staged a coup and assassinated President Ndadaye. In the ensuing violence, as many as 50 000 people were killed, with roughly the same number of Hutu and Tutsi, according to an International Commission of Inquiry, and about 700 000 people, mainly Hutus, fled the country. Negotiations between the different parties, as well as international pressure, led to the appointment by the parliament of President Ntaryamina, also of Frodebu, in February 1994. But he, in turn, was killed in April 1994, together with his Rwandan colleague, when the plane they were travelling in was brought down upon approaching Rwanda's capital, Kigali (an incident which led to the horrendous genocide of Tutsis in Rwanda). In Burundi, the situation worsened. The various political parties, many of which were established by factions and splinter groups of the older organizations, agreed upon a 'Government Convention' in September 1994, to tide the country through a transitional period. In the meantime, sporadic and selective violence continued. Though the coup of 1993 failed, observers now speak of a continuing 'creeping coup' which is designed to achieve the same objectives, by destroying the legitimacy of Frodebu and effectively paralysing the government.[1]

6. PAKISTAN

Another case of protracted and seemingly intractable ethnic conflict is to be found in Pakistan, originating in the Partition of India in 1947 and the subsequent massive transfer of populations. To begin with, as Farida Shaheed and Abbas Rashid report, the politics of ethnicity in Pakistan took the form of sub-nationalism, though subsequently localized ethnic conflict became a dominant feature. Ethnic boundaries have been defined and redefined as the circumstances changed, demonstrating that there is nothing primordial in the identity of the ethnic groups in conflict even though some markers of identity may be more resilient than others. The Indian Muslims, in their struggle for a separate homeland, chose to subjugate other aspects of their identity deriving from territory, language, culture, etc., in favour of their religion. The Muslims from Uttar Pradesh as well as from Bengal articulated their demand for Pakistan not as culturally distinct groups but as Muslims. Once Pakistan came into being however, the competition between different regional elites very rapidly assumed the form of conscious ethnic differentiation that foreshadowed the processes of development and the development of ethnic conflicts.

A number of imbalances attended the very creation of Pakistan. As in other post-colonial societies, the institutions of the state, i.e. the army and bureaucracy, were over-developed in comparison to civil society. Along with differences of language and culture, not to mention unequal levels of interest in the very concept of Pakistan, the regions forming Pakistan also had different levels of social formation. To make matters worse, the elite that assumed power was dominated by two ethnic groups who, even together, did not constitute the majority population. Also of political significance is the fact that this domination came to be seen by the other regional groups precisely in ethno-national terms. Another factor that contributed greatly to aggravating the imbalances was the large-scale transmigration of populations at the time of Independence when the Indian subcontinent was formally partitioned to form the states of India and Pakistan. Over eight million people arrived in West Pakistan from India.

Not only were the regional elites unequally represented in the central elite, the socio-economic structures of the component regions/groups were different. Of all these regions, Punjab had been most integrated into the British colonial structures. It was more urbanized, had the biggest irrigation system and some industrial activity, apart from dominating the army and bureaucracy. Bengal was culturally developed, politically more advanced, had higher educational levels and, of course, constituted the majority. Hence the claim for a share in state power by the middle-class leadership in Bengal had considerable popular support and was well articulated. Consequent to the frustration of these aspirations, the politicization of Bengali ethnic consciousness subsequently led to a bloody confrontation between the central Punjabi elite and the Bengali counter-elite, resulting in an independent Bangladesh.

As in the case of Bengal, the Pakhtuns of the North-West Frontier Province started with a strong sense of ethnic consciousness under the popular leadership of Ghaffar Khan. This soon took the form of a sub-nationalism in opposition to the state of Pakistan, which was now seen as an instrument of Punjabi domination. The situation subsequently changed with the integration, gradually and effectively, of the Frontier population into the state structure and the market economy. The nationalist demand for 'Pakhtunistan', i.e. an autonomous/independent state comprising Pakhtuns on both sides of the Pakistan–Afghanistan border, finally collapsed with the war in Afghanistan and the arrival of nearly two million Afghan refugees in the Frontier region.

In Sindh, the two main features at independence were first, the presence of an oppressive feudal system, and secondly, the sudden vacuum created by the departure of the Hindus who had formed the bulk of the middle class – a vacuum filled, almost entirely, by the Urdu-speaking immigrants from north India who settled in Sindh's urban centres, i.e. Karachi, mostly, and Hyderabad. This effectively left the province of Sindh without an indigenous educated middle class. The net result was a radical alteration of the ethnic landscape of Sindh where Urdu native speakers now made up 50 per cent of the urban population. These migrants also took over the property of the Hindus who had fled to India, further alienating the Sindhis. A substantial proportion of lands mortgaged to Hindu money-lenders did not revert back to its original Sindhi owners, but went to Urdu-speaking migrant refugees, known as Mohajirs, from India. The Sindhis were further alienated when Karachi, the seat of their provincial government, was turned into a separate federal area under the jurisdiction of the central government. As a result, the local feudal elite was able to consolidate their political hold while posing as the champions of peoples' rights vis-à-vis a centre that came to be seen as an instrument of domination and exploitation.

In Sindh, the urban–rural divide widened in terms of development, with Karachi receiving, almost exclusively, infrastructural support as well as new investment in industry and the manufacturing sectors, and rural Sindh being almost entirely ignored. Here, another major source of grievance emerged with the controversial allotments to military and civil bureaucrats, mainly Punjabis, of land brought under cultivation by a number of multi-purpose dams.

After the violent separation of East Pakistan and the establishment of Bangladesh, the Pakistan People's Party (PPP) led by a charismatic leader from Sindh, Zulfiqar Ali Bhutto, came to power in the country. The Bhutto regime sought to address itself to some of Sindh's grievances, notably with reference to government appointments and the language issue. More Sindhis were inducted into lower and middle-level government jobs, while the government tried to enforce urban–rural quotas vis-à-vis Sindh's share in federal jobs and regional quotas in the Provincial Services. Bhutto, however, made no parallel effort to induct Sindhis into the military bureaucracy. The Mohajirs' share in the government services declined as a result, while at the same time they were pushed back in the upper echelons of bureaucracy as a consequence of increasing Punjabi domination at this level. Moreover, the administrative reforms enacted by Bhutto weakened the influence of the entire bureaucracy, allowing even greater domination by the military. However, in other areas the Mohajirs actually gained, as in the field of education where nationalization of private schools, opening of new educational institutions and better salaries for teachers benefited the Mohajirs more than any other group because of their strong presence in the educational services. So while there was no reversal of the upward trend in terms of social mobility, the higher number of educated unemployed among the Mohajirs meant growing frustration among their youth.

Bhutto's removal (and subsequent execution) and the seizure of power by General Zia-ul-Haq in July 1977 meant, under the circumstances, two completely different things to the Sindhis and the Mohajirs. To the former, it suggested that their access to state power and hence the ability to have their grievances redressed had been comprehensively subverted. For the Mohajirs, General Zia's military regime meant a radical shift of the balance in their favour as it did away with Bhutto at the centre as well as the PPP government at the provincial level.

Having seen in Bhutto someone who 'cared for and loved us poor Sindhis', the dismissal of his government would have been shock enough, but his 'judicial execution' at the hands of a Punjabi general had a devastating impact on the Sindhi psyche. Popular opposition to Zia's regime, at first disorganized, grew over the years, and in rural Sindh it included a broad front of peasants, students, middle-class professionals, as well as the Movement for the Restoration of Democracy (MRD). While in rural Sindh a strong opposition developed with a definite presence of Sindhi nationalist sentiments, the Mohajirs in urban Sindh did not support this movement. Under Zia the share of the Mohajirs in the civil bureaucracy was further reduced. Military rule meant increased Punjabi domination of the army. The Mohajirs withdrew, as it were, to urban Sindh for the defence of what they saw as their core interests.

By the mid-1980s, Karachi was a powder keg waiting to explode. Pakistan's active involvement in the Afghan war had meant the formation of an arms and drugs mafia in Karachi, with a strong Pakhtun presence, a community that already dominated transport. There had been a high level of in-migration of Punjabis and Pakhtuns on a large scale into Karachi and the city had become even more unmanageable with power failures, water shortages, uncollected refuse, etc. The fuse was ignited in 1985 when a spontaneous outbreak of rioting, sparked off by a fatal traffic accident in Karachi, was manipulated into the first of the increasing spiral of incidents of ethnic violence. The succeeding years saw a spate of violence involving the Mohajirs, Pakhtuns, Punjabis, Sindhis, and probably the arms and drugs mafia. Initially (between 1986 and 1987), the killings, which pitted Mohajirs against Pakhtuns and then Punjabis, masked the real crisis in Sindh. Two powerful forces had been growing in isolation from each other during the 1970s and 1980s – the urban, mostly Mohajir, middle class and the newly emerging Sindhi middle class. They were on a collision course long before they actually took aim at each other, but the absence of a political voice on either side gave no warning of their impending conflict.

In Karachi itself, which has virtually no Sindhi presence, the clashes were initially between Mohajirs and Pakhtuns, and later Punjabis, and while in many cases the violence was spontaneous, it was then manipulated as an ethnic conflict. Since then, this pattern of spontaneous eruptions of violent protest quickly turning, or being converted into ethnic confrontation frequently repeats itself. It was in Hyderabad actually that Sindhi–Mohajir violence erupted in 1986. Elsewhere, however, the characteristic feature of Mohajir and Sindhi confrontation has not been direct violence so much as heightened antagonism in what has increasingly come to be perceived by both sides as a zero-sum game for control of the resources and the means of livelihood.

A significant dimension of the violence to which these two communities are subjected is that which is perpetrated from within. The battle by the ethnically based political organizations to be recognized as the sole representatives of their respective communities means that members, especially students, of a particular ethnic group belonging to 'other' organizations or parties are at times severely beaten up, inhumanly tortured and killed. This happens, for instance, to the PPP's Mohajir members in Karachi at the hands of the MQM (The Mohajir Quami Movement, founded in 1984) and, though less often, to its Sindhi members in rural Sindh at the hands of the extremist nationalists. In some instances, however, there have been examples of restraint as well. In Sukkur, for example, local Sindhi leadership was able to prevent an exodus of Mohajirs to Hyderabad and Karachi, which is what the MQM leadership would have wanted, to reinforce its assertion that there is no alternative to an effective partition of Sindh between Mohajirs and Sindhis. Under the circumstances, the role of the state as a mediator has become crucial, for the issue now cannot be resolved purely at the local or provincial level given the bitterness and hostility that inform the environment in Sindh. Unfortunately, the state apparatus suffers from a profound lack of credibility.

7. GUATEMALA

After the overthrow of the democratic regime in 1954 in the name of anti-communism, the Guatemalan military embarked upon a policy of counter-revolution and political terror against anybody suspected of subversive activities. In fact, the military became the leading force in Guatemalan politics, even if an occasional honest election was allowed to be held. By the mid-1960s a number of right-wing paramilitary death squads, closely linked to the military, began physically eliminating and terrorizing intellectuals, students, labour leaders, peasant organizers, progressive priests, lawyers and just about anybody who opposed the army's high-handed methods or demanded democratic reforms. Up to 40 000 people are estimated to have 'disappeared' between 1954 and the early 1980s.[2] The brunt of the terror was borne by workers and peasants, particularly in rural areas.

In the early 1960s a first guerrilla movement challenged military rule. Inspired by the Cuban revolution and Che Guevara's revolutionary strategies, and linked to political parties of the Left, it was mainly based in *Ladino* peasant areas with urban support in Guatemala City. Torn by factional strife and shifting alliances, the Fuerzas Armadas Rebeldes (FAR) and other guerrilla organizations completely ignored Indian ethnicity. Their leaders theorized about Guatemala's problems purely in terms of the then fashionable 'class struggle'. Massively aided by the United States, the Guatemalan military launched a major counter-insurgency campaign which, together with the guerrilla movements' own internal weaknesses, soon led to the defeat of the revolutionary groups.

The attempts at modest agrarian reform undertaken by the democratic government before 1954 had long been undone by succeeding regimes, when a new economic crisis hit the Indian peasants during the 1970s. A 'modernization' strategy which promoted non-traditional agricultural exports (winter crops, vegetables) helped create a new, dynamic commercial and agribusiness sector, in which the military were actively involved as land-owners and entrepreneurs, but it also pulled the rug from under the traditional peasant subsistence economy, already destabilized by high population growth and the decreasing average size of their minuscule landholdings (*minifundios*). Indian peasants had to leave their communities in ever larger numbers to seek subsistence elsewhere, and began to migrate massively to urban shanty-towns and commercial plantations.

During the 1970s and 1980s the military consolidated their power over the political system and institutionalized the 'counter-insurgency national security state'. Despite increasing repression and military terror, labour and peasant unrest spread, and popular mass organizations, such as the Committee for Peasant Unity (CUC), the Consumers Defence Committee, the organization of urban shanty-town dwellers (MONAP) and others, mobilized widespread popular support around demands for social and democratic reforms. The ruling classes (urban bourgeoisie, landed oligarchy and their military allies) rightly perceived these movements as threatening their vital interests and retaliated with increasing ferocity. In the late 1970s the army perpetrated a number of massacres of Indian villagers that caused hundreds of victims and focused international attention on the massive human rights violations occurring in Guatemala.[3]

By the early 1980s renewed guerrilla activity challenged the Guatemalan state. This time, the revolutionaries were able to count on a new social base and developed different strategies from those of the 1960s. Jonas argues that changes in the productive and social structure of the highlands during the 1970s transformed the class position of the Indian population, mainly because of expulsion from the land and the changing organization of agriculture, producing a migrating semi-proletariat.[4] Moreover, these highland Indians were not only among the most impoverished sectors of the rural population, but also an oppressed ethnic group. If many of them joined the revolutionaries it was because they had no other recourse, as all legal avenues of redress were closed. The indigenous population was excluded from regular 'party politics' (the fiction of which was continued even under military rule) and the exclusion of independent social actors virtually guaranteed that the popular movement would have to reconstitute itself outside the political party spectrum. A number of distinct guerrilla groups organized themselves in the late 1970s and early 1980s, and in 1982 joined together to form the Unidad Revolucionaria Nacional Guatemalteca (URNG). Its broad political programme included, among other objectives, an end to repression and a guarantee of basic rights for all citizens, an end to discrimination, full equality for Indians and an end to their cultural oppression. In contrast to earlier guerrilla movements, the leadership of the URNG and its constituent political groups actively sought the support of the Indian population. According to Arias, between 250 000 and 500 000 highland Indian people participated in the war in one form or another. Paramilitary organizations, forms of self-defence, were organized to provide food and clothing for the permanent guerrilla units whose members were mostly Indians with relatives in the various villages.[5]

Once again, the army countered with unspeakable violence and terror against the population.

There is no more painful chapter in the history of modern Guatemala than the events of 1980–1983. At the human level, it is a tale of wholesale slaughter and genocide by the new death squads, the counterinsurgent security forces . . . without the façade of legal constraints. That this holocaust was almost unknown and unimagined in most Western countries, is a testament to the 'great silence' about Guatemala – an indifferent, at times complicitous silence, perhaps because the victims were overwhelmingly Indians.[6]

In order to stem the rising revolutionary tide, the government carried out a scorched earth war from 1981 to 1983, the goal of which was to 'drain the sea' in which the guerrilla movement operated and to eradicate its civilian support base. This included massacres and burning of entire villages and massive forced relocations. In those years, over 440 villages were destroyed, between 100 000 and 150 000 civilians were killed or 'disappeared', there were over one million displaced persons (internal refugees plus over 250 000 refugees in Mexico). 'The war took on the character of an assault by the ladino state against the Indian population.'[7] As a result of this 'total counter-insurgency war' the revolutionary forces were almost entirely destroyed, the consequence of the carefully planned policy of genocide by the government.

To consolidate its victory, the army organized the Indian peasants into mandatory paramilitary 'civilian defence patrols' to report on their fellow villagers and to keep independent political activity under complete control. At one point around one million youths and men, 25 per cent of the total adult population, was involved in these PACs (*Patrullas de Autodefensa Civil*). The government also created forced resettlement camps, known as 'model villages' in so-called 'development poles' (imitating US policy in Vietnam), in which every aspect of the people's lives was subject to direct military control.

According to some observers, the violence that gripped Guatemala in the early 1980s caused a demographic, social and cultural 'holocaust' in Maya communities similar to that experienced by their ancestors after the Spanish invasion of the sixteenth century. Davis reports that Indians began joining the guerrilla organizations as a means of individual and community defence against the selective killings and acts of terror by the army and the death squads. In response to the Indian mobilization, however, the army stepped up its counter-insurgency efforts in the highlands, killing suspected community leaders, burning houses and fields, and attempting to drive a wedge between the indigenous population and the guerrilla organization.[8] International organizations documented the massive human rights violations occurring in Guatemala during the 1970s and 1980s. The UN Human Rights Commission and the Inter-American Commission on Human Rights published reports and adopted resolutions citing human rights abuses, and so did numerous non-governmental organizations.[9] The US government, which had supported, financed and organized the military's anti-communist crusade in the 1960s and 1970s, began to have second thoughts about its Guatemalan allies and withheld further direct military aid, at the same time pressing for 'democratic elections'. Hardly anybody in the Indian communities of the western highlands has been unaffected by the violence and the repression. Anthropologists report the spread of a 'culture of fear' throughout the country and the destruction of the moral basis of community solidarity which was for centuries the mainstay of Maya cultural identity.[10]

The violence and instability took an enormous toll on the economy and society of Guatemala. After a constitutional assembly reformed the national constitution, democratic elections put a civilian president in power in 1985 for the first time in decades. Though he had promised to curb the army's excesses and stop human rights abuses, the Christian Democratic president, Cerezo, and his civilian successors have been unable to escape from the tight control of the military who actually continue to run the country. Refugees in Mexico began to return home under international guarantees, only to find their villages destroyed, their families dispersed and their lands ravished. In the mid-1980s, a reorganized and chastened guerrilla movement again took the initiative, and the civil war continued, as well as the military repression, albeit on a lesser scale than before. In the early 1990s peace talks between the URNG and the Guatemalan government were being held under the auspices of the United Nations and other third party agents, but no final agreement had been reached by the end of 1995.

8. THE FORMER SOVIET UNION

The break-up of the Soviet Union in 1990 and its transformation into the Commonwealth of Independent States, as well as the establishment of numerous independent countries which had formerly belonged to the USSR, brought to light a number of ethnic conflicts which had been simmering for decades within its borders. Valery Tishkov reports that the first violent ethnic conflict on the territory of the Russian Federation took place towards the end of October 1992. This confrontation involves the Ossetians and the Ingush, who live in the central part of the northern Caucasus in two administrative districts of the former USSR and the present Russian Federation, North Ossetia and the Chechen-Ingush Republic. The Ossetians form the majority (53 per cent) of the population of North Ossetia. The Ingush live for the most part in the Chechen-Ingush Republic (where they number 13 per cent of this republic's total population) and in North Ossetia (where they represent only 3 per cent of that republic's total population). The Ingush are a majority in some regions and villages, but have also settled in two of the area's major cities. The total Ingush population was around 215 000 in 1990, whereas the Ossetians numbered around 600 000 altogether.

Under the Soviet nationalities policy, every republic had a 'titular' or majority nation, whereas other nationalities were considered as minorities. Thus, the Ossetians constitute the titular nation of North Ossetia,[11] whereas the Ingush were considered a minority without status, that is, they did not possess any form of territorial autonomy in this republic. By contrast, the Ingush together with the Chechen constitute the two titular nationalities of the dual Chechen-Ingush republic. However, in both republics the Ingush are a minority, and are made to feel as such by the other groups, in the first place, because in each republic the dominant majority (Chechen and Ossetians, respectively) has controlled the local power structure. The Ingush have been kept away from prestigious and influential positions in public office and in other social spheres, and Ingush youth have experienced certain restrictions on their enrolment in secondary and higher educational institutions. Complaints by Ingush have been addressed increasingly in recent years to the Russian federal government, but to little avail.

Being under-represented in the power structure at the republic level, and not having the possibility of attaining a voice in the framework of the existing system, the Ingush have been attempting to create an ethnic territory of their own where they would constitute an actual majority. In fact, in some western Ingush-dominated regions of the Chechen-Ingush republic, they have already been able to achieve political and administrative predominance. But they have been unable to obtain similar privileges at the republic's centre and control of the centre is important for access to, and distribution of, economic and political resources.

Both the North Ossetian and the Chechen-Ingush republics have, in turn, long been competing for resources from the federal (Russian) centre. As it turns out, North Ossetia was consistently favoured by Moscow over its Chechen-Ingush neighbour (in socialist and post-socialist times as well). In terms of various socio-economic indicators, the Chechen-Ingush republic lags behind North Ossetia, and in both republics the Ingush show lower indices than the rest of the population. Among the Ingush, particularly the youth, unemployment rates are exceptionally high.

In 1991, radical Chechen forces staged a coup and proclaimed a separate Chechen republic, leaving the Ingush out in the cold. This can be interpreted as a response to earlier radical Ingush demands for their own separate republic. Chechnya then tried to take over some Ingush territory, whereas an independent Ingushetia was recognized by the Russian Federation in the summer of 1992. By the end of 1995, the central Russian government had broken the back of the Chechen Separatist attempt with a brutal military campaign that left thousands of civilian victims dead and massive destruction.

Tishkov, who as Russian Minister for Nationalities at that time was directly involved in some of the negotiations, considers that

> on the whole, in our view, the Ingush's humiliated position in former Chechen-Ingush created the fundamental reason for an ethnic movement which favoured administrative separation in order to acquire the right to direct distribution of resources from the center and to widen nomenclature administration. The reluctance of the dominating group of Chechens to ensure a comfortable status to the Ingush minority strengthened this movement. It was supported by leaders of the Ingush minority in Northern Ossetia, where political discrimination supplemented a policy of covert and overt cultural oppression.

Across the border in North Ossetia, Ingush had been the object of discrimination and marginalization all along. Their situation deteriorated with the influx of 60 000 to 70 000 Ossetian refugees from Georgia in 1991 and 1992, who were fleeing the Georgian–South Ossetian conflict. Some of the South Ossetian refugees behaved with particular brutality towards the local Ingush, and the North Ossetian government preferred to support their 'ethnic kin' from the south rather than their own 'non-ethnic' citizens. In the ensuing violent clashes over land and other resources, the ideologies and practice of 'ethnic nationalism' (Ossetian solidarity) triumphed over the principles of civil society and government.

Thus, in both republics, the stage was set for the emergence of the 'vocalization' (as Tishkov calls it) of Ingush demands against the respective dominant majorities. But there is a long history to this 'vocalization', which explains to a certain extent the emergence of the conflict. After having obtained some regional autonomy during the early years of the Soviet Union, the Ingush, together with the Chechen, became one of Stalin's 'repressed' peoples, that is, they were deported *en masse* to Central Asia in the 1940s. It was only years later that they were allowed to return and partly resettle in their old homelands. The traumatic experience of deprivation and deportation left permanent scars on the Ingush's collective memory. But resettlement was not easy, as the Ingush had to compete with the Ossetians and other nationalities for control over what each group considered its own legitimate territory. Soviet policy, over many years, did not facilitate the solution.

On the other hand, Soviet nationalities policy did stimulate the emergence of a highly educated, skilled Ingush professional stratum, who as an intellectual elite now find themselves in the forefront of Ingush nationalist claims. In the spring of 1992, the Ingush leaders presented the Russian federal government with a collective letter in which their grievances are set out: loss of land and government, discrimination. The letter complains that 'the Ingush people are outside the law, outside the constitution; it is permissible to crush, rob and hack up their homeland . . . poverty and tyranny oppress Ingushetia', and they demand the restoration of 'the historical homeland of the Ingush people with Ingush Republic status . . .' Earlier, in 1991, a referendum among the Ingush had produced a massive vote in favour of the formation of a sovereign Ingush republic within the Russian federation. Finally, in the summer of 1992, the Russian Supreme Soviet passed a law re-establishing Ingush autonomy (though the question of borders was left open to later negotiations).

Immediately, a political struggle broke out between different Ingush factions (based on traditional local clan structures) for the control of administrative positions. At the same time, and in the face of North Ossetian resistance to granting the Ingush their due, Ingush young men began to arm themselves, as did the Ossetians on the other side, including South Ossetian refugees from Georgia. Violence broke out in October 1992, and irregular fighting continued for several weeks, particularly in the Prigorodny district, which the Ingush wished to annex to their new republic and which the Ossetians decided not to give up. By the end of 1992, almost 40 000 Ingush nationals had been driven out of North Ossetia, about 5000 homes had been burned and the number of victims was estimated at approximately 300. Mediation efforts by the Russians had failed.

9. CONCLUSIONS

There seems to be some agreement among scholars that ethnic conflicts constitute a particular kind of social and political conflict which is more related to questions of identity and deeply rooted values than to issues of rational interest. While the latter frequently become the object of bargaining, negotiations and agreements of various kinds, within the framework of established 'rules of the game' (for example, labour negotiations, industrial bargaining, electoral competitions in democratic polities, etc.), the former tend to be protracted, linked to collective historical memories and their reinterpretations, suffused with highly charged emotions and passions, imbued with myths and fears and perceived threats, entwined with deeply held beliefs and aspirations, and thus much more difficult to reduce to the ordinary give-and-take of political bargaining or negotiation. While a trade union may negotiate on wage levels, it would be more difficult for an ethnic group that feels slighted or discriminated against to bargain over more or less 'ethnic' identity in any given setting.

This is not to say that other kinds of social or economic conflict are always free of passion (they are certainly not), nor that rational interest or calculus does not play a role in ethnic conflict (as we have seen in this chapter, it does). It is suggested, however, that ethnic conflicts often revolve around the self-perception (and the perception by others) of an entire people within the framework of the modern nation-state, and that therefore their dynamics involves competing concepts of the nation and contrasting ideas about the very structure of the state itself.

Outbursts of ethnic violence may occur under the most diverse circumstances. If they are short-lived, one-off events, they are not usually considered as ethnic conflicts in the way these are referred to in this book, though they may express underlying pre-existing tensions. The sudden outbreak of violence between Mauritanians and Senegalese in 1991 may be a case in point.

Generally, ethnic conflicts pass through a period of incubation and build up over time, before they actually shake the foundations of the social edifice, or before violence becomes part of the 'discourse' of conflict. While some conflicts escalate in almost linear fashion (the events leading up to the Nigerian civil war in the 1960s are an example), others wax and wane in cycles according to multiple and sometimes unpredictable circumstances.

As we can see from the cases studied in this chapter, ethnic conflicts vary in duration, intensity and extension. There are also multiple layers of society which become involved: conflict involves individuals, groups, institutions and the state, and frequently neighbouring states as well. However, not all these elements necessarily intervene at the same time and in the same way. Individual involvement occurs, for example, when members of different ethnies compete for jobs, power or privileges, or when ethnic animosities, stereotypes, prejudices and rivalries condition interpersonal relations at the local level in everyday activities. This seems to be the case, certainly, between Fijians and Indians as well as between Guyanese Indians and Africans, as we have seen in preceding sections of this chapter. It has also occurred between Mohajirs and Sindhis in Pakistan, and between Hutus and Tutsis in Burundi. The violence which erupted in 1992 between Ossetians and Ingush underscores these aspects as well.

Interpersonal conflict and tensions in ethnic relations are not uncommon in other situations. In countries where racist ideologies are characteristic among dominant ethnic groups, ethnic violence at the interpersonal level may occur fairly frequently, as in xenophobic outbursts against Turks, Arabs, Africans and other foreigners in Germany and other industrialized countries. It also occurs when subordinate ethnic groups compete for a niche in the economic system, such as the rivalry and confrontation between Blacks, Hispanics and Asians in the urban ghettos of the United States.

Interpersonal ethnic tensions do not necessarily become collective conflicts nor do they always involve the dominant institutions of society. On the contrary, most organized groups as well as the institutions of the civil society and the state may be systematically opposed to such confrontations (which is the case in the democratic polities of the industrialized North). On the other hand, as we have seen in some of the cases studied in this chapter (Burundi, Lebanon, Pakistan), ethnic confrontations fostered by political groups or state institutions may in turn trigger intensive interpersonal ethnic animosities, which frequently turn violent and become most difficult to control. Such is the case in Ayodhya, India, where self-serving political groups instigate ethnic riots which then induce personal hatreds and violence that result in hundreds and thousands of victims. Violence becomes, indeed, part of the discourse of conflict.

While interpersonal ethnic conflict may be latent and of generally low intensity (usually limited to subjective feelings of rejection, exclusion, discrimination or animosity), but always holding a great potential for violence, the inter-ethnic conflicts that characterize relations between groups tend to become structured, though they do not always appear to be so.

For example, ethnic riots, rampages, massacres, which cost many innocent lives and cause major material damage (such as have occurred in India, Pakistan, Burundi), may seem at first glance to be irrational, emotional outbursts, unrelated to the formal institutions of society and therefore unpredictable and uncontrollable. Yet many studies show that riots and massacres are more often than not instigated by ethnic 'entrepreneurs', fanned by ethnic ideologues and political profiteers, and are actually fine-tuned and fairly well controlled by local power-brokers and manipulators.

If such is indeed the case, then one of the issues that requires careful analysis is the relationship between ethnic leaders and their followers, between the ethnic entrepreneurs and the ethnic 'masses'. In the cases studied in this chapter, as well as in others, it is clear that before group conflict erupted, the ideological underpinnings of confrontation were established by ethnic organizations, political parties or sundry groups which developed a rationale for the conflict. The killings in Burundi, as Lemarchand demonstrates, emerge directly from the way the Hutu see the Tutsi, and the Tutsi perceive the Hutu. The conditions are set, and at any moment a haphazard event can set off a cycle of violence which, in turn, feeds into the crystallization of mutual fear, distrust and antagonism. This drama was played out once again in 1994 in the killing-fields of Rwanda.

Collective inter-ethnic violence – riots, massacres and genocidal killings – are usually short-lived, though their implications are far-reaching. If unchecked, they may escalate into open warfare and the eventual break-up of the state. When the state intervenes, it ends up by setting the political parameters whereby the ethnic groups in conflict are supposed to work out their differences. More than interpersonal animosity and mutual rejection, ethnic group conflicts involve power relations between the disputing parties. This is where the issue of leadership becomes particularly salient. For the issue of power relates, on the one hand, to the position that the ethnic group as such occupies in the wider society, and, on the other, to the kind of control that an ethnic leadership can exercise over its own constituency. These issues are related, but they are not the same.

In this respect, the role played by political 'outbidders' is particularly crucial for the evolution of any ethnic conflict. In Fiji, for example, the extremists in both the Fiji Indian and the native Fijian segments of the population draw the more moderate elements towards intransigent positions. The native Fijians feared an Indian political takeover, and the Indian Fijians feared total disenfranchisement. The outbidders on both sides made an inter-ethnic alliance of moderate elements increasingly difficult, and helped push the system to the point of confrontation.

The most intensive and protracted ethnic conflicts involve the struggle between structured ethnic organizations (political parties, nationalist movements, armed militias or guerrilla groups) and the institutions of the state, generally the central government. The Guatemalan case illustrates this well. As a result of historical circumstances, Guatemala's Maya Indian peasants, the country's majority population, have found themselves to be the perennial victims of economic exploitation, social discrimination and political exclusion. Since the 1960s a relentless, intermittent civil war has pitted military governments against leftist guerrilla movements. While the Indian civilian population have been the principal victims of the war and especially of the military's genocidal counter-insurgency tactics, during the early years the indigenous peoples were not active participants as such in the conflict.

The leftist guerrillas and their political allies concentrated on the class aspects of the struggle and ignored or neglected the ethnic component of Guatemala's oppressive social system. Beginning in the 1970s, however, the Left reviewed its position on the 'national question' and pursued a strategy of incorporation of the indigenous peoples into the revolutionary movement. For reasons mentioned earlier, many Indians joined the guerrillas, while others adopted non-violent tactics of furthering ethnic goals through the building of social and political organizations within the system, particularly after the return to nominal civilian rule in 1985. To be sure, numerous Indians were also forced to join the ranks of the army's civilian patrols, while a budding Indian bourgeoisie, as well as some of the Indians newly converted to one of several proselytizing Protestant sects, sensing where their individual interests lay, threw in their lot with the ruling elites and the army (whose recruits are principally lower-class Indians). Thus, it can be said that the 'class conflict' in Guatemala, in which the military oligarchical state is a prime actor, is also fundamentally an ethnic conflict. At the same time, Indian identity is fragmented and socio-economic differentiation within the indigenous communities themselves also produces intra-ethnic rivalries and conflict.

As we have seen in this and earlier chapters, certain conditions must be present for a conflict to emerge and to persist. An occasional protest or outburst of ethnic violence does not, according to our view, constitute a conflict. An ethnic conflict is a continuous form of collective action between ethnic groups over ethnic issues, and involves a certain degree of organization. The conflicts studied in this chapter all involve some form of ethnic organization; they are high on what the social theorist Tilly calls 'catness' and 'netness' (that is, they involve a specific category of people who operate within structured networks of relationships).[12]

For an organization to become effective in the pursuit of its group objectives or interests, it must also be able to mobilize, in other words, to go from being a passive collection of individuals to an active participant in public life. The Mohajirs in Sindh were at first simply the refugees from India, who later became a political force in Pakistan. The Hutu in Burundi have become politically active through their mobilization in several Hutu political parties. Kurdish identity has found expression over the decades in various militant nationalist movements. The degree and scope of mobilization is an essential ingredient in all forms of collective action, and this is particularly the case in ethnic conflicts. The Derg regime was overthrown in Ethiopia by a coalition of highly mobilized ethnic organizations. Mobilization here refers to the acquisition of collective control over resources.

But organizations may also demobilize. For example, the continuous fragmentation of Kurdish organizations along tribal rivalries and ideological shifts, which the states in the region have used to their own advantage over the years, has constantly weakened the Kurdish nationalist movement, making any kind of regional overall solution almost impossible to achieve.

A recent survey of major ethno-political conflicts in the world concludes:

since 1945 more than 200 groups have openly resisted the terms of their incorporation in states controlled by other groups. Their grievances about discrimination and threats to group identity have motivated hundreds of protest movements. The same grievances, coupled with historically grounded demands for the restoration of lost autonomy, have triggered rebellions by 79 groups . . . some of which escalated into protracted conflicts that have had profound political and humanitarian consequences. In ten instances since 1945, regimes threatened by autonomy movements have resorted to mass political murder in separatist regions. . . . At the beginning of 1992 more than half the world's 40 million refugees were fleeing from civil wars and repression arising out of communally based conflicts.[13]

Of the 233 communal groups surveyed, 180 used nonviolent protest as the main form of communal political action, 96 groups used violent protest, and 114 groups initiated some form of rebellion. In 37 instances, the survey reports protracted communal conflict (that is, spanning at least three successive five-year periods), which Gurr considers to be among the most severe conflicts of the modern world, concentrated almost entirely in the Third World. There are important regional differences in the patterns of communal conflict. Nonviolent protest has been the most common form of communal action in the industrialized countries and Latin America;

violent protest occurs more frequently in the Middle East, whereas communal rebellions have occurred mainly in Asia, the Middle East and Africa. The survey also shows that since the 1950s all forms of communal conflict have increased markedly.

6 Ethnic Conflict and Economic Development

To say that ethnic conflict (or, for that matter, any kind of major political and social conflict) is inimical to economic development is to state a self-evident truth. The economies of many countries ravaged by civil war and other kinds of political strife have been set back by years, if not decades. The economic destruction and disorganization wrought by ethnic conflicts are no exception. Material wealth and resources are often destroyed or consumed in the process. Strategic economic targets are frequently prime objectives of the warring parties. Investors are scared away and take their capital with them. Fields may lie uncultivated for years; irrigation systems, transportation and communications networks break down. Scarce foreign exchange is no longer used for infrastructure or productive purposes, but for arms and 'security' needs. Unemployment rises and the labour force abandons the war zones to join the struggle or to find refuge elsewhere, often in the capital cities. Public services are stretched to the limit. The flow of refugees increases and strains national and international resources. Ethnic riots, whether in Bombay or Los Angeles, involve looting, destruction of property and vandalism.

The social and economic costs of ethnic confrontations tend to be high. But that is only one side of the picture. If national economic development were the only, or even the principal concern, of a country's political elites, then ethnic conflict would be actively avoided, prevented or kept in check, given the high economic cost that is generally associated with it. That economic considerations take a back seat to other politically valued gains is a frequent component of such drawn-out conflicts.

But, on the other hand, it is often in the economic sphere itself that we find the roots of so many conflicts. Resources, jobs, income and wealth are seldom distributed equally in any society. Rural property may be concentrated in the hands of a few large land-owners. Financial and industrial capital may be held by certain elites. Commercial and middleman activities may come to be identified with particular ethnic groups. Some regions may benefit greatly from productive investments by the state or private entrepreneurs, whereas others may lag behind. Extractive activities may in fact impoverish some regions by generating outflows of resources to other areas. In ethnically heterogeneous societies, such distributions, concentrations and cleavages very often occur along ethnic lines. In other words, the socio-economic differentials may coincide with ethnic differences. Social class stratification often overlaps with ethnic stratification. In the Caribbean region, there is a general awareness of the existence of a 'colour-class continuum', where class position in the society is directly related to racial-ethnic identification. In Latin American history, landlord and peasant in the agrarian structure generally means white land-owner and Indian farmer. In Sri Lanka, the Indian Tamils became the workers on the tea plantations and make up the poorer segments of the country's population.[1] Tribal and indigenous peoples everywhere, distinguished by their cultures and way of life, are among the most vulnerable and exploited groups of any population.[2]

While there are numerous cases of ethnically segmented societies in which socio-economic differentiation does not inevitably occur along ethnic lines, there are probably many more in which ethnic economic and social stratification is widespread. Scholars have analysed and theorized about the cultural division of labour both on the world scale and in individual countries. In the industrialized nations an ethnically differentiated split or dual labour market has arisen as a result of widespread international migrations which are the consequence of the dynamics of the world economy.[3] This, in turn, sometimes produces the 'racialization' of social relations and generates ethnic and racial competition and tensions.[4] As a result of earlier historical processes of conquest, colonization and settlement, relations between dominant and subordinate ethnic groups can in some instances be understood in terms of internal colonialism.[5]

When ethnic divisions are associated with competition and struggles over natural resources, land, investments, wages, jobs, education, health care, public services, and in general with economic opportunities and standards of living, then it is clear that the issues of economic development cannot be tackled either in theory or in practice as if ethnicity did not exist. Yet for many years such has been precisely the approach of mainstream social science. The economic implications of a number of ethnic conflicts in this project illustrate many of these issues.

1. LEBANON

After gaining independence in 1943, capitalist development occurred in Lebanon at a much faster rate than in other Arab countries. Economic growth began in the mid-nineteenth century in the Mount Lebanon region, which was the first to witness the break-up of the large, feudal, landed estates. The process continued under French colonial administration, with investment in infrastructure and the emergence of a strong commercial and services sector. This dependent development in the 'modern' sector of the economy, concentrated in the urban area of Beirut, furthered the predominance of Christian families in the ranks of the rising Lebanese bourgeoisie.

After independence, the external influence of France diminished while that of the United States increased. Capitalist development extended into other areas of the country, producing not only general economic growth but more significantly, profound distortions and imbalances in the country. Several factors account for this development:

1. Massive expenditures in the country during the world war by the Allied war effort.
2. After the creation of the state of Israel in 1948, the influx of highly qualified Palestinian labour, which helped stimulate banking and insurance activities as well as agriculture.
3. In 1950, the break-up of the long-standing customs union between Lebanon and Syria, which favoured the growth of the Lebanese bourgeoisie's import–export activities in subsequent years.
4. The growth of the oil-exporting economies in the Middle East during the 1950s, which stimulated the development of the Lebanese financial and commercial networks, bolstered in later years by the arrival of flight capital from other Middle Eastern countries. Beirut became a major financial centre in the region.

The combined effect of these various factors contributed to a relatively important economic boom during the three decades following independence. The benefits from these activities were, however, not evenly distributed among the different economic sectors, and imbalances soon became apparent. While agriculture and manufacturing activities declined, employment in the tertiary sector increased, stimulating a massive rural exodus and the rapid and disorganized urbanization of metropolitan Beirut. Low productivity in petty trade, handicrafts, personal services, as well as in public administration, surged. The social costs of what was at one time called the 'Lebanese miracle' became too high and eventually turned into one of the principal causes of the destabilization of the political and social system.

While Beirut and the Mount Lebanon area became the 'developed' pole of the country, the North and the South remained 'non-' or 'under'developed. This geographical–economic division became closely linked to parallel social and communal cleavages. In fact, the great majority of the Mount Lebanon population consists of Maronite Christians, whereas most of the Sunni Muslims live in the north, and the large majority of the Shi'ite Muslims in the south and the Bekaa Valley.

Communal religious distinctions are also apparent in the distribution of capital and wealth in the industrial sector. Most of the industrial establishments are owned by Christians, and the larger and more complex industrial organization becomes, the higher is the concentration of ownership among Christian family groups. A similar degree of economic concentration was to be found in the banking sector, at least until a special effort was made by Arab Muslim interests in the early 1970s to establish a foothold in this activity. Disparities of wealth and income became progressively more acute in the post-war years. In the 1970s, household income and standard of living surveys showed that on the average Christian households had higher levels of living than Druze, Sunni and Shi'ite households (in that order). Similarly, of the households living in poverty, the Shi'ites were most numerous (22 per cent), followed by the Sunnis (15 per cent), Druzes (11 per cent) and Christians (6 per cent). A similar pattern emerges from data on high- and low-skilled, and high- and low-wage, jobs. While these figures reflect averages, there are also great disparities within each community.

Despite these patterns, there is no clear overlap between religion and class in Lebanon, there is no 'religion – class' continuum. Social and economic disparities occur as a result of unequal capitalist development, principally in the post-Second World War period. Criteria of class relate only secondarily to religious and communal affiliations. But the social unrest generated by these disparities found fertile political ground in the traditional communal structures of the society.

2.   HORN OF AFRICA

Impoverishment is a striking feature of recent Ethiopian and Sudanese history, both countries are to be counted among the 'least developed' economies. However, the burden of impoverishment is not evenly shared, for there are striking differences between regions and ethnic groups within each country. Such disparities are a key contributing factor in the generation of conflict.

The arid region is the home of wandering pastoralists. Sudan and Ethiopia rank first and fifth respectively in the world in terms of pastoral population size. It is estimated that pastoralists represent 12–15 per cent of the total population of Ethiopia and Sudan. The available seasonal grass and shrub growth in the arid zone supports only periodic grazing; consequently grazing systems must be based on the constant movement of both animal and human populations.

Typically, the pastoralist social structure is highly segmented, with the lineage as its cornerstone and the household as the unit of production. Designed for subsistence, pastoralism does not produce a surplus and is not linked to the market, though pastoralists regularly barter goods with their sedentary neighbours. Lack of surplus rules out the emergence of non-producing classes, therefore, pastoralist society is notably egalitarian in comparison with sedentary societies. Although relatively well-endowed in comparison to the lowlands, the Abyssinian homeland in the northern plateau of Ethiopia suffers from an age-old process of physical degradation, the work of natural forces abetted by human and animal action. Along with rainwater, its many river and streams carry away the plateau's topsoil. The result of relentless human and animal population pressure is monumental erosion and declining land productivity. The most drought-prone regions in Ethiopia are also the ones where conflict has occurred: Eritrea, Hararge, Bale, Sidamo, Tigrai, Wolo. Inevitably, drought has been followed by famine, a regular visitor to these regions. Tigrai experienced three major famines in less than three decades, in the 1970s and 1980s, and again in 1991.

Productive land in Ethiopia and Sudan is under heavy and steadily increasing human and animal population pressure, though neither country is overcrowded in relation to its size.[6] Development in independent Sudan followed the colonial blueprint. Investment continued to be channelled into commercial agriculture, with state and foreign capital providing the major share. There was no investment at all in the South, where the sole venture of the colonial era, the Zande Scheme, fell apart during the civil war. Not surprisingly, many southern Sudanese blamed the regime in Khartoum for the plight of their region.

Modern economic development in Ethiopia did not start until the mid-1950s. Although Ethiopia was an independent state, the evolving modern sector of its economy was typically neo-colonial in its dependence on primary product exports, foreign capital and imported technology and management. The imperial regime exerted itself to attract foreign capital, and the state itself invested heavily in infrastructure and joint ventures with foreign investors. The distribution of investment was concentrated in three regions: the Addis Ababa region in the centre, a cluster around Asmara in Eritrea, and Dire Dawa in the southeast.

A geographical bias was noted also in the emerging sector of commercial cultivation. The production of coffee, Ethiopia's main export, was concentrated in the southwest, sugar and cotton production was undertaken by foreign capital in the eastern lowland region. There was no change at all in the Abyssinian provinces in the north, which remained among the most backward regions of the empire. The most neglected province in the north was Tigrai. Its people are predominantly subsistence cultivators, working a land ravaged by ecological degradation and drought. There was little investment for economic development in the Abyssinian provinces under the imperial regime, and none at all in Tigrai. Many of its people were forced to migrate in search of seasonal or permanent employment.

Both Sudan and Ethiopia built their economic foundations on cultivation, especially commercial cultivation of export crops. Linked to the world market, this new economic sector supported the emergence of towns, which provided the required technical, economic and administrative services. The material base of pastoralist production, however, was seriously eroded by the loss of valuable pastureland to irrigated cultivation. Nearly all irrigation schemes in the two countries displaced pastoralists and forced them into less favourable and more crowded terrain. Restrictions on their freedom of movement imposed by state borders, provincial boundaries and grazing zones, coupled with the great growth of herds, resulted in congestion, overgrazing and the degradation of the pastoralist habitat.

The marginalization of pastoralism bred widespread dissidence, especially in Ethiopia. The alienation of the pastoralists there is reinforced by the fact that nearly all are Muslims and belong to ethnic groups with which the Abyssinians have fought since time immemorial. Pastoralists have no access to the state whose language they do not speak, and no way to express grievances other than through violence. As a result, pastoralists participated in most conflicts that have broken out in that country.

By contrast with the regions and groups mentioned above which experienced relative deprivation, highland Eritrea was at one time more highly developed than Ethiopia. The period of economic expansion ended in the second half of the 1940s, and Eritrea entered the federal period with a depressed economy, lack of domestic capital and widespread unemployment. Many thousands of Eritreans migrated to Ethiopia and the oil states of the Arabian Gulf to seek work. After its annexation by Ethiopia, Eritrea fell well behind the central region of Ethiopia, where the bulk of capital investment was concentrated. Unemployment and migration became permanent features of Eritrean life.

In agricultural areas peasant participation in regional and ethnic political movements is considered indispensable to their success, because the peasantry is expected to provide manpower, supplies, transport, intelligence and refuge for the armed force. Securing peasant support is a priority for the leadership of these movements, and a form of populism is the usual means employed to attract it. Inevitably, this tends to emphasize ethnic or regional cultural values and social institutions, to extol a mythical past and construct an imaginary future. Thus, Eritrean propaganda invented a regional history a few centuries old, the Tigrai named their rebellion 'Woyane' in order to link it with a local peasant uprising against Addis Ababa in 1943, and the Oromo make much of the *gada*, the extinct institution whereby their ancestors governed themselves.

To induce the peasantry to risk rebellion, the movement has to promise a future that is much brighter than the present for the ordinary man and woman. It was in this connection that socialism became the dominant fashion in the Horn of Africa. The peasants' response to the appeal of ethnic and regional movements is determined by a variety of considerations. The critical factor is likely to be the material condition of the peasantry at the time, and this depends directly on access to land and, to a lesser extent, on the level of taxes and prices for agricultural produce. The contrasting response of the peasantry in northern and southern Ethiopia offers a vivid illustration of this factor.

Prior to the land reform of 1975, the situation of the peasantry in the two regions was quite different. The Abyssinian peasantry in the north enjoyed inalienable customary rights to land derived from the individual's membership in the kinship group. Such rights changed hands only through inheritance, and land could be neither sold nor amassed through purchase. Large land-ownership and landlessness were rare in this region. Though heavily taxed and living on the margins of subsistence, the Abyssinian peasant was the indisputable possessor of a plot of land, however tiny.

By contrast, the bulk of the land in the south had been expropriated after the conquest of the region and was distributed to Abyssinians. A large section of the indigenous peasantry had become quasi-serfs of Abyssinian landlords, who exacted not only rent and taxes but various other fees and services as well. In the late 1960s, the land tenure system in the south was abolished, turning most of the feudal landholdings into private property, and the serfs into tenants.

The material plight of the peasantry in the south was obviously related to the imposition of Abyssinian rule. The conjunction of class and ethnic contradictions produced an explosive situation that was nearing the critical point in the twilight years of the imperial regime. It was commonly expected that alienation among the peasantry in the south would lead to mass violence when the regime began to lose its grip. It was, however, the peasantry in Tigrai and Eritrea in the north that rallied to the call for rebellion, and not in the south. The reason for this dramatic turn of events was the 1975 land reform. By abolishing land-ownership and tenancy, the reform dissolved the link between class and ethnicity. The tenants in the south acquired usufruct rights to the land they tilled, and the Abyssinian landlords left the area. The former tenants were relieved of landlord exactions, and gained secure access to land. By contrast, the Abyssinian smallholders in the north gained nothing from the land reform, since there were few large landholdings to be expropriated so that their smallholdings could be enlarged. Although the land reform proclamation confirmed their customary rights to the land they tilled, inevitably it aroused fears that such rights were no longer sacrosanct to those who ruled the country from Addis Ababa.

Fanned by famine, dissidence in Tigrai reached a high pitch in the late 1970s, making it easy for the Tigrai People's Liberation Front to raise a peasant guerrilla force which proved more than a match for the government forces. Similarly, the Eritrean peasantry, which suffered greatly from the indiscriminate violence of the Ethiopian army, provided a steady flow of recruits to the nationalist movement. By contrast, the land reform took the wind out of the sails of the Oromo Liberation Front, whose appeal to Oromo ethnicity received a faint response. Instead, for 15 years, the Oromo peasantry provided cannon fodder for the Ethiopian army.

In Eritrea another story unfolded. The former Italian colony had attained a high rate of urbanization and a sizeable urban workforce by the end of the Second World War. A trade union association was formed in the brief period of freedom that obtained when the federal scheme went into effect in 1952. After annexation, the imperial regime officially banned the trade union movement, and the Eritrean workers were permanently alienated from Ethiopia. This was a period of serious hardship for Eritrean workers, due to the deflation of the local economy. Unemployment and emigration became their lot. Muslims went to the oil-rich Gulf states and Christians to Ethiopia, where they dominated the construction, transport and service sectors. Those who stayed home participated in the nationalist movement from the outset. Eritrean workers abroad provided crucial financial support for the movement, many of them contributing regularly a percentage of their wages. Both nationalist fronts had affiliated worker organizations.

3. FIJI

The land issue is perhaps the most significant flashpoint of Fijian–Indian ethnic conflict. Fijians own most of the country's land under a system of traditional communal tenure which prohibits private individual alienation to non-Fijians. They equate ownership of land with their heritage and identity. In a modern cash economy dominated by Europeans and Indians, land constitutes the Fijians' most powerful pillar of political bargaining. Being mainly farmers, Indians view land as the indispensable means for their survival. Since they own very little of it, however, they require predictable access to land use since alternative avenues of employment are practically non-existent. The struggle, then, between Fijian owners and Indian lessees is cast in terms of vital needs over a very limited resource generating unusual emotional intensity around the issue.

Fiji has about 4 500 000 acres of land; at the time of cession, the Europeans had claimed about 1 000 000 acres. A land commission subsequently recognized as legal only 415 000 acres. Nevertheless, these tracts represent the best agricultural land in Fiji. With brief interruptions, land policy has remained very tight. Essentially, the government intervened to terminate all private sales in an effort to preserve the Fijian way of life.

The freezing of the tenure pattern has bequeathed a legacy of wide disparities in land-ownership among the races. Fijians constituting about 46 per cent of the population retain ownership over 84 per cent, of which less than 10 per cent is cultivatable. Europeans constituting about 4 per cent of the population own in freehold 5.5 per cent of prime commercial land. Indians forming about 48 per cent of the population own 1.7 per cent. The overwhelming majority of Indians are tenants and sub-tenants who depend on Fijians for leased land. About 62 per cent of the leases issued by Fijians are held by Indians. Indians utilize the land mainly for sugar farming; about 80 per cent of the sugar farmers are Indians who continue to demand more land. This latter fact has launched Fijians and Indians on a collision course, which continues to the present.

Fijian fear of losing their land as well as their desire to retain land unencumbered by long leases for future use led to the enactment of the controversial land reserves policy in 1940. For over three and a half decades, year after year, land leased to Indian families who had no other alternative source of income was taken out of cultivation and placed in reserves. The more land placed in reserve, the more the country lost revenue from taxes, fewer people were employed, and more people moved into already overcrowded urban areas in search of work.

Fijians defend the land reserves policy by pointing out that the availability of land would provide the incentive for them to cultivate the soil commercially. Because of long leases, many Fijians in a single lifetime may not have the opportunity to use their land. Indians see the reserves policy as an expression of jealousy of their growing prosperity and the

Fijians' fear that, in the long run, Indian economic power may be translated into political power. Fijian interests in land were safeguarded in the 1970 independence constitution which validated all Fijian land claims to 84 per cent of the country's land and entrenched Fijian land rights. The deterioration of Fijian–Indian relations following the military coup in 1987 throws the renewal of the leases in the mid-1990s into an incendiary zone of uncertainty.

Employment, especially in the public sector, has emerged as a vicious arena in which competitive claims for ethnic shares have attained a special intensity. While the two areas, representation and land, were bound by colonial precedent and yielded to formal compromises, jobs from the modern commercial sector and from the public bureaucracy, both spheres expanding significantly in the post-Second World War period, were left wide open for competition by the ethnic communities. In the absence of a formula, each group staked its own claims guided by its own interests. Employment opportunities in the modern non-agricultural public and private sectors were, however, limited. It would be in this crucible of scarcity for a very highly prized value that government policy would play a pivotal part in determining the distribution of benefits.

The public service, including the education service, has become the largest single source of employment in Fiji. Until independence, the highest posts were occupied by European personnel. Because of their lack of land and insecure leases, Indians spent heavily on upgrading their schools. To them, education was the only alternative to land scarcity; it held the promise of employment in the emerging modern public and private sectors. Indian expenditures in education were reflected after the Second World War in the steady incremental displacement of many Europeans in position that required skills. Fijian educational achievement was retarded by comparison.

As the state undertook an increasing number of development projects and more services were extended to citizens, the public bureaucracy expanded. In a scheme where merit determined appointments, the public service was swamped by educated Indian personnel. But the concept of balance entered into the picture. After independence, a Fijian-dominated government offset Indian preponderance in the private business sector by higher Fijian employment in the public bureaucracy.

After the coup in 1987 in the name of Fijian paramountcy, the issue of preferential allocation of jobs, projects, scholarships, etc., in favour of Fijians became mired in intense controversy. Fundamentally, the Fijian communal social structure which gives priority to collective endeavours and sharing is inconsistent with the individualistic and more materially-oriented social structure of Europeans, Indians and Chinese. From these causes has emerged the condition of relative deprivation among Fijians in the modern sector. Hence, the Fijian community displays less conspicuous signs of prosperity than the Indian, European and Chinese communities. In turn, this has thrown up comparisons reflecting badly on the social status of Fijians relative to other groups in Fiji. But more importantly, over the years, the relative wealth of Indians, Europeans and Chinese has outstripped that of the Fijian community. To Fijians, the latter factor may have significance in the political arena where the immigrant groups will eventually yield *de facto* greater influence on government decision-making. In effect, the greater economic wealth of non-Fijians will undermine and make a travesty of the substance of Fijian political paramountcy.

For Fijians, it was more than reasonable that 50 per cent or more of civil service positions have been assigned to them since Indians find employment much more easily than Fijians in the private sector. Hence, Fijian over-representation in the public sector was offset by Indian over-representation in the private sector. As a result of all of this, many Indians had to migrate to seek job opportunities overseas. However, many remain in Fiji, qualified but unemployed or under-employed. To offset these tendencies, the Fiji government has undertaken policies to strengthen the economic position of the Fijians. By setting quotas and underlining privileges, the affirmative action programme actually institutionalizes the practice of ethnic discrimination. It both confirms Fijian economic inferiority and frustrates Indian economic efforts. Statistically, the concessions made to Fijians in these areas were not very large. The larger problem is the dual economic citizenship that has been created so that the effort and industry of one section is made to pay for the under-achievement of another group. The prospect of permanent discrimination confers an aura of depressed behaviour that could affect the well-being of all.

4. GUYANA

In Guyana, as in other typical multi-ethnic societies, one of the most crucial part of the economic legacy of colonization is its ethnic specialization and complementarity. The specialized parts of the economy have emerged as areas of ethnic concentration so that over time each economic sector becomes the *de facto* preserve or territory of one or another ethnic group. To be sure, there are inter-ethnic overlaps, but what is significant is that preponderant ethnic concentrations occur in different economic sectors and that this is reinforced by ethnically-oriented residential and occupational patterns and preferences.

While, on the one hand, this system of ethnic separation has tended during most of the colonial period to maintain a substantial level of political order and stability in Guyana, on the other hand, each ethnic section, because of its preponderance in one essential sector of the economy, can by that fact disrupt the entire system by withdrawing its role. In the post-independence period when ethnically-based parties were formed, this was done repeatedly to sabotage and destabilize the government in power.

The creation of an economy of ethnic enclaves and economic spheres of influence also resulted in important communal disparties in the distribution of material benefits. Most wealth was controlled by Europeans in combination with a handful of Chinese and Indians. The Africans as a whole were excluded, but in the twentieth century, many on them, including a mixed race category, occupied strategic positions in the public service. Nevertheless, the greatest amount of poverty, unemployment and economic deprivation was found among Africans. Although there were many poor Indians, generally most Indians emerged as better-off than Africans. The colonial heritage, then, bequeathed an economic order of inequality that was preponderantly ethnicized.

To the extent that Guyana's economy was based on sugar cane plantations, many rural investments in support of this activity provided benefits to Indian families. Similar benefits accrued to African workers and their families in the bauxite mines. In the urban areas, however, there was a general neglect of housing and community services. The major companies were managed by imported European executives who lived as a privileged upper caste in separate residential areas. Any attempt by the socialist-minded political parties to confront the issue of economic dominance, quickly turned into a conflict between whites and non-whites. What endowed the colonial market strategy with a peculiarity of its own was the close association that the factors of production bore to the ethnic groups and status system in the society. Later, as the governmental administrative system evolved, Africans would come to dominate the public bureaucracy.

The impact of this ethno-capitalist colonial model was disastrous for the colony in the long run. Clearly, the economic ascriptive caste system did not rely on the maximum utilization of human resources. It relied on race and ethnicity as variables in the assignment of labour in the productive process. The best investors and the finest workers were not market-determined. Nor were the sources for the disposal of the final product. A distorted capitalist market system institutionalized ethnicity around productive activities and the distribution of benefits. It laid the foundation for future ethnic conflict built around the allocation of resources as the colony moved towards a more achievement-oriented order at a later date.

The unified independence movement under the joint bi-ethnic leadership of Cheddi Jagan and Forbes Burnham was socialist in commitment but lasted barely six months before it was evicted from office by British troops. An ethnically unified independence movement using a socialist ideology could have redirected the use of resources for development. But the movement was destroyed. In the immediate aftermath, two ethnically polarized parties evolved, and each in turn would govern a state whose ethnic seams were severely inflamed. After the departure of the British, Africans and Indians confronted each other in a deeply divided state.

The Indian-based Jagan-led PPP government won two successive elections (in 1957 and 1961) and it had the opportunity to design an economic strategy consonant with its ideological premises for the transformation of the society. The choice by Jagan of an economic strategy that emphasized agricultural production and diversification and rural development, although it could be vindicated by economic arguments, entailed the emphasis of budgetary expenditures on Indians who were mainly rural residents. The fall of the Indian-based PPP regime under Jagan was followed by the Burnham–D'Aguiar coalition, which obtained strong support from the United States. It proceeded to implement a policy that was unequivocally committed to the market mechanism with heavy emphasis on private, especially foreign investment. At the same time, the security forces and public service bureaucracy were shored up, providing jobs for an increasing number of principally African urban residents. All of this elicited a strong opposition response from the Jagan forces which mounted strike after strike in the sugar industry to destabilize the government. In turn, many of Jagan's activists were imprisoned without trial under the Emergency and Security Regulations of the regime.

The full articulation of an ethno-economic strategy and its devastating counter-responses would however not come until after Burnham's PNC virtually seized power in the fraudulent elections of 1968. In sole control of the government having jettisoned its coalition partner, the PNC proceeded to enunciate and implement a strategy of economic development consonant with its own views of socialism. Guyana officially was declared a Co-operative Socialist Republic.

Through a series of nationalizations, some 80 per cent of the economy was placed under this vision of co-operative socialism. In practice, most of the nationalized companies simply became state enterprises, largely under African control. The upshot was a series of boycotts and strikes by the

Jagan forces which literally frustrated the experiment in co-operative socialism. Indians saw the government's policies as masterminded by ethnic jealousies. Farmers lost their previous government supports and subsidies and their political leaders were frequently harassed and jailed. Rice production plummeted. The sugar industry, the backbone of the economy, was hamstrung. In control of an integral aspect of the economy, Indians practically paralysed the economy in the same manner as Africans did when Jagan was in power. As in Jagan's case, internal ethnic divisions and external ideological interests combined to reduce the economy to virtual shambles.

The persistence of ethnic conflict with its economic effects saw Guyana tumble from a prosperous country in the 1950s to the lowest rung in the Western Hemisphere in 1990. Per capita real income declined by about 33 per cent between 1975 and 1986. To maintain an ethnically dominant regime, the economic costs were considered secondary to that of poverty. In due course, the adverse economic effects meant loss and degradation for all ethnic sections. About a third of the population consisting of its best trained and educated persons migrated overseas. Social indicators of levels of living and basic needs satisfaction (health, education, housing, nutrition, etc.) diminished sharply as a result.

5. NIGERIA

By the time of national independence in 1960, Nigerian politics had become synonymous with an inter-ethnic struggle for power. Political power was widely perceived as an important instrument in the struggle among ethnic groups for the division of the national wealth.

When in 1951 the various ethnic factions of the nationalist movement assumed governmental powers in the regions, public wealth was the chief source of private capital for Nigerians. Therefore, the emergent businessmen in the various regions supported the party in power there. For example, the Northern Contractors Union and the Northern Amalgamated Merchants Union were closely connected with the Northern Peoples Congress, NPC; the Union of Niger African Traders at Onitsha and the Eastern Nigeria Civil Engineers and Building Contractors of Enuga strongly backed the National Council of Nigeria and the Cameroons, NCNC. And the Federation of Civil Engineering Building Contractors of Yaba, the African Contractors' Union, the Nigerian Produce Buyers Union and the Nigerian Motor Transport Union supported the Yoruba-led Action Group. Government loans, licensing and contracting were channelled through public agencies that were ethno-political in character. The avowed goal of creating local capitalists through the use of governmental power was part of the nationalist struggle against colonialism. But as part of the emergent inter-ethnic rivalry among the nationalist leaders, ethnicity played a strong role in deciding who would be the beneficiaries of this policy. Each ethnic group sought to mobilize its own businessmen in this way in the hope of achieving economic ascendancy over the others in the post-colonial order.

The commodity marketing boards played a significant role in the policy of creating a class of local entrepreneurs in Nigerian society. In every region, the governing party maintained an extensive system of patronage that was financially anchored in the funds and activities of the regional marketing boards, which set the prices for local cash crops. By the time of independence in 1960 a sizeable group of Nigerian businessmen had emerged to conduct business side-by-side with foreign entrepreneurs. They were involved in various fields ranging from trading to manufacturing, road building and trading. Regional rivalry for public funds in all fields spurred industrial development. Similar specialized enterprises were set up in more than one region to placate local interests, but they often created duplication and inefficiency.

Ethnicity and regionalism serviced the interests of the local elites, who held to the widely used, ethnically-laden slogan of 'West for the Westerners, East for the Easterners, North for the Northerners and Nigeria for All'. The rivalry in the formulation and execution of community development projects in health, education and other services led not only to progress in various fields in both rural and urban areas; it also gave rise to a culture of community self-help, thus ensuring socio-economic progress for the vast majority of the population. Wanting in any shared economic activities, the regional business classes lacked national class consciousness. They perceived one another essentially as potential rivals to be eliminated rather than as peaceful competitors. Mutual exclusionism as well as cross-class ethnic solidarity prevailed.

By far the most important and persistent struggle among the ethnic groups for federal resources was carried on over revenue allocation. The various ethnic groups seek advantages through it in the distribution of the national wealth. Those who believe that they have lost out will often protest and call for a review of the allocation formula. One of the latest ways through which ethnic leaders seek to improve their advantage over others in revenue allocation is to have their state split up into more states, whereby they will then receive additional portions. Similarly, the census became an arena for intense inter-ethnic struggle. It affected revenue allocation through the application of the principle of need, based on size of population. Thus, with the politicization of ethnicity, regionalization of politics and consolidation of ethnically-based political parties, inter-ethnic struggle for national wealth found expression in the inter-regional/inter-state struggle for maximum advantage from the allocation of revenues in the country.

Some regions received more benefits from federal resources than others. Between 1962 and 1966, the northern region was thus favoured, whereas in the south unemployment was more than twice as high. Similarly, the Nigerianization of the federal public service favoured the north because the NPC was a leading partner in the coalition government, even though there were many more qualified people in the south.

The defeat of the Igbo in the civil war effectively eliminated them as major competitors for federal resources. In the immediate post-war period the centre-stage was occupied by the Hausa-Fulani, the Yoruba and the minority ethnic groups. Just before the war, the country was split into 12 states to accommodate the political aspirations of the minority groups. Ethnic groups put a premium on securing advantages for themselves in the distribution of the national wealth. The major strategy for achieving these advantages relied on the control of governmental power. All ethnic groups became involved in the struggle for power at all political levels, in order to increase their economic share. Inevitably, some groups would feel shortchanged, a frustration which ethnic leaders knew how to exploit, thus paving the way for conflicts and confrontations. The highest social and economic costs were paid by the country as a result of the Nigerian civil war, in which ethnic confrontation played a crucial role.

After the war, 30 new states were created out of the three original regions in the country. This political change, it can be argued, quickened the pace of investment and growth in certain areas. Yet the creation of states has also contributed to the proliferation of tertiary activities through the expansion of public administration and new state bureaucracies. These activities have not furthered healthy economic development. Moreover, manufacturing and other productive activities continue to be concentrated around the capital, Lagos, in the south.

Okwudiba Nnoli argues that the alleged benefits derived from the creation of 30 states are mere rationalizations of the interests of the privileged classes in the various ethnic homelands. It is not the farmers or low and middle income workers but the bureaucrats, contractors and businessmen who are able to take advantage of the new state administrations. Nnoli concludes that the creation of numerous states did not contribute to overall growth and development nor to the improved distribution of wealth among the different ethnic groups and regions.

One of the most significant developments in the ethnic situation in Nigeria is the increasing salience of politicized ethnicity in the rural areas of the country. Until recently, the ethnic phenomenon was essentially urban, where people from the various regions competed for jobs and resoures. They also bonded together in ethnic associations for self-help and solidarity. Today, many rural areas have become theatres of inter-ethnic struggles, some of which have become violent. Border disputes in the northern part of the country have steadily risen in number over recent years, often over land rights for farming and grazing. Politicized ethnicity has now affected all sections and sectors of the country. The creation of new states, argues Nnoli, has succeeded in spreading rather than containing the problem.

6. YUGOSLAVIA

Contemporary analysts seem to agree that one of the factors contributing to the disintegration of Yugoslavia was the persistence of regional economic disparities between the constituent republics of the federation and the inability of the federal government to come to terms with these inequalities. Dragomir Vojnić analyses these questions in his study for UNRISD. A time sequence of the country's gross domestic product since 1952 shows that there were vast differences in the level of economic development between the republics and provinces of the former Yugoslavia. The greatest extremes were to be found between Slovenia and Kosovo, the latter's per capita product in that year amounting to no more than a quarter of the per capita product of the former. In subsequent years, despite the federal government's compensatory policies, the differences between the two regions increased. In terms of disposable income per family, a Slovene family disposes of an amount (per family member) five times higher than in Kosovo, almost three times higher than in Bosnia-Herzegovina, Montenegro and Macedonia, more than twice higher than in Serbia and a good third higher than in Croatia and Vojvodina. This is to be attributed to the considerable differences in the quantity of the social product, as well as in the number of family members, particularly the number of children.

Vojnić considers that these disparities contributed to major demographic movements over the years, which in turn had a significant influence upon the process of disintegration. Generally speaking, the less developed republics and provinces increased their total share of the population, while the share of the more developed ones decreased. Thus, Croatia's and Slovenia's share of the total population decreased, whereas Montenegro, Macedonia and Kosovo increased theirs. Differential birth rates in the various regions account partially for these tendencies. In the more developed regions of Slovenia, Croatia and Serbia, low birth rates contributed to population decline. In Kosovo, Montenegro, Macedonia and Bosnia-Herzegovina, on the other hand, the population of Muslims and Albanians grew rapidly between the late 1940s and early 1980s, as a result of high birth rates.

On the other hand, internal migration flows pointed in the opposite direction: Muslims and Albanians as well as other national groups from the poorer areas migrated towards the more developed ones. However, Serb migration into Kosovo was furthered not so much for economic as for political and ideological reasons (Kosovo, though inhabited mainly by Albanians, is considered by the Serbs to be an integral part of historical Serbia).

From the early 1950s, after Yugoslavia split from the socialist bloc, accelerated economic development became of the highest political priority. Workers' self-management was introduced as an alternative to central planning, and large-scale investments were required to carry out this policy. The former Yugoslavia was counted among the rapidly developing economies, and the UN classified it among the ten newly industrialized countries. Vojnić considers, however, that this effort was expensive and ineffective, if the Yugoslav economy during that period is compared to developed market economies. The Yugoslav government put considerable emphasis on the accelerated development of the less developed republics and provinces. Kosovo, for example, had extremely high investment rates (50 per cent of the total social product during almost 40 years). The Federal Credit Fund redistributed financial assets from the more developed republics and provinces to the less developed ones, and so did the federal budget for the purpose of decreasing disparities in the standard of living. Total redistribution amounted to approximately 2 per cent of the social product of Yugoslavia.

The programme stimulating the rapid development of the less developed republics and provinces was the cause of continuous conflict with the more developed republics and provinces who had competing interests. Among other causes for contention, the developed republics of Croatia and Slovenia, as well as the Serbian province of Vojvodina, were inclined towards greater market activity which involved economic and political decentralization, whereas the less developed republics and provinces saw their interests in an increased administrative centralization of assets for investment and foreign currency. By means of the assets which were accumulated through administrative redistribution, the less developed regions created bureaucratic structures which became centres of economic and political power. Thus they opposed the market reforms which would weaken their position. They saw that the more centralized redistribution of investment assets and foreign currency was to their benefit, but the more developed republics and provinces resisted such a policy, not so much because of the size of the redistributed assets, but because of their irrational use. In this political context, inter-republic and international tensions thrived. Nobody was satisfied in such a situation, and everybody felt like losers. Vojnić argues that the rise of nationalism in the former Yugoslavia was rooted in relations which created the perception among all of injustice and exploitation. This not only contributed to the process of disintegration, but it destroyed the areas in which co-operation was possible as well.

In general, investment efficiency was much lower in the less developed republics and provinces than in the more developed areas. Kosovo, for example, which received large tranches of redistributive assets through the Federal Credit Fund, realized only modest growth-rates in social product. While Kosovo and the poorer republics demanded more federal support, Croatia and Slovenia expressed their increasing dissatisfaction with these arrangements. The long-run political implications of these tensions were not lost on analysts as long ago as the 1960s.

Beginning in the 1950s with the workers' self-management system, the Yugoslav economy was geared to accelerated development through export promotion as opposed to import substitution, and operated on the basis of decentralized economic decisions. However, under the influence of Soviet economics, during the first phase of industrialization in the 1950s, each of the republics wanted to have a self-contained economic structure with an emphasis on heavy industry. Whereas the more developed republics were more involved in the manufacture of final products, the less developed ones, especially Bosnia-Herzegovina and Kosovo, were more involved in the production of energy as well as intermediary and raw materials. This led to continual conflicts concerning pricing policy, customs duties and protection. The tendency toward autarkic development at all levels, argues Vojnić, contributed to the disintegration of the federation.

Major reforms tending towards the development of an open market economy were introduced in 1965 and, after some wavering, were pushed forward during the 1970s. Nevertheless, the great regional disparities continued to haunt the political system, even after the introduction of the new Constitution in 1974.

7. THE FORMER SOVIET UNION

Economic factors were involved in several of the developing inter-ethnic conflicts in the Soviet Union. Events in Estonia may be looked at as an example of this process. In 1988, the ethno-national Estonian movement, which was later to become the National Front of Estonia which spearheaded the drive for independence, organized the first mass actions aimed against the mining of phosphates, by challenging the plans of the Union central ministries to mine significant areas of the country for phosphorous. It was a protest against what the population perceived to be the removal of part of the republic's territory to the control of Union, that is non-Estonian, organs of power. The protests, which began with concern over the environment, soon turned to political and economic issues (whether the mining of phosphates was in the best interests of Estonian development, whether it was necessary and convenient to bring in Russian workers, whether the central Union or the republic would control these resources, etc.). Similar protests occurred in other parts of Estonia, and thus a struggle detonated by ecological concerns turned into a conflict over the defence of the population's ethnic interests.

Similarly, the so-called 'small peoples' (numerically) of the north and in Siberia, whose economy is based to this day to a significant degree on deer husbandry, fishing and hunting (as well as some larger nationalities such as the Yakuts and Buryats), resent the loss of their hunting, fishing and herding grounds as a result of industrial development of mineral deposits, the building of hydro-electric dams, oil and gas pipelines, railways and highways. In many cases, this not only sharply weakens the possibilities of their traditional economic activities, but makes the very preservation of the primary systems of livelihood and cultural continuity impossible. The resulting protests easily become ethnic conflicts, as the local (sometimes poly-ethnic) populations unite against the newcomers who are associated with the new economic activities. In the Yakutsk region, for example, ecological deterioration was considered as one of the main reasons leading to the emergence of an ethno-national movement. The Association of Nationalities of the North Kamchatka Region, made up of several ethnic groups, also appealed to the All-Union Congress of Peoples Deputies

> to object to the development of a gold-mining industry in our region ... which will turn our region into an uninhabitable scrap of land. Deer pastures, spawning rivers, hunting grounds will all be destroyed.... With the disappearance of our traditional livelihood, will disappear our

national cultures and native tongues ... the indigenous nationalities of Kamchatka will disappear.

The demands of the northern peoples in Russia are not dissimilar to those of other indigenous peoples around the world, whether in the Arctic region, the Amazon or Southeast Asia.

8.   CONCLUSIONS

For the last half-century the main objective of national and international economic strategy has been to further economic development, particularly in the so-called less developed or developing parts of the world. The United Nations produces sophisticated measurements to monitor the performance of countries in terms of their development. Gross domestic or national product and per capita income are probably the most widely used and accessible indicators and they give us a good idea of national averages. These indicators are useful when making international comparisons and also to trace growth rates over time.

But aggregate growth provides only a partial picture of development. The other important aspect, which complements GDP and per capita income figures, refers to distribution. How the national product, the incomes of individuals and families, and the principal resources of a country (its wealth) are distributed among the population is as much an indicator of 'development' as growth rates and investment coefficients.

As is well known, high growth rates do not necessarily go hand in hand with better distribution of wealth. On the contrary, recent experience has indicated that accelerated growth will usually produce increasing income inequalities between regions and among a country's population. This easily leads to different forms of social protest and political turmoil. When social and economic classes that are differentially affected by economic growth strategies are also identified in ethnic terms, then the ensuing social and political confrontations may take on the characteristics of an ethnic conflict. Precisely because economic growth is not to be mistaken for development in the broader sense of implying an increasing flow of goods and services to a widening circle of people, the United Nations and other agencies consider that 'social and human' development is just as important, if not more so, than economic growth. There is much debate and relatively little consensus about the exact meaning and scope of terms such as 'social development' and 'human development'.[7] These concepts generally refer to issues such as urbanization, composition of the labour force, employment and unemployment, child labour, age structure of the population, distribution of land and other productive resources, housing, education, family structure, health, culture, leisure activities, information and 'communication, criminality and violence, democratic elections, political parties, human rights and, in general, what is now referred to as the satisfaction of 'human needs'. How to put all these items (and others) together in a single meaningful indicator, or on a ranked index that means something real to whoever reads it, is actually next to impossible, and at any rate, an extremely challenging, task, yet the United Nations has valiantly tried to do exactly that.

Of the countries covered in this study, the UN's Human Development Report (1993) ranks most of them within the range of countries with Medium and Low Human Development. Their situation on the Human Development Index (HDI) ranges from 0.790 for Malaysia (the highest) to 0.152 for Sudan (the lowest).[8] Generally, a country's rank on the HDI corresponds roughly with its rank on the GDP per capita index, but this does not always hold. Among the rich countries, while Canada, Australia and the United Kingdom rank significantly higher on the HDI than on the GDP per capita index, the reverse is true for Switzerland, Germany and Finland.

Among some of the countries in this study which rank higher in HDI than in GDP per capita we find Malaysia, Fiji, Turkey, Guyana, Pakistan, India, Nigeria, Burundi, Ethiopia and Sudan. Among the countries in which the per capita GDP ranks higher than the HDI, we see Iraq, Lebanon, Iran, Guatemala and Senegal.[9]

In general, violent and protracted ethnic conflict is less likely in countries high on the HDI, whereas it occurs more frequently at the other end of the scale. The 'Minorities at Risk Project' concluded that of 233 instances of politicized communal groups, 74 were found in Africa south of the Sahara, 43 in Asia, 31 in North Africa and the Middle East, 32 in Eastern Europe and the USSR, and 29 in Latin America and the Caribbean. Only 24 were located in the Western democracies and in Japan. Again, this survey indicates that more minorities at risk are to be found in the less developed countries or countries of middle-level development than in highly industrialized states. Perhaps because highly industrialized states are fewer and have fewer minorities among their population. Gurr argues that ethnic grievances in the West have in general been solved through political accommodation and economic redistribution of resources over a long period of time, and this has diminished the potential for conflict.[10]

As suggested earlier, aggregate figures can be misleading. For example, in the United States, which ranks sixth in the Human Development Scale,

Whites rank higher than Japan at the world level (first place), whereas Blacks (African-Americans) are placed at about equal with Trinidad and Tobago (31st place), and Hispanics rank next to Estonia (34th place). Further disaggregation shows that white women rank highest and black men lowest on the HDI, but the latter have higher scores than most of the people in the rest of the world.[11] In Mexico, the Human Development Report finds that the state of Chiapas, bordering on Guatemala, ranks considerably lower than the national average as far as per capita income and adult literacy is concerned. This is borne out by other national statistics on social and economic indicators. It comes as no surprise that Chiapas was the scene of an Indian peasant uprising at the beginning of 1994.

While economic deprivation may not have been the only cause of ethnic conflict in Ethiopia, it is clear that the Tigrai and Eritrean Liberation Movements had their origin in some of the poorest regions in Ethiopia. Markakis shows that the most drought-prone regions in Ethiopia are also the ones where conflict has occurred. Tigrai was the most impoverished of the provinces, and many of its people were forced to migrate in search of employment. Likewise, many Eritreans blamed the central government for the economic plight of their region.

In Lebanon, the regions inhabited mainly by the Shi'ites, who later became one of the more active politically mobilized groups in the civil war, were traditionally among the most impoverished, and those who migrated to Beirut increased the ranks of the marginalized population and the urban underclass. The Amal movement, one of the militant Shi'ite factions in the civil war, was founded in 1973 as the 'Movement of the Deprived'. The focus of Shi'ite mobilization efforts, writes one student of the problem, 'remained in the south, where the human misery was a stark contrast to the opulence of the city-state (Beirut). This impoverished area was the chief victim of the war ...'[12]

While 16 years of civil war wreaked vast destruction on Lebanon, estimated at roughly US$ 20 billion, it also became a major source of income for numerous particular interests. As in other wars, there developed a major market for arms in which numerous weapons merchants from East and West were actively involved. Another group that benefited were the members of the militias. After the collapse of Lebanon's financial system between 1984 and 1986, says Picard, militia pay in hard currency became a major source of income for tens of thousands of families from all Lebanese communities. The Hizbollah militia, for example, received a monthly allocation from Iran of roughly US$7 million, and a militiaman's salary was much higher than that of a schoolteacher, or even of the members of the Lebanese national army. Hizbollah was also able to lure away members of the rival Amal militia by offering them higher monthly salaries. After the Taef Agreement provided for the demobilization of the militias and their partial incorporation into the newly regenerated national Lebanese army, many militiamen signed up for the army, but others were deprived of their incomes. Early in the conflict, the Amal high command began receiving considerable resources for 'reconstruction' in the south, thus creating an incentive for maintaining clientelistic relationships which only strengthened the political control of the communal Shi'ite elites.

We see from the case of Lebanon that violence wreaks destruction, but also creates vested interests that have a stake in the continuation of the conflict (similar situations prevail in all countries where ethnic and regional conflicts occur). Money and resources poured into a conflict by outside interests, as happened in Lebanon, may be 'lost' for development purposes, but there are many who know how to profit from them.

How to take advantage of 'the national cake' is also, according to Okwudiba Nnoli, one of the permanent features of politicized ethnicity in Nigeria. The various ethnic groups perceive the 'national cake' as being essentially limited, and the main goal of the inter-ethnic struggle for power at the level of the central government is to draw away resources to benefit this or that particular ethnic region. The splitting up of the country into numerous states smaller than the three original regions, while it may serve important political purposes, has simply increased the disputes over federal resource allocation and has led to useless duplications in expenditures which actually hamper development efforts.

In ethnically bipolar states such as Fiji, Guyana and Malaysia, the two major ethnic groups have long struggled over the distribution of economic resources. Sometimes the major focus of conflict has been control of the land, as in Fiji, or jobs and employment opportunities in the civil service and public enterprises as in Malaysia and Guyana. Here also, as in Nigeria, the role of the central state as dispenser of resources, is paramount. Consequently, among the issues in so many conflicts 'preferential' or 'affirmative action' policies stand out, frequently demanded by aggrieved groups, and often resisted by the dominant ethnies.

A particularly poignant situation is that of indigenous and tribal peoples, whose revolts, rebellions and uprisings all over the world are directly related to economic deprivation, exploitation, land-loss, ecological degradation and other hardships imposed on them by traditional capitalist unequal development, reinforced by the neo-liberal policies of the 1980s and 1990s. Economic and social hardship was the principal cause of the Indian peasant uprising in southern Mexico in 1994. Indian mobilization in Ecuador, which has had significant political impact on national society since the mid-1980s, is motivated essentially by economic grievances, as are similar movements of tribal peoples in South and Southeast Asia as well as Native Americans in Canada and the United States.

In conclusion, generally speaking, economic causes can be said to be among the major factors generating ethnic conflicts. They in turn tend to have a negative impact on a country's economy as a whole, but frequently turn out to benefit certain ethnic elites and their providers, who then develop an interest in the perpetuation of the conflict. When outside economic support dries up, pressures build up for a reduction in violence and the search for peaceful solutions. The state and its resources become a principal bone of contention between ethnic groups in conflict, not only because of the political power it represents, but also, and sometimes mainly, because of the economic wealth it can provide. A rich state can better provide the resources and services that disadvantaged ethnic groups claim, but only if it is not already an instrument in the hands of a particular ethnic group that wields political power in its own benefit. Thus, in order to reduce the potential for ethnic conflict, a distributive state needs to be a democratic one. On the other hand, a poor state with limited resources may not become the prey of particular ethnic appetites, but then again it may not have the institutional power to keep ethnic conflict in check.

7 Ethnic Policies

We have seen in previous chapters how ethnic conflicts are shaped by the way states and governments deal with ethnic diversity within their borders. Government ethnic policies sometimes generate or excacerbate conflicts, but they may also be designed to lessen, solve or avoid them. The conflicts may lead to the formulation and modification of specific ethnic policies. Governments have rarely been neutral outsiders to such confrontations, and they often are active participants in their dynamics and evolution. The shaping of government ethnic policies is frequently one of the principal issues around which such conflicts occur in the first place.

1. KURDISTAN

Some of the root causes of the Kurdish conflict were explored in Chapter 3. The continuation of this struggle under different forms in the various states in which the Kurdish people live (Turkey, Iran, Iraq, Syria) is directly related to the policies which these governments have adopted at different times in relation to their Kurdish populations.

In *Turkey* the first nationalist expressions of anti-Kurdish sentiment occurred in the 1920s under Kemal Atatürk, the founder of the modern Turkish state. Official rhetoric held that the Kurds were actually 'Mountain Turks' and had no claim to an independent identity, an assumption which Kurdish nationalist movements have hotly contested. Notwithstanding the Treaty of Lausanne of 1923, by which Turkey accepted the obligation to protect its 'minorities', the Kurds did not benefit from these provisions. The current constitution, adopted in 1980, prohibits the expression of any opinion which counters Turkish national interests, the integrity of the Turkish state and nation, Turkish historical and moral values, and the principles and reforms of Atatürk. Articles 26 and 28 of the constitution prohibit the publication of any text in a language 'forbidden by law' (meaning the Kurdish language). Special laws and decrees of 1926, 1967 and 1983 prohibit the use of any language not officially recognized by the Turkish state (i.e. the Kurdish language) in public. Another 1983 law forbids the existence of political parties based on non-Turkish religious, racial, linguistic, cultural or national criteria. It actually prohibits political parties from mentioning the existence of such 'minorities' in Turkey. Turkish is considered the only 'mother tongue' of all Turkish citizens, and the use and dissemination of any other mother tongue is forbidden. Over the years, Kurds, Turks and even foreigners in Turkey have been persecuted and jailed for allegedly violating these laws.

The eastern provinces (*vilayets*) of Turkey, usually referred to as eastern Anatolia, are the home of most of the Kurdish population. This area is under direct administration by the political centre through a Turkish prefect who has almost absolute powers. For many years it has been massively militarized to prevent any Kurdish political or military opposition from taking root. The military presence in Kurdistan produces numerous human rights violations which have been widely documented and denounced over the years by human rights organizations inside and outside Turkey.

Government ethnic policy in the region has had two principal objectives: deportation and Turkification. Deportation of Kurdish populations by the government began in 1927 in the aftermath of the Kurdish revolt of 1925, and continued well into the 1980s (involving family members of Kurdish political prisoners). Demographic and economic changes in Turkey are also generating massive out-migration from eastern Anatolia, and rural Kurds have flocked in great numbers to regional urban centres as well as to the large cities of central and western Turkey where they become more or less integrated in the national population. The policy of 'Turkification' includes the changing of names of villages, linguistic and educational programmes in the school system, the diffusion of governmental nationalist ideology at all levels. In other words, accelerated, government-directed assimilation of the Kurds into the Turkish national mould. To some extent this policy is successful in that numerous Turkish citizens of Kurdish origin have completely adopted the Turkish language and culture as well as the official nationalist ideology. Others, however, resist the process of Turkification and are involved in the various manifestations of the Kurdish nationalist movement.

As a result of the Kurdish resistance movement, extensive international criticism and the instability provoked by the Gulf War of 1990–1, the Turkish government softened its stance on the Kurdish issue in 1991 and now expresses greater tolerance for Kurdish culture on its territory. It is possible that the more repressive laws will eventually be repealed and government policy reversed.

Relations between the Kurds and the government of *Iraq* have been tense, often violent, ever since the creation of the Iraqi state by the Western powers after the First World War. Generally, a weak Iraqi government negotiates with the Kurds and offers autonomy and partnership; a strong Iraqi state reneges on previous agreements and pursues a repressive policy. Over the decades, the various Kurdish nationalist movements, sometimes beset by internal conflicts and rivalries, following different ideological lines and playing along with different international sponsors (Great Britain, United States, Soviet Union), were able to challenge the Iraqi government but have been unsuccessful in achieving their desired goal: an autonomous or perhaps even independent Kurdistan. Periods of open warfare and massive military repression alternate with periods of relative calm and political accommodation. Iraqi Kurdistan occupies less than 20 per cent of Iraq's territory and holds about 3 million people. Unlike Turkey, Iraq formally recognizes the existence of a Kurdish minority, and the Accords of 1970 between Kurdish insurgents and the government guarantees the autonomy of Kurdistan. The Iraqi state, however, has been unwilling to grant the Kurds all the territory which they claim for themselves, basically because some of the area is rich in oil reserves. Despite the 1970 agreement, violent military repression of Kurdish nationalists and civilian population continued off and on into the early 1990s, when the Kurdish areas were protected by the United Nations following the Gulf War.

Whereas different Iraqi governments have tried at times to impose a policy of Arabization on the Kurdish population, the 1970 agreements and subsequent laws establish that Iraq is composed of two communities, the Arabs and the Kurds. Kurdistan possesses its own legislative and executive councils which are responsible for the government of the region. In fact, however, they have been more or less controlled by the central government. As a result of the persistent armed conflicts between the Kurdish nationalists and the Iraqi government, massive violations of the human rights of the Kurds have taken place, including the razing and destruction of Kurdish villages, the use of chemical gases against civilian populations (1987, 1988), the forced deportation of tens of thousands of people, and the 400 000 refugees created by the war in the early 1990s.

Kurdish nationalist revolts have also taken place in *Iran*, where the only attempt at the establishment of an independent Kurdish state, the Republic of Mahabad, flourished briefly for less than a year in 1946 with the support of the Soviet Union. The Iranian state has steadfastly pursued a policy of assimilation of the Kurdish people (who represent about 15 per cent of the total population, i.e. 7 million), through the forced settlement of nomads, the imposition of teaching in Farsi in the schools and tight central governmental control over the administration of the Kurdish regions. In general, Iranian Kurdistan is a poor, marginalized agricultural area whose average income and standards of living are by and large lower than in the rest of the country.

About one million Kurds live in *Syria*, making up 10 per cent of the country's population. Historically, the Kurds in Syria were well integrated in the country's social life. But in the 1960s and 1970s Kurdish cultural life in Syria suffered from the pan-Arab policies of the government. Nevertheless, a certain flexibility and tolerance allows the Kurds to participate in the country's political life.

Government ethnic policies regarding their Kurdish minority vary in each of the four countries, and they have also differed over time. As a result, the Kurdish nationalist movement likewise adopted different strategies and pursued separate aims according to the circumstances. Government policies extend from total denial of Kurdish identity (Turkey) to occasional granting of formal regional autonomy (Iraq) and relative tolerance, at times, of Kurdish cultural distinctiveness alternating with attempts at cultural destruction and forced assimilation (Iran and Syria). While Kurdish political movements have tried to negotiate with the various governments over the years, they have also resorted to armed struggle to achieve their goals. Hundreds of thousands of Kurdish exiles and refugees abroad, as well as numerous local and regional political groups and parties, continue to engage in their decades-long struggle for recognition, autonomy and identity.

2. HORN OF AFRICA

Ethiopia

The conflict that broke out in Tigrai was unexpected, particularly in view of the dimensions it took. Surprise was due to the fact that Tigrai is the heartland of Abyssinia, and its history is part and parcel of Abyssinian history. The Tigrai-speaking population extends northwards onto the Eritrean highlands, the northern frontier of Abyssinia where many wars were fought to keep invaders out. A century ago, a Tigrai noble, Yohannes, became emperor of Abyssinia (1872–89) and waged war against the Egyptians and the Sudanese Mahdists. Other Tigrai nobles married into the royal family and held important posts under the emperors Menelik and Haile Selassie.

Nevertheless, there are sharp differences within the Abyssinian family between the Tigrai branch, much smaller in size, and the dominant branch, the Amhara, who built and ruled the empire, and mixed uninhibitedly with other ethnic groups. A basic difference is language. The Tigrai language is related to but quite distinct from Amharigna, and the two are not mutually intelligible. This difference reinforces a provincial consciousness and sense of identity which set Tigrai apart from other Abyssinian provinces. When the Tigrai language was banned, it became the cause for grievous resentment and the symbol of Amhara domination. The population of Tigrai is not homogeneous. Nearly one-third are Muslims, and relations between the rival faiths in this province have never been easy. Eastern Tigrai is the home of Oromo agro-pastoralist groups, while the eastern flanks of the plateau and the lowlands are inhabited by Saho and Afar pastoralists.

Tigrai was always a provincial contestant in the dynastic struggles of Abyssinia, ruled by its own nobility who were restless vassals of the Abyssinian crown. With rare exceptions, the head that wore the crown was Amhara, a fact that did not inspire loyalty among the Tigrai. Historically, Tigrai provincialism was manifested in strong opposition to the Amhara monarchy and the central government's claim to absolute authority. In 1943, when the recently restored imperial regime sought to strengthen central control in Tigrai, by appointing Amhara governors and imposing taxes that had lapsed under the Italian occupation, it provoked a major uprising which was put down after heavy fighting. Central control was imposed afterwards, along with taxes, and the most painful cut of all was the banning of the Tigrai language in a region where, as late as the mid-1970s, only 12.3 per cent of the males claimed to speak Amharigna and only 7.7 per cent could read it.

Stark impoverishment underlay Tigrai political alienation. With a population estimated in the 1984 census at 2.4 million, Tigrai is the poorest Abyssinian province and probably the poorest in Ethiopia. Its land is devastated by soil erosion, and yields are half of what they are elsewhere in Ethiopia. Land fragmentation has rendered peasant holdings minuscule. Producing one crop annually, these were barely sufficient to maintain the peasantry at subsistence level in good years. There were major famines in this province in 1958–9, 1972–4, 1983–5, and minor ones in between. Tigrai peasants were accustomed to trekking far and wide during hard times to find work and food. By outlawing hired labour, the 1975 land reform closed this outlet during the crisis of 1983–5, and forced the stricken peasantry to seek refuge in Sudan *en masse*.

Like its imperial predecessor, the military regime in Addis Ababa had never considered a political solution to the manifold conflict that threatened the Ethiopian state with disintegration, because such a solution would require structural reforms, especially decentralization and regional autonomy. Like its counterpart in Khartoum, the military regime in Addis Ababa was intent on even greater centralization of state power and, rhetoric aside, the political structures it created were designed to achieve just that. More than once it offered regional autonomy to the Eritreans, and the constitution it adopted in 1987 included an elaborate design for local self-rule. However, all such offers were propaganda ploys, and not a single step was taken to implement them. Moreover, the insurgents rejected them because they had nothing to do with their formulation. As the decade drew to a close, it became quite obvious that it would be impossible to reach a negotiated solution to the conflict with the incumbent regime in Addis Ababa.

As the 1980s came to an end, it became obvious that the military regime in Ethiopia was no longer able to contain the armed opposition by force. The end came with unexpected swiftness in the summer of 1991, through an irresistible advance by the combined forces of the Tigrai People's Liberation Front and Eritrean People's Democratic Movement, now joined in the Ethiopian People's Revolutionary Democratic Front (EPRDF). They routed the regime's demoralized forces, isolated Addis Ababa, and left the dictator Mengistu Haile Mariam with little choice but to flee the country. With his departure, the 400 000 strong Ethiopian army disintegrated overnight, and the rebel forces entered Addis Ababa without opposition. The defunct regime's elaborate political edifice dissolved equally fast, leaving no political heritage after a reign of 16 bloodstained years. Unlike other Africans, Ethiopians had never tasted political freedom, having passed from the absolutism of imperial rule to the tyranny of the pseudo-Marxist military regime. The unexpected swiftness of the latter's collapse did not allow time for political mobilization among the population, and gave the EPRDF an opportunity to lay the foundations of a new state structure.

Moving cautiously, the EPRDF did not form a government. Instead, barely a month after entering Addis Ababa, it called a national conference to form a transitional government. About 20 groups participated, 15 of which represented ethnic constituencies, most of them newly formed in order to take part in the conference. Taking part also were most of the older, though not necessarily active, ethnic and regional dissident movements. The EPRDF scored an initial success in persuading the Oromo Liberation Front to take part. This seemed to indicate a change of policy on the part of the OLF, whose avowed goal until then had been unconditional separation from Ethiopia. The Oromo were also represented by the remnants of the Somali and Abo Liberation Front, now renamed the Abo Oromo Liberation Front.

Working with a draft programme submitted to it by the EPRDF, the national conference in Addis Ababa drew the charter for the transitional government and approved its make-up. Besides the TPLF and EPDM, OLF and other organizations were represented in the government. Seats to a council of representatives were allocated to groups participating in the conference, and the council was given the task of drafting a new state charter. By the end of the year, the council had prepared a draft constitution which divided Ethiopia into 14 self-governing ethnic units enjoying wide powers of self-government. Ethnicity and decentralization were to become the basis for the restructuring of the Ethiopian state.

The restructuring had already begun with the recognition by the national conference of the *de facto* separation of Eritrea, now under complete EPLF control. The conference decided to maintain this status quo for two years, when a referendum in Eritrea would decide its future. Wisely, the Eritreans not only refrained from a unilateral declaration of independence, but also defused an explosive issue by agreeing to make Asab a free port for Ethiopia.

3. MALAYSIA

In examining the ethnic conflict between Malays and Chinese, the visible difference between the two groups is an important factor contributing to the maintenance of ethnic boundaries. The racial distinctions between Malays and Chinese are reinforced by other cleavages based on almost every conceivable difference: language, religion, customs and way of life.

The attitude of the colonial masters to the different groups had a considerable effect in the shaping of policies which in turn adversely affected Malay–Chinese relations. As the population was mobilized on ethnic lines informal alliances were made between groups based on their similar cultures or perceptions regarding their political rights. As Malay claims for special privileges as the indigenous community became more vociferously expressed, the two groups who were identified as the non-indigenous communities in contrast to the indigenous Malays, the Chinese and Indians, formed an informal alliance to fight for their common interests.

For the Malays, who saw a significant correlation between the extent of colonial penetration and the size of the Chinese population, efforts to maintain Malay numerical majority were directed at controlling Chinese immigration and at the same time encouraging the assimilation of culturally similar groups.

During the early years of Chinese immigration, relations between the Chinese and the Malays were cordial and mutually beneficial. The expansion of colonial rule into the country brought about significant changes in relations between Malay rulers and the Chinese leaders. The colonial government set up political and administrative structures that dealt directly with the Chinese community while continuing to retain the traditional structures for dealing with the Malays. Among others, this resulted in the establishment of an education policy which allowed each ethnic group to have their children educated in their own mother tongue. But at the same time there was also a demand for English-educated technicians and clerical workers to fill middle level positions especially in the expanding public sector. This resulted in the establishment of English medium schools in the town, thus giving opportunity for the non-Malays to take advantage of these opportunities to gain the necessary education to participate in the modern sectors of the economy.

All these developments contributed to differential rates of social mobility between the Malays and Chinese. In order to offset the economic advantages of the Chinese, the Malays were given special privileges with regard to jobs in the public sector and scholarships to receive training in the special school set up to train Malays for the Malay administrative service.

The end of the Second World War brought far-reaching changes to the situation of the Malays. Some of the traditional Malay rulers and members of the Malay middle class were accused of having collaborated with the Japanese occupying forces. The Chinese, on the contrary, seemed to be in the ascendant. The introduction of the Malayan Union brought the nascent Malay consciousness that had been growing since the 1920s into sharper focus giving rise to Malay nationalism.

After the war, the Federation of Malaya Agreement between the British and the Malay leaders introduced a new balance of power between Malays and Chinese. By excluding non-Malays from the negotiations, it in effect confirmed and strengthened the Malay claims that they had special rights. The constitution of independent Malaya in 1957 was adopted after lengthy disputes and negotiations between the different ethnic communities and political parties. It was finally accepted by all the parties and became the basis for inter-ethnic co-operation in the country, even though by giving official recognition to group membership, through a provision relating to special rights for Malays, it set the stage for future ethnic conflict in the country.

One of the issues that was hotly debated in subsequent years was that of language. The small but extremely influential section of the English-speaking Malays believed strongly in making Malay the national language as it was tied to the whole question of Malay claims for recognition of their special position. In this they were supported by the Malay school teachers. This policy, in turn, was opposed by the Chinese community. The politically dominant Malays were able to amend the constitution in 1962, to make it more difficult for non-Malays to acquire citizenship. The formation of Malaysia brought a new dimension into ethnic relations, by adding new categories of people who would share the privileges of being Malay. Before the formation of Malaysia the Malay population was just under one-half of the total population; but as a result of Malaysia the Bumiputra population formed 55.5 per cent of the population.

When Singapore joined the Federation (for a few years), it furthered the call for a 'Malaysian Malaysia', which is what the non-Malays and the Chinese in particular had been fighting for. This concept was in direct contrast to the ethnic preference policies which treated one group differently from another, bringing into sharper focus ethnic differences. While Malays insisted on national integration through the development of a common school system with Malay and English as the language of instruction at the secondary and tertiary levels, the Singapore government had allowed the development of multi-lingualism in the school system. Thus the 'Malaysian Malaysia' concept became a symbol of Chinese rights. Again, the Malay community, headed by the Malay school teachers, felt that there was a threat to Malay privileges. In 1964 a National Language Action Front was formed to pressure the government to oppose the demands from the non-Malays.

The language issue became important once more as the ten-year period given for the continuation of English as an official language was coming to an end. On the one side, there were those who wanted the Chinese language to become an official language together with Malay, English and Tamil, and on the other side those who wanted Malay to be made the national and sole official language.

A key role was played by the Malay civil servants, who had worked closely with the Malay political leadership in formulating ethnic preference policies and this, together with the ethnic quota system to ensure Malay dominance in the administrative service, has given the civil servants a highly political role. If Malay became the official language many non-Malay officers who had been educated in English would have little opportunity to further their career. It was in the self-interest of this group to support the policy of making Malay the sole official language. Thus the various subgroups within the Malay community began to coalesce around the language issue. The most vehement opposition to the National Language Bill of 1967, which provided for the continuation of English as an official language for an indefinite period came not from the Chinese as in the past but from the Malays.

In 1969 the ruling Alliance lost much of its erstwhile electoral support. After ethnic riots in Kuala Lumpur had taken a heavy toll, the government declared a National Emergency. This led to the establishment of authoritarian rule which concentrated powers in the hands of a Malay leader. For the Malays, the abandoning of the democratic system was seen as necessary for the re-establishment of Malay claims for exclusive political rights as the indigenous community. Gradually, Malay political dominance began to be expressed in a wide range of government policies, especially in the appointment of personnel in key policy-making positions in the cabinet, in the civil service, in the armed forces and in the judiciary. As a result of the Emergency, the government introduced changes in the constitution to ensure that the non-Malays would not be able to challenge the political dominance of the Malays in the future. It identified what was called 'entrenched provisions' in the constitution which related to the rights of Malays, to Malay as the national language, to the special position of the Malays in the constitution and to the position of the Malay rulers. The parts of the constitution guaranteeing fundamental liberties which the non-Malays had believed to be the core of the constitution were given subordinate status to these 'entrenched provisions'. At the time that these constitutional amendments were made, the government also made amendments to the sedition laws making it illegal for anyone to criticize what were called 'sensitive issues'. These covered all aspects of the constitution which directly or indirectly gave expression to Malay hegemony, the status of Malay as the national language, the constitutional position of the Malay rulers and the special position of the Malay community. In addition, a 'national ideology' was drawn up which, it was hoped, would become the basis for the development of a common set of values for all the people, the *Rukunegara*.

Measures were also taken effectively to curtail the political participation of the non-Malays, a process which had already begun in the 1960s. Not only were citizenship laws made more restrictive, but changes in the electoral system which allowed rural constituencies to be much smaller than urban constituencies in a first-past-the-post electoral system had the effect of reducing the 'value' of the urban, largely non-Malay vote. Thus Malay political dominance was guaranteed both in the constitution and through the electoral process.

Determination by Malays to retain hegemony was also dictated by economic considerations. Up to the mid-1970s an implicit agreement had prevailed between the government and the non-Malay political leadership: that Malay political power was to be exchanged for Chinese economic power. Now the situation was to be changed. The unevenness of development between the fast-growing modern sectors of the economy dominated by foreign and Chinese interests and the traditional agricultural sectors dominated by Malays was identified as the major cause of ethnic conflict. The government argued in an official paper in 1970 that the 'average' Malay had a lower standard of living than the 'average' non-Malay, that Malays formed a much higher proportion of the population in rural areas than in towns; that Malays populated the relatively poorer states and occupations to a higher degree than non-Malays; that Malays formed a higher proportion of the workforce in low productivity traditional agriculture and lower proportion in modern industry and commerce; that Malays had a significantly lower share of ownership of industrial and commercial capital; and that Malays suffered from other apparent disadvantages as well. The government paper thus gave the impression that there was a ranked social system in which all Malays were poor and all non-Malays rich.

The government made a concerted effort to justify its actions by emphasizing the 'immigrant–indigenous' dichotomy. There was an attempt to delegitimize the political rights of non-Malays by making assertions about their inability to speak the national language. The Chinese, as the 'middleman minority', provided a convenient target to deflect possible Malay criticism against government policies by indirectly implying that the Chinese have been responsible for the relative poverty of the Malays.

4. PAKISTAN

Pakistan became an independent Islamic state after the partition of India in 1947. Since its inception, however, it had to deal with the fact that its eastern portion, separated from Western Pakistan by 1000 miles of Indian territory, was inhabited by a population which was ethnically and culturally quite distinct from the peoples of the Western segment. The fact that East Pakistan was almost entirely Bengali and contained 54 per cent of the total population became a major stumbling block in the framing of a constitution and in the democratic process. Before the 1956 Constitution, and in response to the central government's insistence that Urdu would be the only official language of the country, language riots broke out in the Eastern wing in 1952. The way the central government in Western Pakistan handled the language issue and other problems concerning regional identity in the East led finally to the dismemberment of the country, a bloody war of liberation, military intervention by India, and the emergence of Bangladesh as an independent state in 1970.

In what remained of Pakistan (the Western portion), the relationship between the various ethnic and regional elites shaped the evolution of the country in later years. The Punjabis maintained a dominant position over other regional/ethnic elites. While this dominance was tempered somewhat between 1971 and 1977, when Zulfiqar Ali Bhutto (from Sindh) was the country's prime minister, it greatly intensified after General Zia's coup d'état.

As already noted in Chapter 5, after the partition of India in 1947, millions of Muslim refugees from India came to Pakistan. While most of them remained in the Punjab, the province of Sindh was particularly affected by the migration pattern of these refugees, known as Mohajirs, most of whom settled in the urban areas. By 1951, 50 per cent of the urban population of the province was made up of Urdu-speaking Mohajirs, whereas only a few years earlier, 95 per cent of the population consisted of Sindhi-speaking natives.

Even though the Mohajirs came to Sindh from five different regions, they had enough in common among them in cultural and ideological terms for the development of a sense of common identity. Immigration to Punjab did not create much of a problem. But in Sindh the situation was very different. The massive influx of the Mohajirs in Karachi to the exclusion virtually of other areas created a ghetto-like situation. Further, the potential for integration was undermined by the lack of an indigenous Sindhi middle class. On the other hand, the Urdu-speaking Mohajir elite brought with it a cultural and ideological arrogance that further aggravated the issue.

It believed its own language to be far superior to the regional languages spoken in the areas that now constituted Pakistan. It also put forward the theory that the adoption of a single language, Urdu, guaranteed national integration. In doing so, of course, the elite managed to put all those whose mother tongue was Urdu at a real advantage in terms of education, jobs, and so on. Finally, because of the Mohajirs' critical role in the creation of Pakistan, this elite also saw itself as the standard-bearer of the Pakistan 'idea'.

The predisposition of the Mohajirs to view themselves as natural rulers of Pakistan, their lack of contact with a corresponding Sindhi urban middle class, and their partnership with the Punjabi ruling elite, all meant that their political and cultural perspective was centre-oriented with an almost complete absence of identification with the culture and concerns of the people of the province in which they found themselves.

In supporting Urdu as a national standard while de-emphasizing its own mother tongue, the Punjabi elite also sought to bolster its claim of being eminently suited to the task of governing not just Punjab but the entire country. Unity in uniformity was the watch-word. All were Muslims and Urdu was to be the only official language notwithstanding the fact that the Bengalis, constituting the majority, possessed a homogeneous culture and a well-developed language. Urdu and Islam were, in fact, woven into one, and by implication a non-negotiable, framework of identity.

The initially accommodating Sindhis saw their province and resources literally taken over by others, first Mohajirs and then the Punjabi elite, and found themselves in a constant battle with the centre and with the centre's representatives in the province. The centre's partisan policies aggravated existing imbalances.

Barring Karachi, practically no representation was given to Sindh in the upper echelons of the most powerful organs of state, i.e. the army and the bureaucracy. The outcome of such policies has coincided with the scramble for scarce resources – such as education, employment and basic amenities – at the local level to produce the present conflict in which the Mohajirs are fighting to maintain an earlier privileged position and the Sindhis, experiencing the phenomenon of an emerging middle class, are laying a vociferous claim to what they consider to be their due.

The central elite, in competition with regional elites, saw in language and religion the effective instruments not only for countering the Sindhis' demands, but also the means by which to deny the legitimacy of their distinct cultural identity. As early as 1948, Pakistan's prime minister said: 'Pakistan is a Muslim state and it must have as its lingua franca the language of the Muslim nation ... it is necessary for a nation to have one language and that language can only be Urdu and no other language.'

Even though in the first decade after independence there was a democratic form of government in the country, it was clear that the central elite sought to maximize its privilege and power regardless of democratic norms and the rights of the 'outsiders'. This approach found its most dramatic expression in the so-called 'one-unit' formula, by virtue of which, under an order issued in 1955 by the Acting Governor-General of Pakistan, the unified province of West Pakistan came into being. This formula was incorporated into the constitution of 1962. Under this provision ten formerly distinct administrative units were integrated into the new province. During the years of martial law and then limited democracy, regional elites were even more comprehensively blocked from participating in the process of governance and the sharing of power. Politicians were subjected to arbitrary bans and arrests under laws unilaterally devised and promulgated.

The so-called language controversy was a watershed in terms of the Mohajirs' alienation from the Bhutto regime (it will be recalled that Bhutto was from Sindh). The status of their mother tongue had been a primary concern of the Sindhis all along. The Sindh Assembly in July 1972 passed a Bill to promote Sindhi in the province, providing for little that would appear to have been radical or extreme. It required Sindhi to be taught as a second language to students for whom Sindhi was not the medium of instruction and made it essential for provincial government officials to learn the language in a specified period. More than a century earlier, the British colonizers had laid down such a policy. The Bill made it clear that the status of Urdu would in no way be compromised and that the policy would be implemented 'without prejudice' to the 'national language' (Urdu).

The Mohajirs, however, took strong exception to the Bill and responded with rioting, attacking the Sindhis and attempting to bring down the government. The 1977 elections and the agitation which followed, aggravated the division between the Sindhis and Mohajirs into two hostile camps. Even before Bhutto took power, the Mohajirs were in a state of shock on two counts: with the break-up of the one-unit system under Yahya Khan, Karachi had been returned to Sindh. One of the lessons that they learned was that the centre was not always an adequate guarantee for their welfare or even survival.

5. YUGOSLAVIA

The break-up of Yugoslavia in 1991 and the ensuing civil wars and violent ethnic conflicts in what used to be the Yugoslav Federation are still awaiting an objective, historical assessment. However, a partial understanding of the conflicts can be gained through an analysis of ethnic policies as they were set down in Yugoslavia's constitutional development and other governmental measures over the years before the catastrophe occurred.

Ethnic plurality and problems inherent in inter-ethnic relations have been present in Yugoslavia's constitutional development from the very founding of the Yugoslav federation; the constitution of 1974 simply reflected trends which already existed. It is also true, however, that by emphasizing ethnic pluralism and (at least to a certain degree) enabling its manifestations in the political system, Yugoslavia's constitutional development influenced the subsequent course of events and the social situation.

It is particularly significant that the constitution of 1974 defined the constituent republics as national states, based upon the principle of national sovereignty. Accordingly, the republics were given practically all the attributes of statehood. They were entitled not only to their own national symbols (the national anthem, the coat of arms, the flag) but more importantly, to their own constitutions as well as the entire structure of the organs of state authority (the Assembly, the Executive Council, the presidency, regular, self-management and constitutional courts). These were sovereign within their own formally widely established competences. Individuals had the right to original citizenship in their republics, on the basis of which they also automatically assumed Yugoslav citizenship. Furthermore, the republics had certain competences in the field of international co-operation and defence.

In the 1974 constitution, only the Yugoslav nations were considered directly as founding members of the Federation. Other nationalities (national minorities) were referred to only indirectly, as when, besides the republics, the two autonomous provinces of the Republic of Serbia (Kosovo and Vojvodina) were also classified as the constitutive elements of the federation. Formally, the Federation was distinctly decentralized. In practice, however, Yugoslavia was rather more centralized than anticipated by the constitutional system. It was the actual political and social role of two key centripetal factors that made this possible: the personal authority and reputation of President Tito, and the social influence and role of the leadership of the League of Communists of Yugoslavia in the processes of political life and decision-making.

Certain specific features in the treatment and regulation of inter-ethnic relations began to appear in the constitutions of the individual republics and provinces. The provision of ethnic rights (particularly those pertaining to national minorities), were designed to ensure the existence and development of ethnic pluralism in individual communities. Thus the constitution of the Socialist Republic of Slovenia (1974), in a special sub-chapter dealing with human rights, classified the special rights of the Italian and Hungarian nationalities, which ensure and regulate their existence and integral national development, their partaking in the political system, and the responsibility of the republic for the implementation of these special rights.

The constitutions of the Autonomous Provinces of Kosovo and Vojvodina in the Republic of Serbia determined that nations and nationalities are equal in their rights and duties, and were guaranteed the right of expression and development of their own language, culture and history and their ethnic characteristics, the right to national symbols, the official use of their national language, etc.

Different concepts of development began to manifest themselves, particularly in 1988, in the discussions concerning the adoption of constitutional amendments to the 1974 constitution. When the political scene became more pluralistic, particularly in Slovenia, this caused sharp reactions in the political summit of the Federation and, above all, in the southeastern parts of Yugoslavia. The changes to the constitution of the Republic of Slovenia, adopted in 1989, in which the political opposition co-operated, laid the groundwork for political pluralism and multi-party elections. The normative part of the constitution of the Republic of Slovenia, which included the provision on 'the permanent, all-embracing and inalienable right of the Slovene nation to self-determination, including the right of secession and union', provoked considerable indignation in the rest of Yugoslavia. This constitutional provision represented the basis for the full emancipation of Slovenia only three years later. The Italian and Hungarian nationalities are ensured (irrespective of the number of their members) at least one representative in each chamber of the Assembly of the Republic as well as adequate representation in the assemblies of the communities, populated by their members.

In December 1990, a new constitution was also adopted by the Republic of Croatia, which regulated the basis for the introduction of a multi-party presidential political system. However, it failed to bring any new provisions related directly to inter-ethnic relations within the republic. These relations deteriorated seriously in 1991 and resulted finally in armed struggle – civil war. Only during the war did the Croatian parliament finally pass the constitutional law on human rights and freedoms and the rights of national minorities in Croatia. Apart from certain asserted minority rights (language, cultural development, education), minorities are given the right of cultural autonomy as well as their proportional representation in elected political bodies. The possibility of the founding of communities and regions with special autonomous status is also foreseen. The law is not likely to contribute to the resolution of the worst ethnic conflict in Croatia so far, because the Serbs, having demanded political autonomy of the Serbian Krajine (regions) are dissatisfied with it. The Serbs seem actually to have obtained more benefits through the armed struggle.

Language issues have been another major contributing element to ethnic tensions and conflicts in Yugoslavia. The national census includes 28 different nationalities reflecting the extreme variety of the ethnic composition of the former Yugoslavia. The fact that the number of ethnic groups does not match the number of languages represents an additional element of this complex situation: on the one hand, four Yugoslav nations shared a common standard language (Serbo-Croat) with two alphabets (Cyrillic and Roman), and on the other, there are several linguistic islands.

Yugoslavia has always been an historic crossroads between West and East, a situation which is reflected in the level of socio-economic and cultural development of the individual ethnic groups, as well as in the development and the course of language planning of individual languages. The search for a standard written form for some languages took place at the same time that the peoples who spoke these languages developed into modern nations at the end of the nineteenth and the beginning of the twentieth centuries (Serbo-Croat, Slovene). The written form of other languages was decided upon only recently. Thus, for instance, the first grammar of Macedonian was prepared only after the Second World War. The Albanians agreed upon the features of a common standard Albanian language only around 1970; and the languages of some ethnic groups have not yet fully developed a standard written form (Valacs) or are just on the way to developing one (Romany/Gypsy). From the point of view of language policy, and especially from the point of view of planning language status, this historically conditioned variance in the development of individual languages has had a considerable influence on the realization of linguistic rights foreseen in political declarations and legal documents.

The sociolinguistic features noted above demonstrate the significant role of language policy in Yugoslavia as an indivisible component of Yugoslav policy towards inter-ethnic relations. Inter-nation relations played an important role from the very establishment of Yugoslavia as a sovereign state. After all, the very reason for the creation of a multinational state after the First World War was the aspirations of the nations it united to safeguard and develop their national (ethnic, cultural and linguistic) characteristics. In the multi-cultural and multi-linguistic reality of Yugoslavia, however, the question of how to achieve harmonious coexistence among different ethnic groups was given different answers in different periods. At the beginning of the newly created state, the regulation of relations among the languages of the three constituent nations – Croats, Serbs and Slovenes – was the most pressing question. Owing to their ethnic similarity, these three nations were considered merely three tribes of one nation.

Language policy in fact reflected the centralist conception of the Yugoslav state at the time, and a theory in which the concept of nation was closely related to the concept of language was accepted as a basic premiss. Hence the four modern nations which spoke Serbo-Croat in common were considered only one nation. The Slovenes with their own language were supposed to merge sooner or later into the single emerging Yugoslav nation, while Macedonian was considered either a Serbian or a

Bulgarian dialect, depending on the nationality of the linguists who analysed its structure. The smouldering conflict between Croats and Serbs on the linguistic issue was only aggravated by such a policy. The basic premiss of the Serbo-Croat norm, set out by a group of pan-Slavic-oriented linguists in 1850 in the so-called Vienna Agreement, that the Serbian and Croatian languages were but two varieties of a common language, suited the official centralist policy very well.

Subsequent historical experience contributed to the evolution of the national question in Yugoslavia, and step by step, the principle of the equality of nations and ethnic groups was introduced. On the rhetorical level, cultural and linguistic differences in Yugoslavia were considered a source of enrichment for the development of each ethnic group and of all of them together. Cultural pluralism became the basic principle of inter-ethnic relations in Yugoslavia, and 'unity in diversity' was proclaimed as a common goal and value. Such an approach was intended to eliminate both ethnic stratification and assimilation, and was thought to bring about equal opportunities of social promotion to members of minority and majority nationalities, regardless of their ethnic origin. Linguistic pluralism, of course, represents a salient component of cultural pluralism. The role of languages was based on the equality of relations among the various ethnic groups, with the language of each serving as the means of a group member's involvement in all social processes.

The language policy model in Yugoslavia was a directive one with an admixture of self-management features. Yugoslavia was among those multi-lingual states which based their language policy on the territorial principle, but in addition respected the right of an individual to maintain and use his or her mother tongue. This right was safeguarded for the individual, for example, in judicial processes, regardless of whether the individual's mother tongue was an official language in the area where the trial was being held. On the other hand, the languages of nations and ethnic groups were accorded the status of official languages in the regions inhabited by them.

The territorial principle also meant developing a system of institutional support to enable any ethnic group's language to function on equal terms with the majority language in all channels of public communication, both official and unofficial. The territorial principle relative to languages in public communication required an agreement on the status and use of individual languages in communication between different subjects on both the local and wider socio-political levels. For the sake of analysis, three levels of language contact and relations among the languages of Yugoslav nations and ethnic groups could be observed:

1. The first is the level of relations and contacts of languages and alphabets of Yugoslav nations and ethnic groups as subjects of sociopolitical entities. This sphere comprised communication on the federal level, communication between federal institutions and republics and/or autonomous provinces, and direct communication between republics/autonomous provinces.

2. The second was the level of relations and contacts between languages of Yugoslav nations and of autochthonous ethnic groups in the territory they inhabited. This is the level of republics and autonomous provinces, but in fact the bulk of these relations were actualized and realized at the district level, where the actual interaction and communication between members of a majority and a minority was a matter of everyday life and work.

3. The third level can be designated as the level of contact between the language of a nation and the languages of migratory members of nations and national minorities from other republics or autonomous provinces.

The equality of a language, however, is judged by the extent of its social function, which in turn depends on the degree of its use as a means of communication in social intercourse. For example, the Slovenes and Macedonians struggled to ensure that their languages had equal access with Serbo-Croat to all channels of social communication within the framework of the Yugoslav federation. Besides having an exclusive status for communication with socio-political organs at the federal level, in practice Serbo-Croat held the status of the state language. Although this role was not granted formally to Serbo-Croat, it was used in public communication even in Slovene and Macedonian linguistic territory.

With the constitution of 1974, however, Serbo-Croat acquired an absolute position. In spite of formally regulated relations among languages of the Yugoslav nations, there were misunderstandings and conflicts even after 1974. The question of the language of command in the army remained open. On the other hand, the resolution of the Serbo-Croat linguistic dilemma was far from settled. All the Yugoslav constitutions from 1946 to 1974 dealt with the linguistic situation and the status of languages in Yugoslavia. In the 1963 constitutions, the language of the four nations is called 'Serbo-Croat' in the constitutions of Bosnia-Herzegovina and of Serbia, as well as in Montenegro, but it is called 'Croato-Serbian' in the constitution of Croatia. The 1974 constitutions spoke of 'Serbo-Croat' in Serbia, while in Croatia it was referred to as the 'Croatian literary language – the standard form of the national language of Croats and Serbs living in Croatia, which is called Croatian or Serbian'. In Bosnia-Herzegovina it was 'Serbo-Croat' or 'Croato-Serbian', while the constitution of Montenegro did not refer to an official language at all.

These expressions reflect the apparent regulation of the status and use of both versions of Serbo-Croat, which was defined as the common literary language according to the 1850 Vienna Agreement and again in the 1954 Novi Sad Agreement. But for many, the idea of two versions of the Serbo-Croat literary language is contentious. While many Serbian linguists and writers deny it, a fear prevailed on the Croatian side that the Serbian version of Serbo-Croat was being imposed on public communication. The fear of one version predominating is particularly acute in Bosnia-Herzegovina, where the linguistic situation is by far the most complex. After a heated debate at the 1965 Congress of Yugoslav Slavists, the conflict sharpened, and in 1966 the Declaration on the Name and Status of the Croatian Language, demanding the consistent name and use of Croatian in schools, press, public and political life, was published in Zagreb, signed by some 140 Croatian intellectuals, including members of the Central Committee of the League of Communists of Croatia, as well as by 18 Croatian cultural and scientific institutions.

This attempt to distinguish was termed nationalistic and suppressed through a strong political campaign (many members of the Communist Party were expelled or otherwise punished). While in Serbia and Croatia the language problem was pushed into the background, in Bosnia-Herzegovina the concept of linguistic tolerance, equality and the naming of both language versions began to emerge in the 1970s.

In the hope of becoming a more efficient and more just state than the 'old' Yugoslavia, socialist Yugoslavia also attempted to modernize and transform its educational system. In doing so, it inevitably had to encounter the problem of national diversity. Since it based its own political organization on a federal framework, the Yugoslav state therefore also attempted to decentralize education. However, the most pronounced trait of the educational system was its strict control by the ideological centre. Centralism and uniformity in the content of the curriculum overshadowed the flexibility and decentralization of the system. The integrative role of (dogmatic) Marxist ideology implied a supernational ideological linking of the Yugoslav people, which entailed no understanding for the fuller expression of national diversity and feelings.

The right to education in one's mother tongue was guaranteed by the 1974 constitution to all peoples and nationalities (national minorities) as an expression of their equality within the Yugoslav federation (article 171). Since there was no common language in official use in Yugoslavia, all languages had equal status in all the federal units, which at the same time meant that members of each and every people or nationality – in every republic, province or municipality in which they lived – had the right to education in their own language. Nevertheless, although the Law on Education and Instruction in the Languages of Nationalities regulated the rights of members of the nationalities (i.e. national minorities) to education, there were no special regulations in regard to the schooling of members of the six constitutive South Slavic peoples (Croats, Macedonians, Montenegrins, Muslims, Slovenes and Serbs) living outside their 'mother' republics.

In other words, members of any constitutive Yugoslav nation, if they lived outside their 'mother' state (republic) had the formal right to be educated in their mother tongue and to be taught about their national cultures, but in fact, generally, they had little opportunity to enjoy this right. By 'forgetting' the various constitutent nations, in a certain sense, the ruling elite considered itself as supranational (yet it was selected according to specific 'national criteria') as it attempted to educate towards Yugoslavism, and not towards national communities, to suppress particular national feelings and to develop a certain type of supernational identity (Yugoslavism as a meta-nationality). One of the possible indicators of the results of this educational practice was the increase in the number of individuals who declared their nationality as 'Yugoslav'. According to the 1971 census, there were only 273 000 Yugoslav 'nationals', but in 1981 their number had increased to 1 220 000. This may be the result of an amalgamation, of the use of Yugoslav as a useful identification for social promotion, of close identification with the 'Yugoslav dream', or else resistance to the fragmentation of Yugoslavia, but it also may be an artifact of the educational system.

The so-called common Yugoslav programme core in the school system was a means to this end. The creation of the so-called common programme core and the strengthening 'Yugoslav socialist patriotism' within a unified educational system was the result of the tenth Congress of the League of Communists of Yugoslavia in 1974. Although that year was marked by the passing of a constitution which led to the decentralization of the federation, in this context it was also a period of repression in regard to national movements and demands for pluralism after the so-called 'Croatian Spring' of 1971. The 'Proposal' for a common core in pre-school education and elementary instruction, and the 'common foundations in education', was realized at the beginning of the 1980s, but was never fully harmonized (not even after several years of debate and despite pressure exerted during the subsequent party congresses). This Yugoslav project provoked a series of reactions, with the fiercest opposition in regard to the 'programme core' in the language–arts domain. Fear was expressed in relation to the domination of content from the Serbo-Croat language. It was felt that this would make members of smaller nations feel inferior, due to relatively less attention being given to their cultures. In a 1986 Memorandum of the Serbian Academy of Science and Arts, Serbian politicians and academics complained about language and cultural discrimination in Croatia, a posture that furthered the mobilization of Serbian ethnic ideology in later years.

Another conflict in the educational sphere took place between the Albanian nation and the Serbian government, and this is not unrelated to the ethnic conflict in Kosovo. In fact, one of the roots of the conflict were the measures taken by the Serbian authorities to introduce changes in the education of Albanians in Kosovo, particularly a change of the teaching programme in the Albanian language and the introduction of a unified programme and unified textbooks in all of Serbia (translated into the languages of the 'nationalities'), as well as the reduction of the number of places in secondary schools reserved for Albanians in Kosovo. These restrictions were obviously intended to counteract the drive towards affirmation of the minority national identity. The Albanians have had a long history of such pressures, so that one might find in their educational situation one of the causes of the ethnic conflict in Kosovo.

In 1918, all Albanian schools had been closed. In later years, it was possible to be educated only in Serbian, but when this proved to be an inadequate method of assimilation, the authorities limited education only to the religious sphere, where it was carried out by Muslim imams and Catholic priests. It was believed that this 'would keep the Albanians behind and ignorant'. An especially difficult phase (also in regard to education) was experienced by the Albanians in Socialist Yugoslavia between 1948 and 1966 (many schools were closed due to a 'lack of personnel', the work of cultural institutions was forbidden). After 1966, educational and cultural activities began to flourish in Kosovo, but after the disturbances of 1981 a new period of pressure on Albanian 'nationality' began. The present state of education of Albanians in Kosovo makes education at the same time both a cause and consequence of ethnic conflict.

Closely related to the problems which were being faced by their own ethnic groups or nations, the religious communities in the former Yugoslavia often became involved in disputes and conflicts. Indeed, they sometimes played a not unimportant role in the formation of ethnic identities and the accession to independent status (including state independence) by the various peoples in this area. So it is not surprising that ethnic differences overlap with religious distinctions. While it should not be claimed that religions actually 'created' nations or ethnicities, yet in a given historical period they acted as a type of cultural cohesive factor, or one of the constitutive elements of nation-formation.

It should be remembered that in the Balkan area, for historical reasons, three great Mediterranean traditions have come into contact: Roman Catholicism, Eastern Christian Orthodoxy and Sunni Islam. Professing the faith of one of these religions was usually of crucial importance for the cultural and political content of a given nationality. In a certain sense, the Balkans were a 'frontier', and to a certain degree they have remained so.

It can be argued that religion played a role in the ethnonational formation and differentiation of the 'central' South Slavic space, i.e. the territory of the 'Croato-Serbian dialect system', among most Croats, Bosnian Muslims and Serbs. This was especially so, according to some opinions, on the territory of Bosnia and Herzegovina, populated today mainly by Croats, Muslims and Serbs, which in a certain sense represents the core area of the 'frontier'. It seems that the role of the religious-cultural factor was significantly less in the fringe areas of the former Yugoslav territory, i.e. in regions were linguistic-cultural specificities were more crucial – in other words among Albanians, Macedonians and Slovenes.

The religious and ethnic mosaic of the Balkans is in many respects unique. Many peoples, cultures and religions meet in a relatively small territory. Throughout the centuries the major conflicts based on religion occurred between Islam and Christianity on the one hand, and Christian Orthodoxy and Catholicism, on the other hand.

As is generally the case in Orthodox Christianity – namely, that it expressly binds itself to an ethnic group – so it was in the case of the Serbian Orthodox Church. After the Serbian people lost their national independence during the Ottoman occupation in the sixteenth century, the national Orthodox Church (later renewed by the Turks themselves in 1557), attempted to overcome this loss by blurring the distinction between state and Church. The Patriarchate of Pec, based on the millet (or indirect rule) system during the Turkish occupation, combined the roles of religious and national (secular) leaders of the Serbian people. When the Turks suppressed the Patriarchate of Pec once more (in 1766), the Serbian religious-national centre had already been transferred to southern Hungary. During that period there were also strong Serbian and 'Vlach' migrations to the west and to the north, and these movements came to have an influence on the formation of the ethnic picture of the whole area. The millet system, which the Serbs, in a fashion, transplanted to the Hapsburg

Monarchy, was a great instrument for the spread of Serb national identity in the western Balkans. Wherever they exercised jurisdiction, Serbian church organizations promoted Serb nationhood.

To the extent that Catholicism, in distinction to Orthodoxy, views man not only through his ethnic and cultural specificity, but fundamentally through his human universality, it may be argued that the Catholic Church could not be nearly so 'national' – neither among Croats, nor among Slovenes.

Islam is the third religion in the South Slavic area. It is important to note its decisive role in the national, ethno-cultural formation of the Bosnian Muslims. However, in this case, the interconnection between religion and the nation has come to be crystallized in the very ethnonym, which for many years was a cause of disputes and stress. Besides the ethnonational Muslims of Bosnia (and the Sanjak), the greater part of the Kosovo Albanians also profess the Islamic faith.

In summary, the main contemporary focal points of tension in the Balkans in which religion (or rather, the Church) is significantly involved, are the following:

1. between Serbian Orthodoxy and Croatian Catholicism;
2. between Serbian Orthodoxy and Islam (the Kosovo Albanians and the ethnic Muslims in Sanjak and Bosnia and Herzegovina);
3. between Serbian Orthodxy and Macedonian Orthodoxy;
4. between Serbian Orthodoxy and Montenegrin Orthodoxy.

They may be considered focal points of tension or conflict, to the extent that the Serbian Orthodox Church can be said to entertain more or less veiled aspirations of supporting the realization of the idea of a Greater Serbia ('where there is a Serbian church, here is also Serbian land'). The fact that the Serbian Orthodox Church and the Great Serbian political programme have quite successfully made use of religious-mythical symbols (Saint Sava, the Kosovo myth) in the ethnic mobilization and homogenization of 'Serbianism' at the end of the 1980s and the beginning of the 1990s probably stems from the circumstance that the Balkan area still has many of the traits of a relatively closed traditionalist and agrarian society. In other words, religion in closed agrarian societies seems to have a greater role in ethnomobilization than in industrial Western societies.

6. SENEGAL

Senegal, on the coast of west Africa, is a linguistic and religious mosaic. Islam and Christianity, as well as a number of other religions with fewer followers than the former, have coexisted here since colonial times. Since gaining political independence from France in the early 1960s, Senegal's democratic politics have not been interrupted by military coups or civil wars. Despite regional and linguistic differences among the population, no major conflicts have shattered the polity, although a number of lesser ethnic conflicts do exist.

The country's intellectual elites, mostly French-educated, are justly proud of their tradition of multi-ethnic and multi-cultural national integration. According to Makhtar Diouf, the factors explaining national integration in Senegal are several: social and cultural structures, the impact of the Wolof language, inter-ethnic marriages and relationships, the importance of the cosmpolitan capital city of Dakar, and the policies of Senegal's first president, Léopold Sedar Senghor.

Senegal's various population groups speak 15 different languages, which are classified by specialists into two major linguistic families, the West-Atlantic and the Mande groups. However, Wolof is considered the major vehicular idiom in the country, and it has become widely used in recent years, to such an extent that it is possible to speak of a process of 'Wolofization'. The reason for the hegemony of Wolof is that the first European colonial contacts took place in Wolof-speaking areas, thus establishing a privileged position for Wolof speakers in trade and dealings between the native population and the early Portuguese and later French colonialists. Wolof became associated with the expansion of the groundnut economy introduced by the French. As the principal native language, Wolof enjoyed a special statute during colonial times. The use of Wolof as a 'national' language has been considered a factor of 'ethnic peace' in the country.

In contrast to some other African cities which have a distinct original ethnic population Dakar soon became a mixture of ethnic groups coming from the rest of the country, so that today at least 90 per cent of the city's population is made up of immigrant ethnic groups. This urban environment also encourages inter-ethnic marriages, particularly among the middle classes.

Religion seems to be another stabilizing factor. Islam, which is professed by almost 95 per cent of the population, was established in Senegal almost a thousand years ago. It superseded the animistic religions which distinguished the various ethnic groups, by universalizing a monotheistic creed. The structure of Islam in Senegal has permeated economic and social life in the country for centuries. Four major brotherhoods, or confrèries, each led by a respected religious leader known as Khalif or Marabout, controlled most of the population in such a way that religious or ethnic conflict became almost impossible.

A fairly rigid and widely accepted caste system permeates Senegalese society. Caste membership is mainly occupational and crosscuts ethnic identification. Only one caste is coterminous with an ethnic group; in all other cases people from different ethnies belong to the various castes. And caste consciousness appears to be a much stronger factor of social identification than ethnic criteria. Caste differences are more prone to generate conflict than ethnic distinctions, and caste conflicts have in fact occurred more than once in the country's recent history. Not even the universal monotheistic creed of Islam has been able to diminish the importance of caste and caste consciousness in Senegal.

During the colonial period, the Senegalese were divided into two political-administrative sectors: the population of the 'four communes' (Dakar, Gorée, Saint-Louis, Rufisque), who were granted French citizenship, and the Protectorate of the interior, whose population had obligations but hardly any rights. The inhabitants of the protectorate were discriminated against by the colonial system in several ways, notably in the administration of justice, taxes and their place in the army. While the citizens of the four communes were mainly of Lebu and Wolof ethnic origin, the distinction between citizens and subjects was not strictly maintained along ethnic lines. The four communes did not become ethnic enclaves, and members of different ethnies as well as people from other parts of Africa were in fact able to integrate in these urban centres. On the other hand, a large majority of Wolof are also concentrated in the groundnut-producing areas, which belonged in colonial times to the protectorate. The population of the protectorate has harboured resentments against the privileged position of the citizens of the four communes, but these feelings did not develop into expressions of ethnic animosity.

In contrast to some other African countries (e.g. Nigeria), in Senegal political parties are not ethnically based. While the country's political system was formally democratic, for many years a single official party dominated the political scene, and observers pointed to numerous cases of electoral fraud. The governing elite, however, was careful not to concentrate power in the hands of a single ethnic group nor to exclude different ethnic groups from participation in the political process. A new electoral law adopted in 1991 heralded a period of renewed democratization. The concept of national unity, bolstered by an early commitment of the Senegalese leaders to the ideal of Pan-Africanism, also became a powerful integrating force. A survey of African students in the 1960s (many of whom belong to today's political and economic elites) indicated that Senegalese students had a higher degree of identification with a general African identity than those of other African countries.

Senegal is a pioneer in African trade union organization. From the 1920s, Senegalese rail workers – regardless of ethnic origin – were engaged in labour struggles. The Pan-African labour movement received strong support in Senegal; it struggled not only for the traditional rights and demands of the workers, but also against racism and discrimination and for national independence.

After independence, the Senegalese government attempted to accommodate the different ethnic groups of the country. President Senghor, who belonged to a minority ethnic group and a minority religion (Christianity), handled ethnic problems with great prudence. The country's first political constitution, which guarantees a multi-party regime, nevertheless prohibits parties from becoming identified with any religion, race, sect, ethnie, language or region. To prevent linguistic conflict, French was made the official language and Diola, Malinke, Pular, Serer, Soninke and Wolof were declared to be national languages. These national languages are used in radio and television broadcasts and are taught in schools and literacy campaigns. In order to prevent the proliferation of official languages, the government actually removed a number of minority languages such as Bambara, Mankagn, Manjak, Basari, Ndut, Safen and others, from official protection. Even so some are still occasionally used in radio broadcasts. While Wolof could have been declared the country's official language, given its status as principal vehicular language, this was never attempted to avoid offending minority groups.

Despite a fairly successful policy of national integration over the years since independence, Senegal has not escaped ethnic tensions and conflicts, albeit of a relatively minor nature compared to some other countries in Africa covered by the UNRISD study. Since colonial times, tensions existed between the Peul livestock herders and the Wolof and Sereer farmers, which at times became violent. Conflicts over resources between pastoralists and agriculturalists are of course widespread, and Senegal is not unique in this. To the extent that the populations who practise these two distinct ways of life are also distinguished in ethnic terms, the conflict takes on at times an ethnic aspect. During the 1940s, the Peul organized to struggle for their common interests, mainly the maintenance of their traditional herding grounds and the pastoralist way of life, but they also included the preservation of their culture and customs which were being endangered. However, specific socio-economic objectives overrode any ethnic-cultural demands, and soon the organization became known as the Movement of Senegalese Cattle-raisers, with no reference to their Peul ethnicity.

A much more serious ethnic conflict has arisen around the separatist demands of political groups in the region of Casamance, which occupies about 15 per cent of the country's area (the size of Belgium) and has about an equal proportion of the total population. Political demands for independence met with strong repressive measures by the central government, and since 1990 incidents of violence have multiplied. Serious human rights violations (imprisonment, refugees, torture, killings, summary executions) were noted by international human rights organizations such as Amnesty International. The policy of repression by the central government, in the name of national security and national unity, has only furthered adherence to the separatist movement in Casamance, mainly fostered by the Joola ethnie, who make up about 32 per cent of the region's population.

The Casamance issue, as in the southern Sudan, seems to be more of a regional problem rather than a strictly ethnic conflict. In 1984, the central government proceeded to divide the Casamance region into two new administrative units, within the framework of a country-wide administrative reform. This redrawing of the map did not, however, dampen the spirits of the separatist movement nor the regionalist sentiments of the population, who had always identified with Casamance as a distinct entity, having a particular history within the larger Senegal. To stop the further spread of violence, in 1991, the parties in conflict agreed to participate in political negotiations, the government released several hundred political detainees and decreed a general amnesty.

7. CONCLUSION

It should be clear from the foregoing that the nature of ethnic conflicts, as well as their dynamics and intensity, can be traced back to the relationship between the state and the different ethnies that make up a country's population. We have made this point on several occasions in this book. The resources of the state have increasingly become the focus of competition between ethnic groups. The post-colonial state is frequently controlled by a dominant ethnie, a situation which provokes the political reaction of other excluded ethnies and which may lead to accommodation or conflict according to particular circumstances.

The policies that states have implemented to deal with such situations are many and may vary over time. Sometimes different policies are carried out simultaneously or sequentially to deal with conflicting and changing situations. A simple scheme of such policies would give us three major prototypes: (1) assimilation or incorporation; (2) exclusion; and (3) pluralism.

1. Assimilation or incorporation

Assimilationist policies have probably been the most common approach used by states to deal with ethnic diversity within their borders. Assimilation occurs when there is a dominant model of what constitutes a nation, usually furthered by a strong nationalist ideology, and when specific measures are adopted with the purpose of incorporating members of distinct ethnic groups who do not originally conform to this model, into the mould of what is defined as the 'nation'.

For many decades, assimilation was the avowed objective of the process of national integration in the United States. It was assumed that the multitude of immigrant groups who came from all over the world would within a generation or two become fully 'Americanized' and conform to the dominant model characterized as WASP (White, Anglo-Saxon, Protestant). This has been described as *Angloconformity*.[1] More popularly, the process has often been referred to as the 'melting pot', the idea being that immigrant groups would progressively lose their cultural distinctiveness and identity and take on a new national identity as 'Americans'. The principal vehicle for this transformation were the schools, but an important role was to be played by the occupational structure, the electoral system, the mass media and in general, the rather fuzzy domain of 'changing values'. To a great extent the assimilationist model has been highly successful in the United States over the decades, though some ethnic groups have had a more difficult time in becoming assimilated than others (African Americans, Native Americans, Hispanics, Orientals), and critics have pointed out that it worked best with European immigrants who were already culturally closer to the early colonial settlers from northwest Europe.

In recent years the 'melting pot' ideology has come under critical scrutiny, and observers point out that US society more closely resembles a 'salad bowl'. Indeed, *E pluribus unum* (unity in diversity), the national motto of the United States, derives from Virgil's description of a vegetable salad.[2] Now ethnic diversity is celebrated among many sectors of US society and the earlier assimilationist model has been widely criticized. The widespread debate over assimilation versus multi-culturalism is one of the crucial elements of the 'culture wars' being fought in the United States, with implications for all aspects of the social and political system (education, politics, the legal system, the labour market, etc.).

Assimilation has also been the stated objective of government policies related to the indigenous peoples in most Latin American countries for the better part of this century. In the 1940s a continental state-sponsored ideology of *indigenismo* set about to develop policies designed to 'integrate' the Indians (indigenous populations) into the national society, through processes of accelerated and directed culture change.[3] Thus, vernacular indigenous languages were shunted aside in favour of the official Spanish or Portuguese. The school system was charged with the task of turning the Indian peasantries into 'useful citizens' of their countries. Local customs and social structures were disparaged and 'national' values were thrust upon the indigenous communities. Even in countries such as Guatemala, in which the indigenous Maya peoples make up more than half the total population, the dominant model of the nation-state ignored and rejected the Indian cultures as less than adequate in the process of building a modern nation. In Latin America, as elsewhere, the virtues of governmental assimilationist policies are being challenged by critics and, foremost, by indigenous organizations themselves. Alternative policies are hotly debated in official and unofficial circles, and regional conferences of many kinds have formulated the need for new approaches.

In the countries included in the UNRISD study, the most notorious example of the assimilationist ideal as process and policy is the situation of the Kurdish people in Turkey, who are officially referred to as 'Mountain Turks'. The state has long pursued a policy of 'Turkification', just as in Iraq and Syria governments have occasionally pursued a policy of 'Arabization' and in Iran one of 'Persianization' of their respective Kurdish populations. In the process, the Kurds have had to struggle to maintain their language, culture and identity as a distinct people.

Official assimilationist measures undertaken by the Sudanese state are likewise at the root of the protracted ethnic conflict in southern Sudan. The central government's attempt to impose the Islamic shariah law on the southern non-Islamic peoples, as well as the tendency of 'Sudanization' of the civil service, were among the factors triggering the first southern uprising in 1964, followed by a negotiated agreement in 1972 which lasted for a decade, only to lead to subsequent renewed fighting in the early 1980s.

The grievances of the various minority groups (Eritrea, Ogaden, Oromo, Tigrai) who fought the military dictatorship in Ethiopia for many years likewise resulted from resistance to the assimilationist policies pursued by the central government, such as its attempt to impose Amharigna (the tongue of the dominant minority) as the national official language.

John Markakis points out that in both Ethiopia and Sudan the purpose of state policy was a campaign of 'national integration', intended to eliminate cultural differences which were perceived to be the cause of dissidence. Not surprisingly, what the ruling groups in Ethiopia and Sudan perceived as the 'national' identity was their own ethnic identity writ large. Accordingly, Christianity and Amharigna became the hallmark of Ethiopian nationalism, Islam and Arabic of Sudanese nationalism. National integration, therefore, was premissed on assimilation. Not surprisingly also, this premiss was rejected by other ethnic groups, and when the regimes sought to impose it by force, it became a potent source of alienation and a great boost for dissident movements.

The Albanians of the region of Kosovo have been the object of various attempts of more or less forced assimilation by the Serbian state, before, during and after the existence of communist Yugoslavia. The tension between the Albanian population in this province and the Serbian government led to disturbances in 1981. After the break-up of the Yugoslav federation in the early 1990s the situation deteriorated even further.

When assimilation is a natural process, so to speak, such as that of voluntary immigrant groups in a host society, particularly when the cultural distinctions between immigrants and natives are not large, then it may be viewed as a positive factor in social integration and national cohesion. However, when the assimilation of a minority (or majority) by a dominant nation or nationality is the specific objective of state policy carried out without the consent of the target group, then the seeds of discord and dissidence may be sown. This is particularly the case when assimilationist policies are implemented by force or bureaucratic coercive measures. For example, when a native language may not be taught in schools or spoken in public; when traditional ethnic place names must be changed or when family names are 'nationalized' by government decree. (This happened, for example, in Romania and Bulgaria during the communist period.) Assimilationist state policies are perceived as particularly burdensome on non-immigrant native populations or territorial minorities whose right to local or regional identity precedes the overriding claims of the nation-state.

The merits and demerits of assimilationist policies are currently widely debated in different forums. There is no lack of arguments in favour of assimilation, the basic one being the plea for 'national unity' in the face of what some perceive to be the dangerous centrifugal and disintegrating forces associated with ethnic and cultural diversity. As 'nation-builders' have long known, a common language, a standardized school system, a homogeneous legal system, an integrated bureaucracy, among other elements, are powerful weapons in the development of modern states, and were no doubt essential in the early stages of the post-agrarian economy.

On the other hand, the heavy-handed state-building that has taken place in so many parts of the world in recent decades (let alone in nineteenth-century Europe) can best be described, as Walker Connor pointed out many years ago, as a process of 'nation-destroying',[4] because on the ground of the modern state and the ideology of nationalism many peoples with their own distinct cultures and identities, histories and traditions have been ploughed under so that new nations might sprout. Consequently, whereas assimilationist policies may look attractive from the perspective of the national state, they frequently look less than satisfactory to the peoples at whom these policies are directed.

2. Exclusion

Exclusionary ethnic politics may take many forms. The most extreme policy of ethnic exclusion is genocide, an international crime according to the Convention on the Prevention and Punishment of the Crime of Genocide, adopted by the General Assembly of the United Nations in 1948. The worst case of genocide in modern times (and which gave rise to the term itself as a new concept in international law) was the intended extermination of the entire Jewish people by Nazi Germany (the Holocaust). Other instances of genocide have been perpetrated in history (some indigenous peoples in the Americas in the nineteenth century; the Turkish genocide of the Armenians during the First World War, the genocide of the Herero tribe in South West Africa by the German colonial army in 1904). Genocide is not always a stated government objective, but may be perpetrated by one ethnic group on another with the connivance or tacit approval of government. Other policies may be akin to genocide though they are not to be labelled as such. The 'ethnic cleansing' carried out by the Serbs and Croats against the Muslims in the framework of the war in Bosnia-Herzegovina has been widely regarded as falling within the scope of the Genocide Convention.

Among the countries covered by the UNRISD study, Burundi has been the scenario of the genocidal killings of Hutu populations by the dominant Tutsi ethnie on several occasions between the 1960s and 1980s. While not necessarily the outcome of specific state policies, ethnic massacres and pogroms within the framework of ethnic conflicts are widespread phenomena. Their purpose may be to eliminate the political or cultural leadership of the victimized ethnic group, to wreak revenge for real or imagined offences, to repress an insurrection or uprising (this sparked the killings in Burundi in 1972, the massacres of Igbos in the Nigerian civil war in the 1960s, the pogroms against Tamils in Sri Lanka in the mid-1980s), or to terrorize the targeted group into submission and passivity.

Whereas genocidal massacres of one kind or another are more widespread than is generally assumed, the Genocide Convention has never been invoked by the United Nations against any state.[5] The International War Crimes Tribunal set up by the UN in 1995 to investigate such crimes in Bosnia and Rwanda is the first crack in a long-standing taboo.

Still, physical genocide of an ethnic group is less common than what is sometimes called cultural genocide, also known as ethnocide. This refers to state policies designed to destroy the cultural identity of a group through various kinds of coercive measures such as forced religious conversion, destruction of cultural monuments and sites, land expropriations, massive relocation of populations, imposition of a new language, etc. Often coercive assimilationist policies are in fact forms of cultural genocide. Indigenous and tribal peoples around the world, who are particularly weak and vulnerable in the face of more powerful societies and technologies, have been victimized in recent decades by policies of ethnocide.

Exclusionary policies may take various other forms. The apartheid system in South Africa constituted an extreme case through which the dominant white minority were able to subjugate the majority native African people for decades. Less rigid forms of segregation exist in other parts of the world. Caste discrimination in south Asia is a traditional form of exclusionary policy, but it would not generally be considered as a form of ethnic discrimination because the caste system belongs to a single cultural area. Still, certain lower castes who are victims of prejudice sometimes are also identified with specific cultural or ethnic characteristics, which set them apart from the rest of society. This is not the case, however, of the Burakumin in Japan who suffer discrimination and prejudice but are not ethnically distinct from the rest of the population. Segregation was long the hallmark of race relations in the United States, where until the 1960s the African-Americans (then called Negroes) suffered severe legal and institutional handicaps. The assimilationist policies which favoured the integration of immigrant groups from Europe did not apply to Black Americans. Even though legal segregation and discrimination has now disappeared in the United States, exclusionary practices are still widespread and observers agree that African-Americans continue to suffer the handicaps and disabilities of various forms of racism and discrimination.

In some countries of Latin America, indigenous people have suffered the indignities of exclusionary policies, by being treated as minors, denied citizenship rights and considered as wards of the state rather than free and equal citizens. True, these policies are sometimes carried out in the name of the protection of vulnerable minorities, but they nevertheless impose severe disabilities on the populations concerned. For example, 'protected' Indians cannot enter into legal contracts, they have no control over their land and resources, they do not enjoy freedom of education, cannot participate in political activities, etc. As a result, Indian organizations have mobilized to struggle for their human rights in recent years, with various degrees of success.[6]

Exclusionary policies have re-emerged in the last few decades, particularly in Western Europe, in relation to immigrants from Asia, the Middle East and Africa. Turks, Arabs, Africans and South Asians are the main objects of restrictive immigration laws as well as the victims of racist activities carried out by right-wing groups (skinheads, neo-Nazis, extreme nationalists, etc.).[7]

3. Pluralism

Despite the widespread occurrence of exclusionist and assimilationist practices, the most common category of ethnic policies are of the pluralist variety. Here we distinguish between pluralism as a sociological fact and pluralism as policy. As a description of the composition of any particular national society, pluralism of course can be said to exist all over the world. Most so-called nation-states are in fact made up of different ethnic groups and therefore can be referred to as plural societies. Colonial and post-colonial societies in particular are frequently identified as plural societies. Specialists have devised all sorts of complex schemata for the classification of different types and degrees of pluralism which need not concern us here.[8]

More to the point for our purpose is pluralism as the stated policy of governments within the framework of a pluralistic society. This means that official policies and practices are generally geared more or less successfully to the accommodation of the diverse and sometimes conflicting interests of the principal ethnic groups. This is most commonly the case when the demographic, political and economic weight of any one ethnie is too important to be ignored by the state or by the other collectivities, and when a particular ethnic group is able to neutralize state policies which it perceives to be contrary to its own interests. Conflict (especially violent conflict) arises when a particular ethnic group ignores such correlations of power and attempts either to impose its own particular ethnic interests on the whole of the national society (ethnocracies) or when, on the contrary, it attempts to wrest state power from others for its own purposes (ethnic insurrections) or to secede from a state in which its own particular interests are not well served (secession, wars of liberation).

Among the countries studied in the UNRISD project, there are numerous plural societies which have attempted different kinds of pluralistic ethnic policies. Malaysia, for example, has struggled for decades with government strategies designed to cope with the undeniable fact that Malaysian society is made up in almost equal proportion of native Malays and Chinese, in addition to a number of smaller ethnic populations. We have already mentioned some of the policies adopted by the Malay government over the years to deal with cultural diversity (some of which might be labelled as assimilationist or even exclusionist). In general, however, the political system has to deal with this bi-polar situation through the electoral process, the application of preferential policies in the civil service, the acceptance of a multi-cultural and multi-lingual educational system, and the recognition that Malaysia can only survive as a multi-ethnic plural society. Malay ethnic forces try to impose an exclusive 'Malay identity' on the nation, whereas the Chinese and other groups favour a 'Malaysian' identity (meaning all the peoples who live in the country). At times during the last few decades Malaysia has been on the brink of major outbreaks of ethnic violence over these issues, but moderate forces on both sides of the ethnic divide have been able to avoid the worst.

Some observers believe that by judicious 'electoral or constitutional engineering' the diverse ethnic interests can be accommodated. Others consider that more than electoral politics is involved and that permanent arrangements to safeguard the interests of the major ethnic groups must be the purpose of a national consensus.

In Guyana the dominant African-Guyanese and Indian-Guyanese communities have faced each other in a virtual political and economic stalemate, but both ethnic communities and their political organizations recognize that Guyana as a state must necessarily come to grips with the reality of its multi-cultural, multi-ethnic composition. The 1992 elections brought to power again after many decades the old Indian-Guyanese leader, Jeddi Jagan, who had been ousted from government by the British in 1956. This event has opened the possibility that Guyana may yet become a democratic, multi-cultural, pluralistic society.

Inter-communal strife in the political arena has also beset the island state of Fiji, particularly after the military coup in 1987 and the rewriting of the Fijian constitution. The native Fijians feel besieged by the Indian Fijians, and these in turn consider themselves to be marginalized and excluded from the political process. Both communities, however, realize that they must live together on a small island; neither can hope to incorporate the other through a process of assimilation, nor can they realistically expect to exclude the other entirely from the polity or the economic system. How Fiji will finally work out this ethnic dilemma is still an open question at the time this book is being written.

Nigeria had to go through a traumatic civil war before it could develop measures by which the political system might effectively deal with ethnic pluralism and diversity. The lack of political democracy makes this task much more difficult, and local and regional ethnic conflicts are quite frequent in the country. Possible future attempts by some group at regional or ethnic secession should not be discounted, though the multiplication of regional administrative units (33 states instead of the earlier three major regions) should discourage such a possibility. Despite linguistic assimilationist policies, Pakistan reognizes ethnic and cultural pluralism within its borders, and pluralistic policies seem to be the only alternative to chronic ethnic violence in Sindh, Karachi and other areas.

Senegal is only one among many African countries which has been able to deal successfully with ethnic and linguistic pluralism. The triumph of the revolution in Ethiopia in 1991 has put the pluralist approach on the table, in contrast to the earlier ethnocratic policies carried out by Haile Selassie and the military regime which succeeded the fall of the emperor.

Likewise, it is hoped that recent negotiations in Burundi will lead to political arrangements between the majority Hutu and the dominant Tutsi within a framework of ethnic and political pluralism. However, the fragility of these efforts became clear once again in the autumn of 1993, when yet another military coup in Burundi led to renewed ethnic violence which produced thousands of victims, and which has continued sporadically well into 1995.

Pluralistic policies may be of two kinds:

1. In the framework of liberal democracies (one citizen, one vote), ethnic differences may be irrelevant to public policy and politics, and ethnic collectivities as such receive no legal or formal recognition of any kind. Here pluralistic policies are of a *laissez-faire* kind in the sense that no particular ethnic group is privileged over any other, and members of all and every ethnic group are endowed with the same rights and prerogatives. This seems to be indeed an ideal situation, but as many students of liberal democracies have observed, it does not work that way in practice. As a result of historical process and socio-economic differentiation (so-called structural factors) even in the most liberal of pluralistic democracies, certain ethnic groups are in fact victims of discrimination, exclusion and marginalization, whereas others find themselves in dominant, superior or privileged positions. As a result, affirmative action or preferential policies are adopted to offset the unequal and/or unjust consequences of the workings of the liberal economy. And affirmative action then becomes what some authors decry as 'affirmative discrimination',[9] that is, certain individuals receive special entitlements because of the supposed historical

disadvantages of the ethnic group they belong to, thus depriving others, who are deemed equally or more meritorious in individual terms, of their rightful due.

In the United States, for example, public opinion is severely divided on the virtues of affirmative action policies first adopted in the late 1960s. Representatives of minorities (Blacks, Hispanics, Native-Americans) strongly support affirmative action and maintain that this is the only means by which they can overcome the historical handicaps they have had to face. Others contend that this 'reverse discrimination' does more harm than good by establishing quotas in education and employment, and that it goes against the grain of the traditional individualistic meritocracy of American society. A strong conservative backlash against affirmative action policies is also present in the United States, which denounces public support for the 'undeserving' and blames the minorities themselves for their predicament.

2. A second policy approach to ethnic diversity consists in explicitly recognizing the existence of ethnic groups and fashioning the political system accordingly. Here it is assumed that the needs, claims and interests of the various ethnic groups will find accommodation through rational and judicious negotiations, as well as the operation of a democratic electoral system with equanimous rules which are scrupulously adhered to by all parties concerned. Again, we can find a variety of pluralist policies which address these issues with varying success under different circumstances.

Affirmative action measures to redress the historical disadvantages of ethnic minorities have already been mentioned in the case of the United States. Other countries, such as India, have adopted similar policies. Among the countries in the UNRISD study, preferential policies have been adopted in Malaysia to favour the native Malay people against what they perceive to be Chinese dominance in the country. The Malay dominated administrative service has worked closely with the Malay political leadership in formulating ethnic preference policies and this, together with the ethnic quota system to ensure Malay dominance in public administration, has given the civil servants a highly political role. Gradually, over the years, Malay political dominance began to be expressed in a wide range of government policies, especially in the appointment of personnel in key policy-making positions in the cabinet, in the civil service, in the armed forces and in the judiciary. The belief that the Malays had special politial rights as the 'sons of the soil' is held by a wide cross-section of Malay elites. In Malaysia, preferential policies go beyond merely redressing historical imbalances (as they do in India, for example, where Harijan untouchables receive preferential treatment); here they help ensure the political dominance of the Malay elites and therefore have contributed to heightening ethnic tensions in the country.

In numerous cases, more than preferential policies are involved. How to consolidate a democratic polity in countries with a long history of ethnic divisions and rivalry continues to be one of the major challenges facing the world today. Arend Lijphart, some years ago, developed the theory of consociational democracy to account for the political arrangements which maintained a certain degree of stability in plural or segmented societies. Lijphart not only used the concept of consociational democracy to interpret a given situation, but he also proposed it as a model to solve ethnic conflicts in ethnically divided states. Basically, he defined consociational democracy in terms of four characteristics. The first and most important element is government by a grand coalition of the political leaders of all significant segments of the plural society. The other elements are the mutual veto or 'concurrent majority' rule, which serves as a protection of vital minority interests; proportionality as the principal standard of political representation, civil service appointments and allocation of public funds; and a high degree of autonomy for each segment to run its own internal affairs.[10]

Lijphart had in mind, among others, several European countries such as Holland, as well as Third World countries such as Lebanon and Malaysia (during specific periods). However, the long civil war in Lebanon between 1975 and 1991, and dramatic conflicts in other countries to which the model has been applied, underline the flaws of the 'consociational democracy' approach. Moreover, the model has been criticized on theoretical and practical grounds by a number of political scientists, among them Donald Horowitz, who questions the validity of the 'grand coalition' of ethnic elites. He rightly points out that in many plural societies it is precisely the tensions, rivalries and struggles between ethnic elites which lead to conflict. Furthermore, says Horowitz, ethnic groups may have different leaders, some of whom might favour a coalition but others not. Thus, there is also intra-ethnic conflict to take into account when political arrangements are devised. As an alternative to consociationalism Horowitz favours what he terms 'the grand settlement' between adversarial ethnic groups, which involves bargaining, reciprocity, give-and-take, in a carefully timed sequential pattern. But as Horowitz himself recognizes, grand settlements and diverse electoral techniques to reduce or solve conflict may work at times but may just as easily fall apart at other times. Upon closer examination, the differences between the 'consociational democracy' and the 'grand settlement' models are more in emphasis than in substance.[11]

More lasting arrangements are sometimes attempted through territorial divisions. Federalism is often proposed as a convenient solution for regional-ethnic conflict, and the case of Nigeria shows that under certain circumstances it does in fact work quite well (particularly after the Biafra war and the increase in the number of states). On the other hand, the federal state of Yugoslavia broke up into its constituent national units with unexpected speed in 1991. Federalism as such is no guarantee for ethnic harmony and accommodation in the absence of other factors. The same can be said about autonomy and devolution, which are sometimes adopted as half-way measures between the unitary and the federal or confederal state.

Regional autonomy has been attempted with varying success in a number of cases. In southern Sudan, autonomy was granted in 1972, but it did not last. The Kurds of Iraq and Syria have at times enjoyed a degree of regional and cultural autonomy, but the basic conflict endures. Democratic Spain, after the Franco dictatorship, has experimented successfully with regional autonomy in Catalonia, the Basque province and other areas. In Nicaragua the indigenous populations of the Atlantic Coast succeeded in obtaining a measure of formal regional autonomy, yet their basic situation in relation to the political centre has not changed appreciably in the few years since the new constitution was adopted in 1987.

Summarizing, what we can learn from a comparative survey is that pluralistic ethnic policies are certainly better for dealing with ethnic conflict than assimilationist or exclusionist policies. But there is a variety of possible pluralistic policies and the effectiveness of any particular policy will depend on a number of specific circumstances.

8 International Dimensions of Ethnic Conflicts

For a long time it was held that ethnic conflicts were to be considered a purely domestic matter and that the international community had no business getting involved in them. During the post-war years, except for conflicts related to the process of decolonization, the United Nations Organization and other international regional organizations were not eager to intervene in what were deemed to be internal matters of member states in good standing. In fact, however, ethnic conflicts the world over have, in most instances, always had an international component. There is hardly a case in which some neighbouring state, or a regional or world power, has not had a hand in some aspect of these conflicts, even when they appear at first glance to be purely 'sub-national' rather than 'inter-state'. Some of the cases of conflict covered by the UNRISD project are typical examples of external intervention and the internationalization process. This is not to say that the conflicts were actually caused by external interests (though in some cases this might have been the case), but only that other than purely local or national interests have also played a not insignificant role in their origins, their dynamics and their eventual outcome. We shall look at some of the evidence from the UNRISD case studies, provide some additional material from other areas in the world and attempt some generalizations.

1. KURDISTAN

Kurdistan provides a good illustration of how ethnic conflicts are generated, fostered and manipulated by great power and geopolitical concerns to the detriment of the real interests of the peoples concerned. Outside intervention has been a part of Kurdish history ever since the Kurdish region was incorporated into the Ottoman empire. In fact, the Kurdish question today can only be understood as the historical result of complex international power-plays since the end of the First World War. Like many other peoples from the defeated empires, the Kurds sent delegations to the Versailles Peace Conference to plead for their nationalist cause, but they did not receive much of a hearing, and even less Great Power support.

The allied powers signed the Treaty of Sèvres with the Turkish government in 1920, whereby the Kurdish population of Turkey was guaranteed regional autonomy. However, the republican government of Kemal Atatürk, proclaimed in 1923, did not recognize or implement these provisions and the Kurds were left without any international guarantees. The new treaty of Lausanne, in 1923, in fact sanctioned Turkish sovereignty entirely and while it recognized the rights of some minorities, the Kurds were not included. Thus, after the new borders had been drawn in western Asia, the Kurdish people were divided between five different nations: Turkey, Iraq, Iran, Syria, and a small number in what were then the southernmost border regions of the Soviet Union.

As detailed in Chapter 3, Kurdish nationalist or separatist revolts took place over the following decades in several of these countries. They were usually forcefully repressed, amidst massive violations of human rights, the most recent such instance taking place in Iraq during the Gulf War of 1990–1. The fact that the Kurdish regions constitute geographical enclaves with no access to the sea made it imperative for Kurdish political organizations to seek external alliances, particularly since the 1960s. First the British and French, then the Soviet Union, the United States and more recently Israel, pushed the generally weak and fragmented Kurdish political organizations in one direction or another in order to weaken some regional adversary.

After the Second World War, the Kurdish Republic of Mahabad was proclaimed in northern Iran, with support from the Soviet Union, but it collapsed after a year. One of the strongest Kurdish nationalist movements was headed for many years by Mustapha Barzani in Iraq, who first received encouragement from the Soviet Union, but later turned to the United States for aid. During the Gulf War the United States first half-heartedly encouraged a Kurdish revolt, and then back-pedalled, which only incurred the wrath of the Iraqi government and produced several million refugees. As a result, the Kurdish areas in northern Iraq were placed under the protection of the United Nations.

Iran supported the Iraqi Kurds during the 1970s, and the Kurds in enemy territory were supported by each one of the adversaries in the war between Iran and Iraq in the 1980s. Yet none of the outside actors will accept a unified Kurdish movement and none wishes to see a Kurdish military or political victory. Regionally, one government may support the Kurds in a neighbouring state while suppressing Kurdish activity at home. All four of the region's states have been actively involved in such activities for many decades, and in the end the only losers are the Kurdish people. Though the international community had taken up the Kurdish question at the end of the First World War, it ignored the plight of the Kurds for many years thereafter. The United Nations refused to deal with the issue time and again. It became involved during the Gulf War, and mainly because of humanitarian concerns, not political considerations. That is, neither the right of self-determination nor the political status of the Kurdish people or regions are raised as international issues, but only human rights violations. In 1991, both the UN Security Council and the European Parliament adopted resolutions voicing their concern over the situation of the Kurdish victims of the war, together with other civilian populations. The US Congress approved a number of non-binding resolutions about the human rights of the Kurds in Turkey and Iraq, yet in its recent dealings with Turkey the US administration has quite clearly marginalized human rights concerns.[1]

2. LEBANON

The new international situation during the Second World War which made the French mandate over Lebanon, established by the Anglo-French agreement of 1916, obsolete, led to the independence of Lebanon in 1943 and gave the United States its chance to impose its hegemony in the Middle East. The ruling elites of Lebanon agreed on the National Pact of 1943, which was to govern relationships between the two major religious communities over the next 30 years. According to this agreement, in exchange for certain political privileges which they had held for a century, the Christian Maronite elites renounced Western, particularly French, protection and agreed to the 'Arab identity' of the country, a concession which would lead in later years to a foreign policy of neutrality between Arab nationalist aspirations and the interests of the Western powers. The Muslims in turn, both Shi'ites and Sunni, while recognizing that Lebanon would remain a sovereign and independent state, renounced the cherished ideal of merging with Syria to form a larger Arab nation, and were assured a share in the political system.

The short-lived civil war of 1958 became the first open and violent political confrontation between the two major communities since the nineteenth century. While the war was triggered by popular opposition to President Chamoun's intention to stay in power beyond the end of his legal mandate, the underlying conflict pitted the Christian Maronite dominant conception of Lebanon's national identity (closely identified with France and the West) to the increasing involvement of the Muslim popular masses with pan-Arab nationalism identified with Nasser's Egypt. Muslim anger was heightened when the Lebanese government refused to make common cause with its Arab neighbours after the Anglo-French-Israeli attack on Egypt in 1956. Chamoun could no longer count on the loyalty of the Lebanese army and had to call in US troops, supplied by the Eisenhower administration, to prop up his shaky regime during the last months of his mandate. Succeeding governments would declare their solidarity with the Arab cause, but maintain their pro-Western policies.

Further tensions between the two communities built up during the 1960s and early 1970s, when the Palestinian resistance movement increased its military presence in southern Lebanon. The political impact of the Palestinians further deepened the cleavages between the Muslim and Christian communities, and these were not lessened when Israel's military operations in the south produced a flow of Lebanese and Palestinian refugees to the metropolitan area of Beirut. As the Muslim elites felt themselves increasingly marginalized from power by the political strategies of Maronite presidents Chehab and Frangie, they were tempted to play the Palestinian card and ally themselves with the Palestinians and their external supporters. Thus, external power struggles were mirrored and internalized into Lebanese politics. The various communal groups reached out to an external reference group for inspiration, identity and support in their domestic struggles, further complicating the Lebanese situation.

The three principal external actors were the Palestinians, Syria and Israel. By 1975 about 300 000 Palestinians were living mainly in the various refugee camps near Beirut, Tripoli and Saida. Before 1965, they were strictly controlled by the Lebanese state and were unable to play a political role in the country. But as soon as they began to organize armed resistance after 1965, they became increasingly involved in Lebanese politics. By siding with the Progressive-Islamic camp, the armed Palestinian groups, who established increasingly independent para-state institutions for themselves, incurred the wrath of the Maronite elites and eventually lost the support of the Shi'ites who had aided them for nearly ten years. In the aftermath of the Israeli invasion in 1982, the Palestinians were forced to retreat from active participation in domestic Lebanese politics, which by that time had hardened around the violent confrontations between the various armed communal factions. Still, several armed encounters occurred well into the early 1990s between the Palestinian resistance, the Amal militias and the Lebanese national army. During the 16 years of civil war in Lebanon, the Palestinians made and unmade alliances with various political groups and armed militias, and they finally managed to establish a relative neutrality with respect to the different local actors.

The second external actor in the conflict, the Syrians, have long been linked economically and culturally to Lebanon. Syria, being one of the major regional players in the Arab–Israeli conflict, was concerned with the way the Lebanese civil war would affect its role in the geopolitics of the area. Within a year of the outbreak of the civil war, Syrian troops intervened in favour of the Maronite faction, but they soon became involved in confrontations with the more radical Maronite 'National Forces' as well as the various 'progressive parties' and Islamic groups. While its major adversary in Lebanon was the Israeli army which it wished to contain, Syria maintained shifting alliances with the various Lebanese factions in a complicated balancing act.

In its attempt to counter and restrict the Palestinian resistance and contain the Syrian advance, Israel's military operations in Lebanon deeply affected the situation of the country even before the start of the civil war. The air raids and the tens of thousands of internal refugees had a devastating effect on Lebanese society, economy and politics. At first Israel simply tried to weaken the Palestinian resistance, but after the beginning of the civil war, its main objective was to establish a security zone in southern Lebanon, which it finally achieved with the 1982 invasion. By openly siding with the Christian forces, Israel played a pivotal role in the development of the Lebanese conflict and the disintegration of the Lebanese state.

Syria's presence in Lebanon was challenged by other forces as well. Both Iraq and Iran supported rival Shi'ite militias and this weakened Syria's position, at least until the Gulf War for the pro-Iraqi groups, while Hizbollah, the pro-Iranian group, was mainly concerned with attacking Western interests in Lebanon. Within the wider international context, cold war rivalry between the United States and the Soviet Union were clearly present in the Lebanese conflict by way of the super-powers' support for Israel and Syria respectively. Finally, the old colonial protector, France, tried hard but failed to influence the outcome of the conflict.

3. HORN OF AFRICA

The Horn of Africa provided both the motivation and the opportunity for foreign intervention in the affairs of the countries there in the past few decades. Intervention has come from three sources, each with its own motives and means. First, immediate neighbours in the Horn became inextricably involved in each other's political conflicts, not solely due to proximity, although this was a major factor, but also through a crude exercise of *Realpolitik* intended to help suppress domestic dissidence. Second, states in the Red Sea and the Middle East, a region whose international relations are dominated by the Arab–Israeli conflict, saw the Horn as a natural extension of their battleground, where the struggle could be fought by proxy. Third, the protagonists in the cold war became involved in the Horn because of their interest in the Red Sea, one of the world's most important sea lanes.

It is an axiom of revolutionary strategy in the region that an armed struggle against the state cannot succeed unless it has access to the territory of a neighbouring state, where it can find refuge, establish bases and supply routes, disseminate propaganda and conduct its foreign relations. Nearly all dissident movements in the Horn have been able to secure such access, and in doing so they have turned inter-state relations in the region into a complex game of reciprocal blackmail, in which all the players ultimately have come out the losers.

It all began in the early 1960s, when the Eritrean Liberation Front launched a guerrilla struggle. Its first recruits came from the Beni Amer pastoralist group, the Eritrean branch of the Beja people, most of whom live across the border in eastern Sudan. The leaders of the first ELF field units were deserters from the Sudanese army. Until 1970, the headquarters of the ELF field force were in the Sudanese border town of Kassala, where it operated rest camps, hospitals, repair shops, foreign relations offices, and even commercial enterprises in Sudan. The 605 km-long Sudan–Eritrea border was wide open to the Eritrean nationalists.

The first military regime in Sudan (1958–64) was hostile to the Eritrean rebels, and went as far to hand some of them, who were arrested in Sudan, to the Ethiopians. However, with the rise of rebellion in the South, the Eritrean issue became a card Sudan could play to counter Ethiopian support for the Anya-nya. Ironically, Ethiopia chose to support the Anya-nya purely as a retaliation for Sudan's open door policy for the Eritreans, there being no domestic political reason for doing so. Southern Sudanese refugee camps inside Ethiopia became Anya-nya bases and recruiting grounds, and Ethiopia became a conduit of Israeli support for the southern Sudanese rebels. Despite formal agreements between the two states intended to end such mutually harmful policies, nothing was done.

Ethiopia helped arrange the negotiations that led to the agreement signed in Addis Ababa in 1972 ending the civil war in Sudan. As a reward, it expected the second military regime in Khartoum to seal the Eritrean border and to close down rebel enterprises in Sudan, but the Nimeiry regime did not oblige. Understandably, when the southern Sudanese took up arms again, Addis Ababa was eager to assist them. Both the Anya-nya Two and the Sudanese People's Liberation Movement were formed inside the Ethiopian border by deserters from the Sudanese army. Heavily armed by the Soviet Union, the military regime in Addis Ababa offered them modern weapons and other supplies, as well as broadcasting facilities to advertise their victories and carry their message to the people of Sudan. Sudan retaliated by providing access to the Tigrai People's Liberation Front and to the Oromo Liberation Front. It was only then that the latter was able to establish a credible military presence in western Ethiopia. More meetings followed between the Ethiopian and Sudanese regimes, and more agreements were signed pledging them to cease supporting each other's enemies, but nothing in fact happened.

Intervention from states in the Red Sea and Middle East region has been a factor of considerable significance in the manifold conflicts in Ethiopia and Sudan. Though fairly complex, the motivation for intervention is related to two issues of primary regional importance; that is, control of the Red Sea, and the Arab–Israeli struggle. Having been drawn early into the Western orbit, Ethiopia was regarded as an imperialist pawn by radical Arab regimes. Worse yet, Ethiopia was drawn into an ill-concealed alliance with Israel.

Ethiopia became the recipient of considerable military aid from Israel. After the overthrow of the monarchy, despite its formal denunciations of Zionism and the breaking of diplomatic relations with Israel, the military regime in Addis Ababa could not dispense with Israeli assistance. Initially, it required help to maintain the American aircraft of the Ethiopian air force until they were replaced by Soviet planes. Hard-pressed for funds, it allowed a group of Ethiopian Jews, the Falashas, to emigrate to Israel in exchange for money. Israel also became involved in the Sudanese civil war. A general concern was to diminish Arab influence among black African states, and the conflict in Sudan offered an opportunity to highlight what the southern Sudanese themselves depicted as a struggle between Arabs and Africans.

By far the most overt, flamboyant and massive, though hardly the most effective, intervention in the Horn came from the rival super-powers in the cold war; the United States and the Soviet Union. Neither the United States nor the Soviet Union had any desire to see the Red Sea become an Arab lake. They both made strenuous efforts to preserve the Ethiopian state, and opposed movements which aimed to divide or weaken it. Suspicious of Britain's colonial designs after the Second World War, and aware of that country's economic weakness, the imperial regime in Ethiopia eagerly sought US patronage. The United States provided the wherewithal to equip four army divisions, by far the largest military force in sub-Saharan Africa at the time, and by 1970, Ethiopia had received 60 per cent of US military aid funds for Africa.

A dramatic switch of patrons and clients was to take place in the second half of the 1970s. Alienated by the Marxist rhetoric and strident denunciations of the West by the new rulers of Ethiopia, as well as the nationalization without compensation of American investment in that country, the United States began to curtail weapon deliveries to Ethiopia and asked for payment. The Ethiopian regime approached the Soviet Union for aid towards the end of 1976. Though heavily involved in Somalia, the latter seems to have thought it possible to bring both countries under its wing and resolve their differences in the spirit of socialist solidarity.

However, soon the Soviet Union was forced to choose sides. It chose Ethiopia, probably because it was believed that a genuine social revolution had taken place in that country which could lead to socialist transformation. Moreover, Ethiopia was a much larger and more important country in the region than Somalia. Once the die was cast, a massive airlift of weapons to Ethiopia was organized by the Soviet Union and financed by Libya, with South Yemen providing air and naval staging facilities at Aden. Within a short time, the value of Soviet military aid came to dwarf the aid granted to Ethiopia by the United States over two decades. Thousands of Soviet military and technical personnel were dispatched to help Ethiopia assimilate the new arsenal.

The Soviet Union's allies also came to the aid of Ethiopia. Cuba outdid the rest by sending combat units to take part in the offensive that expelled the Somali forces from Ethiopian territory in the spring of 1988. Afterwards, Cuban units remained on guard in the Ogaden and Bale. Inevitably, the United States moved into the vacuum created by the Soviet Union's loss of influence in Somalia and Sudan. During the last years of the Nimeiry regime, Sudan joined Egypt as a client of the United States and received military and economic assistance, as did the regime in Somalia.

What was the impact of foreign intervention in the conflict? It was quite common for post-colonial regimes to credit hostile foreign circles with fostering, or at least manipulating, ethnic and regional opposition. However, foreign intervention is unlikely to materialize unless a conflict is already in progress. If it can be called intervention from abroad, the bad neighbour policy in the Horn was most effective in supporting ethnic and regional conflicts, by affording secure bases across the border to movements challenging the armed might of the modern state. Such bases play a most important role at the outset, when an armed movement lacks secure bases inside the contested region. Free access to the territory of a neighbouring state remains highly important for bringing in supplies and maintaining communications with the outside world. Access to Sudan was most important for the Eritreans for most of the period of their struggle.

The case of the Sudanese People's Liberation Movement (SPLM) demonstrates best the importance of access to a neighbouring state. The

SPLM itself was founded inside the Ethiopian border and benefited greatly from having a generous host in the regime that ruled that country from 1974 to 1991. Not only did it enjoy sanctuary and a steady supply of arms, it was also able to maintain a high profile regionally thanks to the availability of radio broadcasting facilities, and internationally thanks to the easy access to the world communications media available in Addis Ababa where the SPLM maintained offices.

The most massive and overt intervention came from the two super-powers, and it was directed to the defence of the centralized post-colonial state. It can hardly be said to have been effective, since the state in Ethiopia and Somalia was overwhelmed by the centrifugal forces represented by ethnic and regional political movements. In the end, both super-powers were forced to accept the inevitable, and by cutting off support helped to bring the conflict to an end. In the final analysis, the effect of super-power intervention was quite negative. On the one hand, it helped to prolong the conflict far beyond the inherent capacity of the states to defend themselves. On the other, by providing modern weapons on credit, it raised the technology and violence of the armed conflict to levels far beyond what the parties involved could afford, had they been left to their own devices. The result was a protracted struggle waged on a massive scale, which took a terrible toll in lives, laid waste the regions where it was waged and bankrupted the countries involved.

4. BURUNDI

Burundi's existence as a national entity precedes by centuries that of some European states. For as far back as can be remembered the monarchy served as the prime focus of popular loyalties. Its legitimacy as an institution was never seriously questioned. Yet the net effect of the social impact of German (1889–1918) and Belgian (1918–62) colonization was greatly to intensify the potential for conflict inherent in the traditional order. Despite unmistakable evidence of ethnic tension behind the violent eruptions of the 1920s and 1930s, social protest during this period was never exclusively defined in an ethnic vocabulary (even though ethnic references occasionally came to the surface as part of a broader catalogue of grievances).

As we saw in Chapter 5, at the time of decolonization in the late 1950s and early 1960s, two major political parties were struggling for power: the Parti Démocrate Chrétien (PDC) and the Union pour le Progrès National (Uprona). The decisive role played by the Belgian administration in lending its full support to the PDC against Uprona brought the full panoply of resources available to the local colonial delegate into the hands of the PDC, while at the same time imposing crippling restrictions on Uprona candidates. When the victorious Uprona candidate, Rwagasore, was assassinated by a hired gunman in 1961, victim of a PDC plot, many observers saw the hand of the Belgian administration behind the tragedy.

No other event did more to sharpen ethnic hatred in Burundi than the Hutu revolution in neighbouring Rwanda. In the months following independence a number of Hutu politicians, at first mostly outside the Uprona, began to feel the contagion of republican ideas. By identifying their political aims and aspirations with their Rwanda kinsmen they imputed to the Tutsi of Burundi hegemonic motives which they (the Tutsi) at first did not possess but to which they eventually gave a substance of truth. Conversely, many were the Tutsi who saw in the Rwanda upheaval an ominous prefiguration of their future destinies.

Especially significant in fanning the flames of ethnic animosities was the sudden influx into the country of thousands of Tutsi refugees from Rwanda. By early 1965 as many as 50 000 had found refuge in Burundi. Brutally uprooted from their traditional habitat, many haunted by memories of homes destroyed and relatives killed, the Tutsi refugees added a potent source of ethnic hatred to a social arena already ripe for a Hutu–Tutsi confrontation. While many Tutsi already feared the advent of a Rwanda-like republican order based on majority rule, the presence in the country of thousands of Tutsi refugees, homeless and destitute, was immediately seen by their Burundi kinsmen as living proof of the horrifying implications of the Rwanda model. The tragic human dimension of the refugee problem is inseparable from its political aspects. For the vast majority who hoped some day to return to Rwanda maximum support from the host government was essential to enable them to fight their way back into their homeland. Only through a Tutsi-dominated government in Burundi could Tutsi rule be restored in Rwanda. In time increasingly close ties of interdependence developed between the two communities, each relying on the other's help to attain its own political ends. Just as the refugees saw that it was in their interest to aid the accession and maintenance in power of Tutsi elements in Burundi, the latter quickly understood the tactical advantage they could reap from the effective manipulation of the refugee population.

Another critically important factor has to do with the 'neo-colonial' overtones of the Hutu revolution in Rwanda. The success of the revolution was due in no small part to the massive support it received from the Catholic Church and its affiliate organizations, all closely connected with their parent organizations in Belgium. Tutsi perceptions of a 'Hutu danger' were thus greatly magnified by the identification of Hutu trade unionists with a neo-colonial, Church-sponsored movement.

During much of 1963 and 1964 Burundi politics took the form of a three-cornered fight between the Crown, the Hutu and the Tutsi. What eventually brought this fragile balance of power to the verge of collapse was the sudden intrusion of East–West rivalries into the cauldron of Hutu–Tutsi competition. The key to this situation lay in the rapid expansion of the 'Congo rebellion' (1963–4) to eastern Zaire. Its repercussions were felt immediately in Burundi, setting in motion a complex pattern of mutually supportive relationships between the Tutsi elites, the rebel army in Zaire and the Chinese embassy in Bujumbura. No sooner did the Chinese receive diplomatic recognition (in 1963) than their embassy became a major conduit for the transfer of arms and equipment to the Zairian rebels. In this complex pattern of trade-offs the Tutsi refugees from Rwanda acted as major brokers. Their overriding strategic objective was to create in Burundi a 'safe' environment for the launching of military operations against Rwanda: what better way to achieve this goal than by throwing their weight behind the Tutsi faction, and co-operate with them in their struggle against Hutu and the Crown? The refugee problem in Burundi cannot be dissociated from its broader regional context. Just as the Tutsi refugee problem in Rwanda is in part linked to the nature of Hutu–Tutsi relations in Burundi, the same is true of the question of Hutu refugees in Burundi. For every outbreak of anti-Tutsi violence in Rwanda, one can expect a similar explosion of anti-Hutu sentiment in Burundi, and vice versa.

Recent events confirm this fearful symmetry of violence. For if there is little question that the attacks launched from Uganda by the refugee-led, Tutsi-dominated Rwanda Patriotic Front (RPF) in October 1990 were directly responsible for the subsequent anti-Tutsi backlash in Rwanda, much the same scenario occurred in November 1991 in Burundi, when armed Hutu activists trained in Rwanda joined local Hutus to strike against military installations, in turn triggering a violent repression against Hutu civilians. The appalling genocide of Tutsi in Rwanda in 1994, ending with the victory of the Rwanda Patriotic Front and the exodus of over 1½ million mostly Hutu refugees to Zaire, again sent waves of foreboding to neighbouring Burundi, where observers once more spoke of a genocide waiting to occur.

5. CONCLUSIONS

The interplay between domestic and external factors is frequently a crucial element in the dynamics of ethnic conflicts. While the non-interference in the internal affairs of sovereign states is a universally accepted norm of international law and constitutes the basic principle of the contemporary inter-state system upon which the United Nations itself was founded, it is equally true that this principle is often violated not only by various political interest groups, but sometimes by states themselves.

Depending upon the nature and the intensity of the conflict concerned, several levels of external involvement may be seen to operate at different times.

(a) Kin group support

Ethnic groups that struggle against established states may seek and obtain support from their ethnic kin abroad. The minority Tutsi in Rwanda garner help from the dominant Tutsi in neighbouring Burundi, whereas the Hutu in this country look for support from the Hutu in Rwanda. In the Horn of Africa, Somalia provided support to the Somali irredentist movement in Ethiopia, and the Eritrean rebellion received help from ethnic kin across the border in Sudan. Similar relationships are found in other parts of the world. The Irish nationalists in Northern Ireland have received support from Irish organizations in North America, and so do the Basque nationalists from Basque communities in Latin America and France. Members of numerous Sikh communities around the world sympathize with the Sikh separatist movement in the Punjab, and Sindhi organizations in the United Kingdom and Canada co-operate with the regional Sindh movement in Pakistan. International public opinion would not have become as concerned with the Tamil–Sinhalese conflict in Sri Lanka had it not been for the information campaigns in support of the Tamils launched by Tamil organizations in the United Kingdom and other Western countries. Similarly, the Kurds in Turkey and Iraq count on the active support of Kurdish associations in Western Europe. Greece and Turkey support their respective ethnic kin on the politically divided island of Cyprus. More recently, indigenous organizations at the international level have voiced public concern and organized activities in support of indigenous struggles in Guatemala, Nicaragua and southern Mexico.

Premdas calls the geographical overlap of ethnic groups into two or more states the *ethnic affinity link* and he suggests that ethnic communities are kept together by networks of communications, renewing and reinforcing ethnic struggles thousands of miles away, involving many more countries in the conflict.[2] The role of ethnic diasporas has thus become more important in recent years, particularly as the development of electronic communications networks (instant TV coverage, computer networks, e-mail, fax machines, satellite transmissions, desktop publishing, home video recordings) make information exchange readily and cheaply available to individuals and organizations alike.

Ethnic diasporas (Sindhs, Tamils, Sikhs, Kurds, Armenians, Tibetans, Irish, Palestinians, Basques, Mapuches, Indo-Guyanese, Guatemalan Maya among many others) are not only nuclei of cultural preservation and identity, but they have increasingly become political lobbies in their host countries for ethnic causes in their nations of origin, and in the process they constitute new kinds of transnational communities that transcend the traditional inter-state system.

(b) Political power links

It is not only ethnic groups and diasporas that tend to become involved in ethnic conflicts. Frequently, neighbouring states, regional hegemons and, of course, the world's super-powers play active roles in such confrontations. Premdas refers to these as political power links which involve unrelated, non-ethnic actors pursuing their own political interests. We have seen how different regional states and super-powers became participants in the struggles over Kurdistan as well as in Lebanon, and how the ethnic confrontations in Ethiopia and Sudan attracted the participation of neighbouring countries as well as the super-powers in their time.

The world's imperial states have a long history of stirring up ethnic troubles in countries over which they wish to exercise influence or control. The British were masters at this game in Africa and Asia during the nineteenth and early twentieth centuries. The Nazi regime used ethnic Germans in Central and Eastern Europe to further its aggressive *Ostpolitik*. More recently, during the Vietnam war, the United States organized and armed the Hmong and other mountain tribal peoples, while in the mid-1980s it openly supported the Miskito Indians against the Sandinista government in Nicaragua. China complains that India and the West are fomenting unrest among the Tibetans, whereas India accuses Pakistan of doing similar mischief in the Punjab and Kashmir. The Sri Lankan government requested the military presence of India in order to subdue – unsuccessfully as it turned out – the Tamil secessionist struggle in the north. India's military intervention in Sri Lanka's civil war was a disastrous adventure and cost Prime Minister Rajiv Ghandi his life in a Tamil terrorist attack. The Indian army withdrew within two years, and the ethnic conflict in Sri Lanka continues well into the 1990s.

Neighbouring states and regional middle powers may have a variety of interests in intervening in an ethnic conflict in another country. Sometimes this occurs in order to maintain the peace and regional stability, or to avoid the extension of the conflict across the border. India's interest in the Sri Lankan struggle may be of this kind, in so far as radical elements in Tamil Nadu in southern India, where Sri Lankan Tamil guerrilla organizations receive support, also pose a challenge to India's unity as a state. Nigeria is the major power in western Africa, and though it has a long history of ethnic strife within its borders, it attempted to play a stabilizing role in other ethnic conflicts in west Africa, such as the civil war in Liberia in the early 1990s.

However, regional powers are not only interested in maintaining peace and stability. They may, in fact, have expansionist or geopolitical ambitions of their own, and such objectives sometimes draw them into ethnic conflicts nearby in order to consolidate their regional hegemony, weaken rival states, enable them to control access to valued resources or simply strengthen their political hold on their own populations. This seems to have occurred in Libya's intervention in Chad, and as already mentioned, in Iran and Iraq in relation to the Kurds, or Israel's support of various ethnic movements in Arab states in order to weaken its regional enemies. In the post-world war period, the internationalization of ethnic conflicts through the involvement of neighbouring states or regional powers has rarely led to full-fledged inter-state wars, though it sometimes comes close to it. There are a few exceptions, however. Pakistan became involved in a war with India because of the latter's support for Bangladeshi secession in the early 1970s. Turkey invaded Cyprus to help establish the Turkish Cypriot Republic in 1974. During the 1960s and 1970s, Somalia and Ethiopia fought several short but brutal wars over the former's support for the Somali secessionist movement in Ethiopia's Ogaden and Oromo regions. Since the break-up of the Soviet Union in 1991, ethnic conflict has emerged in a number of the former Soviet republics, but open warfare has erupted only between Armenia and Azerbaijan over the status of the ethnic Armenian enclave of Nagorno-Karabakh in the latter country.[3] The war in Bosnia-Herzegovina following the disintegration of the Yugoslav Federation was seen by international observers as an act of aggression by the Serbian Republic against the independent state of Bosnia-Herzegovina rather than as a civil war between Serbs, Croats and Muslims.[4]

Until the disintegration of the Soviet Union, super-power involvement in domestic ethnic conflicts was related more to the ideological imperatives of the cold war than to ethnic affinities. Thus the Soviet Union could support first Somalia and then Ethiopia whereas the United States did exactly the reverse. Cuba, then a Soviet client-state victimized by the United States, sent troops to help the Ethiopian military regime fight against the various ethnic and regional rebellions on its territory, which were supported by the United States. In turn the United States, armed and guided the Guatemalan military in its genocidal war against the Mayan peasants, ostensibly to prevent a 'Communist takeover' in Central America.[5] Similarly the United States supported the Indonesian takeover of East Timor, whose people are still struggling for self-determination, because the Indonesian government was staunchly anti-Communist.

(c) The United Nations

Peace-keeping, peace-making and peace-building
There are basically two reasons for involvement by the international community, as distinct from individual states, in domestic ethnic strife. The first concerns threats to international peace and regional security. This has always been a major concern to international organizations, and when an ethnic conflict is perceived as essentially or potentially destabilizing across international boundaries, then a number of mechanisms and procedures may be brought into action by other states in the system to keep or bring the conflict in check.

The other factor is of more recent interest to the international community, and there is still no widespread consensus about how it should be handled. This relates to flagrant human rights violations within the framework of ethnic conflicts, often accompanied by massive refugee flows. International intervention for human rights reasons is a relatively recent phenomenon, and the legal framework to support such intervention either by regional organizations or the UN system is still being thrashed out in the halls of inter-governmental assemblies.

The United Nations was not set up to deal with ethnic conflicts within states, and this has hindered its effective participation in dealing with them. U Thant, who was Secretary General of the United Nations during the civil war in Nigeria in the mid-1960s, wrote in his memoirs that he never had any doubt that the conflict was strictly an internal matter and, therefore, outside the jurisdiction of the United Nations.[6] It took many years and the end of the cold war for the UN to become more active in attempting to mediate in, or prevent the escalation or further the solution of, ethnic conflicts. Within its mandate of peace-keeping, the UN has sent observer missions or peace-keeping forces to numerous ethnic hotspots around the world, including Cyprus, Lebanon, Kashmir, Rwanda, Bosnia and Somalia. While UN intervention may have prevented further escalation of conflicts in some cases, it has been less successful in resolving them. This is not, of course, the fault of the UN or its Secretary General, but rather the fact that the major powers (through the Security Council) are not providing the necessary mandate or means for it to carry out such tasks, which were not originally foreseen in the Charter.

Regional inter-governmental organizations have fared little better than the UN. Perhaps no collective failure has been more dismal than that of the European Community to stop the butchery in Bosnia-Herzegovina after the break-up of Yugoslavia. The Organization of African Unity (OAU) attempted to mediate conflicts or to keep the peace by sending a peace-keeping force in various parts of Africa (Chad, Sudan, Liberia, Ethiopia, Somalia) but the results have been meagre. The Arab League provided a peace-keeping force for Lebanon after the outbreak of the civil war in that country, but this contingent disintegrated shortly thereafter. The League has attempted, rather unsuccessfully, to broker peace efforts in other conflictive situations in the Arab region.

Besides attempts at peace-keeping, the UN, as well as regional organizations, have at times tried their hand at peace-making and peace-building. Peace-making is defined as the attempt to help the parties to a conflict to negotiate a peaceful solution to their problems. While the UN has been mainly involved in conflicts between states, it has also had to respond increasingly to growing ethnic conflicts where at least one of the parties is a non-state actor. But as numerous observers have pointed out, the Security Council and the General Assembly are inappropriate arenas for the settlement of ethnic conflict because they are composed of states and exclude ethnic groups that do not represent sovereign states.[7] Some ethnic groups in conflict will find state sponsors to present their case before the UN (such as the Cypriot Turks in the voice of the Turkish delegation, the Palestinians through the Arab representatives, the South African Blacks through the the African states), other ethnic groups have not been so fortunate. Nobody ever spoke for the Kurds in the UN, nor have the Sri Lankan Tamils found a state sponsor to speak for them at that forum. Few states raise their voices to speak for the indigenous peoples, except for an occasional rhetorical aside, or purely formal resolutions such as those on the International Year (1993) and the International Decade (1995–2005) on Indigenous Populations.

As Ryan rightly states, there are also more general problems associated with UN peace-making by the General Assembly and the Security Council. Even when they do pass resolutions relating to ethnic conflict, there will be no enforcement mechanism to ensure that they are put into practice. Even the Secretary General admits that the UN often finds itself unable to take decisive action to resolve conflicts, and its resolutions are increasingly ignored by those who feel themselves strong enough to do so. Rather than setting up mechanisms to negotiate, the Security Council and the General Assembly tend to pass resolutions, which do not solve anything. The temptation at the UN, says Ryan, is to approach problems in a parliamentary style, rather than adopt an approach based on negotiation. An attempt is made to outvote the opponent rather than to sit with him to discuss conflicting interests.

In contrast to peace-keeping, which may require the use of military force, and peace-making which calls for negotiating and political skills, peace-building is a long-term process which involves developmental and confidence-building mechanisms. The UN and some of its specialized agencies, such as UNESCO, have tried their hand at setting up peace-building projects in which the contending parties can come together to tackle and solve common problems.

More recently, and in the face of an increasing number of ethnic conflicts around the world, there has been talk at the UN of preventive diplomacy, that is, identifying potential areas of violent ethnic conflict and deploying diplomatic efforts to nip the violence in the bud. Boutros Boutros Ghali, the UN General Secretary, proposes that preventive diplomacy be given high priority during the 1990s.[8] This is a timely and promising development in international diplomacy and it may involve not only the UN and its member states, but also the efforts of non-governmental organizations and private parties (see below). In order to start a process of preventive diplomacy in the area of ethnic conflicts, it will be necessary to institute a system of early warning of such conflicts. Some efforts have already been made in this direction (meetings, publications, data-banks) but the problem of early warning of ethnic conflicts is highly controversial and the UN has not yet stepped firmly into this field. It is widely felt that this is an area better left to non-governmental organizations.

Human rights intervention
While peace-keeping and peace-building efforts are necessary and worthwhile, they are handicapped by the political interests of the states and parties involved. Ethnic conflicts, as mentioned before, frequently involve human rights violations of various kinds. The human rights machinery of the UN and some regional inter-governmental bodies provide mechanisms for the international surveillance of individual and collective human rights violations, and for the implementation of universal human rights standards.

The Human Rights Commission of the United Nations, established by the Economic and Social Council in 1946, is empowered to receive periodic reports from UN member states on human rights. But as one specialist notes,

> in its consideration of the periodic reports, the Commission on Human Rights had to proceed slowly, as some states considered that the reporting procedure violated the Charter's prohibition of intervention in matters which are essentially within the domestic jurisdiction of a state, while others simply did not present any reports.[9]

Furthermore, it was unlikely that states would report on human rights violations committed by them against ethnic minorities within their borders.

Separate reporting systems by states were set up within the framework of: (a) the Committe on the Elimination of Racial Discrimination, which monitors the implementation of the International Convention on the Elimination of All Forms of Racial Discrimination, adopted by the General Assembly in 1965; (b) the Committee on Economic, Social and Cultural Rights, which monitors the implementation of the International Covenant on Economic, Social and Cultural Rights, adopted by the General Assembly in 1966; and (c) the Human Rights Committee, which monitors the implementation of the International Covenant on Civil and Political Rights (as well as its Optional Protocol), which was also adopted by the General Assembly in 1966. A number of other UN committees, such as the Committee on the Rights of the Child, the Committee on the Elimination of Discrimination against Women, and the Committee against Torture may also, as the case may be, become involved in human rights reporting and monitoring under circumstances of ethnic conflicts.

Reports by states, as already noted, are not particularly useful as far as international activity to prevent human rights violations is concerned. The various UN committees are also empowered to receive complaints by a member state about non-compliance of the provisions of any of the covenants by another member state. When a 'consistent pattern of gross violations of human rights' occurs, as is frequently the case in situations of ethnic conflict, then action by one or several member states in the Human Rights Commission or one of the committees, is fully justified and may lead to a resolution or the appointment of a special rapporteur to look into the matter.[10]

Under special conditions, the commission and the committees may consider private communications or complaints, that is, presented not by a member state, but by individuals or non-governmental organizations. However, mechanisms for the consideration of private communications are more flexible in UNESCO and the ILO than in the UN proper.

The UN body that concerns itself directly with problems related to ethnic minorities and indigenous peoples is the Sub-Commission for the Prevention of Discrimination and the Protection of Minorities, established in 1947, which reports to the Human Rights Commission. The Sub-Commission's main function is 'to undertake studies and make recommendations to the Commission on Human Rights concerning the prevention of discrimination of any kind relating to human rights and fundamental freedoms and the protection of racial, national, religious and linguistic minorities'. Under certain specified conditions, the Sub-Commission may consider communications (i.e. complaints) regarding 'a consistent pattern of gross and reliably attested violations of human rights and fundamental freedoms within the terms of reference of the Sub-Commission'.[11]

After many years of debate, the Sub-Commission prepared the draft of what became, after its adoption by the General Assembly in 1992, the Declaration on the Rights of Persons Belonging to National or Ethnic, Religious and Linguistic Minorities. A number of existing UN human rights mechanisms may be used to further the principles and rights set out in this Declaration. Other mechanisms must be found in the future. Asbjørn Eide, a Sub-Commission member and special rapporteur, recommends that a global and system-wide strategy for peaceful and constructive solutions be adopted. He particularly suggests that the Sub-Commission

should now consider the feasibility and usefulness of the preparation of a comprehensive programme of action that would include measures for the elimination of racial, ethnic and religious discrimination combined with measures to promote the rights of members of ethnic, religious and linguistic minorities, based on respect for territorial integrity and the promotion of the political and social stability of states.

More specifically, Eide recommends that the Commission on Human Rights establish a Working Group on minority issues, which should provide access to representatives of both governments and minorities. 'By providing a voice for the groups concerned it would serve to facilitate communication between minorities and governments and to develop methods for conflict resolution or direction of the conflict into peaceful channels.'[12]

The Sub-Commission's Working Group on Indigenous Populations has been preparing a draft Declaration of Indigenous Rights which it is hoped will also be adopted by the UN General Assembly in the near future. For over ten years, since the early 1980s, the annual sessions of the Working

Group are attended by scores of representatives of indigenous organizations from all over the world, who present their grievances and demands and take an active interest in the drafting of this new international document.

In the field of indigenous rights, mention must also be made of ILO's Convention 169, adopted in 1988 (which supersedes ILO's 1957 Convention 107). The ILO Constitution establishes procedures for examination by a special committee of complaints about non-compliance by member states of any of its Conventions. However, indigenous peoples as such are not represented in the ILO, and if complaints about non-observance of Convention 169 should be made, then they would have to be channelled through government, employer or worker delegates, the only ones that the ILO recognizes. This is obviously a complex procedure for any indigenous people having cause to make a representation to the ILO. Complaints may also be filed by private parties under UNESCO's Convention on the Elimination of Discrimination in Education.

In general, the UN's role in ethnic conflict resolution and the protection of collective human rights in situations of ethnic conflict has been rather limited, but everything seems to indicate that it will become more active in the future.

(d)   Other inter-governmental organizations

It would seem that as far as domestic ethnic conflicts are concerned, regional organizations might be better placed to play a constructive role than the more universal UN system. In fact, regional organizations have at times become involved in them. Mention has already been made of the Arab League's involvement in the Lebanese conflict and the attempts by the Organization of African Unity (OAU) to help solve ethnic conflicts in Africa.

Though not strictly a regional organization, the British Commonwealth took a stance on the conflict in Fiji after the military coup in that country in 1987. While the Commonwealth Heads of Government meeting did not issue a strong condemnation of the military coup, it viewed developments 'with sadness' and offered the 'good offices' of the Commonwealth in trying to solve Fiji's problems. Fiji withdrew from the Commonwealth, at least for the time being.[13]

A more constructive role has been played by the Conference on Security and Co-operation in Europe (CSCE) which now comprises over 50 states. According to Eide, the CSCE has developed significant mechanisms for the prevention of ethnic violence. It established an office of the

High Commissioner on National Minorities in 1992, whose mandate is conflict prevention and the search for long-term sustainable solutions.

Prevention is considered to require as a first step de-escalation of tensions followed by a process of reconciliation of the interests of the parties concerned. The mandate of the High Commissioner is to provide early warning and, as appropriate, early action, at the earliest possible stage in regard to tensions involving national minority issues which have the potential to develop into confllict within the CSCE area, affecting peace, stability or relations between participating states. It is intended as an instrument of preventive diplomacy. The task is therefore not directly the protection of minorities, but to be an instrument for investigation and resolution of ethnic tension at an early stage. During the brief period since the office was established, the High Commissioner has already dealt with a number of situations, significantly contributing to the reduction of tension: the Baltic states, particularly Latvia and Estonia; Slovakia and Hungary; Romania; Macedonia; Albania, and the situation of the Roma (Gypsies).[14]

As a result of increasing ethnic tensions in Europe, the European Union has also become more concerned about these issues. For example, in response to the political conflict in former Yugoslavia, it convened a peace conference at The Hague, where it also set up an Arbitration Committee, which has developed, in the course of its opinions, a small body of doctrine on self-determination and minority rights. According to one author, the Union also contributed to international state practice in this field by the adoption, within the framework of European Political Cooperation, of a Declaration on the Guidelines on Recognition of New States in Eastern Europe and the Soviet Union. Recognition of new states in those areas of the world was made conditional on a number of commitments from the side of the applicants, including respect for human rights and guarantees for the rights of the ethnic and national groups and minorities in accordance with the commitments subscribed to in the framework of the CSCE.[15]

On the American continent, the Inter-American Commission of Human Rights, a subsidiary body of the Organization of American States (OAS), has occasionally taken up the issue of indigenous peoples' rights. It has published reports and adopted recommendations relating to the human rights of the indigenous Maya people of Guatemala, the Miskito Indians in Nicaragua and the Aché population in Paraguay.[16] Following upon the example of the United Nations, it is studying the possibility of drafting an Inter-American legal instrument on the rights of indigenous peoples.

(e)   Non-governmental organizations

In recent years, so-called non-governmental organizations, that is, private associations of various types, church bodies, trade unions, business interests, but mainly international voluntary associations committed to human rights, humanitarian aid, conflict resolution and development issues have come to play an important role in guiding ethnic conflicts towards peaceful solutions.

To the extent that ethnic conflicts are deemed to be purely internal matters of sovereign states in which other states are loath to intervene, non-governmental organizations have seen a role for themselves. For example, numerous human rights associations inform public opinion about human rights violations occurring within the framework of ethnic conflicts. They not only gather and disseminate information, but they also prepare and distribute reports, lobby governments, inform the United Nations and other intergovernmental agencies, and they sometimes provide their good offices to facilitate dialogue between the contending parties, or to mediate and conciliate when this is feasible.

At the international level, the work of Amnesty International is perhaps best known in the field of human rights. Amnesty International's missions and published reports on human rights violations are among the most respected worldwide, though numerous governments which have been criticized in AI's reports attempt to disqualify the organization. Similar work is carried out by many other organizations such as Human Rights Watch (in the United States), the International Commission of Jurists, the Anti-Slavery Society (London), Minority Rights Group, and in the area of indigenous peoples' rights, Cultural Survival, Survival International and the International Work Group for Indigenous Affairs (IWGIA). Most of these organizations have NGO consultative status at the United Nations, UNESCO and the ILO, where they can submit briefs, make occasional oral statements, lobby government representatives (at the ILO, they also work with workers' and employers' delegations), and this helps to get their message across, and sometimes aids in putting a particularly serious situation or the special plight of a vulnerable ethnic group on the agenda of one of the UN committees.

In the recently more relevant area of international conflict resolution, linked to the newly developing field of preventive diplomacy, alluded to above, a number of non-governmental organizations have become quite actively involved. Former US president Jimmy Carter's Carter Center in Atlanta, Georgia, organizes seminars, missions, etc. to help find and further solutions to internal conflicts. The London-based organization,

International Alert, was established in the mid-1980s to help find peaceful solutions to ethnic conflicts in which massive human rights violations occurred. It has since moved in the direction of preventive diplomacy, convinced that it is even more important to try to prevent conflicts than to help manage or solve them after they have erupted. It has carried out activities in east Africa, some of the republics of the former Soviet Union, Sri Lanka, the Philippines, Fiji and other areas. In Fiji, for example, it has helped bring together the various parties in the ethnic conflict to discuss the possibility of reaching agreement on constitutional changes in that country which would not penalize the Indian Fijians as second-class citizens. In the Philippines, International Alert organized round table discussions between representatives of the government, the military, the universities and guerrilla groups linked to a number of tribal minorities.

Among other Church-linked associations, the World Council of Churches, in Geneva, has played an active role in brokering peace talks in a number of ethnic conflicts around the world. Non-governmental organizations can be particularly useful in bringing the points of view of ethnic groups in conflict, indigenous peoples and other minorities to public attention, particularly as these are so-called 'non-state actors' who do not usually find a voice in the world's inter-state organizations. One such organization, which was established in 1991, is the Unrepresented Nations and Peoples Organization (UNPO), a membership association of, precisely, unrepresented peoples such as the Tibetans, the Kurds, the East Timorese, tribal groups in India and indigenous peoples of the Americas. In the words of UNPO's secretary-general,

> With the exception of the observer status granted to the PLO and the Pan African Congress and the ANC by the United Nations and other organizations, peoples without their own state, as well as minorities, are excluded from participation in the foremost international bodies. Regardless of the size of the population concerned, or of its territory, or of its strategic or cultural importance, representatives of peoples or minorities are not permitted to take part in debates, let alone decisions, which concern their own fate. Most importantly, in today's legal order as understood and implemented by states, nations and peoples without a state, as well as minorities, have no right to a voice simply because they do not constitute an internationally recognized state.[17]

UNPO is an organization whose membership is composed of nations, peoples and minorities not adequately represented in the international community. Its two primary objectives are to provide a legitimate international forum for unrepresented nations and peoples, and to provide services to the members, enabling them more effectively to advance their causes by peaceful means. It serves as a link between its members and international organizations and governments. Thus, it can play a pivotal role in international debates on ethnic conflicts to the extent that it can carry the representation and voice of the 'unrepresented' party or parties in the conflict.

9 The Seeds of Conflict: Racism, Anti-Semitism and Xenophobia

Throughout this book, we have been examining different cases of ethno-political conflict which arise and develop under particular conditions. We have also seen that the dynamics of conflict contribute to the forging of ethnic identities and the creation of images, stereotypes and prejudices through which members of the groups in conflict see each other, and often come to fear, reject and even hate the members of the adversarial group. How negative stereotypes about the 'other' become generalized and influence social action is one of the persistent issues in the social psychology of mass behaviour.

Another strand in the complex tissue of ethnic confrontation relates more to the conscious forging of ethnic and racial ideologies, fostered by small groups of ideologues for their own particular purposes. In modern times, such ideas were developed specifically in the West and they relate directly to two issues which have beleaguered the Western mind for centuries: on the one hand, assumptions and theories about race; and on the other, beliefs and notions about Jews. Racism and anti-Semitism, while historically linked, can nevertheless be treated as two distinct instances of ethnic ideology. The intellectual roots of the former are ancient, yet they can be considered to have consolidated during the period of European colonial expansion. Anti-Semitism, on the other hand, also has deep roots in Christian Europe, but it found its major and most lethal expression in modern Nazi ideology.

Conscious of the danger to peace and human rights of racism, anti-Semitism and other intolerant ideologies, the international community in the post-war years attempted to create legal, educational and cultural structures to counter their influence. The International Bill of Rights specifically outlaws discrimination based on race and other criteria. In its early years, UNESCO brought together prominent scholars from around the world to examine the so-called 'racial question', and they unanimously reported that ideas of racial superiority and inferiority had no basis in scientific fact.[1] More recently, the UN proclaimed two international decades to combat racism, within the framework of which a vast array of activities to educate the public about racism were undertaken.

Despite these and other efforts, racism, anti-Semitism and xenophobia continue to flourish, particularly in Europe and North America. In 1988, the European Parliament issued a report on the subject, followed by another a few years later. Committees of Inquiry in Britain and France have investigated the activities of political groups that promote racist policies. In the United States, non-governmental organizations, which monitor the topic, report on the rise of racist and anti-Semitic incidents in the 1980s. After the collapse of communism, anti-Semitic and xenophobic beliefs have found political expression in various countries in Eastern Europe.

While the persistence and recurrence of racist and anti-Semitic incidents are troubling in themselves, equally troubling, though less well known, are the means whereby racist and anti-Semitic ideology is disseminated and propagated. To the extent that such ideologies are kept alive and are able to recruit new adherents, their potential for violence remains a constant threat. Many of the tendencies dealt with in this chapter could also be reported upon in other Western democracies, but we shall concentrate here on the situation in the United States, a country whose political institutions and official ideology are committed to human rights and equality between its citizens.

1.   RACISM, RELIGION AND THE EXTREME RIGHT IN THE UNITED STATES

Although overt racial discrimination in the United States has declined in the twentieth century, racism and anti-Semitism still exist, as do a great number of extremist groups that espouse either openly or thinly-veiled racist views, many of them violent. Polls indicate that the number of Americans holding openly racist or segregationist views fell considerably in the 1960s and 1970s. Surveys have found similar declines in anti-Semitic sentiments.[2] These tendencies notwithstanding, civil rights monitors noted an upswing of racist incidents and race-related violence in the 1980s, and the successes of David Duke, a former Ku Klux Klan leader, in a series of Louisiana elections in recent years makes it clear that racism is still well entrenched in US society.

Documented racist incidents have taken place all over the country, but particularly on college campuses. Over 3000 violent occurrences (including 138 bombings) were reported between 1980 and 1986, and more than 250 colleges and universities have reported acts of ethno-violence since that time. Violent white supremacist underground movements began to emerge in 1983, particularly in the western part of the country. In the 1990s, the political success of David Duke, the growing anti-immigration movement, and the nationalist and xenophobic positions of presidential candidate Pat Buchanan indicate that there is still a disturbingly large potential base of support for extremist causes. In 1990, the existence of 67 different hate organizations with a combined membership of about 20 000 and an estimated 200 000 followers, was reported.

Historically, the base of right-wing extremist movements in the United States has tended to be the 'once-hads' or members of groups that are in relative socio-economic decline. Right-wing extremism is most successful during periods of social flux, as people struggle to preserve their declining economic and social status.[3] Members of extremist groups are sometimes thought to be mainly drawn from lower socio-economic spheres and to have lower levels of formal education. Such conditions lend themselves to 'monist' or absolutist thinking, which in the United States has often been tapped by Christian fundamentalism. Organizations like the John Birch Society tell Americans that their society is neatly divided 'between good and evil, freedom and slavery . . . sin and virtue', and that 'either communism or Christian-style civilization must emerge with one triumphant and one completely destroyed'. Such thought allows no tolerance for people or ideas that lie outside 'Christian-style civilization'. Although the groups targeted by extremist organizations as 'distorters' of 'American' or 'Western' culture have changed during the course of US history, the underlying monism and nativism that spawns such attacks has remained more or less constant.[4]

Nativism, defined as 'an ideology of racial-cultural homogeneity and hierarchy that employs conspiracy, culture and race theories', and instils in its adherents a profound fear of new (particularly non-Western) immigrant groups, has influenced US politics throughout US history. In the nineteenth century it was directed first against Catholics and immigrants; later it focused on newly emancipated Blacks and Jews; in more recent times it has targeted Asians and Latin Americans. In the 1930s American nativism was closely bound up with the pro-Nazi activities of numerous organizations which were subsequently severely limited and dismantled during the Second World War.

(a) From segregation to separatism

The Supreme Court's school desegregation ruling (*Brown* v. *Board of Education,* 1954), and the increasing prominence of the civil rights movement, provoked a strong segregationist backlash in the US. The Ku Klux

Klan, a virulent racist, anti-Semitic and anti-Catholic organization, which first emerged in the nineteenth century after the American Civil War, resurfaced in the 1950s, and at least 90 other 'protective societies' with names like Americans for the Preservation of the White Race, White Men, Inc., White Brotherhood, American States Rights Association and the Christian Civic League, emerged in the American South.

The most prominent of the segregationist groups in the South were the White Citizens Councils, organized in 1954 to prevent racial integration in the schools and public places. The movement attracted a wide following; it influenced local elections and produced anti-integrationist material for distribution in schools in which it argued that 'White men built America' and that 'mixing races makes America weak'.[5]

Ku Klux Klan activity also increased after the Supreme Court decision, and its membership continued to grow in the 1960s as masses of poor, rural Blacks migrated to the large cities both north and south. For a few years the KKK adhered to 'old-style' thinking of the pre-civil rights era, in which 'niggers' were viewed as less than human and the 'pure white' race had to be protected by all means. In the 1970s, however, the KKK underwent a face-lift, largely due to the efforts of a neo-Nazi, David Duke, a young college graduate who tried to create a 'sanitized version of the Klan'. Under his influence, the Klan became more open, marching publicly and seeking out media coverage, but ideologically it remained devoutly white supremacist. The Klan's membership and sympathizers increased rapidly in those years.

Anti-immigration fervour also continued to grow in the 1980s, as nativist organizations such as Stop Immigration Now (SIN) and the Federation for American Immigration Reform (FAIR) emerged to call for stricter immigration controls, and 'English only' activists fought against bilingual education.[6] As concern over the 'rising tide of colour' continued to grow, many in the white supremacist movement began to search for more radical solutions. Rather than simple segregation or an end to immigration, some groups began to call for the expulsion of all non-Whites from the US, or for the creation of an all-White nation within US territory. Such proposals were based on the perception that the US was being 'overrun' by non-Whites and that due to mixed-race marriages and low birth rates, the white race was in danger of extinction. This idea was disseminated in a widely read book, *The Dispossessed Majority*, whose author argued that only 'racially homogeneous' societies can survive and prosper and that the growth of 'minorities' in the US has led to a 'decline of the majority'.[7]

Duke, who left the Klan in 1980 to form the National Association for the Advancement of White People (NAAWP),[8] became a leading exponent of 'white people's rights' and racial separatism in the 1980s. The NAAWP Newsletter, with a circulation of 30 000, proposed a kind of 'racial cleansing', whereby the United States would be divided up into racial homelands: New York would become 'West Israel' and 'Minoria' for Puerto Ricans, Italians, Greeks and other 'unassimilable minorities'; much of the Southeast would become 'New Africa'; south Florida, 'New Cuba'; New Mexico might be 'Navahona' for Native Americans, while the rest of the Southwest would become a homeland for Mexicans. Finally, the Northwest would be the 'White Bastion'. Anyone caught crossing borders would be shot. The NAAWP also called for the use of eugenics to develop a 'super-race' of blond, blue-eyed people with an average IQ of 144.[9]

(b) Racism, the Right and violence

After a surge in activity in the late 1970s, white supremacist activity dropped off in the early 1980s. Further marginalization pushed the movement in a more radical (and violent) direction. The 1980s witnessed the emergence of a number of groups with 'revolutionary' ideologies that put them 'at war' with the government. The decline of the Klan corresponded closely to the rise of the mainstream American Right. In the 1980s, the Reagan Republicans addressed the racial issues that had strengthened extremist groups like the Klan, thereby coaxing away much of the Klan's support.[10]

Unlike his Republican predecessors, Reagan openly embraced much of the radical Right's agenda, including its fierce anti-communism, support for school prayer, and its strong opposition to abortion, bussing, affirmative action and welfare spending. He thus became the first president in the post-civil rights era to oppose what was the essence of the civil rights/Great Society agenda. Such a platform obviously appealed to the Klan's constituency, but the Republican shift to the right hurt the Klan, for many extremists were lured back into the Republican fold.[11]

The fundamentalist Christian movement also encroached on the Klan's base. Though the revival of Protestant fundamentalism may have given the Klan a boost in the late 1970s, the money, organization and media power of conservative Christian groups like the Moral Majority ultimately attracted many extremist fundamentalists out of the Klan and into the New Christian Right (NCR). The NCR moved into the political arena in the late 1970s and early 1980s, throwing its considerable weight behind ultra-conservative politicians and leading an assault on 'secular humanism' which targeted communism, abortion, feminism, homosexuality, welfare, immigration, bussing, affirmative action and other important issues on the extreme Right agenda. These issues, as well as strong support for the white government in South Africa and occasional anti-Semitism, appealed to extremists, even if NCR leaders themselves were not explicitly racist.

The New Christian Right's fundamentalist moralism was not confined to Protestants. The conservative Catholics for Political Action declared that when the Christian majority took over, pluralism would be seen as immoral and evil.[12] Unlike the extreme Right, the NCR reached a mass audience, successfully combining pre-existing networks such as church and ministerial links with modern means of communication like direct mailings and radio and television programming to build a constituency of millions of conservative Protestants. By the mid-1980s, New Christian Right 'televangelists' Falwell and Swaggart claimed audiences of 25 million and 8 million respectively. A 1985 survey found that 61 million people (40 per cent of all households with televisions) watched one or more of the top syndicated religious shows.[13]

Fundamentalist organizations became multi-million dollar enterprises. Pat Robertson's '700 Club' raised enough money in contributions to cover a $230 million annual operating budget and finance Robertson's surprisingly strong bid in 1988 for the Republican presidential nomination.[14]

By appealing to their issues in the early 1980s, Reagan and the NCR brought many extremists back into the mainstream Right, further marginalizing the Klan. Klan membership dropped significantly, from a peak of 11 500 in 1980 to 6500 in 1984.[15] Other extremist organizations lost support as well. The racist and anti-Semitic Liberty Lobby, one of the largest extremist organizations in the US, saw the circulation of its newspaper, *The Spotlight*, fall from more than 300 000 in 1981 to some 124 000 in 1985.[16] The Reagan revolution had stolen its thunder.

As membership dwindled, white supremacist leaders grew desperate – and more radical. As it became clear that even the Reagan government favoured the 'integrationist' status quo, many leaders abandoned the last vestiges of law and order mentality. These leaders urged Klan members to move back underground and rejected the idea of building a non-violent political movement. One of them formed the paramilitary Texas Emergency Reserve in the late 1970s. Another broke away to form the more secretive and increasingly violent and racist 'Invisible Empire'. Proclaiming their willingness to 'spill every drop of blood in our veins to maintain white power in the United States', Invisible Empire leaders organized secret paramilitary training camps and created Klan 'Special Forces' in preparation for a 'race war'. By 1980, such paramilitary units existed in Mississippi, Alabama, Tennessee and Georgia.

Another organization, the United Klans of America (UKA), also stepped up its violence in the early 1980s, leading to the lynching of a 19-year-old black man in Alabama. In court testimonies, UKA members claimed they had received orders to harass, intimidate and kill blacks. These extremist groups laboured to transform the Klan into a violent revolutionary force. In their newsletter, the *Inter-Klan Newsletter and Survival Alert*, they called for the Klan to enter the 'fifth era' of its history, which they envisaged as a period of revolutionary warfare. In calling for revolution, the 'fifth era' advocates had made an important ideological shift. Having given up all hope of working within the system, they began to view the principal enemy not as Blacks or other minorities, but rather the state itself, which they saw as being controlled by 'Antichrist Jews'.

Such an anti-government sentiment lends itself to conspiracy theories, and racists are no exception. Drawing from the anti-Semitic conspiracy theories of *Protocols of the Elders of Zion*, Henry Ford's *The International Jew* and the preacher Father Coughlin who was active in the 1930s and 1940s, as well as from the emerging Identity movement (see below), many white supremacists argued in the 1980s that the US government, media and financial institutions were controlled by Jews and that Jews were promoting racial integration in an effort to create chaos and take over the country. White supremacist leaders claimed that Jews had 'infested every White Nation' and referred to the US government as the 'Zionist Occupied Government' (ZOG).[17]

The violent, conspiracist and anti-state attitudes that predominated in the white supremacist movement in the mid-1980s were firmly rooted in the emergence of a racist religious sect called the Christian Identity movement. Christian Identity teaches that Anglo-Saxons are the true Israelites of the Bible and that modern Jews are therefore 'impostors'. According to Identity literature, the fact that Anglo-Saxons are God's 'chosen' people 'explains why the Anglo-Saxon–Celtic nations have been the only successful colonizers' and 'why the United States occupies the position it does'. The virulently anti-Semitic Identity Christians believe that a worldwide Jewish conspiracy seeks to exterminate the white race, and claims that Jews instigated the two world wars and fomented the Russian revolution. Race is the foundation of Identity Christianity. Followers view the 'chosen ones' as the the Anglo-Saxon 'race', and they consider the Bible to be 'the family history of the white race'. The stated goal of a parallel movement, calling itself the Aryan Nations, is to 'eliminate the members of the Jewish faith and the Black race from society' and create a 'national racist state'.[18] The group seeks a 'territorial sanctuary' in the Northwest where Whites can 'protect' their 'seed line'. Since the late 1970s, Aryan

Nations has served as the hub of the Identity movement, providing it with leadership and a national organization. By the mid-1980s it had become an umbrella organization for white supremacist groups, claimed a mailing list of 6000, and published three national newsletters.

The Identity movement spread in the 1980s through churches, prisons, mail, cable television, radio programmes and computerized bulletin boards, and reached a nationwide audience via the magazine *Identity*. The racist radio programme 'America's Promise' was broadcast on 30 radio stations. By the early 1980s, an estimated 75 Identity churches went active across the country, particularly in the Midwest and the West, with a total membership of between 7000 and 20 000, although the movement's general following was much larger. The movement's current following has been estimated at up to 30 000 nationwide.[19]

The Aryan Nations serves as a national coordinator of Identity churches and has become an important unifying force among white supremacist groups in general. Identity provides the ideological foundation for racist organizations such as the Posse Comitatus, the Order, the White Patriot Party and the several Ku Klux Klan groups. The 'Christianity' that shrouds the Identity movement's racist ideology gives it added force in two ways. First, Identity churches provide channels through which non-racist Christians can be brought into contact with the white supremacist movement. More importantly, the Identity religion legitimizes racist and anti-Semitic thought by telling followers that white supremacy is God's will. In the 1980s, such zealotry often turned into violence, and this too was encouraged by Identity preachers, who told their congregations to prepare for the 'coming racial war' or 'the terrible day of destruction'. Convinced that a 'race war' or the 'day of destruction' was imminent, several Identity churches formed Christian 'survivalist' groups, stockpiling food and weapons and engaging in wilderness survival exercises. In 1985, the FBI reported that it had located 16 paramilitary training camps across the country.

One of the oldest survivalist groups is the Christian Patriots Defense League (CPDL), founded in 1959. The CPDL opposes 'humanism, modernism, communism, regionalism, Judaism, integration and taxation' and is preparing to confront the 'almost certain and inescapable collapse of the present structure', to be brought about by the 'Christ-hating International Jewish Conspiracy'.[20] The paramilitary White Patriot Party (WPP) had an estimated 120 armed members and claimed a total membership of 2500 in the mid-1980s. Other paramilitary groups to emerge during the 1980s include the Arizona Patriots, the Oklahoma White Man's Association and the Citizens Emergency Defense System.

The largest and most widely supported paramilitary group in the 1980s was the Posse Comitatus, a loosely organized secret organization, founded in 1959, which refuses to recognize all federal authority. By 1976, it was reported to have at least 78 chapters in 23 states, with between 12 000 and 50 000 members and up to 500 000 supporters. The Posse's base was strongest in the Midwest, particularly among farmers.[21] This virulently anti-Semitic and racist organization sponsored paramilitary training camps and trained 'killer teams' in guerrilla warfare tactics during the 1980s.

Between 1983 and 1985, much of the white supremacist movement was literally 'at war' with the government. Rather than simply preach or prepare for violence and revolution, Aryan Nations, Posse and Klan leaders actually began to plan and carry it out. In a widely circulated book, one of the Klan leaders spoke of an 'armed party' of racist 'ultras' who would make 'war against the US government'. He also warned that the US 'will be white or will not be at all'. Another Klan leader wrote a pamphlet entitled *Essays of a Klansman*, which outlined an elaborate point system for the assassination of government officials, civil rights leaders and 'recipients of policy', meaning Blacks, Mexicans and Cubans.[22]

Most important among the 'inspirational' works was a novel called *The Turner Diaries*. Written in 1978 by William Pierce, a longtime fascist who heads the neo-Nazi National Alliance, *The Turner Diaries* is a detailed account of a white supremacist guerrilla movement (called the Order) that overthrows the US government and ultimately leads a world revolution through a series of increasingly violent acts between 1991 and 1999.[23] At the end of the novel, the US is reduced to 50 million Aryans, and a 'Christian' paradise is established. Widely read throughout the white supremacist movement, *The Turner Diaries* was viewed by many as a blueprint for revolution. This novel actually inspired the formation of an underground military organization which named itself the 'Order', in the state of Idaho. After staging a number of armed bank robberies, the proceeds of which went to various white supremacist movements, it also began assassinating its perceived enemies. 'The end goal', one of the Order's leaders later testified, 'was the annihilation of the Jewish race.'[24] The US government prosecuted its leaders, and by the late 1980s the Order's influence had declined, but other organizations, such as the Bruderschweigen Strike Force II, continued along the same lines, engaging in robbery, arson and murder.

In the spring of 1995 the terrorist bombing of the Federal Building in Oklahoma City, causing over 160 deaths, drew public attention to the paramilitary vigilante groups that peddle anti-federal government hate ideologies. While the perpetrator of the attack was not personally identified as a racist or white supremacist, his links to such organizations clearly proved that extreme right-wing ideologies in the United States as elsewhere have the potential to generate extreme violence.

In addition to farmers, white supremacist paramilitary organizations actively recruited among soldiers, police and prisoners. The Invisible Empire and the Klan recruited at various navy bases and military camps in the United States, Japan and the Philippines. The Aryan Nations has been particularly effective in recruiting prisoners, telling convicts that they are actually 'prisoners of war' of the Zionist Occupied Government. The Klan distributes a racist prison newsletter called *Beyond the Bars...The Stars!* (allowed into prisons as 'religious' material).

A federal crackdown and a series of successful civil suits against the Klan decimated violent white supremacist groups in the second half of the 1980s. With most paramilitary leaders behind bars and other key racist leaders bankrupt, many of organizations that grabbed headlines in the mid-1980s disappeared, to be replaced by new types of groups. The nativist base did not disappear. Anti-immigration fervour continued to build in the late 1980s. In 1989, a southern California group organized a series of 'Light up the Border' vigils to demonstrate how the government had 'lost control' of the southern border with Mexico. In November 1994, voters in the state of California approved by a wide margin Proposition 187, which denies social, medical and educational services to 'illegal' (that is, undocumented) immigrants and their families. Though based on economic arguments, namely that illegal immigrants were benefiting from taxpayers' money, observers noted that Proposition 187 was mainly targeted at immigrants from Mexico and Central America, and labelled it as racist in outcome, if not in intent. The Bill was promptly challenged in the courts by human rights activists as unconstitutional, but other states were said to be preparing similar legislation.

Skinhead gangs first appeared in Europe in the 1970s. Tough-looking youths with shaved heads and combat boots, skinheads galvanized white working-class youth with their nationalist, anti-immigrant and often violent rhetoric, as well as by the so-called skinhead culture, which involves unique styles of dress and music. Skinheads began to appear in the US in the 1980s, particularly on the West Coast, and the movement spread rapidly in the second half of the decade. Like their European counterparts, American skinheads tend to be anti-immigrant, anti-Black, anti-homosexual and prone to violence. Many skinhead groups subscribe to neo-Nazi ideologies and are linked to neo-Nazi parties. Whether openly

Nazi or not, most skinhead groups are violent and white supremacist. Incidents of skinhead violence became more numerous as skinhead membership expanded in the late 1980s. One organization that was able to capitalize on the skinheads is the California-based White Aryan Resistance (WAR). Formed in 1983, WAR quickly expanded into ten states. It is a virulently racist, anti-Semitic and anti-immigrant organization, which calls for the overthrow of the 'Zionist Occupied Government'. It was eventually brought down by the legal system. In 1990, a grand jury awarded $12.5 million to the family of an Ethiopian immigrant who had been beaten to death by skinheads affiliated with White Aryan Resistance. The organization's leaders were forced to sell their homes and other assets to pay off the award, and WAR was essentially bankrupted. A year later, its founder was imprisoned. WAR membership has fallen significantly since these court rulings.

(c) Recurrent anti-Semitism

Although anti-Semitism in the US has declined considerably since the 1920s and 1930s, it has not disappeared. One monitoring agency reported 1879 anti-Semitic incidents in 1991, including 929 cases of vandalism or desecration, 950 cases of harassment, threat or assault, 60 cases of physical attack and one murder.[25] Organized anti-Semitism also continues to exist, as witnessed by the following trends.

The Liberty Lobby
The largest and most influential anti-Semitic organization of the post-war period is the Liberty Lobby, founded in 1957. A self-described 'pressure group for patriotism', the Lobby has long advocated nativist, xenophobic and racialist policies. Unlike other extremist organizations, however, it has always remained legal and above ground, never explicitly endorsing violence or using blatantly racist language. It has constantly striven to legitimize itself, working within the system in an attempt to gain a foothold in the mainstream conservative movement. Though it never succeeded in gaining respectability, it has effectively served as a bridge between the conservative Right and the extremist movement. It has also succeeded in reaching a much larger constituency than that of the Klan or any other paramilitary group.[26]

The Liberty Lobby is a network of organizations which include the Populist Party, the Institute for Historical Review, Noontide Press and *Spotlight* magazine. It promotes race and culture theories that purport to show Anglo-Saxon superiority over other races; it is also staunchly anti-

Semitic. All of the Lobby's publications espouse conspiracy theories in which 'International Zionism', through Israel, American Jewish organizations and large financial institutions, dominate the government and threaten to take over the world. The LL's electoral arm is the Populist Party, founded in 1984, which runs candidates on an anti-immigration, isolationist, anti-Israel, anti-tax and anti-Federal Reserve platform. The party fielded a presidential candidate in 1984 and again in 1988, and ran candidates for lower offices in 16 states that year.

The Holocaust denial

One of the most insidious forms of contemporary anti-Semitism, which the Liberty Lobby and other similar organizations around the world are promoting, is so-called 'Holocaust revisionism' or 'Holocaust denial'. Under the guise of historical scholarship, Holocaust denial argues that the Holocaust never took place, and that the extermination of the European Jews was not the policy objective of Nazi Germany. These arguments are disseminated through the California-based Institute for Historical Review (IHR) and the Noontide Press, both affiliated with the Liberty Lobby. The IHR, founded in 1979, is composed of a small circle of Americans and Europeans, some of whom hold university positions, whose declared objective is to further 'scholarly research' on the history of the Second World War, and particularly on the genocide of the Jews. In fact, however, while protesting that they are only doing what respectable historians should do, the Holocaust deniers consistently espouse anti-Semitic, anti-Zionist and pro-Nazi views.

The IHR publishes the quarterly *Journal of Historical Review*, which is dedicated almost entirely to Holocaust denial and the rehabilitation of Nazi Germany. Despite its claims to be a 'historical journal', few JHR contributors are professional historians, and nearly all of them are known to be longtime anti-Semites. The Organization of American Historians criticized the JHR contributors for making 'highly selective use of their data', dismissing 'massive evidence of extermination', building arguments on 'the flimsiest of evidence' and using 'obsolete materials or rumours, often in line with Nazi ideology and propaganda'. For more than ten years, the IHR and Noontide Press have published materials, sponsored annual conventions and organized debates and speaking tours in a relentless propagation of its single anti-Semitic message. The Institute for Historical Review also places advertisements in respectable college journals, defending its positions on the basis of the 'freedom of inquiry' and the 'freedom of expression', which are dear to academics the world over. Holocaust deniers are quick to argue that opposition to their views is orchestrated by powerful pro-Israel interests who benefit from exacting compensation for the Holocaust from an innocent and vilified Germany. They have founded a Committee on Open Debate on the Holocaust (CODEH), which calls for 'free enquiry' and 'open debate' on the issue. But their arguments do not resist serious scholarly criticism, and their views are not generally accepted as representing *bona fide* academic research, but rather the biased ramblings of politically motivated ideologues.[27]

Other pro-Nazi groups

Another influential political movement with anti-Semitic tendencies is that of millionaire Lyndon LaRouche, a former Trotskyite, who embraced fascism in the 1970s. His National Caucus of Labor Committees (NCLC) raised millions of dollars across the country and boasted affiliates abroad. His publications and lengthy nationwide television commercials reached a wide audience. His movement came close to electing several members to office in Illinois and other states, and LaRouche himself ran for president in 1988.

LaRouche's ideology is a complex web of conspiracy theories which links the British royalty, international bankers and drug cartels to a Zionist plot to take over the world.[28] The LaRouche movement, which has ties to the Liberty Lobby, seeks to unite various ethnic groups in an anti-Jewish front which LaRouche describes as 'the sort of large organization which US fascism must become to be taken seriously'.[29] Like other anti-Semitic groups, LaRouche tried to recruit farmers during the agricultural depression of the mid-1980s, but the movement weakened considerably following LaRouche's conviction and imprisonment on charges of fraud and conspiracy.

Since the US entry into the Second World War, support for pro-Nazi organizations in the US has been extremely low. Nevertheless, Klanwatch reported the existence of at least 30 neo-Nazi organizations in 1991. Most of them openly celebrate Hitler and the Holocaust and publicly display Nazi regalia in an effort to attract media attention. Estimates of the total membership of these groups range from 400 to 2000.

A descendant of the original American Nazi Party, one of the factions is a Milwaukee-based group, the New Order, which calls itself 'the movement of Adolf Hitler' and describes itself as 'the vehicle for the fulfillment of Adolf Hitler's great mission on this earth'. The National Socialist White Workers Party (NSWWP), located in the San Francisco Bay area, calls for an 'all-out war against non-whites'. Another group, based in southern California, distributes fliers reading 'White Power – Death to Race

Mixing' and swastika-emblazoned stickers reading 'Niggers Get Out!'. Several other white supremacist organizations defend or support Nazism and distribute Nazi propaganda, and call for the creation of a 'racially and culturally pure' white nation.

Anti-Semitism and the American farmer

One region in which anti-Semitism seemed to rise during the 1980s was the farm belt. The farm crisis of the mid-1980s was devastating to many small and medium-sized farmers in the US. As an increasing number of farmers saw their livelihood taken away by banks or by the government, discontent and anti-government sentiment grew. The farm belt became a fertile recruiting ground for extremist groups, many of which espoused anti-Semitic conspiracy theories about Jewish control of the financial system. One such organization was the Heritage Library, an Identity-linked paramilitary group, which protested against farm foreclosures throughout the Midwest and South, while at the same time promoting conspiracy theories about Jewish control of the government.

No extremist group, however, was as successful at recruiting farmers as the Posse Comitatus. After convincing farmers they were genuinely concerned with the plight of the family farm, Posse leaders argued that 'Jewish banking' had caused the crisis, and the government had been 'captured and occupied by Jews', who also sought to 'control the food supply'.[30] The conspiracy theories spun by the Posse and other extremist groups during the 1980s did not fall on deaf ears. A 1986 poll in Nebraska and Iowa found that 70 per cent of farmers believed that 'international bankers' were at least partly responsible for the farm crisis, while 27 per cent believed that farmers had always been exploited by 'Jewish bankers'.[31]

Black anti-Semitism

The Black community was also linked to anti-Semitism in the 1980s. Surveys found that anti-Semitic attitudes among African-Americans increased between 1964 and 1981.[32] Two theories have been set forth to explain the rise in Black anti-Semitism. One is what Quinley and Gluck called the 'Jewish economic presence in ghetto life'. A disproportionate number of employers, business owners and landlords in urban centres are Jewish, and therefore many urban Blacks work for, rent or buy from Jews. Some observers argue that what Blacks are expressing is hostility to those with power over them and to Whites in general. Jews just happen to be the Whites that Blacks come into contact with. One study found a considerable degree of overlap between anti-Semitism and anti-White attitudes.

For the most part, those highly intolerant towards Jews were also intolerant towards other Whites.[33]

Others argue that Black anti-Semitism is more organized. One author has noted that the Black 'movement' is 'developing an anti-Semitic ideology', and another claims that anti-Semitism is a 'carefully introduced transplant' by 'Black racists' who are 'exploiting the myth of the malevolent Jew' as a 'means to personal power'.[34]

(d) Spreading hatred: recent white supremacist tactics

White supremacist groups utilized a number of emerging technologies, such as cable and public access television, to disseminate their ideas in the 1980s. With few costs or restrictions, extremist groups like the Klan, WAR and the Liberty Lobby were able to air overtly racist programmes, which reached a potentially wide audience. By 1991, such programmes were being broadcast in 24 of the largest 100 media markets in the US. One of the most successful of these programmes was 'Race and Reason', a talk show produced and hosted by the White Aryan Resistance, which in 1989 was being viewed by millions of people in 35 cities.

Several Identity ministers have also produced and broadcast television programmes, and so has the Ku Klux Klan. Extremist organizations use radio broadcasts to disseminate their views to wider audiences as well. Radio stations in Spokane, Portland and other cities in the Northwest have sold airtime to Identity ministers, who describe Blacks as 'mud people' and claim the US is 'poisoned by Jewish money'.

One of the most important forms of communication utilized by white supremacist groups in the 1980s was the recorded telephone message. Inexpensive, easily accessible and difficult to monitor or control, telephone messages are now used by dozens of neo-Nazi, skinhead and other extremist groups. A 'Dial a Nazi' service exists in northern California, and in South Carolina, one can listen to the Southern National Front attack Martin Luther King's birthday celebration as a holiday to 'honour a nigger communist'. In addition to recording hate messages, white supremacist leaders regularly use phone messages to disseminate logistical information about meetings and rallies. For many small groups, such messages are a primary means of communication.

Another innovative means of communication utilized by white supremacist leaders in recent years is the computer bulletin board. These are inexpensive and easy ways to spread messages, and many white supremacist groups have found them to be particularly effective in recruiting youth, and in circumventing the Canadian ban on the importation of hate material.

The Klan Youth Corps, which is active in at least nine states, has distributed fliers in high schools asking for white students who are 'fed up to here' with 'Black, Chicano and Oriental criminals who break into your lockers and steal your clothes and wallets'. In 1985, the Youth Corps produced a 'Five Point Program', which called on white students to: (1) organize 'white youth' in every school; (2) 'get tough' with 'arrogant non-whites'; (3) 'force school administrators to drop their appeasement policy to minorities'; (4) adopt a 'tit for tat' policy of demanding 'equal rights' for whites (such as 'white culture' courses); and (5) demand segregated classes, towards the ultimate goal of segregated schools. The 'Five Point Program' declared that the Youth Corps recognizes that there are fundamental and biological differences between the white race and other races. It also recognizes that 'integration has been responsible for much of the racial strife in America ... integration is a prelude to miscegenation which will lead to the down breeding of the White Race'.

(e)   Racist scholarship

Scholarship has long been used as a means of legitimizing oppression. For centuries, scientists have sought to 'prove' white superiority by demonstrating biological or genetic differences among the races. In the US in the 1920s, Madison Grant tried to prove 'Nordic superiority' by virtue of the Nordics being 'dolichoephalic' or long-headed. Grant also argued that Nordics had played a disproportionately critical role in US state building, and he called for the sterilization of minorities and creation of other 'conditions' under which Nordics could thrive and dominate. During the same period, Ernest Sevier Cox claimed that Nordic Teutons were superior to other races because they had contributed disproportionately to the development of music, physics, chemistry, astronomy and other sciences. Cox, who once declared that 'the white man is the sun that lights the world', called repeatedly for the repatriation of American Blacks to Africa so that the 'blood of Africa' would not 'seep' into the United States.

Although racist theories are far less accepted in academia today than they were in the 1920s, a number of scholars continue to engage in research on race differences. William Shockley, who won a Nobel Prize for his work on transistors, announced in the mid-1970s that he had reached the 'inescapable opinion that a major cause of the American Negro's intellectual and social deficits is hereditary and racially genetic in origin'. He was joined by the psychologist Arthur Jensen of the University of California, who argues that about 80 per cent of the 'intelligence variation' found between Blacks and Whites is of a hereditary nature, a result that he says 'flatly contradicts the notion that the pattern of black–white differences in test performance merely reflects the overall black–white difference in socio-economic status'.[35]

One scholar writes that Whites are 'on average significantly more intelligent than Blacks' (a difference that is 'probably innate'), citing global data from a variety of intelligence tests to show that the 'two races with the highest intelligence levels are the Mongoloids and the Caucasoids', while 'the Negroids are ranked lowest'.[36] Another researcher attributes Blacks' (supposed) low intelligence levels to 'genetic lesioning accumulated over many generations from protracted exposure to retroviral infections endemic to Southern Africa'.[37]

Shockley, Jensen and others studying race differences claim their research is not motivated by racist attitudes but is rather legitimate scholarship. Yet the conclusions drawn by at least some of them have strong political implications. One author, for example, warns that 'blacks are reproducing more rapidly than whites and will constitute an increasing proportion of the workforce' in the future. This increase, he claims, will lead to a 'corresponding drop in productivity and living standards' and will leave the US 'unprepared for problems of unprecedented seriousness as it enters the next century'.[38]

Academic scholarship purporting to show that Whites are more intelligent than Blacks continues to fuel political arguments against welfare policies in the United States. In 1994, widespread controversy was generated by the publication of *The Bell Curve*, a thick tome of highly technical data on comparative 'intelligence testing' of different 'racial' groups, which draws policy conclusions from dubious scientific studies which provide support to racist groups.[39] Even if scholars studying race differences are themselves not racist, their work has been widely used by white supremacist groups to legitimate their views. However, some scholars and pseudoscholars have very clearly used a façade of scholarship to promote a racist or racialist agenda. Such is the case of Roger Pearson, a university professor and member of several respected conservative mainstream organizations, who has been active in racist politics in Europe, the United States and Latin America. In his book, *Eugenics and Race*, he proposes eugenic policies to 'preserve' or 'purify' the white race. The anthropological journal *Mankind Quarterly*, edited by Pearson, has the trappings of a truly scholarly publication but devotes most of its space to articles on race differences and eugenics, as does the *Journal of Social, Political and Economic Studies*, also edited by Pearson.[40]

2. CONCLUSIONS

Racism, anti-Semitism and xenophobia are recurring themes in contemporary Western culture, though the rejection of foreigners (xenophobia) is not exclusive of the West. What does seem to be peculiar to the modern West is the erection of racism and anti-Semitism as structured ideologies which serve specific political purposes. Long associated with Nazism, it was expected that these ideologies would disappear in the postwar years. As the examples in this chapter show, this has not been the case. Indeed, it may be argued that racism as a collective form of behaviour and anti-Semitic individual and group attitudes find renewed strength and inspiration in their underlying ideologies. That is why the study of these ideologies and the ways and means with which they are generated, disseminated and transmitted from generation to generation is crucial to an understanding of the dynamics of ethnic antagonisms.

Racism may be defined succinctly as: (a) the belief in the superiority and inferiority of different 'races', which (b) is expressed through systematic mechanisms of exclusion and discrimination against the 'races' deemed to be inferior. There are currently three major ideological strands in racist thinking:

1. Christian religious racism, which holds that the white race is superior by God's design. This conviction justified African slavery in the United States in the nineteenth century, it was used by Afrikaaner white supremacists to prop up the apartheid system in South Africa and, as we have seen in this chapter, it is propagated by a number of Christian Identity churches in the United States. Christian racism is not only one more form of religious intolerance, it is a world-view that holds the potential for conflict and violence.

2. 'Scientific' racism, which attempts to provide support for racist attitudes and behaviour by marshalling data from various scientific disciplines such as biology, genetics, psychology and anthropology. The invention of 'races' and their study by the various sciences occurred in the nineteenth century and reached its most refined expression in Third Reich 'raciology'. It attained a certain degree of academic respectability mostly in Anglo-Saxon universities during the first half of the twentieth century, and has since been quite discredited.[41] Still, there are a handful of scholars in the world who continue to argue that there is a scientific basis to the 'superiority' and 'inferiority' of the various races. As it turns out, being white themselves, they generally conclude that the 'white' race is superior in all respects. While no longer propounded by serious scholars, the idea that there exists scientific proof of the superiority and inferiority of the various

'races' of the world is still being popularized, and therefore reaches an audience much larger than that which might follow the debates in scientific or professional journals.

3. 'Nationalist' racism, which argues that there is some profound 'essence' in the ethnic nation that distinguishes it from all others. Thus, being an ethnic German or Englishman or Frenchman makes one inherently superior to the newcomers or immigrants from different ethnic stock who may happen to share one's citizenship. When ethnic nationalism is strong, then ethnic characteristics are often framed in racial or 'blood' terms, and whoever does not possess them is not only considered to be an ethnic outsider, but may also be rejected as racially impure or different. Translated into social attitudes and political action, this has led to attaching racial categories to the cultural 'other', thus actually 'freezing' distinctions which are neither genetic attributes nor immutable. A case in point is the tendency in the United Kingdom to lump all current and past immigrants from various continents together as 'Blacks' and deal with them accordingly.

Xenophobia, the 'fear of the foreigner', is a phenomenon much more widespread than racism, and to the extent that it deals with individual subjective feelings and attitudes of rejection which may not specifically target people who are biologically different, some authors consider it as having nothing to do with racism at all. Nevertheless, in so far as it becomes a recurrent collective phenomenon, which may be anchored in one of the racist ideologies already mentioned, xenophobia has all the trappings of racism. A good example is provided by xenophobic incidents against Turkish immigrants in Germany.

Anti-Semitism in its various guises has different ideological components as well. The oldest and most persistent form of anti-Semitism also stems from the Christian religious tradition, having been most virulent during the European Middle Ages, but lasting well into modern times. A second, more prominent expression is the political anti-Semitism of the nineteenth and twentieth centuries, which achieved notoriety precisely during the period in which ethnic nationalism became the driving force in many countries. In Germany as well as in Austria, during the 1920s and 1930s, for some nationalist political elites or populist parties, the identification of Jews as an 'alien body' was a highly useful political tool, particularly in times of crisis. Finally, in its obsession with racial purity, Nazi Germany constructed the 'racial' Jew, only to impose the Final Solution.

Though anti-Semitism and conventional racism may share some ideological roots, the peculiarity of the former is that Jews are always placed in the role of scapegoats, whether this happens among American farmers in the 1980s, or the depressed urban middle classes in Depression-era Austria and Germany, or in post-communist Poland and Russia. More recently, anti-Semitism has been nurtured by other events as well. The Arab–Israeli conflict and the Palestinian question have generated a current of political anti-Zionism in the Third World and the intellectual Left, which sometimes shows clear anti-Semitic overtones. And, in an ironic reversal of the tables, the desire by new (and old) generations of Germans and Austrians to overcome the past and deal with 'historical memory' (the Holocaust), Jews are being metamorphosed from victims into 'culprits'.[42]

We have seen in this chapter how many of the ideological undercurrents of racism, anti-Semitism and xenophobia are being kept alive and revitalized through various social and political mechanisms. While the hard-core of racism finds a place undoubtedly in a small group of extreme right-wing fringe groups, many of the racist and xenophobic arguments are made today by political movements which aspire to play a legitimate electoral role (as, for example, Le Pen's Front National in France). Their message spreads well beyond their immediate constituencies, and populist movements, cashing in on people's fears and insecurity, thrive on the simplistic categories of racist, xenophobic and anti-Semitic dogmas (as is well shown in the case of the Russian politician, Zhirinovsky).

Moreover, it is as well to keep in mind that these ideologies are not only political platforms, but pervasive social and cultural (sometimes religious) world-views, which are easily assumed by different sectors of the population who do not necessarily think of themselves as politically active. This is well understood by the racist ideologues themselves, who make excellent use not only of the mass media (television and radio shows, journals, newsletters and bulletins), but also of the latest communication technologies (such as computer bulletin boards, direct phone-mail campaigns and even interactive video games).

While the dissemination of racial and ethnic hate messages is legally prohibited or controlled in most countries, those who propound them have always found ways around the legal system, and their voice is as threatening today as it ever was.

10 Conflict Management and the Multi-ethnic State

Like other types of social and political struggles, ethnic confrontations seem to undergo cycles during which they wax and wane. In earlier chapters we have seen that the emergence of ethnic conflicts can be the result of multiple causal and contingent factors, and their eventual solution also depends on a series of circumstances. Much has been written about conflict resolution, management, regulation and reduction, and there now exists an array of academic institutions devoted to research and training in this field. Sometimes resolution, regulation and reduction are seen as alternative or even mutually incompatible approaches. In some of the relevant literature, it seems as if there were a basic contradiction between the proponents of conflict resolution and those of conflict management.[1] Horowitz, however, only calls for techniques of *conflict reduction*. He argues that the reduction of ethnic conflict depends on two prior crucial conditions, namely, the motives of policy-makers and the timing of policy innovation. The motives of policy-makers may be fickle: they may indeed tend to favour the solution of a conflict, or then again they may simply favour the advantage of a particular ethnic group. As regards timing, Horowitz rightly points out that there is a greater chance of success if reciprocal concessions between the groups in conflict, sometimes referred to as a 'grand settlement', are agreed upon before a pattern of conflict emerges which makes going back especially difficult. He suggests that inter-ethnic conflict may be reduced by:

1. Dispersing it, by proliferating the points of power so as to take the heat off a single focal point.
2. Arrangements that emphasize intra-ethnic conflict instead.
3. Policies that create incentives for inter-ethnic co-operation.
4. Policies that encourage alignments based on interests other than ethnicity.
5. Reducing disparities between groups so that dissatisfaction declines.[2]

Other authors see ethnic conflicts as somehow 'intractable', that is, they are considered as either not solvable at all or so 'stubborn' in their persistence that their solution within a given social and political unit is extremely difficult. Agnew, for example, argues that ethnic conflicts 'generate practices, interests, goals and symbols that cannot be mediated discursively.

The sources of intractability are of both a spatial and temporal order; they reflect both the spatial and temporal dimensions of specific conflicts.' He concludes that 'Intractability ... is generated by the dynamics of the conflict rather than by the reasoning processes of the parties to it ... only by changing the conditions that create intractability in a specific case can an intractable conflict be resolved. Resolution, therefore, is always beyond reason alone.'[3]

One of the characteristics of ethnic conflicts is their protracted nature, and this makes their resolution particularly difficult. Azar attributes this to the denial of security, distinctive identity, social recognition of identity and effective participation in the society, in other words, the denial of those human needs that are common to all. He argues that these human needs and long-standing cultural values will not be traded, exchanged or bargained over. They are not subject to negotiation. In order to work towards conflict resolution in such cases, it will be necessary to take the identity (i.e. ethnic) group rather than the nation-state as the analytical unit, and explore the needs of the opposing parties and the ways and means of satisfying them, rather than bargain over interests.[4]

Gurr, in his survey of 233 ethnopolitical conflicts around the world, suggests that policies associated with regional autonomy, assimilation, pluralism and power-sharing have the potential for accommodating the essential interest of most disadvantaged and politically active communal groups. He concludes that there are two keys to the constructive management of ethnopolitical conflict. One is to seek out politically and socially creative policies that bridge the gaps between the interests of minorities and states. The second is to begin the process of creative conflict management in the early stages of open conflict.[5]

In this, Gurr concurs with Horowitz and others that conflict reduction and management, including group accommodation, can be achieved by the judicious and timely use (presumably by governing elites) of specific techniques. Agnew and Azar, among others, seem to be saying, on the contrary, that unless basic issues of needs and identity are addressed (which cannot be reduced to 'interests'), protracted ethnic conflict will continue to exist.

Some of the conflicts studied in the UNRISD project did in fact come to an end during the period of study (Ethiopia and Lebanon); others continued unabated or re-emerged (India, Pakistan, Burundi), and still others (as in the former Soviet Union and Yugoslavia) blew up into full-scale warfare during the course of the study itself. What can we learn from some of these experiences about the solution and management of ethnic conflicts?

1. FAILED SOLUTIONS IN BURUNDI

With the army, the government and the economy virtually purged of Hutu elements after the 1972 killings, Tutsi hegemony seemed impregnable. Yet in the autumn of 1987, President Buyoya seized power and promised a process of liberalization. His failure to deliver was partly responsible for renewed massacres in 1988.

First and foremost on Buyoya's agenda was the normalization of Church–state relations: most of the catechism schools were reopened; all restrictions on the holding of church services were lifted. Freedom of expression was no longer stifled. All of this carried important implications from the standpoint of Hutu–Tutsi relations. While raising the anxieties of Tutsi hard-liners, these early signals nurtured Hutu hopes for a further acceleration of the move toward liberalization. If initially the regime denied altogether the existence of ethnic conflict, by the end of 1988 the issue of ethnicity had been dragged out of the shadows. The immediate result of Buyoya's reforms was to set in motion a movement towards the depolarization of the Hutu–Tutsi conflict while at the same time deepening incipient divisions within each group. In 1988, Buyoya appointed a National Commission for the Study of the Question of National Unity, consisting of an equal number of Hutu and Tutsi. The aim, in essence, was 'to conduct a sustained investigation into the historical and socio-cultural foundations of Burundi unity, to trace its evolution, and identify the reasons and manifestations of present divisions so as to propose appropriate solutions'. Six months later, the Commission issued its eagerly awaited report. For the first time in the history of independent Burundi an official statement was issued which explicitly recognized the centrality of the Hutu–Tutsi problem.

The report is a profession of faith about the country's capacity to recover its national unity; it is a diagnosis of the roots of ethnic conflict; and it is a set of prescriptions 'aimed at protecting and strengthening the unity of the Barundi'. The roots of the Hutu–Tutsi problem, we are told, lie exclusively in the legacy of the colonial state; not only was the traditional society free of social tension, but bore no traces whatsoever of a potential rift between Hutu and Tutsi; as for 'the rift in national unity over the past 30 years' it is the work of 'selfish' and 'self-serving politicians' who 'took advantage of colonial stereotypes to undermine the age-old unity of the Burundian people'; if the future is to hold any promise, it is imperative to avoid confusing a 'political majority' with an 'ethnic majority'; in short, to recognize the claims of the Hutu as an ethnic majority would be tantamount to 'a denial of the Burundian nation and a misconception of democracy'.

The report emphasizes the 'cultural homogeneity' of pre-colonial Burundi, and makes no mention of the potential for conflict inherent in the Hutu–Tutsi cleavage. If the 1972 massacre is duly reported, remarkably little attention is paid to the circumstances that lie in the background of the violence. With regard to the 1988 killings, the report argues that this was essentially the work of outside agitators. The report's recommendations relate to 'the organization and management of employment and of the public services in a spirit of equity', and based on merit, but it is unlikely to bring about social integration, because the legacy of decades of discrimination in the educational system has produced a social pyramid in which the top positions within and outside the government are largely the monopoly of Tutsi elements.

Ironically, the first serious manifestation of dissent from the Commission's conclusions did not come from the Hutu, but from the Tutsi-dominated military. The army, after all, has never ceased to be involved in the Hutu–Tutsi struggle, so it was not surprising that it did not entertain serious reservations about the wisdom of Buyoya's 'grand settlement' strategy. The Hutu too were divided, between those who were willing to accept the compromise outlined in the report, and those who rejected it out of hand as a thinly veiled attempt to perpetuate Tutsi hegemony. The former cast their lot with the official, ethnically mixed, though Tutsi-dominated, Uprona, the latter with the all-Hutu Palipehutu. Taking exception to both the exclusivist, pro-Hutu outlook of the Palipehutu and the official, pro-regime stance of the Uprona, a third group, identified with the Front des Democrates Burundi (Frodebu), sought to enlarge the scope of reforms initiated by Buyoya, and in so doing prepare the ground for a genuine multi-party democracy in which both Hutu and Tutsi would have a meaningful share of power.

Led by an exceptionally bright Hutu intellectual, Melchior Ndadaye, Frodebu was born as an underground movement in 1986. After the publication of its manifesto in 1990 it became the first legitimate opposition movement seeking to attract an ethnically mixed following, and openly rejecting intimations that it is a Hutu party (even though its top leadership is largely Hutu). The events of November 1991 dealt a body-blow to Buyoya's 'national unity' campaign. Once again violence became a mode of discourse – a rejectionist, counter-hegemonic Hutu discourse directed at the entire train of reforms introduced since 1988. The repression, likewise, through its sheer brutality and arbitrariness, served to articulate the regime's hegemonic response, conveying an ominous message to anyone seeking to challenge the status quo.

What appeared to be emerging was a limited form of consociational participation based on the belated (and reluctant) recognition that ethnic identity matters. Recent political reforms in Burundi might be said to reflect a consociational or power-sharing approach to ethnic conflict. But the wide numerical disproportion between Hutu and Tutsi makes Burundi the worst possible candidate for the application of a consociational solution. Indeed, in the situation of 'proportionality' assumed by the model the Tutsi minority would find itself totally at the mercy of the Hutu majority, whose incentive to share power is far from evident.

Many observers consider that the economic disparities between Hutu and Tutsi are a more powerful obstacle to democracy than their ideological differences. The absence of even the sketchiest form of statistical data on the distribution of income and occupational activities between, and among, Hutu and Tutsi is itself a commentary on the extreme sensitivity of Tutsi elements to accusations of economic domination. After the 1972 bloodbath and for the next decade the only qualified applicants for positions of responsibility in the private and public sectors were drawn from the Tutsi stratum; meanwhile, much of the wealth previously owned by the victims of the massacre, including that of the refugees, passed into Tutsi hands. Subsequent restrictions on the admission of Hutu children to secondary schools meant that by 1988 only a tiny fraction of the Hutu population had the requisite skills for employment in the modern sectors of the economy. Among those few Hutu who, in spite of these restrictions, were able to gain a secondary or university education, many were either killed or forced into exile during the 1988 and 1991 massacres.

All this is not meant to suggest that poverty is unknown among Tutsi, or that among Tutsi ethno-regional identities make no difference. But in an environment of economic scarcity, if the Tutsi claim the lion's share of what little wealth the country has to offer, this can only be at the expense of the Hutu community. Whether public policies designed to bring about a more equitable distribution of resources are politically feasible remains an open question. What seems reasonably clear, however, is that no power-sharing arrangement can survive the strains and stresses generated by such profound socio-economic inequalities between Hutu and Tutsi.

Equally plain is that the merits of federalism as a strategy for conciliation are largely irrelevant to Burundi. Neither is 'ethnic separation', i.e. partition into separate, ethnically homogeneous units, a possible solution. Given the extent to which Hutu and Tutsi intermingle in most rural settings, 'ethnic separation' is singularly unrealistic. The massive transfers of population which it implies are far too impractical and politically objectionable to deserve serious consideration. Given the statutory and constitutional restrictions concerning the organization and platform of political parties, all of which stress the imperative of co-operation across ethnic lines, electoral competition is unlikely to translate into a straight Hutu–Tutsi confrontation. However, it is difficult to think of any major public policy issue in today's Burundi that does not have a significant ethnic dimension, and whose impact on social groups does not carry momentous implications for the future of Hutu–Tutsi relations.

After the renewed violence on 1993 and 1994, the political landscape became even more radicalised and fragmented. Extremist elements amongst both the Tutsi and the Hutu have made agreement among the moderate elements in both camps increasingly difficulty. International observers warned in 1995 of impending genocide on Burundi, where the atmosphere became even more poisonous as a result of the massacres in neighbouring Rwanda and their consequences. However, as a result of the crisis of 1993, Tutsi public opinion now recognizes the relevance of ethnicity, and that the Tutsi constitute an ethnic minority in need of protection.[6]

There is the growing commitment on the part of both Hutu and Tutsi intellectuals to what is referred to in Burundi as 'l'Etat de Droit' (the Rule of Law). The bloodshed of the past has at least served one major purpose in Lemarchand's opinion: however traumatic the learning experience, it serves as a permanent reminder that there is simply no alternative to peaceful coexistence. How this can best be achieved remains an open question.

2.　EXHAUSTION IN LEBANON

In Lebanon, many efforts were made during the civil war to end the violence and launch a dynamic for peace. These efforts produced innumerable initiatives for a solution to the conflict, since its very beginning. There were almost as many peace proposals as there were local contenders in the struggle. Up to 1989, however, none of these initiatives had been carried to a successful conclusion, not even those that were proposed by the most neutral of Lebanese mediators, who were not involved directly in the conflict. Just as unsuccessful were other regional and international actors who tried their hand at putting forth proposals for peaceful conciliation. It looked, Kamal Hamdan argues, as if the war, or rather the 'war system', would continue indefinitely as if obeying some 'divine injunction' rather than the will of human beings.

More than 50 proposals to bring peace to Lebanon were proposed over the years. The most important were the following:

1. In 1976, a 'constitutional document' was presented under the auspices of Syria, which recommended reforms to the traditional system whereby the three religious communities were each entitled to one of the three presidencies: the presidency of the republic, held by the Maronites; the presidency of the chamber of deputies, occupied by a Shi'ite; and the presidency of the cabinet, that is, the post of prime minister, going to a Sunni. This constitutional document proposed parity between Christians and Muslims in the parliament, the consolidation of the role of prime minister and his cabinet at the expense of the president of the republic, and the creation of new constitutional institutions. The document also favoured administrative decentralization and the abolition of religious representation within the administration, except for posts at the highest level. However, by failing to deal with the external dimensions of the conflict, particularly the presence of the Palestinian army in Lebanon and its role in the Arab–Israeli conflict, the document fell flat.

Between 1976 and 1980, a number of partial and temporary solutions were attempted. One was proposed by two Arab summit conferences in November 1976, and it actually ended the two-year war of 1975–6. The summits created an 'Arab deterrent force' in Lebanon, whose main objective was to help restore central presidential power and regulate the relations between the Syrians and the Palestinians on Lebanese territory. The plan was rejected by the Maronites, who considered it as the legitimation by the Arab states of the Syrian presence in Lebanon. Neither was the Arab peace-keeping force greeted with much enthusiasm by the Progressive Palestinian Coalition, who feared Syrian control over the territories they occupied.

A second plan was presented by the Lebanese parliament in April 1978. This was basically a Declaration of Principles, stating that the Lebanese people wished to live together. Despite its symbolic value, this Declaration was no more than a ritual act which reflected the goodwill of the traditional leadership to compromise, at a time when they were being pushed aside by the new leaders rising from the ranks of the various militias. The Declaration, moreover, completely ignored the external dimensions of the conflict. Two years later a new project, the 'National Consensus on Fourteen Points' emerged, presented by the president of the republic and his prime minister. It was an only slightly improved version of the earlier parliamentary Declaration, strong on good intentions and general principles, but weak on practical solutions.

After the Israeli invasion of southern Lebanon in 1982, the Lebanese and Israeli governments signed an agreement in May 1983, under the patronage of the United States, which refers mainly to the external aspects of the conflict. This agreement basically addresses the security needs of Israel, it stipulates Lebanon's disengagement from the Arab world and the Palestinian question, and proclaims the total normalization of relations between the two states. Despite its attempted neutrality as regards the internal aspects of the conflict, the agreement in fact contributed markedly to the sharpening of intra-Lebanese contradictions.

Riding on the wave of the profound changes produced by the Israeli invasion, President Gemayel attempted to re-establish Maronite hegemony over the country by resorting to strong arm tactics. This 'solution' to the problem merely ended up by concentrating more power in the hands of the president and his political clientele. It finally fell apart at the beginning of 1984, as a result of internal opposition, supported by Syria. This failure led to the annulment of the agreement with Israel, even before it was a year old.

Another attempted solution, the establishment of a Government of National Unity, which was to include the increasingly powerful chiefs of the various armed factions, resulted from the Lausanne conference of 1984, which brought together for the first time the traditional political elites and the leaders of the new militias, particularly the Muslims. This government adopted new forms of power-sharing between the communities, but being the outcome of intense political bargaining under the pressures of the moment, it was scarcely more successful than previous attempts in promoting a lasting peace. While it gave the various factions some breathing space, nobody took the new government seriously. As each of the major communities attempted to take advantage of the lull in the fighting to establish its own political hegemony over the state, the new government was soon faced with the rebellion of the Lebanese Forces army in the spring of 1985, and the civil war continued.

If the earlier solutions to the conflict were mainly conceived and haggled over by the institutions of the state itself or the traditional political figures, the latter were almost completely brushed aside by the country's three principal militias, the Lebanese Forces, the Amal movement and the Progressive Socialist Party, who signed a tripartite agreement in Damascus in December 1985, under the patronage of Syria. This very general agreement dealt with both the internal and external aspects of the conflict.

Externally, Lebanon's special relations with Syria were to guarantee its Arab identity through bilateral accords covering military, economic and even educational matters. Internally, the tripartite agreement significantly limited the prerogatives of the presidential institution, which for a long time embodied the hegemonic role of the Maronite leadership at the central state level. It also established a previous non-existent senate, lowered the voting age to 18 years, and insisted on parity between Maronite, Sunni and Shi'ite parliamentarians. The earlier equilibrium between two major players, the Maronites and Sunnis, would now evolve into a new balance between three actors, thus associating the Shi'ites with the collegial government, while at the same time reshuffling the Christian leadership in favour of non-Maronite political elites. As expected, the Maronite factions were not happy with the tripartite agreement and they were not willing to make the necessary concessions and share their traditional power. Once again, the proposed solution fell through. Several months after the signing of the tripartite agreement, another military rebellion broke out, this time within the Lebanese Forces themselves. Bloody fighting took a heavy toll of the two factions of this militia which had signed the tripartite agreement.

Kamal Hamdan concludes that the various proposed solutions between 1976 and 1984 failed because they did not take into account either the internal or external dimensions of the conflict, which are nevertheless closely interrelated. Thus, the constitutional document of 1976, the Declaration of the Lebanese Parliament of 1978, the National Consensus on the Fourteen Points (1980) and the Ministerial Declaration of the Government of National Unity were almost exclusively centred on the internal dimension. In contrast, the Arab summits in Ryad and Cairo of 1976, as well as the agreement of 17 May 1983, imposed on Lebanon by Israel, were basically concerned with the external aspects of the conflict.

Second, many of the proposed solutions were really only short-term agreements and disregarded the true nature of the power relations between the contending actors, who merely wanted to maximize their own short-term benefit, rather than come to terms with the deeper realities of the country.

By 1988, political life in the country had come almost to a standstill. Parliament was unable to elect a new president and the last vestiges of central power disintegrated. For the first time since the beginning of the armed conflict, two rival governments were set up. Parliament was no longer able to meet and became totally paralysed.

In February 1989, armed encounters between the two Christian parties fuelled a new explosive phase of the internal conflict. The Army commander General Aoun, supported by a majority of the Christians and the military, seeing that the political forces were unable to control the country, tried to seize political power. In March 1989, Aoun started his War of

Liberation against the Syrian forces, in an attempt to establish himself as the sole leader of the country. For six months, there was horrendous violence, which stimulated the Arab countries and the super-powers to double their efforts in trying to end the armed conflict and fill the constitutional void into which the country had fallen.

Yet another Arab summit conference was held in Casablanca in May 1989, at which a High Tripartite Commission to mediate on the Lebanese crisis was created. This Commission prepared a project which it presented to the Lebanese parliamentarians who gathered for three weeks at Taef, in Saudi Arabia, to consider it. They finally adopted the Document on National Understanding in October 1989. The Taef Agreement is not only the end-result of a dialogue between local actors, more or less represented by the Lebanese parliamentarians, it also reflects changing regional and international conditions. In the Arab region, Syria and Egypt had begun to heal their differences and the Arab League returned to its old headquarters in Cairo, while détente between East and West was making progress. In sum, for the first time since the beginning of the Lebanese conflict, internal, regional and international conditions seemed to have come together to facilitate a solution in Lebanon.

Essentially, the Taef Agreement reflects a compromise between the different Lebanese factions, particularly the traditional political leadership on the one hand, and the militias on the other. It also includes an Arab–American compromise on the Lebanese as well as other regional issues. Reflecting both internal and external concerns, the Document on National Understanding is more ambitious and global than the earlier proposed solutions. It includes references to internal reforms, the identity and sovereignty of Lebanon, the Israeli occupation, relations between Lebanon and Syria. Beyond general principles, it also includes a detailed programme and timetable for the solution of the conflict.

While a number of the propositions contained in this document are similar to some of the earlier proposals, it is clear that the understanding reflects not so much new approaches to the solution of the conflict as a changing international environment which made agreement by the different contending parties possible. The first part of the Document on National Understanding includes general principles and reforms. It reaffirms the unitary and definitive character of Lebanon's identity as a country, thereby clearly rejecting the thesis about 'cultural pluralism' held for a long time by the Maronite Christian leadership. Reference to the unity of institutions also sets aside the politics of decentralization and federalism which the same Maronite leadership had occasionally expressed. Furthermore, Lebanon is defined as an Arab state, thus solving (at least for the time being) the vexed question of Lebanese national identity, which has been debated in the country ever since its founding in 1920. Despite the Document's stricture about Lebanon's Arab identity, Kamal Hamdan believes that the religious nature of the two major communities may continue to polarize and 'ethnicize' Lebanese politics in the future.

Some of the other general principles in the Document refer to the democratic and parliamentarian character of the Lebanese republic, public liberties and civil rights, as well as the liberal economy. The Document also includes propositions about social justice and economic reform, the need for regional development and administrative decentralization within the territorial unity of the state. Freedom of circulation and residence is proclaimed, which is important in view of the fact that during the war populations were resettled according to an 'ethnic cleansing' pattern.

One of the major political reforms of the Taef Agreement is the restructuring of the power-sharing arrangements between the president of the republic, the prime minister, the cabinet and parliament. Though the Agreement does not spell it out in so many words, it is clear that the traditional distribution of power between the three major communities is maintained: the president of the republic will be a Maronite, the prime minister a Sunni, and the president of parliament a Shi'ite. But the president of the republic loses some of his prerogatives, whereas the prime minister and the cabinet gain a certain of amount of power. In fact, it is no longer the president of the republic, but the council of ministers (the cabinet) who function as chief executive, there is a trend away from the previous 'presidentialism' towards a more collective, collegiate government which is more likely to reflect the various political tendencies and communal factions in the country. The cabinet and the prime minister retain more executive power than that held by the president of the republic. By strengthening the role of the president of parliament, and extending his mandate from one to four years, the traditional Shi'ite community, which had felt itself to be marginalized from the earlier power-sharing arrangements between the two major communities (Sunnis and Maronites), now has a greater share of political power. This new arrangement is also designed to limit the influence of other, more extremist Shi'ite factions, who had challenged the political system as a whole.

The Taef Agreement establishes parity between the two major religions (Christians and Muslims) in parliament, but only as a temporary measure, because it foresees the abolition of proportional representation on religious grounds in the future. In fact, it establishes electoral mechanisms for non-communitarian representation in parliament, but also announces the establishment of a senate in which religious communal representation would function.

In the future, the country would be divided into decentralized administrative regions with religiously mixed populations. Electoral districts would be enlarged, so that candidates can run for office in multi-communitarian and differentiated environments. The state retains control over public and private education in order to reinforce the process of national integration. A single unified textbook will be used to teach history and national education in the schools. Elsewhere, the Taef Agreement deals with national security questions and provides for the dissolution of the various militias, who are expected to turn over their weapons to the national army. Syria is expected to help this process along. After two years, the Syrian forces were to pull back into the Bekaa valley, near the Syrian border. Israeli troops are required to leave Lebanese territory in accordance with UN resolutions.

The final part of the Taef Agreement insists on the 'privileged relations' between Syria and Lebanon, which will be implemented through bilateral agreements of co-operation, but it is not too clear exactly how this should be done. Kamal Hamdan concludes that the political reforms resulting from the Taef Agreement remain profoundly attached to the system of communal representation and participation which has existed in Lebanon for a long time. The merit of the Taef Agreement is that it was able to put a stop to the armed conflict with the co-operation of all the parties, and that it benefited from regional and international circumstances that helped it along: the Syrian and Egyptian détente, the willingness of the Palestinians to go along with a US-sponsored peace process in the region, which in turn relates to the end of the cold war and the disintegration of the Soviet Union.

The peace process was further strengthened because within Lebanon itself hostilities were breaking out within the Maronite and Shi'ite religious communities, bringing the inter-communal conflict into a quagmire. In fact, Lebanon did not have much leeway for multiple choices. The militias wanted to retain control of the small, fragmented pieces of territory which they controlled in the absence of a strong central state, and they insisted on the withdrawal of all foreign armies before any talks on national reconciliation could begin. As the latter condition was impossible to implement, the Taef Agreement opened the door to some form of internal negotiation which might break the vicious cycle of violence. It was an attempt to reconstruct the power of the central state before the withdrawal of foreign military units could even be broached, by eliminating the various factions and militias from contending directly for power at the centre. The militias agreed to pull back from the Greater Beirut area, as well as other regions, and to hand over their heavy weapons to the newly restructured national army.

While the Taef Agreement has many positive points, Kamal Hamdan also raises some pertinent questions and doubts. There is no assurance that the leaders of the various factions will respect the Agreement, any more than they respected early proposed solutions. The underlying inter-communal tensions may flare up again at any time, and the process of decommunalizing political relations in the country is by no means assured.

The driving force behind the Agreement comes mainly from abroad, from regional and global power pressures. The various factions still hold to their own preferred solutions, which are incompatible with those of the other factions, but if they did agree to come to terms within the Agreement, it is mainly because their various foreign sponsors pushed them into doing this. Yet, if external circumstances were to change once more, it is feasible that the militias might take up arms again. The Agreement did not spell out the procedures, mechanisms and resources whereby the general principles of peace and national reconciliation would be effected. This has since led to haggling and bargaining between the various actors, which has not expe-dited the implementation of the Agreement.

Hamdan believes that the larger part of the civil society has been left out of the political agreement, and that the traditional political elites and the new militia leaders who emerged from the conflict itself are in fact jockeying with each other to establish or re-establish their own political power positions. The presidents of the republic, of the council of ministers and of the parliament, who represent each of the major religious communi-ties, are commonly referred to as the Troika, and though they attempt to work together, they are in fact rivals for power and influence for their respective communities.

The bottom line of the Taef Agreement is whether the attempt to find a new equilibrium between the various religious communities can actually lead to a process of national integration, and whether the new Lebanon can maintain the balance between its Arab identity and its ties to the West. Hamdan is not very optimistic, and answers his own questions with a hesi-tant 'Yes ... but ...'. At least, he argues, the fighting has stopped and a window of opportunity has opened for politics to replace violence.

3. REMEDIES TO ETHNIC CONFLICTS IN NIGERIA

Okwudiba Nnoli argues that 'ethnicity' in Nigeria has hindered economic development and the emergence of a truly democratic polity. By ethnicity he means the competitive assertiveness of ethnic identities in order to obtain benefits and power for contending elites. As we have seen in earlier chapters, ethnicity thus understood led to the Biafra war in the 1960s, to various military coups and struggle over control at the political centre, as well as, more recently, to repeated and persistent boundary conflicts between states. Several remedies have been implemented in order to resolve the problem posed by ethnicity thus understood in Nigeria. All of them started from the viewpoint that 'ethnicity' is an inherent characteristic of Nigerian society. Therefore they sought not to engineer it out of existence but to take it in such a way that it posed no problems for Nigerian unity and development. The objective was to contain not to eliminate ethnicity.

British policy actually strengthened ethnic differences in Nigeria, by embarking on a programme of separate development of the various groups with as little contact with one another as possible. This was reflected in the policy of *sabongari* in northern Nigeria by which not only the southerners but also northern migrants were forced to live apart from the local population. It was also implemented in the various borders between ethnic groups, which became frozen barriers that prevented the kind of inter-ethnic assimilation which took place during the pre-colonial times. The policy of *sabongari*, however, merely fanned the embers of ethnicity.

Another colonial policy on ethnicity was indirect rule, whereby the various ethnic groups were made to take charge of their local administrations, headed by the traditional ruler. Where he did not exist he was created. Thus, the British succeeded in creating a new symbolic focus where none existed in the past with the appointment of brand new traditional rulers, and reinforcing it where traditional rulers already existed. In either case the members of the ethnic group, especially in the urban areas, had a viable reference point for their ethnic identity.

Federalism is another policy designed to contain ethnicity in Nigeria. It was initiated by the British and continued by the Nigerian leaders. It is based on the viewpoint that through the decentralization and devolution of state power to sub-national entities under the control of various ethnic groups it is possible to fashion a cohesive and united country. This possibility is only realizable under conditions in which all the units are legally equal and none of them can dominate the others either alone or in a combination with others. The resultant federation was initially constituted of regional and federal governments but later by state and federal governments. Each level of government had its functions spelt out in the constitution including areas in which it was autonomous and others where it enjoyed concurrent jurisdiction with the other level. The sub-national units were independent of one another and only tenuously linked to the federal unit. This federal arrangement has varied in character from a loose, three-region structure to the present much more centralized 30-state arrangement. In practice, it has operated as a decentralized system during civilian rule and as a centralized system during military rule.Within the federal structure of government different formulas were adopted for allocating national revenue to the various levels of government. It is believed that a fair and equitable system of allocation of the national revenue in this way would reduce the degree of conflict among the various ethnic groups. Over the years several commissions have been set up to perform this task.

. After the Biafra war, a principal policy designed to lessen the danger of renewed attempts at secession was the creation of a large number of states. What is the appropriate number of sub-national units of the federation? The issue arises because there are at least 200 language or ethnic groups in the country. As it is considered unwieldy to constitute each ethnic homeland into one such sub-national unit, there have been difficulties in working out the basis for the formation of new states. The problem is temporarily solved each time by satisfying the most pressing demands for states that it is politically feasible to satisfy. Nevertheless, each exercise has given rise to demands for more states. In fact, such demands have now also come from within ethnic groups themselves. Yet it is still widely believed that state creation has the potential to minimize ethnic conflicts arising from ethnic domination as well as alienation from the society arising from neglect in the division of the national wealth.

In line with the federal character of the country, the government attempts to maintain adequate representation of the various ethnic groups and sub-groups in the public administration. This principle has been applied in appointments to positions at the federal, state and local government levels, in admissions to the federal universities, recruitment into the armed forces, the location of institutions of higher learning such as universities, polytechnics and colleges of education, the organization of the political parties and the location of public projects. It is believed that the successful application of this principle will inculcate a sense of national belonging to the various ethnic groups which would deepen their loyalty and commitment to the nation as a whole. In this way, it is expected, ethnic identity and consciousness will give way to national identity and consciousness as the principal determinant of behaviour at the national level.

Finally, the manipulation of the number and nature of the political parties by the government has been used as an instrument to counteract ethnic fragmentation in Nigeria. During the Second Republic (1979–83) an elaborate set of rules was drawn up designed to ensure that political parties were not organized along ethnic lines. In fact, the 1979 constitution insisted that the executive committee or any other governing body of the party must reflect the federal character of the country. Its members must be drawn from at least two-thirds of the states of the federation. The federal election commission was charged with the responsibility for deciding which parties satisfied this guideline. Nevertheless, most of the political parties whose operation was approved by the electoral commission had ethnic bases, which was widely reflected in their political support in the 1979 and 1983 elections.

As part of the continuing effort to undermine ethnicity in the political parties, the present federal authorities have designed and formed a two-party system as the backbone of electoral politics of the Third Republic (1993–). It is believed that by limiting the number of parties to two, the various ethnic groups, especially the majority groups, would be compelled to co-operate with one another within both parties. This would make it difficult for the political parties to be identified along ethnic lines or to articulate and pursue ethnic interests. In addition, the internal organization of the parties must conform to the principle of federal character. In order to ensure conformity to these guidelines, the government undertook to found the parties, build their offices throughout the country, produce their constitutions and manifestos and provide funding for their political activities. Nevertheless, it may still be possible for the parties to be captured by ethnic champions and for the real governing of the parties to be done by ethnic brokers within their leaderships rather than their formal organs. This was the experience of the parties of the Second Republic which turned them back into ethnic parties. If it happens with the two-party system the consequence would be more deleterious. If only two ethnic groups succeed in capturing the parties, they might feel a sense of loyalty to the system, but the rest would be alienated. Under this circumstance ethnic rivalry would increase rather than decrease.

Thus efforts have been made in the past and are being made today to find solutions to the ethnic problems of Nigeria. Unfortunately, the results have not been encouraging. The problem seems to be spreading and intensifying instead of contracting and diminishing in intensity. In fact, the solutions themselves have acted to produce more ethnic consciousness and demands than before. For example, the creation of states has consistently led to the demands for even more states and the consequent heightening of ethnic consciousness. In some cases it has even provoked the emergence of sub-ethnic identities and consequently ethnic-like antagonisms within the same ethnic group. Part of the problem with these remedies is their lack of understanding of the complex nature of the ethnic phenomenon. They address essentially the political demands of the ethnic groups without addressing the socio-economic organization of the society in which those demands are made.

According to Nnoli, as a result of the implementation of the federal character principle, ethnicity has become more widespread than before. While in the past it was limited to relations among language groups, today it has led to ethnic-like antagonisms within language groups such as between local governments in a state and between communities (villages or towns) within local governments. Consequently, the country is not only faced with the prospects of polarization at the national level but also at the regional and local levels.

The policies on ethnicity have acted to ossify and freeze ethnic group boundaries. It has now become more difficult for an individual from one community to become a full-fledged member of another community either within or across ethnic groups. Similarly, the freezing of ethnic group boundaries has blocked the mixing and assimilation of peoples of diverse ethnic groups at their boundaries which characterized the pre-colonial societies. The individual is increasingly confined to a very narrow space consisting of his or her local government area in the ethnic homeland.

The increased balkanization of the internal space of the country with the creation of states imposes undue burdens on the nation's political system. State and local government bureaucracies have proliferated, giving rise to vastly increased and conflicting demands on the national political system. The society must find resources to maintain over-sized cabinets, political organizations and governmental activities. This has led, according to Nnoli, to the politicization and ethnicization of the government bureaucracy, with consequent loss of professionalism. Compensatory action for members of disadvantaged ethnic groups (for example, in university admissions), leads, according to Nnoli, to a lowering of standards. The programme of affirmative action (federal character) is left in the hands of the ethnic groups which benefit from it. The federal character policies in fact promote a desire on the part of the beneficiaries to remain underdeveloped in order to continue to be declared a disadvantaged area. Indeed, many communities are demanding to be classified in various spheres of life as disadvantaged. It has become popular and desirable to be categorized as disadvantaged because of the benefits accruing from that status in the distribution of amenities.

Federal character policies, says Nnoli, damage the prospects of creating a common citizenship for the country capable of ensuring free mobility of persons, labour, capital and other factors of production. It also frustrates the emergence of a cosmopolitan society based on the intermixing of persons of different cultures, ensuring political stability and national unity. The constant preoccupation with ethnic balancing and the satisfaction of ethnic demands and interests impels the state to de-emphasize the emergence of a viable civil society in Nigeria. Voluntary associations such as the manufacturers' associations, the students' union, the medical associations, labour unions, lawyers' association, civil liberties organization and traders' association which cut across ethnic lines are not given equal or even enough attention.

By emphasizing ethnic criteria in the representation process, especially in recruitment to government posts and the assignment of public responsibilities, policies on ethnicity, especially federal character policies, make it difficult to exact accountability from public officers. Nnoli considers that the result is the perpetuation of bad government with the consequent deterioration in the standard of living of the population.

Attempts to solve the ethnic problem have given rise to multiple centres of ethnic tensions in the country. In the process of demarcating the boundaries of the newly created states, the insecurity arising from land scarcity, land grabbing and land speculation has given rise to ethnic tension and violence in the rural areas, at the borders of some ethnic territories. As a result of the belief that gains accrue to those who successfully play the ethnic game the élite are exploiting even sub-ethnic differences to attract these benefits. Consequently, ethnic-like tensions have been generated within the same ethnic group, which are then exploited by the demands for the creation of additional states in the ethnic homeland. The politics of 'dichotomy' in the old Anambra state between the northern and southern populations of the same state and ethnic group led to the creation of two states out of one. In these ways new poles of ethnicity have developed at both the centre and periphery of the ethnic group.

While attempting to create remedies for ethnic tensions, the central state has actually promoted ethnicity, considers Nnoli, and these policies have great potential for causing the disintegration of the national state. By increasing the growth of ethnicity they provide a basis for increased tension and hostility in the society. Consequently, the possibility for the use of violence increases. The massacres that preceded the civil war as well as the Tiv uprisings of 1959–60 and 1964–5 are illustrative. At the same time violence has spread to the rural areas and caused inter-ethnic border conflicts. Ethno-religious conflicts have assumed a violent character in a number of cities and rural communities in the northern states of the country. At the same time it has become much easier than before to acquire arms for the prosecution of violent actions. These developments spell trouble for the survival of the Nigerian state. The threat may not take the form of secession but of the ungovernability of society because of the existence of intractable poles of violence within the state.

4.   LACK OF CONFLICT IN SENEGAL: A MODEL FOR AFRICA?

Senegal is one of the few cases in Africa of a multi-ethnic state which has been able to avoid ethnic conflict to a large extent. Some of the reasons for this have been spelled out by Mokhtar Diouf in his study, and were referred to in previous chapters. In summary, Diouf mentions, among other factors leading to ethnic harmony in Senegal, the fact that the country has a long history as a 'nation' creating a community of cultural values between the various ethnic groups which became more differentiated as time went on; a national, albeit not an official, language, namely Wolof; a tradition of intermarriage and social relations between different ethnic groups; the impact of monotheistic religions on the behaviour of the population, Islam as well as Christianity; the importance of Dakar, the country's capital, as an ethnic melting-pot; the existence of non-ethnic social contradictions (the problem of the castes, the opposition between the citizens of the 'four communes' and the rest of the country), which not only detracts from ethnic oppositions but also facilitates inter-ethnic co-operation; a tradition of political democracy and militant, Western-style trade unionism, which gives priority to political competition and class interests over ethnic considerations; the early involvement of Senegal's first political leaders in the Pan-African movement, which is seen as incompatible with any kind of ethnic chauvinism; and, finally, the careful management of ethnicity after independence.

The emergence of the separatist movement in Lower Casamance in the 1980s does not really challenge the tradition of ethnic harmony in Senegal. But this movement does call attention to the fact that a number of links in the chain of national integration may not have functioned correctly. These can be found in two contemporary elements: a decline in democratic politics since independence, and inadequate management of ethnicity due to excessive administrative centralization.

While the conflict in Casamance throws a shadow upon the tradition of inter-ethnic harmony in Senegal, it is not a 'structural' conflict rooted in some kind of ethnic tension. There is no basic antagonism between the Joola ethnie and the country's other ethnic groups. Even in the midst of the crisis, there was no hostility between different ethnic groups at the interpersonal level, either in Casamance or in other regions. The conflict in Casamance is not a communal conflict. It should rather be regarded within the tradition of popular struggles in Senegal against the abuse of power at the centre, whether in colonial or post-colonial times. Only in this case, the damage to the country was more serious than usual and the consequences could have been grave. Diouf argues that it is possible to set in place adequate political and administrative measures so that such a conflict cannot happen again.

He suggests that what might trigger ethnic tensions in the future is the 'development of underdevelopment', that is, the fact that since independence and despite relative industrialization, Senegal's economic performance has lagged considerably. Thus, ethnic peace, or rather the absence of ethnic conflict, is a necessary but insufficient condition for development. But the economic situation would have been infinitely worse if ethnic conflict had taken place.

Senegal's emphasis on 'national unity' is the framework of its development policies, based on the idea of modernization and the challenge of wanting to catch up with the developed and industrialized nations of the world. To the extent that economic progress in the industrialized world is seen as resting upon the dynamic role of the nation-state, the major task of the 'new countries' is seen as the construction of the nation-state, that is, the challenge of nation-building. Hence the obsession of promoting national unity at any cost, involving a number of 'anti-development' measures, such as the single political party, autocracy, cult of personality, civil rights abuses, attacks upon democracy and also, cultural mimicry of everything Western as the model to be followed. Among all the leaders of African independence, only Kwame Nkrumah posed the need of continental political and economic integration. All the other heads of state considered 'nation-building' to be more important, as if Africa did not know of other forms of state structures even in pre-colonial times.

5. MALAYSIA – CONTAINING ETHNIC CONFLICT

In assessing the success or failure of particular strategies adopted for reducing conflict in any country it is important not to assume that an absence of ethnic strife means that there is national unity. This was evident in Malaysia in the 1960s when the prime minister announced that ethnic harmony had been achieved, making him the 'happiest prime minister', only to find that country erupting into ethnic riots shortly afterwards. Malaysia's success in being able to contain ethnic conflict so far has been impressive. The primary question is whether this can continue in the future.

As we saw in Chapter 7, the Malaysian government made several changes in its ethnic policies since the 1970s, and Mavis Putucheary argues that these changes have led to increasing ethnic tensions in the country. First, when the Malaysian Federation was formed in 1963, the various constituent ethnic groups coalesced around a 'Malay' and 'non-Malay' dichotomy, pitting mainly native Malays against Chinese (the largest component of the 'non-Malay' group). The Malays, who saw a significant correlation between the extent of colonial penetration and the size of the Chinese population, made efforts to maintain Malay numerical majority and to control Chinese immigration, at the same time encouraging the assimilation of culturally similar groups. The relative size of the Malay and Chinese population was an important factor creating the bipolar pattern which tends to aggravate ethnic conflict as each group considers its own culture to be superior to the others.

The coming together of 41 Malay groups to form the United Malays National Organization (UMNO) in 1946 was the result of a form of 'defensive nationalism'. The British confirmed UMNO as the focus and vehicle for Malay political activity, thus reinforcing the saliency of ethnicity as the basis for political mobilization. The Chinese, in turn, formed the Malayan Chinese Associations (MCA) in 1949 and since that time, Malaysian politics have become more and more ethnically based. Putucheary argues that the British supported this trend, despite its inherent dangers, because they perceived other, more racially tolerant parties as 'communist threats'.

The sharpening of ethnic boundaries tended to produce inter-ethnic relations that were confrontational rather than co-operative. Education policy, as was pointed out in Chapter 7, became one of the more divisive issues between the ethnic communities. Still, political leaders realized that as a first step towards setting up a framework for inter-ethnic co-ordination it was necessary to get the leaders from the different ethnic communities to meet and discuss matters of mutual concern without pressure from their own communal organizations. Thus, committees were formed to debate educational issues in a non-confrontational manner. Similarly, economic policies were debated. In one of the early meetings of the Communities Liaison Committee (CLC), set up by the British, it was agreed that as part of the programme to improve the economic position of the Malays, the Chinese would voluntarily restrict their business activities in predominantly Malay areas in order to allow for the development of Malay businesses in these areas. The CLC did not last long, however, because the UMNO split into different parties and the Chinese Association had difficulty in representing its own factions.

Putucheary considers that Malay nationalism has not only exaggerated the differences between Malays and other communities by focusing political attention on the special position of the Malays as the 'Sons of the soil', but also has had the effect of creating other, communally based organizations which also focused political attention upon the distinct cultural and historical heritage of the Chinese. Thus, while the 'ultras' within the Malay community were insisting on the subjugation of all languages and cultures to the dominant Malay language and culture, the Chinese 'ultras' were focusing political attention upon the distinct cultural and historical heritage of their community and demanding the right to use their own language, go to their own schools and practise their own religion.

According to Putucheary, it is likely that this fundamental difference would have escalated into ethnic hostility and even violence, had it not been for the fortuitous UMNO–MCA election pact which gave rise to the formation of the Alliance Party in 1953. This was formed initially as a strategy to win local government elections, but it continued as a political tool for national elections in subsequent years. The strategy for achieving inter-ethnic co-operation at election time allowed the individual parties to retain their own structure while providing some formula for inter-ethnic co-operation at the top.

The main incentive for turning what was an electoral pact into a permanent arrangement was the prospect of forming the new government after independence. Though no real negotiations on substantive issues had taken place between the different ethnic communities, the first National Conference of the Alliance Party in 1953 promised that the Alliance would reconcile the conflicting claims of various communities and would protect the rights of the minorities.

Things did not quite work out that way though. The fact that the electorate was largely Malay made it imperative for the UMNO to wean votes away from another, strongly pro-Malay party (the Party Negara, which had split from UMNO). This meant that any decisions that had been arrived at through inter-elite bargaining within the Alliance had to be played down. On the other hand, whatever had been agreed upon on the question of Malay rights was given maximum publicity. The contrast between the clear and unambiguous promises to the Malay community and the vague promises and deferred matters to the Chinese community was evident in the Alliance Election Manifesto for the 1955 elections, in which promises about special protection of the Malays were made explicitly, while the offer about citizenship rights for non-Malays and a balanced language policy was kept deliberately vague.

The Alliance won a resounding electoral victory in 1955, despite the unresolved citizenship issue for non-Malays, thus giving Malays a major role in the upcoming negotiations on independence with the British. The result of negotiations in the Constitutional (Reid) Commission was the consolidation of Malay hegemony (special privileges, language, Islam as the official religion of the state). In the new constitution, the Malays got their special rights securely entrenched, Malay became the national language, while the Chinese were given citizenship rights, not as generous as they would have liked, but nevertheless on more liberal terms than before. Many people at the time believed that although in many respects it was one-sided and weighted heavily in favour of the Malays, the constitution was only the beginning in the development of a system which would eventually provide for better inter-ethnic relations and perhaps for a more equal distribution of political power in the future. In this belief, the constitution was accepted and became the basis for inter-ethnic co-operation in independent Malaya after 1957.

But there were fundamental contradictions in the constitution, which became the source of ethnic conflict in subsequent years. While it did seem to provide the framework for a democracy based on individual rights and freedoms, it also incorporated another set of premisses: that in which the state gives official recognition to group membership, in this case solely the privileges of the Malay group.

In spite of the weaknesses of the constitutional bargain, the country enjoyed some degree of inter-ethnic harmony in the first ten years of independence due mainly to the ability of the Alliance Party to hold together and stay in power. And it held together, despite profound differences between the elites of the two main ethnic communities, because their leaders were willing to bargain and negotiate in order to obtain electoral short-term gains for their constituencies. Communal problems were worked out through negotiation and bargaining, rather than through intensification of competition and conflict. The exchange of trades against trade-offs was useful in diffusing the potential ethnic conflict. Because 'palpable gains' were clearly visible in the short run, this 'contract' approach between the members of the Alliance nevertheless created problems for ethnic relations in the future, by strengthening ethnic consciousness and mobilizing support along ethnic lines.

In particular, the inclusion of the special rights clause singled out a particular ethnic group for special treatment, and this legitimized and reinforced ethnic cleavages. Thus, although the privileges given to Malays under the constitution had the objective of assisting to reduce socioeconomic imbalances between the ethnic groups caused by historical circumstances, it further ethnicized the political process and expanded the arena for ethnic competition. The incentives for giving in to communal pressures began to increase, thus threatening the break-up of the Alliance.

Though throughout the 1950s the image of the Alliance as a 'grand coalition' became somewhat tarnished as its votes began to decrease, the Alliance leadership actively promoted accommodative behaviour through formal and informal channels. Nevertheless, it suffered conflicting pressures not only from the two major ethnic communities, but also from the different subgroups within each ethnic community over differential access to resources and social and economic goods. In a sense, conflict between classes was expressed in ethnic terms. A political crisis in 1959 pitted the moderate Alliance leadership against the 'ultras' in each community over the language issue (see Chapter 7). The Alliance leadership found that in order to be effective in playing its mediating role, it was necessary to control the 'ultras' within each party. This was achieved through attempts to restrict democracy within the Alliance Party and through political patronage. Though it was threatened by ethnic 'ultras' in both the Chinese and the Malay camps, who attempted to 'outflank' the mutually accommodating Alliance leadership, the Alliance was able to hold together through the 1959 elections. This it did by shifting salience to non-ethnic issues (national economic development, modernization), and by being deliberately ambiguous on divisive communal issues.

The gains made by more extremist Malay nationalist parties in the 1959 elections (which had accused UMNO of being soft on the Chinese and selling out to them) were a warning signal for the leadership of UMNO and the Alliance. It therefore succeeded in amending the constitution in 1962 in order to give greater electoral weight to rural Malay districts and to make it more difficult for non-Malays to acquire citizenship. The ethnic issue became more highly charged after the creation of the Federation of Malaysia in 1963, which included the north Bornean states of Sabah and Sarawak and (for a time) Singapore. While the inhabitants of the former became *Bumiputra* ('Sons of the soil'), on a par with native Malays, Singapore (whose population is principally Chinese) was incorporated with a large degree of local autonomy.

Throughout the 1960s, the language issue was a major political problem, leading to riots in Penang and Kuala Lumpur, and serious disturbances elsewhere. After the Kuala Lumpur riots in 1969 (in which 248 people died), the government declared a National Emergency, which suspended parliamentary democracy and introduced authoritarian rule. The inter-ethnic elite settlement which had been made at the time of independence had failed, in the opinion of Mavis Putucheary, to provide the basis for a stable democracy for two reasons. First, there was no general agreement among the leaders themselves concerning the kind of political system that they wanted. The constitutional agreement was a simple contract based on a quid pro quo arrangement; a system of exchanges in which each side accepted the arrangement because the deal made it better than before. Second, the democratic system, which was supposed to lower the level of ethnic conflicts basically because whatever rivalry or competition existed would be channelled through the workings of democratic institutions, also provided the opportunity for the kind of intense political competition which became so conflict-ridden as to jeopardize political stability.

Instead of using the 1969 crisis to come to a new inter-elite agreement, the Malay leadership, by declaring an Emergency, and ruling by decree through the National Operations Council (NOC), actually excluded the non-Malay elites from any constructive debate. Henceforth, political participation by non-Malays was severely circumscribed. The abandoning of the democratic system was seen as necessary for the re-establishment of Malay claims for exclusive political rights as the indigenous community. Gradually, Malay political dominance began to be expressed in a wide range of government policies, especially in the appointment of personnel in key policy-making positions in the cabinet, the civil service, the armed forces and the judiciary. While the temptation to establish an authoritarian regime was strong, the Malay leadership opted for the introduction of a limited form of democracy, with some degree of electoral competition, in order to head off future dissent among the Malays themselves. The Alliance Party gave way to a wider coalition, the Barisan Nasional (National Front) in which UMNO continued to play a predominant role.

Within five years of the ethnic riots, the regime had re-established itself. The tension between 'representativeness' and 'governability' was resolved in favour of the latter. The central role of the state in managing ethnic conflict resulted in a tightly centralized structure, which concentrates all power within a narrow ruling circle, and the ethnocratic character of the Malaysian state. The need to establish a tightly centralized structure in order to balance the almost irreconcilable demands of the two communities made it imperative to depoliticize sensitive issues and achieve some degree of 'departicipation' in political decision-making. Thus, the system (and the ruling Alliance Party) went through a process of de-democratization.

In Malaysia, the inter-ethnic elite arrangement is premissed on the assumption that the existing status order is accepted by most if not all the major ethnic groups. One ethnie is assigned a superior status and the other ethnies are assigned a politically inferior status. In this respect, ethnic groups are seen to be status groups. The assumption of such an arrangement is that once the question of who is in control is settled, the main source of conflict is removed, paving the way for a more manageable conflict situation. The political actors recognized the need to focus on output goals of the state and especially on economic development in order to gain legitimacy for the state in the eyes of the non-Malays, and particularly the Chinese. It was felt that the main reason why the Chinese were interested in politics was to guarantee a stable political environment and a free enterprise economic policy, which would allow them enough economic space to operate their businesses. By focusing attention on economic development, the political actors succeeded in shifting attention away from the conflict-prone political arena to emphasize inter-elite cooperation in achieving rapid economic growth which would benefit everyone. The government's New Economic Policy, promulgated in 1970, stressed the importance of achieving a more ethnically balanced distribution of wealth through economic expansion.

The Chinese community, however, had become disenchanted with its leaders in the Alliance, and began switching its votes to the opposition parties. The future of the Chinese language and culture was an issue of particular concern to the Chinese community, which traditional community leaders exploited for political purposes. The MCA found that by being part of the government it was vulnerable to attacks from the non-Malay opposition parties for selling out Chinese rights, and in the 1969 elections the MCA suffered a major defeat.

The MCA's position in the Alliance was increasingly challenged during the 1970s in relation to the issue of the setting up of a Chinese university, a move opposed by the Malay leadership. This politically explosive issue was referred to the courts, where it was 'defused', but still the ethnic preference policies continued to be the cause of considerable resentment among members of the Chinese community. Designed at first to allow the Malays to improve their economic position, preferential policies for Malays contributed to reinforcing ethnic boundaries and provoking a backlash response from the Chinese. Similarly, non-Malays were concerned about the growing influence of Islam, particularly after the clause in the constitution was adopted making Islam the official religion.

The system of coalition politics by its very nature tended to result in highly centralized structures, both within the government and within party organizations. This led inevitably to leadership crises within several of the parties of the Alliance, and later the Barisan Nasional, including the dominant Malay UMNO and the Chinese MCA, as well as to struggles and confrontations between leaders of the various communities. The government, by exercising considerable restraint, was able to prevent or quell ethnically explosive situations during the 1980s, but basic tensions persist. Putucheary is not optimistic: she feels that the situation is deteriorating and that the model of inter-elite coalition politics, which held ethnic conflict in check over several decades, will not be able to manage the complexities of inter-ethnic dynamics in Malaysia for much longer.

6. CONCLUSIONS

An assessment of the way ethnic conflicts are regulated, managed or resolved in different parts of the world does not give rise to much optimism. 'Grand settlements' which will lay the ethnic demons to rest forever are unlikely to be achieved in most instances. Countries in which for decades or generations some sort of 'consociationalism' or power-sharing arrangements seemed to have worked well, as in Lebanon, broke asunder when the system was unable to control the various internal and external forces that emerged as a result of historical changes. After 15 years of bloody, destructive civil war, Lebanon finally succumbed to combat fatigue. The Taef Agreement included 'solutions' that had been proposed many years before, but had been rejected by one or the other of the antagonists. The guns were finally silenced by outside powers (mainly Syria) because it became obvious that the cost of continuing the war was higher than that of any settlement, however unsatisfactory. It cannot be said that the legitimate grievances and interests of the various communal parties are addressed equally in the Taef Agreement, and this suggests that communal tensions may continue to build up over the coming years, creating renewed potential for open conflict. However, the recognition of different communal interests and some form of power-sharing between them (including the fragmentation of communal identities) must be addressed by the central state if Lebanon is to regain a modicum of stability and internal peace. Fortunately for all concerned, the international environment has improved considerably: the East–West conflict has disappeared, and Israel and the PLO are in the process of implementing a peace agreement. This has had a significant impact on the various fighting forces in

Lebanon, and just as a number of countries had an interest in keeping the conflict going for many years, so they now may have an interest in containing it. The effect on local political agents is significant. But while the violence has stopped, and national political and economic institutions are beginning to regain their lost strength, the underlying currents which led to the conflict in the first place are still there. Lebanon's national identity is still, as Kamal Hamdan underlines, hanging by a thread, and its survival as a viable nation-state into the twenty-first century is as problematic as ever. As it has been since its creation in 1920, the Lebanese national state is mainly the institutional framework within which the various communal elites attempt to accommodate their diverse economic and political interests.

Another dramatic instance of failed solutions is provided by Burundi. As René Lemarchand reminds us, hopes were high in 1988, when President Buyoya promoted the Charter of National Unity, which promised some redress to the country's majority Hutu population, though critics observed that it preserved Tutsi hegemony. A breakthrough towards a democratic solution appeared to have occurred when the leader of Frodebu, the moderate Hutu opposition party to the governing Uprona, was freely elected President of Burundi in 1993. But his untimely death, together with the President of Rwanda in the summer of 1994 (when the plane they were flying on was shot down, a dramatic turn of events which led to massive genocide in Rwanda), leaves the situation in Burundi wide open once more.

In contrast to a negotiated settlement in Lebanon and the failed attempt at democratic elections in Burundi, the conflict in Ethiopia came to an end with the military victory of the Ethiopian People's Revolutionary Democratic Front (EPRDF), formerly the Tigrai People's Liberation Front, in May 1991, and the collapse of the Mengistu dictatorship. The newly installed revolutionary government, after holding peace talks in London under the auspices of the United States, quickly adopted a national Charter which set up the Transitional Government of Ethiopia (TGE). The Charter granted Ethiopia's different nationalities or ethnic groups the right to self-determination, including secession. As a result, one observer reports, 'the repressive mechanisms maintained by former President Mengistu Haile Mariam have been released, leading to an upsurge in political tension and ethnic strife ...'[7] The new government proposed to establish a federated Ethiopia of 12 autonomous ethnic zones, but conflict between the various ethnic organizations who had jointly struggled for the overthrow of the Mengistu regime erupted soon after. For one, the Oromo Liberation Front (OLF) withdrew from the new governing coalition, accused the EPRDF of wanting to replace previous Amhara domination with Tigrayan domination and of election rigging and intimidation during Ethiopia's first multi-party regional elections. By the middle of 1992, 'low-intensity guerrilla war' had already erupted in many Oromo areas.

As one observer noted, ethnic resentment against the EPRDF is not restricted to the OLF. Various Amhara groups, such as the All-Amhara People's Organization (AAPO), who had also opposed the dictatorship, and some smaller groups, pulled out of the recent elections as well. 'Amhara resentment of the transitional government is growing . . . calls for an end to "Tigrayan Domination" and a return to a "United Ethiopia" have been circulating among the Amhara middle class.'[8]

In a 1993 referendum, Eritrea voted for its long-denied independence and withdrew from Ethiopia. Even before secession, relations between the new government and Eritrean People's Liberation Front (EPLF), who were close allies before, had become strained. By 1993, one student of Ethiopia's democratization process observed that 'the problems of ethnic division appear to be overwhelming the political landscape of post-Mengistu Ethiopia, thereby leaving the country with an unsettled political future.'[9]

In contrast to open victory or failed solutions, Malaysia shows us that ethnic conflict can be contained and managed through inter-elite arrangements and bargaining between contending communally-based political parties in a formally democratic system. However, such an arrangement lasted for less than 20 years in independent Malaysia, and has since been eroded by increasing ethnic tensions and the temptations of ethnocratic centralized rule by the political dominant Malay segment of the population. One author attributes this continuing 'communalism' to the interests of the Malaysian ruling class.

The current literature on conflict resolution, management, regulation and transformation is abundant. Each of the studies undertaken by UNRISD can provide evidence for any of a number of principles which are referred to in the theoretical literature, yet it is doubtful that blanket recipes for conflict resolution or management are useful or even relevant under the specific and complex circumstances which prevail in most cases.

Referring to armed conflicts in general, Wallensteen notes that many of the wars that were being waged in 1987 and 1988 did not result in a military victory for one of the contending parties, but rather settled down into a pattern of protracted conflict. This, he argues, is a major reason for civil talks to commence at some point. But conflict resolution will only be possible at the right moment, when the parties to the war realize that the struggle cannot be won. It is hard to predict the right moment; it may occur for any number of reasons, but it may also be sparked by the mobilization of popular organizations to exert pressure on both parties to accommodate each other so as to benefit the whole country. This was attempted at one time by peace movements in Northern Ireland, Israel, the Philippines, Sri Lanka, Guatemala and elsewhere.[10]

Moreover, a solution makes it necessary for parties to deal with groups that they would not previously agree to deal with. For example, the white supremacist government finally dealt face-to-face with the formerly outlawed African National Congress (ANC) to bring an end to apartheid and establish a democratic polity in South Africa. So did the government of Israel and the Palestine Liberation Organization (PLO), after decades of mutual non-recognition. In Latin America, the Nicaraguan Sandinistas had to negotiate with the political representatives of the 'contra' military force supported by the United States; peace accords were signed in 1992 in El Salvador between the government and the guerrilla movement (originally labelled by the former as bandits). Similarly, the Guatemalan government began negotiating with the rebel forces in that country in 1993. An Indian uprising in southeastern Mexico in January 1994 was first characterized as a rebellion of outlaws to be quickly put down by the regular army, but within a few days the Mexican government offered to negotiate legitimate grievances with the guerrillas' leadership. Since then, negotiations have stalled and an uneasy armed truce has set in, complicated by political instability in the region.

In the discussion of conflict resolution mechanisms, it is often assumed that the contending parties are in fact willing to negotiate, that it is in their interest to do so rather than to keep the conflict going. This is not always true. The leaders of a militant ethnic group in conflict may feel that they have more to gain by pursuing the struggle than by making peace. This was for a long time the position of the warring factions in Lebanon, of the PLO in its struggle with Israel and of the IRA in Northern Ireland. It is still the posture of the Tamil Tigers in Sri Lanka, the Sikh militants in the Punjab, the Shining Path guerrillas in Peru and ETA in the Basque country. A conflict may also continue when a dominant group or an ethnocratic state is unwilling to grant even minimum demands to a struggling ethnic challenger, which was for a long time (and to a certain extent still is) the situation of the Kurdish rebellion in Turkey. This is also why solutions to the Tutsi–Hutu conflict in Burundi have failed so far and why the conflict in the southern Sudan broke out anew after several years of quiescence.

The ethnic conflicts covered in the UNRISD project have produced thousands and tens of thousands of victims over the years. So have ethnic conflicts elsewhere. Victimization is an essential psychological component of these conflicts. Montville writes that victimization is based on three components: it is the personal experience of stunning violence, which creates a powerful sense of loss; there is no way that the violence can be seen as just and deserved; and the threat of further violence and loss at the hands of the aggressor continues into the future. He therefore concludes that the roots of political violence and terrorism in ethnic and sectarian conflicts come from the conviction that only continued activity in the defence of one's *self*, including one's group self, can reduce the threat of further aggression against the self. Can the wounds of conflict be healed in time? Healing, according to Montville, is one of the psychological tasks involved in resolving long-standing ethnic conflict. Will the Hutu and Tutsi in Burundi, the Maronites, Sunnis and Shi'ites in Lebanon, the Hindus and Muslims involved in communal strife in India, the northern and southern Sudanese, the Igbo, Tiv, Hausa and Yoruba in Nigeria, among so many others, be able to go through this process and get on with the business of life? Only time will tell.[11]

The total defeat of one of the parties and the total victory of another is one of the possible outcomes of an ethnic conflict. Biafra's attempt at secession from Nigeria was defeated militarily in the mid-1960s The revolutionary ethnic coalition of Tigrayans, Eritreans, Oromans and others was able to overthrow the Derg military dictatorship in Ethiopia in 1991. Yet even in conditions of victory and defeat (a zero-sum outcome), the conflict may simmer on for years if not decades, unless the underlying causes and grievances are addressed constructively. This is the lesson to be learned from such disparate ethnic conflicts as the Moro rebellion in the Philippines, the conflict in southern Sudan, the various Kurdish uprisings in Iran, Iraq and Turkey, the protracted guerrilla war in Guatemala, the Kabyle uprising in Algeria in the early 1980s, and many others. Moreover, the apparent victors in the conflict will have to deal with the issues raised by the conflict itself in order to guarantee their victory and, occasionally, to reshape society. This is the complex task faced by the victorious coalition in Ethiopia, and this was attempted, with varying degrees of success, by the Nigerian state after the Biafra war.

Mostly, however, ethnic conflicts do not end on a clear-cut note of victory or defeat for one of the parties. It is common for solutions to be sought, and sometimes achieved, in a process of negotiation between the contenders. Who will start the negotiations, how and when they will begin, how they will proceed and what the outcome will be, are some of the complex issues involved that must be faced.

Ethnic conflicts, like other kinds of struggles and movements, have a lifecycle of their own, and the potential outcome of negotiations will depend on the phase of the cycle in which they are begun. It is usually held that the earlier negotiations begin, the greater their likely success. Yet at an early stage in a conflict's cycle, the parties in struggle may not yet be ready to negotiate, each one feeling, perhaps, that they may have more to gain by continuing the fight.[12] This was the case in the war between Serbians, Croats and Muslims in Bosnia-Herzegovina between 1992 and 1995, and it holds for the struggle between Abkhazians and Georgians, as well as Armenians and Azerbaijanis in the early 1990s. Quite the opposite occurred in southern Mexico in 1994, where the government and the Zapatista Army of National Liberation, a small Indian peasant guerrilla group, agreed to sit down and negotiate within 12 days of the beginning of the uprising. Even here, however, the negotiations were broken off three months later and only resumed one year afterwards.

There are many competing approaches to the mechanics of negotiating the resolution of conflicts and there is a burgeoning literature on the subject. While *how* to negotiate is undoubtedly important, it is even more crucial to concentrate on *what* is to be negotiated. Horowitz, who has made a careful study of the politics of ethnic conflict in Malaysia and Sri Lanka, emphasizes the role of multi-ethnic political coalitions, vote pooling and other electoral mechanisms in multi-party democratic systems, to come to grips with ethnic antagonisms. He advises that

> the most reliable way, under conditions of democratic elections, is to make politicians reciprocally dependent on the votes of members of groups other than their own .... Neither the wishful abolition of ethnic parties nor a solemn admonition to politicians to think of national rather than ethnic interests is a good substitute for providing concrete incentives to multi-ethnic behaviour.[13]

It is surely correct to advance the proposition that the best solutions to antagonism between ethnic groups, or between an ethnic group and the state, will be achieved within the framework of a democratic political system. Malaysia has been more successful in this than Pakistan and Sri Lanka. Both Lebanon and Ethiopia are test cases for this proposition in the mid-1990s. Yet it is precisely when a democratic system is perceived by one ethnic group to work to its disadvantage that ethnic conflict can emerge, as the cases of Fiji and Guyana demonstrate.

In many more cases of ethnic conflict the conditions of a democratic polity are not present, as in the Kurdish regions, Burundi, Sudan, Ethiopia during the war, Nigeria under military rule, Guatemala, among others. Here negotiations leading to the reduction of violence, the management and the eventual solution of conflicts will have to take place between contending parties regardless of the possibility of legitimate electoral politics.

Given the intractable and protracted nature of many deep-rooted ethnic conflicts, John Burton and his colleagues propose a problem-solving approach to conflict resolution, based on the recognition of human needs. Burton introduces the concept of 'conflict *provention*' to signify taking steps to remove sources of conflict, and more positively to promote conditions in which collaborative and valued relationships control behaviours. Problem-solving, according to Burton, implies a concern with the causes that lead to conflict rather than with the overt violence and disruptions that are the manifestations or symptoms of such problems. This requires an understanding of the environment of conflict, which in turn leads to a conflict resolution process that aims at the *satisfaction* of human needs (including the identity, security, dignity and recognition of the individual and the group *self*), rather than the suppression of these needs by power.[14]

Whether ethnic conflicts are merely managed or regulated, whether they are reduced or transformed, or whether they are actually resolved, depends on a multitude of factors. In most instances, however, the final outcome must lead to changes in ethnic policies, or else the conditions for a continuation or re-emergence of the conflict are given. As we have seen in Chapter 7, ethnic policies – that is, the way in which states handle the ethnic diversity within their borders – may vary considerably. Sometimes these policies are specifically designed by governments or ethnic groups in power to contain or prevent ethnic conflict (e.g. preferential policies in Malaysia). Sometimes they are the outcome of previous conflicts, concessions granted by the state to an aggrieved minority or the result of bargaining and negotiation between contending ethnic groups (limited autonomy for the Kurds in Iraq, affirmative action policies in India and the United States). Sometimes they actually give rise to conflicts, when they do not satisfy the needs of a subordinate or minority ethnic group or when they impinge upon what such an ethnic group perceives to be its right (for example, the forced assimilation of Kurds in Turkey, the anti-Tamil policies of Sinhala governments in Sri Lanka). And at other times they are the result of agreements between the various ethnic groups as to how best to handle their differences (regional and linguistic accommodation between Flemish and Walloons in Belgium, ethnic harmony in Senegal).

The outcome of a process of ethnic conflict resolution may be, for example, a shift from ethnic exclusion to inclusion and participation. The civil rights movement in the United States led to legislative changes and increasing equality for African-Americans. The struggle of the ANC finally led to the dismantling of apartheid and a democratic awakening in South Africa where, for the first time, the African majority population has achieved equal rights. Conversely, the Fijian military coup produced a shift away from equality to the exclusion of the Indian-Fijian ethnic group, thus creating ethnic tensions and giving rise to the potential for conflict. A return to equality and democracy is now seen as the only way to prevent conflict escalation in that country.

Similarly, indigenous peoples' organizations (as in Guatemala and Mexico) struggle for an end to discrimination, marginalization and ethnocide, and recent legislative changes in several Latin American countries provide a new framework for indigenous participation. While some indigenous peoples demand equal rights and, in fact, the possibility of integration in the wider society (the principal demand of the Guatemalan Maya, who constitute a demographic majority in their country), others struggle for autonomy and the recognition of diversity (this was the issue between the Miskito Indians of the Atlantic Coast and the Sandinista government in Nicaragua in the 1980s).[15]

Numerous ethnic conflicts around the world might be resolved if certain national governments were to abandon their emphasis on assimilation and integration of subordinate ethnic groups and adopt more pluralistic policies, including various forms of regional autonomy. The issue of autonomy is often at the core of an ethnic conflict, as we have seen in the cases of Kurdistan, southern Sudan, Ethiopia, as well as in Sri Lanka, Nicaragua, Quebec and other areas. The granting and recognition of autonomy to ethnic groups, minorities or indigenous peoples in certain territorial units (regions) is an option that many states could have, but only a few have been willing to take. Autonomy includes a number of basic issues, such as land, territory and natural resources, governmental structures, legal systems, education and culture, language, social and public services, tax revenues, etc. It may occur within unitary state structures as well as federal and confederal systems. In countries where autonomy has been tried, it has proved to be a useful and constructive mechanism for conflict resolution, albeit a complex one. (But then, which conflict resolution mechanism is not?)[16]

If autonomy, as can be argued, is one expression of the right to self-determination, another expression surely is secession, national liberation or the establishment of an independent state. Autonomy, and its accompanying concept of devolution, while designed to address the needs and grievances of specific territorial groups, is basically an administrative instrument used by an existing state. Secession and the establishment of a fully independent political unit, on the other hand, usually occurs as the fulfilment of the aspirations of an ethnic group (or people or nation), regardless of the interests of the dominant groups who control the state. Among the UNRISD case studies, the independence of Eritrea is a direct result of the end of the ethnic conflict in Ethiopia (even though, as pointed out above, new ethnic conflicts may be imminent in that country). The secession of Slovakia brought an end to Czechoslovakia in a non-conflictive 'velvet divorce' in 1993. Other recent attempts at secession have been neither successful nor peaceful. The fear of Tamil or Kurdish secession by the Sri Lankan and Turkish governments are one of the reasons why the ethnic conflicts in those countries continue. The war in Bosnia-Herzegovina and its attendant horrors is the result of the Serbian effort to divide the country.

Of 30 protracted wars for national independence since the Second World War, studied by Ted Gurr in his project on Minorities at Risk, only 14 groups have achieved some success, usually in the form of regional autonomy. Seven groups, on the other hand, have suffered decisive defeats. And in six other instances, conflicts persist or are escalating. On average, serious conflict lasted 14 years before success was achieved by the struggling groups. The seven wars that states succeeded in suppressing lasted an average of more than 25 years. It is obvious from this comparative survey that the human and material costs of protracted conflicts can become very high indeed.[17]

While autonomy and other forms of territorial subdivision may represent arrangements for what Asbjørn Eide calls 'pluralism in togetherness' within the unit of an existing state,[18] the attempt at secession or other forms of territorial separation (including irredentist demands) by an embattled ethnie, may put this group on a collision course with the state (e.g. Northern Ireland, Sri Lanka, Nagorno-Karabakh in Azerbaijan), and may fuel more conflict and violence than its proponents expect to solve. That is why the issue of secession is exceptionally controversial and is rejected by many specialists as a valid outcome of conflict resolution processes, except as a last resort, when all other alternatives have failed.[19]

The emotionally charged issue of secession involves the basic question of the relationship between existing states and subordinate ethnic groups. From the viewpoint of the state, if one adopts the perspective of the *raison d'état*, secession is a dangerous thing, for it challenges the core idea upon which the nation-state is built, and upon which the dominant ethnic group bases its own legitimacy. However, from the viewpoint of a subordinate, disadvantaged ethnie, which may have a long list of accumulated grievances against an ethnocratic state, secession may mean freedom, liberation and the final fulfilment of historical aspirations. In the *Realpolitik* of today's world, the issue of secession as an ingredient of so many ethnic conflicts pits the rights of the state (or the national interest as it is often called) against the rights of peoples.[20] The international system recognizes almost exclusively the rights of states and their territorial integrity and is therefore quite unsympathetic to secession as an outcome of ethnic conflict resolution.[21]

There are, however, numerous other possible outcomes of ethnic conflict resolution, and they mainly point in the direction of increased pluralism, whether this is called *multi-culturalism*, as in the United States and Western Europe,[22] or consociationalism or power-sharing, as proposed by Lijphart and others.[23] Whatever their weaknesses and limitations, pluralistic policies, as we have tried to show in Chapter 7, may go a long way in reducing many of the underlying grievances which give rise to ethnic conflicts. Some observers note that the 'consociational' model, which characterized Lebanon's political system for many decades, showed its limitations because it was unable to prevent the civil war. However, the peace accord which brought an end to this war reaffirmed the basic power-sharing system between the contending communities, and no other feasible alternative has been proposed by the Lebanese themselves.

Lemarchand rightly argues that in Burundi neither territorial subdivision nor outright assimilation nor the denial of ethnicity can provide adequate solutions to the conflict between Tutsi and Hutu, but only the development of power-sharing arrangements that satisfy the legitimate needs and aspirations of both groups will eventually bring peace to this ravaged country. The horrendous massacres which broke out in neighbouring Rwanda in 1994 after the shooting down of the plane in which the presidents of both Rwanda and Burundi died, are probably a lesson that will not be lost on the Burundi people, both Tutsi and Hutu.

Some kind of power-sharing will eventually have to emerge between the rebellious South and the dominant North in the Sudan. Unlike the Eritreans in Ethiopia, as Markakis has shown, the southern Sudanese rebels do not seek secession, but rather greater participation at the centre and respect for their cultural, religious and linguistic differences. Power-sharing will also, most probably, develop out of the conflict in Fiji, just as it has contained and reduced the potential for conflict in Malaysia for a time, as Mavis Putucheary has shown in her case study. In Nigeria, Okwudiba Nnoli proposes that ethnicity (that is, acute ethnic competition for power at the centre and for limited state resources) should make way for greater devolution to the local units (states) and true power-sharing at the federal level.

So separation, secession and the formation of ethnically homogeneous territorial units (whether independent states or components of larger federations) are not the only available solutions to ethnic conflics. They may, in fact, not always be feasible and perhaps not even desirable if all the conflicting rights, desires and interests of all contenders are taken into account. Asbjørn Eide, the UN rapporteur for minority rights, admonishes that:

> The search for multicultural pluralism requires a delicate mix of equality and separateness. It seeks to combine efforts to ensure equal opportunity for everyone in the national society, with programs to allocate resources, power and space for separate groups. It requires tolerance and encouragement of ethnic political parties as part of the political system, in order that the different communal groups can participate in power-sharing or at least have an impact on decision-making, and yet it also requires the existence of brokerage, of cross-ethnic or cross-religious alliances concerned with other issues than ethnicity or religion.[24]

11 Conclusions

At the end of our comparative journey to some of the hotspots of ethnic conflict in the world (and to one or two countries where open conflict was avoided), there are a number of questions which may be posed, and perhaps some which might find an answer. Are we in fact speaking about the same thing when we describe such disparate situations as have been covered in this volume as 'ethnic' conflicts? Has not the the the term 'ethnicity' become a useful but perhaps over-simplifying catch-all for what used to be called 'class struggle' or a 'war of national liberation' or conflict over 'nation-building' or simply a 'power struggle'? Does the 'ethnic' label actually help explain and distinguish a certain kind of conflict from other kinds of conflict, or does it, on the contrary, only confuse the issues?

The research project undertaken by UNRISD in several countries around the globe is comparative in so far as it deals with contemporary situations on different continents. The authors of this collaborative study expected to learn something from each other's research, and by presenting the results to a wider public, it is also hoped that the results will contribute to a better understanding of the dynamics of conflict, change and development in different circumstances. Hard-nosed 'comparativists' will no doubt miss the quantitative data that lends itself to factor analysis and other kinds of comparative techniques. Others might regret the absence of formal analytical models in which the 'political', the 'social', the 'cultural' and the 'economic' could be given their respective weights and assessed for their predictive value. Others perhaps would like to see more micro-level analysis. No doubt the results presented here may not satisfy every reader. We can only refer readers to the original monographs in which breadth of information is matched by analytical depth to an extent which cannot be reflected in this volume.

We may define an ethnic conflict as a protracted social and political confrontation between contenders who define themselves and each other in ethnic terms; that is, when criteria such as national origin, religion, race, language and other markers of cultural identity are used to distinguish the opposing parties. Ethnic identities are made up not only of objective attributes, but also of intensively held subjective feelings and beliefs about them, which contribute to 'freeze' such attributes, or sometimes even create and construct them when they are not actually present. Conflict does not arise naturally because groups of people are different, but because of special meanings attached to these differences which make them appear as irreductible and incompatible. This is clearly the case in some of the bipolar societies studied in this volume. Hutu and Tutsi have lived together without resorting to violence for centuries, yet for reasons set out in previous chapters, their respective identities have turned into focal points of violent conflict in Burundi and Rwanda. Similarly, African Guyanese and Indian Guyanese became arch-rivals in post-colonial Guyana, as did Native Fijians and Indian Fijians in that Pacific island.

Conflicts between ethnic groups are not inevitable, nor are they eternal; those who speak or write glibly about 'ancestral tribal hatreds' as a presumptive explanation of a conflict usually betray more of their own ignorance than knowledge about the situation they report on. Ethnic conflicts evolve out of specific historical situations, they are moulded by particular and unique circumstances, and they are constructed to serve certain interests by idealists and ideologues, visionaries and opportunists, political leaders and 'ethnic power-brokers' of various kinds. There was nothing pre-ordained about the conflict between Croats, Serbs and Bosnian Muslims in the former Yugoslavia, yet a series of events (which could have been avoided in time) led almost inevitably to confrontation.

Usually, these conflicts arise, grow, stabilize, wane and disappear over a period of years. Sometimes they remain dormant, only to re-emerge at a later date. Like other kinds of confrontation, ethnic conflicts go through a period of incubation, of shorter or longer duration according to the circumstances. In the cases analysed in this volume, it has not been possible in most instances to speak of a single causal factor that sets off ethnic conflict in any particular situation. To be sure, the razing of the mosque in Ayodhya by Hindu fundamentalists was the spark that ignited communal violence, but even here it is necessary to refer to predisposing factors, which of course will vary from case to case. The specific importance of a triggering or igniting event, which actually unleashes a conflict, sometimes in violent form, must not be underestimated, but usually there are more underlying causes.

In a number of cases studied by UNRISD, the role of the colonial state in setting the stage for the ethnic conflicts to come cannot be ignored. In several African countries, for example, where inter-ethnic relations in pre-colonial times were usually free of conflict, it was not until direct European rule was imposed that internal political struggle became increasingly identified with the major ethnic groups. In Burundi as well as in Rwanda, 'the colonial state served as the crucible within which collective identities were reshaped and mythologized'.[1] Elsewhere, as in Nigeria, the colonial economy expanded and created new urban nodes, in which politicized ethnic relations emerged.

Different patterns developed in societies where foreign peoples were brought in either as slaves or indentured servants or simply as plantation labour. Whereas in Fiji and Malaysia the natives obtained from the colonial administration certain guarantees regarding what they now consider as their original rights (paramountcy in Fiji, 'Sons of the soil' in Malaysia) thus effectively barring the immigrant communities from full participation in the political affairs of the country, in Guyana, by contrast, the ethnic conflict engaged two immigrant populations, neither of which could lay claim to original occupation of the land. In some cases, the territorial element in the emergence of ethnic conflict is of particular importance. Fijians and Malays derive their ethnicity from territorial attachments, as do the Kurdish people, who have been denied a state of their own. Yoruba, Igbo and Hausa identities in Nigeria have regional roots, as do the identities of numerous other peoples in Africa and elsewhere.

The emergence of ethnicity as a politically mobilizing element has been mentioned by all our authors as being one of the important triggering factors in conflict. Thus, in Guyana the major political parties are identified with Indians and Africans respectively; in Burundi, Tutsi and Hutu each organized their own ethnic parties. A similar political polarization along ethnic lines took place in Malaysia, Fiji and Pakistan. In Nigeria, each of the major ethnic regional groups, the Yoruba, the Hausa-Fulani and the Igbos formed their ethnic party organizations. When, as in so many cases, politicized ethnicity leads to (sometimes violent) conflict, it is no wonder that analysts argue for political solutions and electoral mechanisms that might cross-cut ethnic loyalties. Yet as our case studies show, ethnic identities are often quite resilient to mechanical attempts at 'constitutional engineering' or similar procedures designed to ease ethnic tensions.

While showing certain similarities with traditional colonial empires, the conflicts arising in the aftermath of the break-up of the Soviet Union and the Yugoslav Federation result from specific historical factors. Tishkov notes that in the former Soviet Union social and political disparities and cleavages often coincide with cultural, ethnic, racial or religious boundaries. Representatives of some ethnic groups or nationalities enjoy a dominant political and cultural status, among them the ethnic Russians in the Russian Federation, the Kazakhs in Kazakhstan, and in general the so-called titular nationalities. As the Soviet Union broke up, previously subordinate nationalities became dominant majorities in new multi-ethnic states, while many minorities and ethnically related people were divided by new borders. Now the new dominant groups claim exclusive power over cultural institutions and priority status in the economy and social services. In turn, those who used to be 'double' minorities and the so-called 'new' minorities (such as ethnic Russians in Moldova and the Baltic states) are now challenging their diminished status and what they perceive as discriminatory attitudes against them.[2] The potential for conflict increases as ethnic identities overlap with socio-economic inequalities.

As already mentioned, the evidence presented in this study does not support the hypothesis, often encountered in current political analysis, of 'ancient tribal hatreds', long suppressed, breaking out when some kind of institutional lid is suddenly lifted. Nevertheless, one of the recurring features of the case studies undertaken in this project, focusing mainly on the causes and consequences of ethnic conflict, is the fragility of the institutions that are designed to avoid and hold conflict in check, and the ease with which they tend to break down when conditions emerge which may lead to the exacerbation of ethnic tensions, antagonisms, competition and conflict. Under such conditions ethnic conflicts do not so much break out, like some prehistoric monster pecking its way out of its shell, but rather, as many of our authors have shown, they are in fact created to serve certain quite contemporary and modern (not exactly postmodern!)[3] interests.

In all the conflictive situations analysed in this volume, the issue of ethnic identity formation is certainly an intervening factor of unusual importance. What emerges from the study of several cases in Chapter 4 is the fact that politicized ethnic identities are formed in the heat of struggle as a result of the articulation of group objectives and strategies that are played out on the political scene, within the framework of a modern party system and highly contested periodic elections. The primeval tribal enmities, which are so often referred to in the media when covering ethnic conflicts, are often invented by the contending parties to justify or legitimize their current attitudes. Only in rare circumstances do they have an actual basis in historical facts.

But the politicization of ethnicity cannot be reduced only to the instrumental ends of some 'ethnic entrepreneurs' or to the 'organic intellectuals', who are able to mobilize their followers around newly discovered 'ethnic' issues. As the cases in Chapter 4 show with great clarity, the 'ethnic discourse' – whether it is the self-perception of the Hutu as a victimized indigenous people in Burundi, the mutual stereotypes of Africans and Indians in Guyana, or the search for a Hindu national identity in India – reflects a problematic that has several layers.

(a) The 'ethnic discourse' usually addresses the deep-seated affective, psychic identity needs of a population. While it may be argued that ethnic narratives are constructed or 'invented', it is equally true that they address issues of 'collective consciousness' or 'collective memory', which ethnic intellectuals are eager to take up, and which often justify and legitimize their activities. As Tishkov remarks, the conflict between Georgians and Abhkazians in the Republic of Georgia began as a conflict between philologists-turned-politicians. Serbian and Croat linguists struggled over the respective merits of their idioms from the nineteenth century to the 1986 Memorandum of the Serbian Academy of Science which set the stage for the bitter conflict that erupted five years later. Hindu cultural nationalists organized around 'Hindutva' insist on the primacy of the wholly indigenous cultural tradition of the Hindus.[4] The resurgence of Indian identity in Latin America (Guatemala and elsewhere) coalesces around the shared idea that indigenous Americans have suffered over 500 years of colonial exploitation, which entitles them to the collective redress of historical injustices.

Ethnic narratives, whether passed on from generation to generation or invented at specific times to serve particular objectives, constitute powerful tools that help to reinterpret history, to provide a legitimate basis for ethnic ideologies, to justify ethnic political activities and to mobilize ethnic constituencies around ethnically defined goals. At the same time, they satisfy the need for belonging and identity that individuals can fulfil only through collective and communal action.

(b) Ethnic discourse often emerges as a result of the breakdown of traditional society in which, Jor better or for worse, different ethnic groups had an established and recognized position in a system of reciprocal and relatively stable relationships. Ethnicity, as Okwudiba Nnoli argues, is basically an urban phenomenon in Nigeria and some other African countries, though in recent years it has also extended to rural areas. Ethnicity here means not only the identification of people with their ethnic kin group, but rather the political uses of ethnic identities. It is not surprising that recent urban migrants in the sprawling, disorganized cities of the Third World would find that some of their many problems could be addressed through networks in which ethnic bonds play an important cementing role. The same phenomenon has been observed in the way successive waves of foreign migrants adapt to urban life in industrial North America. When the market economy expands and breaks down traditionally stable economic relationships, one way people react to changing circumstances is through social and political organization along class lines. Thus we see emerging peasant unions, newly formed labour organizations, agricultural workers' syndicates, associations of migrant labourers, artisans or small traders, and so forth. Such forms of collective action are legitimized by ideologies of class. Often, however, these ideologies of class do not penetrate deeply enough in the collective consciousness. When a collectivity perceives itself to have been exploited economically as a cultural, racial, religious or ethnic group, then it may react as an ethnie and develop an ethnic discourse or counter-discourse. This appears to have occurred among the Shi'ites in Lebanon, as Kamal Hamdan describes it. The newly emergent 'Indianist' intellectuals in South America have adopted the slogan: 'We were oppressed as "Indians", and as "Indians" shall we be liberated!', which recalls the equally mobilizing slogan, 'Black is beautiful', which militant Blacks in the United States used effectively for many years as an answer to racial discrimination. When the 'Sons of the soil' feel threatened by non-Malays, or the native Fijians by immigrant peoples from across the seas, then the ethnic ideology surrounding the concept of *Bumiputra* in the first case, and of 'paramountcy rights' in the second, is wielded to defend the interests of the supposedly threatened ethnic group. Ethnic discourses are also fashioned to justify racist and xenophobic ideologies that aim at preserving ethnic dominance and discrimination. The recent successes of xenophobic and anti-immigrant parties in some industrialized states appeal to sentiments of endangered ethnic or national identities in these countries. The new militant nationalisms in Eastern Europe come as a response to the breakdown of the total institutions of communist polity; nationalist and ethnic discourse provides purpose and identification to people who sense a loss of meaning and direction in their lives as the old system crumbles and the new, as the saying goes, is not yet born.

(c) For analytical purposes, we may distinguish between a purely 'ethnic' discourse and an 'ethno-nationalist' one. While the former emphasizes the cultural links and identity of a given ethnic group, the latter is concerned mainly with state power and territorial sovereignty. In both cases, the ethnic discourse relates to the nationalist ideology of the modern state, and therefore to the various differing and sometimes competing concepts of the 'nation'. For example, the 'Hindutva' discourse which Ashis Nandy describes in relation to the conflict over the Babri mosque in Ayodhya developed in support of a certain conception of the Indian nation-state, which Hindu cultural nationalists are actively promoting. In contrast, the ethnic discourse of the Hutu, on which Lemarchand reports, arises in opposition to the dominant Tutsi conception of the modern state in Burundi, which the Hutu consider as being discriminatory against them. As we saw in the case of Malaysia, the Chinese and other non-Malays vie for a 'Malaysian Malaysia' in which all ethnic groups have equal status, whereas the ethnic Malays have been actively constructing a 'Malayan homeland' as their national state.

(d) Ethnic identities in fact compete with 'national' identity for the people's loyalties and involvement, and this has become one of the major problems in multiple areas where ethnic conflicts occur. The reason for this is not hard to find, and it is because so often the 'national' ideology, which attempts to subsume all so-called sub-national identities, is in fact an 'ethnocratic' or at least an 'ethnocentric' one. It is only rarely that the concept of the nation as a whole transcends that of one of its component parts in a multi-ethnic society. Switzerland comes to mind as an historically successful case. When the French-speaking Jurassiens sought to break away from the canton of Berne in the 1970s, they did so on the basis of their perceived ethnic identity, but did not challenge the legitimacy of the Swiss Confederation. By contrast, the French-speaking Québecois who proclaim a 'distinct status' for themselves, may in time end up separating from the rest of Canada despite the separatists' defeat by a slim margin in the 1995 referendum. In most of the UNRISD case studies, we find that the dominant concept of the 'nation' coincides with the self-perception of the dominant or majority ethnic group, from which the subordinate group or groups are effectively excluded, or at least feel themselves to be so. One of the reasons for the fall of the Ethiopian military regime, as Markakis describes it, was the effect of the centralizing policies of the ruling Amhara ethnic group. In Guatemala, as elsewhere in Latin America, the 'national' idea, developed by the white and *mestizo* ruling classes, rejected the participation of the majority indigenous peoples, who are now developing a Maya counter-ideology.[5]

Many of the ethnic conflicts occurring around the world involve levels of intense violence that shock world public opinion. Why do these events occur? Why has political conflict led to genocidal massacres in Burundi and Rwanda? How is it that the demolition of a mosque by Hindu militants produces communal riots hundreds of miles away which cost thousands of lives? Why do Serbs, Croats and Bosnian Muslims end up killing, maiming and torturing each other over the political organization of the post-Yugoslav states? There are no ready-made answers to these questions.

One response is that riots and massacres are not unpredictable, spontaneous outbursts of hatred and rage by masses of people running amok. As the cases of India and Burundi show, interpersonal violence can be planned, instigated and manipulated by politically motivated agitators, who create and then play on the feelings of insecurity and fear of an uninformed or deliberately misinformed populace. While the instigators of violence may play a carefully calculated game, to which many interests may be a party, people who actually commit violent acts may be motivated less by calculated interest than by non-rational emotions.

Whether such motivations should be given explanatory value in the analysis of ethnic conflicts, or whether they are to be seen as smokescreens behind which small groups of 'ethnic manipulators' add up their 'rational interests', is still a matter of much debate. It is clear that the existence of shared attributes among the members of an identifiable ethnic group is not a sufficient cause to fire the common ethnic imagination, let alone trigger ethnic conflict and violence. If conflict involves a challenge to the political system or the state that cannot be resolved by the system itself, the result is frequently a violent confrontation. It is possible, as in communal rioting in India and occasionally in Africa, that conflict between ethnically defined social categories may not have this overall political dimension, although given the all-encompassing nature of the contemporary state, this is unlikely. In Sudan and Ethiopia, the direct cause of conflict appeared to be the monopolization by one ethnic group of the state and its resources. This is probably an essential condition for the emergence of ethnic conflict. Barred from access by the rules of the game, it is understandable that ethnic groups will seek to change the rules. Because it is regarded as introducing subject-ive and irrational elements in the political process, ethnicity is considered to be a destabilizing and divisive factor, and not a few means have been devised to excise its malignant influence, as has occurred in Nigeria.

In Burundi, the wholesale massacre of innocent people occurs on both sides of a socially constructed fault line. Lemarchand describes ethnic viol-ence as a mode of discourse and a mode of political action, a system of definitions of ethnic selves, by which ethnicity is transformed, mobilized and ultimately invested into the horrors and irrationality of genocidal viol-ence. The result has been the emergence among Hutu elements of a new sense of self-awareness as a martyred community, and a vision of the 'other' (Tutsi) as an alien, inherently oppressive minority, capable of extraordinary cruelties. On both sides of the ethnic fault-line, summoning the past to explain the present has become part and parcel of a discursive practice intended to legitimize ethnic ideologies.

The question of legitimacy is also at the heart of the ethnic conflict in Guyana, according to Premdas, who postulates that at any early stage in state building, group consciousness can actually be restrained and made into a positive force of identity formation and group solidarity. But if nur-tured and systematically sustained by personal ambition, elite interests, institutional practices, a momentum in its evolution then occurs, spreads over a widening array of institutions, and a threshold of virtual uncontrol-lable inter-group mass behaviour is achieved. This results in the polariza-tion of the state into an ethnically bifurcated structure laying the foundation for the loss of regime legitimacy.

Ethnic conflicts constitute, according to some scholars, a particular kind of social and political confrontation that is more related to questions of identity and deeply rooted values than to issues of rational interest. Consequently, they tend to be protracted, linked to collective historical memories and their reinterpretations, suffused with highly charged emotions and passions, imbued with myths and fears and perceived threats, entwined with deeply held beliefs and aspirations, and thus much more difficult to reduce to the ordinary give-and-take of political bargaining or negotiation. This is not to say that other kinds of social or economic conflict are at all times exempt of passion (they are surely not), nor that rational interest or calculus does not play a role in ethnic conflict (as we have seen, indeed it does). It is suggested, however, that ethnic conflicts often revolve around the self-perception of an entire people within the framework of the modern nation-state, and that therefore their dynamics involves competing concepts of the nation and contrasting ideas about the very structure of the state itself.

Generally, ethnic conflicts pass through a period of incubation and build up over time, before they actually shake the foundations of the social edifice, or before violence becomes part of the 'discourse' of conflict. While some conflicts escalate in almost linear fashion, others wax and wane in cycles according to multiple and sometimes unpredictable circumstances.

The duration, intensity and extension of ethnic conflicts vary according to the different strata of society which become directly implicated. Individuals may become involved, for example, when members of different ethnies compete for jobs, power and privileges, or when ethnic animosities, racism and xenophobia condition interpersonal relations at the local level in everyday activities. Still, different ethnies will continue to live together and interact, as they have for hundreds and thousands of years, despite outbreaks of violence.

Interpersonal ethnic tensions, which are widespread in the world, do not necessarily turn into collective conflicts. In fact, the dominant institutions of society may be designed to control and prevent them. On the other hand, however, as we have seen in some of the cases studied in this book (Burundi, Lebanon, Pakistan), ethnic confrontations fostered by political groups or state institutions may, in turn, trigger intensive interpersonal ethnic animosities which frequently turn violent. For example, ethnic riots, rampages, massacres that cost many innocent lives and cause major material damage may seem at first glance to be irrational, emotional outbursts, unrelated to the formal institutions of society and therefore unpredictable and uncontrollable. Yet many studies show that riots and massacres are more often than not instigated by ethnic 'entrepreneurs', fanned by ethnic ideologues and political profiteers, and are actually fine-tuned and fairly well controlled by local power-brokers and manipulators.

The actual role of such ethnic leaders and their relation to their followers is not yet very well understood. In numerous cases it is known that before group conflict erupted, the ideological underpinnings of confrontation were established by ethnic organizations, political parties or sundry groups which developed a rationale for the conflict. The role of the media in fanning ethnic hatreds has been widely documented, from Yugoslavia to Sri Lanka to Rwanda. Yet it is also clear that the ideological underpinnings of confrontation often result from the historical accumulation of perceived grievances by at least one of the contenders.

In the various cases in which subordinate ethnic groups struggle for equality, recognition or separation, or conversely, in which a dominant ethnic group feels threatened, there is a crucial role for an ethnic 'intelligentsia' that formulates and disseminates the ethnic ideologies on which collective action is based. Racism, anti-semitism and xenophobia are not irrational subjective outbursts, but the result of ideological constructions carefully crafted by ethnic ideologues.

Violent incidents, such as riots, massacres and genocidal killings, are usually short-lived though their implications are far-reaching. More than interpersonal animosity and mutual rejection, protracted conflicts involve relations of power between the disputing parties. This is where the issue of leadership becomes particularly salient. In this respect, the role played by political 'outbidders' is particularly crucial for the evolution of any ethnic conflict. In some of the cases studied in this volume, the extremists in both adversarial segments of the population drew the more moderate elements towards intransigent positions. The outbidders on both sides made an inter-ethnic alliance of moderate elements increasingly difficult, and helped push the system to the point of confrontation.

The most intensive and protracted ethnic conflicts involve the struggle between structured ethnic organizations (political parties, nationalist movements, armed militias or guerrilla groups) and the institutions of the state, generally the central government. For an organization to become effective in the pursuit of its group objectives or interests, it must be able to mobilize, in other words, to turn from a passive collection of individuals into an active participant in public life. The degree and scope of mobilization is an essential ingredient in all forms of collective action. The longest and most successful ethnic struggles in our case studies are those that were able to maintain a high degree of mobilization.

Economic factors play a crucial role in the generation of ethnic conflicts. When regional and social disparities in the distribution of economic resources also reflect differences between identified ethnic groups, then conflicts over social and economic issues readily turns into ethnic conflict. The Tigrai and Eritrean Liberation Movements had their origin in some of the poorest regions in Ethiopia. In Lebanon, the regions inhabited mainly by the Shi'ites were traditionally among the most impoverished. The Amal movement, one of the militant Shi'ite factions in the civil war, was founded as the Movement of the Deprived. How to take advantage of the nation's economic resources is also one of the permanent features of ethnic competition in Nigeria. The various ethnic groups perceive the 'national cake' as being essentially limited, and the main goal of the inter-ethnic struggle for power at the level of the central government is to draw away resources to benefit this or that particular ethnic region. In ethnically bipolar states the two major ethnic groups have long struggled over the distribution of economic resources, whether this is land as in Fiji, or jobs and opportunities in the civil service and public enterprises as in Malaysia and Guyana.

The struggles of indigenous and tribal peoples are directly related to economic deprivation, exploitation, land loss, ecological devastation and other hardships imposed on them by economic development, reinforced by the neo-liberal policies of the 1980s and 1990s. A recent study undertaken by the World Bank concludes that poverty among Latin America's indigenous population is pervasive and severe, and that the living conditions of the indigenous population are generally abysmal, especially when compared to those of the non-indigenous population. The study attributes this 'economic cost' of ethnicity to discrimination in the labour market and to the unequal distribution of human capital among different ethnic groups.[6] Under these circumstances it is surprising that not more indigenous uprisings have occurred in this region.

Generally speaking, then, economic causes can be said to be among the major factors generating ethnic conflicts. While they, in turn, tend to have a negative impact on a country's economy as a whole, they frequently turn out to benefit certain ethnic elites and their providers, who then develop an interest in the perpetuation of the conflict. When outside economic support dries up, pressures build up for a reduction in violence and the search for peaceful solutions.

Ethnic conflicts do not occur in a vacuum; they usually relate to the policies that states have implemented to deal with ethnic diversity over time. While some types of policy are designed to lessen the potential of ethnic conflicts, other kinds actually foster it. To simplify a very complex panorama, we have identified three major types of state policy in ethnic matters: assimilation, exclusion and pluralism.

Modern nationalist ideologies have furthered different kinds of assimilationist policies for ethnic minorities and subordinate culturally distinct peoples, from the illusion of the American melting pot to the integration of Indians into the dominant nationality in Latin America, to the imposition of an ethnocratic model of nation-building in numerous post-colonial states. National integration, as understood in these instances, requires the non-dominant ethnic groups (indigenous and tribals, former slaves or indentured servants, recent immigrants, territorial minorities and other 'non-state' peoples) to shed their respective identities in order to integrate into a wider 'national' entity. While this may occur spontaneously in some cases, and whereas numerous ethnies do in fact willingly assimilate into a majority or dominant culture, in many other instances national, ethnic, religious or linguistic minorities (and sometimes majorities, as indigenous peoples in a number of Latin American countries) reject this premiss. And when states seek to impose it by force, it becomes a potent source of alienation and a great boost for dissident movements.

The pros and cons of assimilationist policies are currently widely debated in different forums. There is no lack of arguments in favour of assimilation, the basic one being the plea for 'national unity' in the face of what some perceive to be the dangerous centrifugal and disintegrating forces associated with ethnic and cultural diversity. As 'nation-builders' have known for a long time, a common language, a standardized school system, a homogeneous legal system, an integrated bureaucracy, among other elements, are powerful weapons in the development of modern states. On the other hand, the heavy-handed state-building that has taken place in so many parts of the world in recent decades has been terribly destructive to many peoples whose distinct cultures and identities, histories and traditions have been ploughed under the ground so that new nations might sprout. Whereas assimilationist policies may look attractive from the perspective of the elites of the nation-state, they frequently look less than satisfactory to the peoples at whom these policies are directed.

Exclusionary ethnic politics may take many forms. While its most extreme expression, physical genocide, is fortunately rare in our times (though by no means absent, as in Rwanda in 1994), other policies may be implemented with similar effects. Such is the case of the 'ethnic cleansing' in former Yugoslavia. Massacres and pogroms within the framework of ethnic conflicts are widespread phenomena, though they are not always the outcome of specific state-inspired policies. Their purpose may be to eliminate the political or cultural leadership of the victimized ethnic

group, to wreak revenge for real or imagined offences, to repress an insurrection or uprising, or to terrorize the targeted group into submissiveness
and passivity.

More widespread than the physical elimination of an entire ethnic group
is cultural genocide or ethnocide. This refers to state policies designed to
destroy the cultural identity of a group through various kinds of coercive
measures such as forced religious conversion, destruction of cultural monuments and sites, land expropriations, massive relocation of populations,
imposition of a new language, and similar measures. Coercive assimilationist policies sometimes take the form of ethnocide, as so many indigenous and tribal peoples can testify.

Exclusionary policies may take various other guises, such as distinct
forms of segregation, of which the now defunct system of apartheid was
perhaps the most notorious example. Racial minorities are the *prima facie*
victims of exclusionary politics, even when assimilation is being fostered
as an official objective.

In recent decades, pluralism has become the most common category of
ethnic policies. To the extent that most modern states are in fact made up of
different ethnic groups, they can be referred to as plural societies. But it is
only when state policies are geared more or less successfully to the accommodation of the diverse and sometimes conflicting interests of the principal
ethnic groups that we can speak of pluralism as a policy objective. This can
be achieved through the implementation of preferential policies in the job
market, affirmative action in the educational system and the workplace, proportional representation and other kinds of electoral mechanisms in the
political system, or territorial autonomy when so required.

In democractic polities, ethnic pluralism can be respected by scrupu-
lous and fair adherence to a carefully designed electoral mechanism in
which every ethnic collectivity that so wishes can find adequate representation, and can become involved in the continuing give-and-take between
different kinds of interest groups who are more or less equally placed in
the system. To the extent, however, that so many ethnic conflicts result
precisely from the asymmetrical placement of ethnic groups in the national
power structure, observers agree that more than free and fair elections are
required to ensure the success of pluralistic policies. It is not enough for
members of all and every ethnic group to be endowed with the same rights
and prerogatives. Therefore, other approaches recognize the existence of
ethnic groups and fashion the political system according to some inter-
elite arrangement that may be described as 'consociational' or a 'grand
settlement', in which arrangements are made to safeguard the interests of
the major ethnic groups, regardless of the vagaries of electoral politics.

More lasting arrangements are sometimes attempted through territorial divisions. While federalism is often proposed as a convenient solution for regional-ethnic conflict, the break-up of Yugoslavia shows that it is no guarantee for ethnic harmony and accommodation in the absence of other factors. Autonomy can be considered as both a form of territorial administration of a state and as a collective human right. Many contemporary ethnic conflicts, as we have seen, take place within the context of a struggle over autonomy. This is not an end in itself – it is a political tool to ensure that other rights and needs are appropriately addressed. Autonomy arrangements usually contemplate at least one and usually several of the following basic issues: language and culture, education, access to government civil service employment and social services, land and territory, control over natural resources, access to and control over fiscal resources, and representative local government structures (including the judiciary).[7]

Effective autonomy must have a territorial base, and therefore not every 'minority at risk' or ethnic group in conflict can aspire to solve its problems through this political-administrative instrument, though there may be levels of autonomy linked to the exercise of, say, traditional legal customs or religious practices which are not necessarily grounded in a specific territory. This is often referred to as cultural autonomy, when the subject is a culturally defined group and not a given territory. Autonomy, to be effective, must be sanctioned in law and legitimized by a political process agreed upon by the parties in conflict. While the unilateral declaration of regional autonomy may have a certain political impact, it will hardly be implemented if existing government structures are not adapted accordingly, and this can only be achieved through political negotiations.[8]

In the modern inter-state system as it emerged after the Second World War, ethnic conflicts within a given country were usually considered to be an exclusively internal matter for a state. Yet, we have seen that in most cases covered by this study, the interplay between domestic and external factors is frequently a crucial element in the dynamics of ethnic conflicts. The ethnic kin abroad of one of the adversaries may become involved in many ways, particularly as in recent years the development of electronic communications networks makes information exchange readily and inexpensively available to individuals and organizations alike. Neighbouring states frequently have a vested interest in an ethnic conflict, supporting either one or other of the parties according to their particular geopolitical concerns, and frequently disregarding the principle of non-intervention. The same is true of the two super-powers during the cold war period, who became actively involved in many ethnic conflicts in the world, when they did not actually sponsor them.

Regional organizations may be called upon to intervene in a domestic ethnic conflict, basically in order to maintain international peace and regional security. But they are only successful if the member states (and the rest of the international community) actually support their efforts. Otherwise, they are limited to adopting well-intentioned resolutions that have little or no effect on the ground. The UN system suffers from a similar handicap, in addition to the fact that it was not designed to deal with internal conflicts at all. However, as these confrontations tend to multiply worldwide, the UN system is called upon increasingly to intervene. Not only because of the threat to peace and security, but also because of the massive human rights violations that sometimes accompany these conflicts. Faced with the limited effectiveness of *ex post facto* interventions, the Secretary General of the United Nations has recently begun to promote preventive diplomacy, that is to activate diplomatic intervention in domestic conflicts before a shot is fired and thousands of victims are created.

Helping to prevent violent conflict rather than merely providing humanitarian aid is also becoming one of the principal concerns of a number of non-governmental organizations. To the extent that ethnic conflicts are deemed to be purely internal matters of sovereign states in which other states are loathe to intervene (except when they pursue their self-interest), non-governmental organizations have seen a role for themselves, by informing public opinion about human rights violations, gathering and disseminating information, preparing and distributing reports, lobbying governments, informing the UN and other intergovernmental agencies, and sometimes by providing their good offices to facilitate dialogue between the contending parties, or to mediate and conciliate when this is feasible.

The break-up of numerous states in recent years in Eastern Europe and the rise of assertive nationalist movements which attempt to establish new states in various parts of the world, have reopened the international debate on the right to self-determination and the viability of secession as a means of solving ethnic conflicts. The special rapporteur of the UN Sub-Commission on Prevention of Discrimination and Protection of Minorities, Asbjørn Eide, is concerned with the deleterious effects of ethno-nationalism, according to which every ethnic nation (*ethnos*) should have its own state. Eide compares ethno-nationalism to a malignant cancer and contrasts it with civic nationalism, which holds that everybody living within the state should be part of the nation on a basis of equality (*demos*), irrespective of their ethnic background. 'Ideally', he writes, 'civic nationalism should make it possible for those who so wish to have and to assert their double identity and loyalty. They can be nationals within the civic nation, territorially defined, and as such expect to be treated as equals without any discrimination, and at the same time they can be members of an ethnic, linguistic or religious group ...'[9] While mechanisms for 'group accommodation' need to be developed, in which the legitimate interests of states can be accommodated with the legitimate rights of ethnic groups, we cannot ignore the fact that many conflicts arise precisely because the contradictions between state interests and the collective rights of peoples are embedded in the ethnic policies of the states themselves.

For many experts, the issue here is mainly how to implement effectively generally accepted universal human rights standards. However, in most cases of ethnic conflict, the struggle is not only over individual rights, but over collective or group rights, and this has placed the issue squarely within the framework of the right of peoples to self-determination. The conflicting interpretations of this right, fundamentally concerning the definition of 'peoples' and the conception of 'self', has generated an enormous amount of controversy. International legal scholars, basing their reasoning on a number of UN resolutions, usually argue that this right pertains only to peoples of territories under foreign domination (namely, colonies or occupied territories). It does not justifiy secession from an internationally recognized independent state, nor does it apply to ethnic minorities within independent states.[10] Such arguments, however, are not universally accepted. Numerous peoples in the world who consider themselves as 'unrepresented' by existing states claim for themselves the right of self-determination regardless of the narrow interpretations provided by the United Nations. Among such peoples and nations there are many groups classified by states as 'ethnic minorities' as well as indigenous peoples.

Whatever may be the practical solutions to ethnic conflicts in the political sphere (consociational coalitions, negotiated settlements, federal or confederal arrangements, territorial or cultural autonomy), the right of peoples to self-determination continues to be central to the whole question. Ever since it was proposed as a principle of international relations, it has had its defenders and its detractors. As it was after the First World War, and as it was during the era of decolonization, so it is today. Reputable experts have for some time considered that the era of national self-determination came to an end after the period of decolonization. This view has been challenged by events in Eastern Europe since 1989 and by the implications of some of the ethnic conflicts studied in this book.

Even if there were agreement on who is the 'self' in self-determination (the individual alone, or the whole group), we are usually dealing with the claim of a group of people to choose the form of government under which they will live. It need not be stressed that the right of self-determination of peoples harks back to older universal principles such as equality, freedom, liberty and the pursuit of happiness. Since its inclusion in the UN human rights instruments, it is also considered as a fundamental human right.[11] Whereas public opinion usually identifies the right of self-determination with a claim for separate statehood or secession, scholars distinguish between 'external' and 'internal' self-determination.

States and governments fear the self-determination of sub-national groups because to them it means breaking up existing national territorial units. Yet many ethnic groups do not actually wish to separate from an existing state, but only claim the right to equal participation, to manage their own affairs and to preserve their cultural identity within existing state structures. This is internal self-determination. The controversy counter-poses a state-centred and a people-centred approach. 'Separatism' and 'secession', as well as related concepts such as 'autonomy' and 'sover-eignty', relate to the political organization of states. Self-determination, on the other hand, involves the needs, aspirations, values and goals of the social and cultural communities we refer to as 'peoples'. How to relate these two levels of analysis meaningfully is one of the unmet challenges of the times.

The crucial question in this discussion is the nature of the 'peoples' who possess the right to self-determination. If by people we simply mean exist-ing states, then there is no need to discuss the matter any further. If we refer to peoples in colonies who have now (mostly) become independent, then indeed, as some authors argue, the time for self-determination is past. However, today there are close to 50 countries where ethnic conflicts related to self-determination issues are currently taking place, so it contin-ues to be a burning issue on the agenda of world affairs. Perhaps for valid reasons, the drafters of the UN human rights instruments never attempted to define the 'peoples' who are the bearers of the right to self-determination. While this may have been an advantage at the time, the lack of a precise definition has now become an obstacle to further legal and political development in this field. The basic question is whether the 'peoples' who are to enjoy the right of self-determination are all the resi-dents of a specific territorial unit (*demos*), or the members of a national or ethnic community (*ethnos*).

Though they obviously tend to disagree, ethnic minorities are not defined as 'peoples' in current international law, and therefore lack the right of self-determination. Indigenous populations are struggling to be recognized as peoples in international legal instruments, and they were rightly distressed by article 20 of the 1993 Vienna Declaration on Human

Rights, which refers to the rights of 'indigenous people' in general, but not of indigenous 'peoples'.

In this context, what is 'peoplehood'? To define carefully the nature and characteristics of the peoples who are the subjects of the right to self-determination is not merely an exercise in labelling or classification. Surely the right to self-determination entails the right to self-definition, as indigenous organizations argue persuasively. But would this include, for example, any fringe group that decides to define itself as a people? This possibility and its implications are precisely the kind of situation which a 'minimalist' approach would try to avoid. Conversely, conceding general acceptance to each and every human population that might claim self-determination for itself, the 'maximalist' position may not only lead to chaos and anarchy. More than this, a 'maximalist' position will end up demeaning and devaluing the idea of self-determination itself, and will thereby only harm those collectivities who require it the most.

The violence we see around us is not generated by the drive for self-determination, but by its negation. The denial of self-determination, not its pursuit, is what leads to upheavals and conflicts. And the denial of self-determination is essentially incompatible with true democracy. Only if the peoples' right to self-determination is respected can a democratic society flourish, and only within a truly democratic framework, in which all other human rights are given due recognition, will the right to self-determination be freed from the 'demons' – real or putative – which now envelop it. The challenge before us is how to transform these basic principles into effective political and legal institutions. The difficulties are daunting and the pitfalls many. It is of course true that the right of self-determination of one group, however defined, many conflict with an equally valid right of another. And when one minority achieves this right, another minority may arise in its bosom, like so many Russian dolls. There are no magical breakthroughs, no recipes for success.

The struggles for self-determination around the world will probably increase before they diminish in the years to come. They can neither be wished away nor denied or ignored. The emerging international mechanisms that deal with ethnic and civil conflicts will have to find ways to ensure that the right of peoples to self- determination, as set out in the UN human rights covenants, will receive full recognition in theory as well as in practice.[12]

An assessment of the way ethnic conflicts are regulated, managed or resolved in different parts of the world does not give rise to much optimism. 'Grand settlements' which will lay the ethnic demons to rest forever are unlikely to be achieved in most instances. Countries in which for decades or generations some sort of 'consociationalism' or power-sharing arrangements appear to work well break asunder when the system is unable to control the various internal and external forces that emerge as a result of historical changes. Even where one of the parties wins a clear military victory, the future for pluralism and democracy is by no means certain. In contrast to open victory or failed solutions, some countries attempt to contain and manage ethnic conflict through inter-elite arrangements and bargaining between contending communally-based political parties in a formally democratic system. In most cases of violent confrontation, however, a clear-cut military victory for one of the contenders is not likely, and then the result is a pattern of protracted conflict. That is the moment when chances for peace negotiations tend to increase, provided the parties in conflict agree that it is in their interest to do so.

While it is surely true that the best solutions to an ethnic conflict will be achieved within the framework of a democratic political system, it is precisely when a democratic system is perceived by one ethnic group to work to its disadvantage that ethnic conflict can emerge or continue. The recognition of ethnic pluralism as a permanent and widespread form of social coexistence requires the extension of the concept of 'citizenship'. In most of the countries covered by the UNRISD project, formal citizenship rights are shared by all the nationals of a given state, but we have seen that not all individuals and groups share the same qualities of citizenship equally in the wider sense. When people are excluded from power, wealth, distributive justice, cultural identity and human dignity because of their ethnic characteristics, then there is something missing in their formal citizenship rights. To overcome this barrier, the notion of 'cultural citizenship' has been developed, to mean:

> the right to be different and to belong, in a democratic, participatory sense ... . It emphasizes participation and influence in the national and local polity; it stresses local, informal notions of membership, entitlement and influence. The word 'cultural' underscores vernacular definitions of community, identity, and human dignity, particularly those of subordinated minority groups.

In a similar vein, the concept of 'ethnic citizenship' has been proposed for indigenous peoples in Latin American.[13] How to transform such abstract concepts into constructive policies which would help deflect ethnic tensions and prevent ethnic conflicts is one of the challenges facing the world at the end of the twentieth century.

It is always hazardous to try to predict events, but from the tendencies observed in recent years, it is likely that ethnic conflicts will increase in number and intensity before they will wane and be replaced by other kinds of conflict. Conflict is, after all, inherent in human affairs. It is also likely that increasing attempts will be made at both the national and international levels to prevent the violent eruption or continuation of such confrontations, and to find solutions acceptable to the contending parties when they do occur. The human, political and economic costs to society are too high to be sustained for long. The essential point is, however, that existing nation-states and the inter-state system must be ready to accept the legitimate claims of subordinate, excluded and marginalized ethnic groups, on the basis of the universal respect for human rights (including the right of peoples to self-determination) and democratic process. Unless these conditions are met, situations prone to the emergence of conflict will continue to arise on different continents.

Notes

CHAPTER 1   THE ETHNIC QUESTION IN THE WORLD CRISIS

1. For a critique of postmodernism in the social sciences, see Rosenau (1992).
2. Bandyopadhyay (1992).
3. The exception to this statement, of course, was the failed Igbo attempt at secession from Nigeria in the 1960s, known as the Biafra war.
4. Some of the groups surveyed are included in more than one category (Gurr, 1993).
5. Gurr and Harff (1994).
6. Fukuyama (1992); Huntington (1993).

CHAPTER 2   THE PITFALLS OF ETHNICITY AND ETHNIC CONFLICT

1. Stavenhagen (1990).
2. Smith, A. (1986).
3. On Africa, see Amselle (1985) and Nnoli (1989). On India, Devalle (1990). The Miskito case has been studied by Jenkins Molieri (1986). On the Metis, see Peterson and Brown (1985).
4. Isaacs (1975).
5. Van den Berghe (1981, 1986). See also Shaw and Wong.
6. Especially in the United States and more recently in Western Europe (Miles, R., 1982).
7. Gilroy (1987).
8. Hechter (1987).
9. Banton (1983).
10. Tishkov (1994).
11. Connor (1972).
12. Rothschild (1981).
13. Epstein (1978).
14. Banton (1983); Olzak (1992).
15. Darby, 1983.
16. Like all generalizations this one has its exceptions. Irish nationalism attempted unsuccessfully to revive Gaelic in independent Ireland. 'Nation-building' in Africa is being carried out preferably in English and French because the official use of the vernacular languages in those multilingual societies would create a host of practical problems.
17. Barth (1969).
18. Miles, R. (1989).

CHAPTER 3   HOW CONFLICT CAME ABOUT

1.   Chaliand (1992).
2.   A small number of Kurds live dispersed in parts of the former Soviet Union, and about half a million migrants reside in Western Europe. Non-Kurds also live in Kurdish areas, and are sometimes counted as Kurds, thus making an exact estimate difficult.
3.   Woodward (1990: 60).
4.   McCreery (1990: 96–113).
5.   Handy (1990: 179).
6.   Jonas (1991: ch. 2).
7.   Horowitz (1985: 291, 293).
8.   See Milne (1981), who compares Guyana, Malaysia and Fiji.

CHAPTER 4   THE STRUCTURING IDENTITIES

1.   Arias (1990: 251).
2.   Based on survey data taken by Valery Tishkov's associates in Kirgistan.
3.   Gilman (1986).
4.   Bloom (1990: 38, 52).
5.   Volkan (1990).
6.   Bloom (1990: 23).

CHAPTER 5   THE DYNAMICS OF CONFLICT

1.   Reyntjens (1995).
2.   Jonas (1991: 63).
3.   Over 100 peacefully protesting Kekchi Indians were massacred at Panzos in May 1978 and 300 were wounded. In January 1980, 39 peasants who had sought refuge in the Spanish embassy in Guatemala City after petitioning the government unsuccessfully, were burned alive together with Spanish diplomats, after the army attacked the embassy (Jonas: 127–9).
4.   Ibid.: 133–5
5.   Arias (1990: 225).
6.   Jonas (1991: 146).
7.   Ibid.: 149.
8.   Davis (1988b: 23).
9.   Rigoberta Menchu, an Indian peasant leader who was affiliated with the Committee for Peasant Unity (CUC), and whose family had been killed in army massacres, received the Nobel Peace Prize in 1992, the year widely commemorated as the 500th Anniversary of the 'Encounter of Two Worlds'. She achieved fame in the 1980s with her widely acclaimed autobiography, *I, Rigoberta Menchu* (Menchu, 1983).

10.   Davis (1988b: 27). For a detailed description and assessment of the violence on a number of particular Indian communities see Carmack (1988).
11.   Ossetians also live in South Ossetia, which is a part of the now independent neighbouring Republic of Georgia. South Ossetians would like to join their fellow-Ossetians in the North, and this has created a problem with the Georgian government.
12.   Tilly (1978).
13.   Gurr (1993: 92).

CHAPTER 6   ETHNIC CONFLICT AND ECONOMIC DEVELOPMENT

1.   Peiris (1991).
2.   Ghee and Gomes (1990).
3.   Bonacich (1972); Potts (1990).
4.   Banton (1983); Miles, R. (1982).
5.   Stavenhagen (1975); Hechter (1975).
6.   Sudan, the largest African country in area (2.5 million square kilometres), has a population currently approaching 25 million and a growth rate of 2.8. Ethiopia, with half the area of Sudan (1.24 million square kilometres) has almost twice as many inhabitants, with a growth rate of 3.1.
7.   The United Nations has put together an HDI in which the countries of the world are ranked according to indicators such as the population's life expectancy, literacy, average schooling, as well as the government's social expenditures, etc. This is published in an annual Human Development Report (United Nations, 1993; see also Miles, I., 1985).
8.   The highest possible score is 1. The highest actual score is 0.983 for Japan, and the lowest, 0.045 for Guinea.
9.   It is not clear how these differences relate to the problem of ethnic conflict, perhaps because this was not factored in the elaboration of the HDI. It is beyond the scope of this chapter to evaluate the methodology used in the HDI, but its first publication in 1990 by the United Nations sparked a widespread and controversial debate on this problem among specialists.
10.   Gurr (1993).
11.   The Human Development Report does not provide disaggregated figures by ethnic group for other countries (United Nations, 1993: 18).
12.   Picard (1993).

CHAPTER 7   ETHNIC POLICIES

1.   Gordon (1975); Jiobu (1988).
2.   Glazer and Moynihan (1975).
3.   Stavenhagen (1992).
4.   Connor (1972).
5.   Kuper (1981); Horowitz (1980); Van den Berghe (1990).

6. Stavenhagen (1992).
7. European Parliament (1985).
8. Smith and Kuper (1965); Schermerhorn (1970).
9. Glazer and Moynihan (1975)
10. Lijphart (1977: 25).
11. Horowitz (1985: 563–600).

CHAPTER 8 INTERNATIONAL DIMENSIONS OF ETHNIC CONFLICTS

1. For example, it did nothing to stop the Turkish military operations in Iraq in pursuit of Kurdish guerrillas in the spring of 1995.
2. Premdas (1991).
3. The war between the Chechen Republic and Moscow took place within the Russian Federation.
4. Ignatieff (1994).
5. Jonas (1991: 197ff).
6. Ryan (1990).
7. Ibid.: 143.
8. Ghali (1990).
9. Sohn (1984).
10. Medina Quiroga (1990).
11. United Nations (1990: 18).
12. Eide (1994). This Working Group was set up in 1995.
13. Howard (1991).
14. Eide (1994).
15. de Witte (1993).
16. Davis (1988a).
17. Van Walt van Praag (1993).

CHAPTER 9 THE SEEDS OF CONFLICT: RACISM, ANTI-SEMITISM AND XENOPHOBIA

1. UNESCO (1979).
2. Quinley and Glock (1979: xxv, 134–8).
3. Lipset and Raab (1978: 23).
4. Aho (1990).
5. McMillan (1971).
6. Davidson (1990).
7. Robertson (1976).
8. This is a reference to the venerable and respected National Association for the Advancement of Colored People (NAACP), which for many decades was at the forefront of the struggle for civil rights for blacks in the United States.
9. Ridgeway (1990).

10. Bruce (1990).
11. Wade (1987).
12. Zeskind (1986).
13. Coates (1987: 258).
14. Diamond (1989: 2).
15. Anti-Defamation League (1991).
16. Anti-Defamation League (1990a).
17. Center for Democratic Renewal (n.d.).
18. Waters (1987).
19. Langer (1990); Klanwatch (1991); Scigliano (1986).
20. Anti-Defamation League (1983).
21. Ridgeway (1990).
22. Lutz (1986).
23. Aho (1990: 64).
24. Anti-Defamation League (1990b).
25. Anti-Defamation League (1990b).
26. Mintz (1985).
27. Seidel (1986); Lipstadt (1993).
28. Corcoran (1990).
29. King (1989).
30. Rebeck (1987).
31. Corcoran (1990: 118).
32. Quinley and Glock (1979: xxi–xxii).
33. Tsukashima (1978).
34. Kaufman (1988); Barnes (1985).
35. Jensen (1985); Persell (1981).
36. Levin (1990); Lynn (1991).
37. Foster (1990).
38. Levin (1990: 211–12).
39. Herrnstein and Murray (1994).
40. For example, the journal's spring 1991 issue contains an article which calls for eugenics policies as a means of preventing 'genetic deterioration', which, it is claimed, led to the fall of the Roman empire (Lynn, 1991a). Another article in the summer 1991 issue, claims that Blacks are 'more violent, more prone to crime, more excitable . . . less sexually restrained, less inclined to follow rules . . . and less altruistic' than Whites, warns that 'an increasing black presence in a classroom increases disorder', and advocates various forms of segregation, including segregated subway cars, with Black males confined to 'special patrolled cars' (Levin, 1991).

In addition to Pearson's groups, several other organizations disseminate racist ideas under the guise of scholarship. The International Association for the Advancement of Ethnology and Eugenics (IAAEE), supports human breeding to create a 'superior race'. The Pioneer Fund, founded in 1937, has given millions of dollars to support research on race differences, heredity and eugenics.
41. Barkan (1992).
42. Bunzl (1992).

CHAPTER 10   CONFLICT MANAGEMENT AND THE MULTI-ETHNIC STATE

1. Ryan (1990: 102–18).
2. Horowitz (1985).
3. Agnew (1989: 41).
4. Azar and Burton (1986).
5. Gurr (1993).
6. Reyntjens (1995).
7. Biles (1992).
8. McWhirter and Melamede (1992).
9. Engedayehu (1993).
10. Wallensteen (1989).
11. Montville (1990: 538).
12. Zartman (1990).
13. Horowitz (1990).
14. Burton (1987).
15. Vilas (1989).
16. Hannum (1990).
17. Gurr (1993: 295).
18. Eide (1994).
19. The collapse of the Soviet Union and Yugoslavia is not usually considered within the framework of secession because the newly independent successor states did not actually secede but were formerly constituent parts of a federation which collapsed. Some of the conflicts which arose within these new states do, however, involve the issue of secession.
20. Crawford (1988).
21. Murswiek (1993).
22. For a critique of the negative aspects of multiculturalism, from a liberal nationalist perspective, see Schlesinger (1992).
23. Lijphart (1990).
24. Eide (1994: 135).

CHAPTER 11   CONCLUSIONS

1. Lemarchand (1994).
2. Tishkov (1994).
3. See the quaint reference to 'post-modern tribalism' in Franck (1993).
4. Madan (1994).
5. Warren (1994); Solares (1993).
6. Psacharopoulos and Patrinos (1994).
7. Hannum (1990: 474) notes that 'autonomy lies at the end of a progression of rights. While it is perhaps of greatest importance to indigenous peoples and ethnic or other minorities, it may respond to purely regional needs, as well.... Territorially based autonomy arrangements are neither incompatible with, nor do they require, other preferential or "affirmative action" policies

to enable disadvantaged groups to achieve effective, as opposed to only theoretical, equality.'

8. As a consequence of the Indian peasant uprising in southeastern Mexico in January 1994, and of the continuing political conflict in the area, a number of indigenous organizations unilaterally declared the 'autonomy' of several 'multi-ethnic regions' in the state of Chiapas in October. The likelihood of their success seems small indeed if the Mexican government refuses, as it does, to recognize this 'autonomy'.

9. Eide (1994: 6).

10. Hannum (1990); Eide (1994); and Tomuschat (1993).

11. The International Human Rights Covenants adopted by the UN General Assembly declare that all peoples have the right to self-determination.

12. The above paragraphs on the problems of self-determination were adapted from Stavenhagen (1993).

13. Rosaldo (1994); Montoya (1992).

References

Agnew, John, 1989, 'Beyond Reason: Spatial and Temporal Sources of Ethnic Conflict', in *Intractable Conflicts and their Transformation*, ed. L. Kriesberg, T. A. Northrup and S. J. Thorson, Syracuse: Syracuse University Press.

Aho, James, 1990, *The Politics of Self-Righteousness*, Seattle: The University of Seattle Press.

Amselle, Jean-Loup and Elikia M'Bokolo (sous la direction de), 1985, *Au Coeur de l'ethnie. Ethnies, tribalisme et état en Afrique*, Paris: Editions de la Decouverte.

Anti-Defamation League, 1983, *Identity Churches: A Theology of Hate*. ADL-Facts.

Anti-Defamation League, 1990a, *Liberty Lobby: Network of Hate*, Anti-Defamation League.

Anti-Defamation League, 1990b, *Audit of Anti-Semitic Incidents*, Anti-Defamation League.

Anti-Defamation League, 1991, *The Ku-Klux-Klan Today: A 1991 Status Report*, Anti-Defamation League.

Arias, Arturo, 1990, 'Changing Indian Identity: Guatemala's Violent Transition to Modernity', In *Guatemalan Indians and the State, 1540 to 1988*, ed. C. A. Smith, Austin: University of Texas Press.

Azar, Edward E. and John W. Burton, 1986, *International Conflict Resolution. Theory and Practice*, Brighton: Wheatsheaf Books.

Bandyopadhyay, Jayanta, 1992, 'From Environmental Conflicts to Sustainable Mountain Transformation: Ecological Action in the Garhwal Himalaya', in *Grassroots Environmental Action. People's Participation in Sustainable Development*, ed. D. Ghai and J. M. Vivian, London: Routledge.

Banton, Michael, 1983, *Racial and Ethnic Competition*, Cambridge: Cambridge University Press.

Barnes, Fred, 1985, 'Farrakhan Frenzy', *New Republic*, 28 October.

Barkan, Elazar, 1992, *The Retreat of Scientific Racism*, Cambridge: Cambridge University Press.

Barth, Frederick, 1969, *Ethnic Groups and Boundaries*, Oslo: Universitetsforlaget.

Biles, Peter, 1992, 'Living on the Edge', *Africa Report*, March/April 1992.

Bloom, William, 1990, *Personal Identity, National Identity and International Relations*, Cambridge Studies in International Relations, Cambridge: Cambridge University Press.

Bonacich, Edna, 1972, 'A Theory of Ethnic Antagonism: The Split Labor Market', *American Sociological Review*, vol. 37 (October)

Bruce, Steve, 1990, *The Rise and Fall of the Christian Right*, Oxford: Clarendon Press.

Burton, John W., 1987, *Resolving Deep-Rooted Conflict. A Handbook*, Lanham: University Press of America.

Carmack, Robert M., 1988, *Harvest of Violence: The Maya Indians and the Guatemalan Crisis*, Norman and London: University of Oklahoma Press.

311

Center for Democratic Renewal, n.d., *Aryan Nations: the Far Right Underground Movement.*

Chaliand, Gerard, 1992, *Le Malheur Kurde*, Paris: Editions du Seuil.

Coates, James, 1987, *Armed and Dangerous*, New York: Hill & Wang.

Connor, Walker, 1972, 'Nation Building or Nation Destroying', *World Politics*, vol. 24, no. 3.

Cooper, Mary, 1989, *The Growing Danger of Hate Groups*, Editorial Research Reports.

Corcoran, James, 1990, *Bitter Harvest*, New York: Penguin Books.

Crawford, James, 1988, *The Rights of Peoples*, Oxford: Clarendon.

Darby, John, ed., 1983, *Northern Ireland. The Background to the Conflict*, Belfast: Appletree Press.

Davidson, Miriam, 1990. 'The Mexican Border War', *The Nation.*

Davis, Shelton H., 1988a, *Land Rights and Indigenous Peoples. The Role of the Inter-American Commission on Human Rights*, Cambridge, MA: Cultural Survival.

Davis, Shelton H., 1988b, 'Introduction: Sowing the Seeds of Violence', in *Harvest of Violence. The Maya Indians and the Guatemalan Crisis*, ed. R. M. Carmack, Norman: University of Oklahoma Press.

Devalle, Susana B. C., 1990, 'Tribe in India: The Fallacy of a Colonial Category', in *Studies on Asia and Africa from Latin America*, ed. D. N. Lorenzen, Mexico, D.F.: El Colegio de Mexico.

de Witte, B., 1993, 'The European Community and its Minorities', in *Peoples and Minorities in International Law*, ed. C. Brölman, E. Lefebor and M. Ziek, Dordrecht: Martinus Nijhoff.

Diamond, Sara, 1989, *Spiritual Warfare: The Politics of the Christian Right*, Boston: South End Press.

Eide, Asbjørn, 1994, *Peaceful and Constructive Resolution of Situations Involving Minorities*, Oslo: Norwegian Institute of Human Rights.

Elster, Jon, 1986, *Rational Choice*, New York: New York University Press.

Engedayehu, Walle, 1993, 'Ethiopia: Democracy and the Politics of Ethnicity', *Africa Report*, 2nd Quarter.

Epstein, A. L., 1978, *Ethos and Identity. Three Studies in Ethnicity*, London: Tavistock Publications.

European Parliament, 1985, *Committee of Inquiry into the Rise of Fascism and Racism in Europe. Report on the findings of the inquiry*, Strasbourg: European Parliament.

Etzioni, Amitai, 1993, 'The Evils of Self Determination', *Foreign Policy*, Winter: 21, 35.

Foster, John, 1990, 'Retroviruses, Genetic Lesioning and Mental Deficiencies among Blacks: A Causal Hypothesis,' *The Mankind Quarterly*, Fall/Winter.

Franck, T. M., 1993, 'Postmodern Tribalism and the Right to Secession', in *Peoples and Minorities in International Law*, ed. C. Brolman, R. Lefeber and M. Zieck, Dordrecht: Martinus Nijhoff Publishers.

Fukuyama, Francis, 1992, *The End of History and the Last Man*, New York: Avon Books.

Gellner, Ernest, 1988, *Plough, Sword and Book. The Structure of Human History*, Chicago: The University of Chicago Press.

Ghali, Boutros Boutros, 1990, *Agenda for Peace*, New York: United Nations.

Ghee, Lim Teck and Alberto G. Gomes, 1990, *Tribal Peoples and Development in Southeast Asia*, Kuala Lumpur: Department of Anthropology and Sociology, University of Malaya.

Gilman, Sander L., 1986, *Jewish Self-Hatred. Anti-Semitism and the Hidden Language of the Jews*, Baltimore: The Johns Hopkins University Press.

Gilroy, Paul, 1987, *'There Ain't No Black in the Union Jack'. The Cultural Politics of Race and Nation*, Chicago: The University of Chicago Press.

Glazer, Nathan and Daniel P. Moynihan, 1975, *Ethnicity. Theory and Experience*, Cambridge, MA: Harvard University Press.

Gordon, Milton M., 1975, 'Toward a General Theory of Racial and Ethnic Group Relations', in *Ethnicity. Theory and Experience*, ed. N. Glazer and D. P. Moynihan, Cambridge: Harvard University Press.

Greenfeld, Liah, 1993, *Nationalism. Five Roads to Modernity*, Cambridge, MA: Harvard University Press.

Gurr, Ted Robert, 1993, *Minorities at Risk. A Global View of Ethnopolitical Conflicts*, Washington, D.C.: United States Institute of Peace Press.

Gurr, Ted Robert and Barbara Harff, 1994, *Ethnic Conflict in World Politics*. Boulder, Col.: Westview Press.

Handy, Jim, 1990, 'The Corporate Community, Campesino Organizations, and Agrarian Reform: 1950–1954', in *Guatemalan Indians and the State, 1540 to 1988*, ed. C. A. Smith, Austin: University of Texas Press.

Hannum, Hurst, 1990, *Autonomy, Sovereignty, and Self-Determination. The Accommodation of Conflicting Rights*, Philadelphia: University of Pennsylvania Press.

Hechter, Michael, 1975, *Internal Colonialism. The Celtic Fringe in British National Development, 1536–1966*, London: Routledge & Kegan Paul.

Hechter, Michael, 1987, *Principles of Group Solidarity*, Berkeley: University of California Press.

Herrnstein, Richard J. and Charles Murray, 1994, *The Bell Curve*, New York: The Free Press.

Hobsbawm, E. J., 1990, *Nations and Nationalism since 1780*, Cambridge: Cambridge University Press.

Horowitz, Donald L., 1985, *Ethnic Groups in Conflict*, Berkeley: University of California Press.

Horowitz, Donald L., 1990, 'Making Moderation Pay: The Comparative Politics of Ethnic Conflict Management', in *Conflict and Peacemaking in Multiethnic Societies*, ed. J. V. Montville, Lexington, MA: D. C. Heath and Company.

Horowitz, Irving Louis, 1980, *Taking Lives: Genocide and State Power*, New Brunswick: Transaction Books.

Howard, Michael C., 1991, *Fiji: Race and Politics in an Island State*, Vancouver: University of British Columbia Press.

Huntington, Samuel P., 1993, 'The Clash of Civilizations', *Foreign Affairs*, Summer.

Ignatieff, Michael, 1994, 'Homage to Bosnia', *The New York Review of Books* vol. XLI, no. 8: 3–6.

Isaacs, Harold R., 1975, *Idols of the Tribe*, New York: Harper & Row.

Jenkins Molieri, Jorge, 1986, *El desafío indígena en Nicaragua: el caso de los miskitos*, Mexico: Ed. Katún.

Jensen, Arthur, 1985, 'The Nature of Black–White Differences on Various Psychometric Tests: Spearman's Hypothesis' *The Behavioral and Brain Sciences*.

Jiobu, Robert M., 1988, *Ethnicity & Assimilation*, Albany, NY: State University of New York Press.

Jonas, Susanne, 1991, *The Battle for Guatemala. Rebels, Death Squads, and U.S. Power*, Latin American Perspectives Series, No. 5, Boulder, Col.: Westview Press.

Kaufman, Jonathan, 1988, *Broken Alliance. The Turbulent Times between Blacks and Jews in America*, New York: New American Library.

King, Dennis, 1989, *Lyndon LaRouche and the New American Fascism*, New York: Doubleday.

Klanwatch, 1991, *Klanwatch Intelligence Report*, Southern Poverty Law Center.

Kuper, Leo, 1981, *Genocide*, Harmondsworth: Penguin Books.

Lane, Charles, 1994, 'The Tainted Sources of "The Bell Curve"', *The New York Review of Books*, vol. XLI, no. 20: 14–19.

Langer, Elinor, 1990, 'The American Neo-Nazi Movement Today', *The Nation*. 16 July.

Lemarchand, René, 1994, 'The Apocalypse in Rwanda', *Cultural Survival Quarterly*, vol. 18, no. 2, 3, Summer/Fall: 29–33.

Levin, Michael, 1990, 'Implications of Race and Sex Differences for Compensatory Affirmative Action and the Concept of Discrimination', *Journal of Social, Political and Economic Studies*, Summer.

Lijphart, Arend, 1977, *Democracy in Plural Societies. A Comparative Exploration*, New Haven & London: Yale University Press.

Lijphart, Arend, 1990, 'The Power-Sharing Approach', in *Conflict and Peacemaking in Multiethnic Societies*, ed. J. V. Montville, Lexington, MA: D. C. Heath and Company.

Lipset, Seymour and Earl Raab, 1978, *The Politics of Unreason*, Chicago: The University of Chicago Press.

Lipstadt, Deborah, 1993, *Denying the Holocaust*, New York: The Free Press.

Lutz, Cris, 1986, *They Don't All Wear Sheets*, Center for Democratic Renewal.

Lynn, Richard, 1991, 'Civilization and the Quality of Populations', *The Mankind Quarterly*, Spring.

MacDonald, Charles G., 1988, 'The Kurdish Question in the 1980s', in *Ethnicity, Pluralism and the State in the Middle East*, ed. M. J. Esman and I. Rabinovich, Ithaca, NY: Cornell University Press.

Madan, T. N., 1994, 'The Burden of Cultural Identity. On Being a Hindu in India', *Cultural Survival Quarterly*, Summer/Fall: 69–71.

McCreery, David, 1990, 'State Power, Indigenous Communities, and Land in Nineteenth Century Guatemala, 1820–1920', in *Guatemalan Indians and the State, 1540 to 1988*, ed. C. A. Smith, Austin: University of Texas Press.

McMillan, Neil, 1971, *The Citizens Councils*, Urbana, IL: The University of Illinois Press.

McWhirter, Cameron and Gur Melamede, 1992, 'The Ethnicity Factor', *Africa Report* September/October.

Medina Quiroga, Cecilia, 1990, *The Battle of Human Rights. Gross, Systematic Violations and the Inter-American System*, Dordrecht: Martinus Nijhoff.

Menchu, Rigoberta, 1983, *I, Rigoberta Menchu: An Indian Woman in Guatemala*, New York: Verso.

Milne, R. S., 1981, *Politics in Ethnically Bipolar States*, Vancouver: University of British Columbia Press.

Miles, Ian, 1985, *Social Indicators for Human Development*, London: Frances Pinter.

Miles, Robert, 1982, *Racism and Migrant Labour*, London: Routledge & Kegan Paul.

Miles, Robert, 1989, *Racism*, London: Routledge.

Mintz, Frank P., 1985, *The Liberty Lobby and the American Right*, Westport, CT: Greenwood Press.

Montoya, Rodrigo, 1992, *Al Borde del Naufragio (Democracia, violencia y problema étnico en el Peru)*, Madrid: Talasa Ediciones.

Montville, Jospeh V., 1990, 'Epilogue: The Human Factor Revisited', in *Conflict and Peacemaking in Multiethnic Societies*, ed. J. V. Montville, Lexington, MA: D.C. Heath.

Murswiek, Dietrich, 1993, 'The Issue of a Right of Secession – Reconsidered', in *Modern Law of Self-Determination*, ed. C. Tomuschat, Dordrecht: Martinus Nijhoff Publishers.

Nnoli, Okwudiba, 1989, *Ethnic Politics in Africa*, Ibadan: Vantage Publishers.

Olson, Mancur, 1965, *The Logic of Collective Action*, Cambridge, MA: Harvard University Press.

Olzak, Susan, 1992, *The Dynamics of Ethnic Competition and Conflict*, Stanford, CA: Stanford University Press.

Peiris, G. H., 1991, 'Changing Prospects of the Plantation Workers of Sri Lanka', in *Economic Dimensions of Ethnic Conflict. International Perspectives*, ed. S. W. R. d. A. S. a. R. Coughlan, London: Frances Printer.

Persell, Caroline Hodges, 1981, 'Genetic and Cultural Deficit Theories: Two Sides of the Same Racist Coin', *Journal of Black Studies*, September.

Peterson, Jacqueline and Jennifer S. H. Brown, 1985, *The New Peoples. Being and Becoming Metis in North America*, Winnipeg: The University of Manitoba Press,

Picard, Elizabeth, 1993, *The Lebanese Shi'a and Political Violence*, Geneva: UNRISD (Discussion Paper No. 42).

Potts, Lydia, 1990, *The World Labour Market. A History of Migration*, London: Zed Books.

Premdas, Ralph R., 1991, 'The Internationalization of Ethnic Conflict: Some Theoretical Explorations', in *Internationalization of Ethnic Conflict*, ed. K. M. d. S. a. R. May. London: Frances Pinter.

Psacharopoulos, George and Harry Anthony Patrinos, 1994, *Indigenous People and Poverty in Latin America. An Empirical Analysis*, Washington D.C.: The World Bank.

Quinley, Harold E. and Charles Y. Glock, 1979, *Anti-Semitisim in America*, New Brunswick: Transaction Books.

Rebeck, Victoria, 1987, 'Facing up to the Farm Crisis', *Christian Century*, 22 April.

Rex, John and David Mason, 1986, *Theories of Race and Ethnic Relations*, Cambridge: Cambridge University Press.

Reyntjens, Filip, 1995, *Burundi: Breaking the Cycle of Violence*, London: Minority Rights Group (Report MRG 95/1).

Ridgeway, James, 1990, *Blood in the Face*, New York: Thunder's Mouth Press.

Robertson, Wilmot, 1976, *The Dispossessed Majority*, Cape Canaveral: Howard Allen Enterprises.

Rosaldo, Renato, 1994, 'Cultural Citizenship and Educational Democracy', *Cultural Anthropology*, vol. 9, no. 3: 402–11.

Rosenau, Pauline Marie, 1992, *Post-Modernism and the Social Sciences*, Princeton, NJ: Princeton University Press.

Rothschild, Joseph, 1981, *Ethnopolitics, a Conceptual Framework*, New York: Columbia University Press.

Rupesinghe, Kumar, 1993, 'Early Warning and Preventive Diplomacy', *International Alert Discussion Paper*.

Ryan, Stephen, 1990, *Ethnic Conflict and International Relations*, Brookfield, VT: Dartmouth Publishing Company.

Schermerhorn, R. A., 1970, *Comparative Ethnic Relations. A Framework for Theory and Research*, New York: Random House.

Schlesinger, Arthur M., 1992, *The Disuniting of America: Reflections on a Multicultural Society*, New York: W. W. Norton.

Scigliano, Eric, 1986, 'America's Down Home Racists', *The Nation*, 30 August.

Seidel, Gill, 1986, *The Holocaust Denial*, London: Beyond the Pale Collective.

Shaw, Paul and Y. Wong, 1989, *Genetic Seeds of Warfare, Evolution, Nationalism and Patriotism*, Boston: Unwin-Hyman.

Smith, Anthony D., 1981, *The Ethnic Revival in the Modern World*, Cambridge: Cambridge University Press.

Smith, Anthony D., 1986, *The Ethnic Origins of Nations*, Oxford: Basil Blackwell.

Smith, M. G. and Leo Kuper, 1965, *Pluralism in Africa*, Berkeley, University of California Press.

Sohn, Louis B., 1984, 'Human Rights: Their Implementation and Supervision by the United Nations', in *Human Rights in International Law*, ed. T. Meron, Oxford: Clarendon Press.

Solares, Jorge, 1993, *Estado y Nacion. Las demandas de los grupos etnicos en Guatemala*, Guatemala: FLACSO.

Stavenhagen, Rodolfo, 1975, *Social Classes in Agrarian Societies*, New York: Anchor Books.

Stavenhagen, Rodolfo, 1990, *The Ethnic Question. Conflicts, Development and Human Rights*, Tokyo: United Nations University Press.

Stavenhagen, Rodolfo, 1992, 'Challenging the Nation-State in Latin America', *Journal of International Affairs*, vol. 45, no. 2, Winter: 421–40.

Stavenhagen, Rodolfo, 1993, 'Self-Determination, Right or Demon?', *Stanford Journal of International Affairs*, vol. II, no. 2, September: 1–12.

Tilly, Charles, 1978, *From Mobilization to Revolution*, Reading, MA: Addison-Wesley.

Tishkov, Valery, 1994, 'Perspectives on Ethnic Accord in Post-Soviet Space', *Cultural Survival Quarterly*, vol. 18, no. 2, 3, Summer/Fall: 52–7.

Tomuschat, Christian, 1993, *Modern Law of Self-Determination*, Dordrecht: Martinus Nijhoff.

Tsukashima, Ronald, 1978, *The Social and Psychological Correlates of Black Anti-Semitism*, R. and E. Associates.

UNESCO, 1979, *Declaration on Race and Racial Prejudice*, Paris: UNESCO.

United Nations, 1988, *United Nations Action in the Field of Human Rights*, New York: United Nations.

United Nations, 1990, *The United Nations and Human Rights*, New York: United Nations.

United Nations, 1993, *Human Development Report*, New York: United Nations.

United Nations, 1994, *Human Development Report*, New York: United Nations.

Van den Berghe, Pierre, 1981, *The Ethnic Phenomenon*, Elsevier Press.

Van den Berghe, Pierre, 1986, 'Ethnicity and the Sociobiology Debate', in *Theories of Race and Ethnic Relations*, ed. J. Rex and D. Mason, Cambridge: Cambridge University Press.

Van den Berghe, Pierre L., 1990, *State Violence & Ethnicity*, Niwot, Co: University Press of Colorado.

Van Walt van Praag, M. C., 1993, 'The Position of UNPO in the International Legal Order', in *Peoples and Minorities in International Law*, ed. C. Brolmann, R. Lefeber and M. Ziek, Dordrecht: Martinus Nijhoff.

Vilas, Carlos M., 1989, *State, Class & Ethnicity in Nicaragua*, Boulder, Co.: Lynne Riener.

Volkan, Vamik D., 1990, 'Psychoanalytic Aspects of Ethnic Conflicts', in *Conflict and Peacemaking in Multiethnic Societies*, ed. J. V. Montville, Lexington, MA: D. C. Heath.

Wade, Wyn Craig, 1987, *The Fiery Cross*, New York: Simon & Schuster.

Wallensteen, Peter, 1989, 'Theory and Practice of Conflict Resolution: An International Perspective', in *Waging Peace in the Philippines*, ed. E. Garcia and C. Hernandez, Manila: University of the Philippines.

Warren, Kay B., 1994, 'Language and the Politics of Self-Expression. Mayan revitalization in Guatemala', *Cultural Survival Quarterly*, vol. 18, no. 2, 3 Summer/Fall: 81–6.

Waters, Ronald, 1987, 'White Racial Nationalism in the United States', *Without Prejudice*, Fall.

Woodward Jr, Ralph Lee, 1990, 'Changes in the Nineteenth-Century Guatemalan State and Its Indian Policies', In *Guatemalan Indians and the State, 1540 to 1988*, ed. C. A. Smith, Austin: University of Texas Press.

Zartman, I. William, 1990, 'Negotiations and Prenegotiations in Ethnic Conflict: The Beginning, the Middle, and the Ends', in *Conflict and Peacemaking in Multiethnic Societies*, ed. J. V. Montville, Lexington, MA: D. C. Heath and Company.

Zeskind, Leonard, 1986, *The Christian Identity Movement*, Center for Democratic Renewal.

Zia, Helen, 1991, 'Women in the Klan', *Ms.*, March, April.

Appendix

Studies prepared for this project are on file at UNRISD, and include:

Akhavan, Payam, ed., *Towards Disaster and Beyond: Yugoslav Perspectives on the Disintegration of Yugoslavia*, 1994.

Bunzl, John, *Perspectives on Antisemitism in Austria*, 1992.

Chaliand, Gérard, *Le Malheur Kurde*, Paris, Edition du Seuil, 1992.

Diouf, Makhtar, *Sénégal. Les ethnies et la nation*, Paris, Editions L'Harmattan, 1994.

García Ruiz, Jesús, *Historia, etnia, conflicto: La configuración de las identidades entre los grupos étnicos de Guatemala*, UNRISD, 1992.

Hamdan, Kamal, *Ethnicité et développement: le cas du Liban*, 1993.

Lemarchand, René, *Burundi: Ethnocide as Discourse and Practice*, UNRISD, 1992.

Levitsky, Steven, *The Ideology of Racism in the United States*, 1992.

Markakis, John, *Ethnic and Regional Conflict in Ethiopia and Sudan*, UNRISD, 1992.

Nandy, Ashis, *Fear of the Self: Invention of Nationality and the Ramjanmabhumi Movement*, UNRISD, 1992.

Nnoli, Okwudiba, *Ethnicity and Development in Nigeria*, UNRISD, 1992.

Premdas, Ralph, *Ethnic Conflict and Development: the Case of Guyana*, UNRISD, 1992.

Premdas, Ralph, *Ethnic Conflict and Development: the Fascistisation of the State in Fiji*, UNRISD, 1992.

Putucheary, Mavis, *Ethnic Conflict and Management in Malaysia*, 1992.

Rashid Abbas, and Shaheed Farida, *Pakistan: Ethno-Politics and Contending Elites*, UNRISD Discussion Paper 45, 1993.

Tishkov, Valery, *The Mind Aflame. Ethnicity, Nationalism and Conflicts in and after the Soviet Union*, Moscow, 1994.

Türk, Danilo, ed., *Towards Disaster and Beyond: Ethnic Issues, Conflict and Collapse of Yugoslavia* .

Index